The Book of Quotations

The
Book
of
Quotations

Compiled by

Robert I. Fitzhenry

Australian content by

Anthony Barker

ALLEN & UNWIN

First published in 1994
Allen & Unwin Pty Ltd
9 Atchison Street, St Leonards, NSW 2065 Australia

National Library of Australia
Cataloguing-in-Publication entry:

The Book of quotations.

 ISBN 1 86373 633 6.

 1. Quotations, English. I. Fitzhenry, Robert I, II. Barker, A. W.
 (Anthony Wilhelm), 1930– .

082

Set in 9½/11 pt Times by DOCUPRO, Sydney
Printed by McPherson's Printing Group, Maryborough

10 9 8 7 6 5 4 3 2 1

Contents

Preface

It is a privilege to be able to revise and update at decent intervals because quotations, like the words of our language itself, change in relevance and currency. Some are coming: 'We're all in this together—by ourselves.' Some are going: 'Another thing about capitalism—everybody knows who's in Grant's tomb.' Some are staying: 'No matter how old a mother is, she watches her middle-aged children for signs of improvement.'

In collecting quotations one is impressed by the borrowing that has always gone on. Even the great ones. Sir Isaac Newton (1642–1727) implied this when he said, 'If I have seen farther, it is by standing on the shoulders of giants.' Even as he said this he was standing on the shoulders of Robert Burton (1577–1640) who had said, 'A dwarf standing on the shoulders of giants sees farther than a giant himself.'

And the Roman poet, Marcus Lucan (39–65) wrote, 'Pygmies placed on the shoulders of giants see more than the giants themselves.' Was this original with the ancient poet? Anyhow, not much change in 1600 years!

Dean William R. Inge (of St. Paul's) said, 'What is originality? Undetected plagiarism.' Voltaire was softer when he said, 'Originality is nothing but judicious imitation. The most original writers borrowed one from another. The instruction we find in books is like fire. We fetch it from our neighbours, kindle it at home, communicate it to others, and it becomes the property of all.'

Thus Abraham Lincoln, in the immortal words of his Gettysburg Address: 'And that government of the people, by the people, for the people, shall not perish from the earth' borrowed from the general prologue of the Wycliffe translation of the Bible (1384). 'This Bible is for the government of the people, by the people and for the people.'

Quotations get polished just as pebbles do. Oliver Goldsmith's famous couplet from *The Vicar of Wakefield* (1766) says: 'Man wants but little here below/Nor wants that little long.' It is better than 'but owes something more than somewhat,' as Damon Runyon would say, to Edward Young's 'Night Thoughts' (1742–1845): 'Man wants but little, Nor that little long.' James Thurber (1894–1961) took the thought and inverted it in a parody: 'Though statisticians in our time/Have never kept the score/Man wants a great deal here below/And women even more.'

The great Ralph Waldo Emerson, a leading entry in the index of any quotation book, said, 'When you strike at a king, you must kill him.' But an old English proverb said it better: 'Who draws his sword against the king, must throw away the scabbard.'

Borrowing has come down through the mists of history. Aesop, whose homilies are still current—'Who shall bell the cat; union gives strength; appearances are deceiving; don't count your chickens; the grapes are sour; etc'—was a pretty good borrower himself. Around 550 BC in *The Eagle and the Arrow* he wrote, 'And 'tis an added grief that with my own feathers, I am slain.'

Aeschylus (525–456 BC) picked up on Aesop and wrote:

That once an eagle, stricken with a dart,
Said when he saw the fashion of the shaft,
'With our own feathers, not by others' hands
Are we now smitten.'

In Ecclesiastes (1:9) it is said: 'The thing that hath been, it is that which shall be; and that which is done is that which shall be done: And there is no new thing under the sun.'

In the inexact business of quotation collecting, one must be aware that men and women—especially famous ones—may not be the authors of quotations attributed to them. As George Seldes says, 'There are many famous, sometimes brilliant and often very great quotations attributed to notable persons, which though false or incorrect, are usually improvements by anonymous requoters.' Many, many inaccuracies have been buried by tradition, which always seems to prefer the colourful phrase to the accurate one.

'I got there fustest with the mostest' is a misquote of Nathan Bedford Forrest, who said, 'I just took the shortcut and got there first with the most men.'

'Me Tarzan, you Jane' does not occur in the 1932 film 'Tarzan'. It was used by Johnny Weissmuller in describing his style of acting.

'Conscription if necessary, but not necessarily conscription' did not originate with Mackenzie King to whom it is usually attributed, but was adopted from a *Toronto Star* editorial.

'God tempers the wind to the shorn lamb,' usually thought to be from the Bible, is from Laurence Sterne's *A Sentimental Journey*.

The Bible itself is often misquoted: 'Money is the root of all evil' should be 'For the love of money is the root of all evil' (1 Tim. 6:10)—quite a difference.

'Pride goeth before a fall' is not quite right either. Proverbs 16:18 says 'Pride goeth before destruction and an haughty spirit before a fall.'

'God is always on the side of the big battalions' is usually credited to Napoleon and he may have said it, but many said it before him, reaching back to the Roman historian Tacitus (55–120) who said, 'The gods are with the stronger.'

No biographer of Benjamin Franklin has ever been able to establish that he said 'We must all hang together, or most assuredly we will all hang separately.' Tradition says that if he did not say it he should have, and it has gone down in history as his.

Marie Antoinette probably never said 'Let them eat cake.' The remark is in Rousseau's *Confessions* (1766) and traces back before Rousseau to the 1700s. It was accepted by the French, who considered her a wilful and wasteful Austrian, because it sounded like her extravagance and it discredited her.

Creators of epigrams today should do perhaps as Mr. Ashleigh Brilliant (his real name) does. Mr. Brilliant, a professional, copyrights his quotable phrases since a Los Angeles judge ruled that Mr. Brilliant's works were 'epigrams' entitled to full copyright protection. E.g., 'I may not be totally perfect—but parts of me are excellent.' Of the admission standard for his own quotes, Mr. Brilliant says, 'It's got to be universal and perpetual. And further it must not be longer than 17 words and preferably 16.'

All this is to show that sources are not too reliable. The words and the thoughts are the thing. 'The best words in the best order' is the object of all quotations. Who made the order and when is of interest, but not vital as the many quotations by 'Anon.' testify.

When two seemingly conflicting thoughts have made it to proverb or aphorism status, usually, in the ambivalence of life, both are true. Edna St. Vincent Millay says that 'It is not true that life is one damn thing after another—it's one damn thing over and over.' But actually life is both.

Mario Pei says, 'Good architecture lets nature in.' And Leonard Baskin says, 'Architecture should be dedicated to keeping the outside out and the inside in.' Rudyard Kipling sums it up with 'There are 9 and 60 ways of constructing tribal lays, and every single one of them is right.'

Just as O. Henry's short stories are famous for the unexpected twist in their conclusions, many quotable quotes have used this same technique. When Babe Ruth was asked in 1930 how he felt about making more money than the President of the United States he said, 'I had a better year than he did.' When Stalin was asked in 1948 what the Pope would say to a proposed strategy, he responded, 'How many divisions has the Pope?' W. C. Fields said, 'I always keep a supply of stimulant handy in case I see a snake—which I also keep handy.'

Translations, of course, are necessarily inexact and in most cases should be. When Heinrich Heine was told on his deathbed by a priest that God would forgive him, he is reported to have said, '*Bien sûr qu'il me pardonnera; c'est son métier.*' This has been honed to 'God will forgive me. It's his business.' Edmund Wilson, commenting on the *Rubaiyat of Omar Khayyam*, said that the best translations 'are those that depart most widely from the originals—that is, if the translator is himself a good poet.'

A necessary quality for lasting quotations is compression. Michelangelo said, 'Beauty is the purgation of superfluities.' Emerson took longer to say, 'We ascribe beauty to that which is simple; which has no superfluous parts; which exactly answers its ends.' Robert Browning said, 'Less is more.' Jean-Paul Sartre capsulized Freud in two words 'Childhood decides.'

André Maurois said concisely, 'Business is a combination of war and sport.' Rollo May said, 'Hate is not the opposite of love; apathy is.'

Sometimes quotations are similar in thought but so different in expression that there probably was no borrowing.

Thus, Robertson Davies said, 'The eye sees only what the mind is prepared to comprehend.' Louis Pasteur said, 'In the field of observation, chance favours the prepared mind.'

Theodore Reik said, 'Work and love—these are the basics. Without them there is neurosis.' The Parisienne couturier Coco Chanel said, 'There is time for work and time for love. That leaves no other time.'

Bernard Shaw said, 'My method is to take the utmost trouble to find the right thing to say, and then to say it with the utmost levity.'

In his 1992 speech to the Republican National Convention, former president Ronald Reagan quoted Abraham Lincoln as saying, 'You cannot strengthen the weak by weakening the strong. You cannot help the wage earner by pulling down the wage payer. You cannot help the poor by destroying the rich. You cannot help men permanently by doing for them what they could and should do for themselves.' But historians have known for many years that the quote, although often attributed to Lincoln, was originated long after his death by the Reverend John William Henry Boetcker, a minister from Erie, Pennsylvania who was born in 1873, eight years after Lincoln died.

One of the great attractions of quotations is that they are rich in ideas which can be tailored to specific purposes.

For instance, Walter Bagehot's 'A man who has not read Homer is like a man who has not seen the ocean. There is a great object of which he has no idea.' For Homer, one could substitute the Bible or Shakespeare or the Charter of Rights and Freedoms or the U.S. Constitution or whatever it is relevant to substitute. And for 'ocean' one can substitute Paris or New York or the Grand Canyon.

As Voltaire says, 'We fetch it from our neighbors, kindle it at home, etc.'

These quotations represent a distillation from 50 years of reading books and manuscripts and magazines and book reviews and advertisements and epitaphs and signs in store windows. They come from other quotation books and from obituary pages, and from listening to friends and strangers and associates. They come from the Bible and Shakespeare and Ralph Waldo Emerson and Samuel Johnson, but also from Margaret Thatcher and Lily Tomlin and Satchell Paige and Igor Stravinsky, and from Pope John XXIII and Marshall McLuhan.

This book does not have the rich indices of key words or first lines for any of those seeking detailed and valuable aids. I leave these to the great scholarly collections. 'To me, the charm of an encyclopedia is that it knows and I needn't.' The best of these, it seems to me, are Burton K. Stevenson's *Home Book of Quotations, Bartlett's Familiar Quotations*, George Seldes' *The Great Quotations*, Lawrence J. Peter's *Peter's Quotations*, James B. Simpson's *Contemporary Quotations*, Edward F. Murphy's *The Crown Treasury of Relevant Quotations, The Oxford Dictionary of Quotations* and *The International Thesaurus of Quotations*. And now, as an aperitif, here are some quotations I like particularly:

Death twitches my ear. 'Live,' he says, 'I am coming.'   *Virgil*
(quoted by Justice Oliver Wendell Holmes on his 90th birthday)

It is well to remember that the entire population of the universe, with one trifling exception, is composed of others.   *John Andrew Holmes*

There is nothing wrong with America that cannot be cured by what is right with America.   *President William F. Clinton*

A man does what he must—in spite of personal consequences, in spite of obstacles and dangers and pressures—and that is the basis of all morality.   *John F. Kennedy*

No him, no me.   *Dizzy Gillespie of Louis Armstrong*

You can't make anything idiot proof because idiots are so ingenious.   *Ron Burns*

A good catchword can obscure analysis for 50 years.   *Johan Huisinga*

Sex is the poor man's opera.   *Italian proverb*

A person buying ordinary products in a supermarket is in touch with his deepest emotions.   *John Kenneth Galbraith*

I wonder what language truck drivers are using, now that everyone is using theirs.
Beryl Pfizer

I don't deserve this award, but I have arthritis, and I don't deserve that either.
Jack Benny

Literature is mostly about having sex and not much about having children; life is the other way around.   *David Lodge*

The act of writing is the act of discovering what you believe.   *David Hare*

If you educate a man you educate a person, but if you educate a woman, you educate a family.   *Rudy Manikan*

There is a road from the eye to the heart that does not go through the intellect.
G. K. Chesterton

Three o'clock is always too late or too early for anything you want to do.
Jean-Paul Sartre

He looked at me as if I was a sidedish he hadn't ordered.   *Ring Lardner, Jr.*

There is a good deal too strange to be believed, nothing is too strange to have happened.
Thomas Hardy

Change is not made without inconvenience, even from worse to better.
Richard Hooker

If you live long enough the venerability factor creeps in; you get accused of things you never did and praised for virtues you never had.   *I. F. Stone*

A man's most valuable trait is a judicious sense of what not to believe.   *Euripides*

One of the misfortunes of our time is that in getting rid of false shame, we have killed off so much real shame as well.   *Louis Kronenberger*

Book lovers never go to bed alone.   *Anonymous*

One doesn't discover new lands without consenting to lose sight of the shore for a very long time.   *Andre Gide*

Much as he is opposed to law-breaking, he is not bigoted about it.   *Damon Runyon*

The placebo cures 30% of patients—no matter what they have.   *David Kline*

There is one elementary truth, the ignorance of which kills countless ideas and splendid plans: the moment one definitely commits oneself, then Providence moves too. All sorts of things occur to help one that never otherwise would have occurred . . .
Whatever you can do,
Or dream you can do,
Begin it.
Boldness had genius, power and magic in it.
Begin it now.   *Goethe*

Not to transmit an experience is to betray it.   *Elie Wiesel*

The enemies of the future are always the very nicest people.   *Christopher Morley*

You don't hold your own in the world by standing on guard, but by attacking and getting well hammered yourself.   *George Bernard Shaw*

R. I. Fitzhenry,
1993

Ability and Achievement

Although the world is full of suffering, it is full also of the overcoming of it.
Helen Keller

Ambition can creep as well as soar.
Edmund Burke

An expert is a man who has made all the mistakes, which can be made, in a very narrow field.
Niels Bohr

An expert is someone who knows some of the worst mistakes that can be made in his subject and how to avoid them.
Werner Heisenberg

Faith moves mountains, but you have to keep pushing while you are praying.
Mason Cooley

Men achieve a certain greatness unawares, when working to another aim.
Ralph Waldo Emerson

Nothing is too small to know, and nothing too big to attempt.   *William Van Horne*

So there he is at last. Man on the moon. The poor, magnificent bungler! He can't even get to the office without undergoing the agonies of the damned, but give him a little metal, a few chemicals, some wire and 20 or 30 billion dollars and, vroom! There he is, up on a rock, a quarter of a million miles up in the sky.   *Russell Baker*

The best is the enemy of the good.
Voltaire

The difference between what we do and what we are capable of doing would suffice to solve most of the world's problems.
Gandhi

The measure of a master is his success in bringing all men round to his opinion 20 years later.
Ralph Waldo Emerson

The trouble with specialists is that they tend to think in grooves.   *Elaine Morgan*

There are no credentials. They do not even need a medical certificate. They need not be sound either in body or mind. They only require a certificate of birth—just to prove they are first of the litter. You would not choose a Spaniel on these principles. (On aristocracy)
David Lloyd George

Where I was born and where and how I have lived is unimportant. It is what I have done with where I have been that should be of interest.
Georgia O'Keeffe

You commit a sin of omission if you do not utilize all the power that is within you. All men have claims on man, and to the man with special talents, this is a very special claim. It is required that a man take part in the actions and clashes of his time than the peril of being judged not to have lived at all.   *Oliver Wendell Holmes*

I am surprised nothing has been made of the fact that astronaut Neil Armstrong carried no sidearms when he landed on the moon.   *Justice Arthur Goldberg*

'What would you call the highest happiness?' Wratislaw was asked. 'The sense of competence,' was the answer, given without hesitation.   *John Buchan*

The winds and waves are always on the side of the ablest navigators.
    Edward Gibbon

How many 'coming men' has one known? Where on earth do they all go to?
    Arthur Wing Pinero

He is the best sailor who can steer within fewest points of the wind, and exact a motive power out of the greatest obstacles.   *Henry David Thoreau*

They are able who think they are able.   *Virgil*

The biggest things are always the easiest to do because there is no competition.
    William Van Horne

What we do upon some great occasion will probably depend on what we already are: and what we are will be the result of previous years of self-discipline.   *H. P. Liddon*

It's pretty hard to be efficient without being obnoxious.   *Kin Hubbard*

Nothing great is created suddenly, any more than a bunch of grapes or a fig. If you tell me that you desire a fig, I answer you that there must be time. Let it first blossom, then bear fruit, then ripen.   *Epictetus*

Out of the strain of the Doing, Into the peace of the Done.   *Julia Louise Woodruff*

It's them that takes advantage that gets advantage i' this world.   *George Eliot*

Anything you're good at contributes to happiness.   *Bertrand Russell*

I think knowing what you cannot do is more important than knowing what you can do.   *Lucille Ball*

There is endless merit in a man's knowing when to have done.   *Thomas Carlyle*

The worst of all diseases is nervous ability.   *Edward Dyson*

It's the whole, not the detail, that matters.   *German proverb*

Long is the road from conception to completion.   *Molière*

Only those who dare to fail greatly can ever achieve greatly.   *Robert F. Kennedy*

Back of every achievement is a proud wife and a surprised mother-in-law.
Brooks Hays

Noise proves nothing. Often a hen who has merely laid an egg cackles as if she had laid an asteroid.   *Mark Twain*

We judge ourselves by what we feel capable of doing, while others judge us by what we have already done.   *Henry Wadsworth Longfellow*

Do what you can, with what you have, where you are.   *Theodore Roosevelt*

About all some men accomplish in life is to send a son to Harvard.
Edgar Watson Howe

He has half the deed done who has made a beginning.   *Horace*

Give me where to stand, and I will move the earth.   *Archimedes*

The only way round is through.   *Robert Frost*

If a man does not keep pace with his companions, perhaps it is because he hears a different drummer. Let him step to the music which he hears, however measured or far away.   *Henry David Thoreau*

Is there anything in life so disenchanting as attainment?   *Robert Louis Stevenson*

I'm a slow walker, but I never walk back.   *Abraham Lincoln*

That's one small step for a man, one giant leap for mankind.   *Neil Armstrong*

You cannot fly like an eagle with the wings of a wren.   *William Henry Hudson*

In esse I am nothing; in posse I am everything.   *John Adams*

Out of the best and most productive years of each man's life, he should carve a segment in which he puts his private career aside to serve his community and his country, and thereby serve his children, his neighbours, his fellow men, and the cause of freedom.
David Lilienthal

Good is not good, where better is expected.   *Thomas Fuller*

Never look down to test the ground before taking your next step; only he who keeps his eye fixed on the far horizon will find his right road.   *Dag Hammarskjöld*

We promise according to our hopes, and perform according to our fears.
La Rochefoucauld

Practice yourself, for heaven's sake, in little things; and thence proceed to greater.
Epictetus

For a man to achieve all that is demanded of him he must regard himself as greater than he is.   *Goethe*

He that leaveth nothing to Chance will do few things ill, but he will do very few things.   *George, Lord Halifax*

When spider webs unite, they can tie up a lion.   *Ethiopian proverb*

Everyone must row with the oars he has.   *English proverb*

Every calling is great when greatly pursued.   *Oliver Wendell Holmes, Jr.*

Any jackass can kick down a barn, but it takes a good carpenter to build one.
Sam Rayburn

God gives the nuts, but he does not crack them.   *German proverb*

Let me tell you the secret that has led me to my goal. My strength lies solely in my tenacity.   *Louis Pasteur*

What one has to do usually can be done.   *Eleanor Roosevelt*

The world is all gates, all opportunities, strings of tension waiting to be struck.
Ralph Waldo Emerson

I confess that altruistic and cynically selfish talk seem to me about equally unreal. With all humility, I think 'whatsoever thy hand findeth to do, do it with thy might,' infinitely more important than the vain attempt to love one's neighbour as one's self. If you want to hit a bird on the wing you must have all your will in focus, you must not be thinking about yourself, and equally, you must not be thinking about your neighbour; you must be living with your eye on that bird. Every achievement is a bird on the wing.   *Oliver Wendell Holmes, Jr.*

Sometimes it is more important to discover what one cannot do, than what one can do.   *Lin Yutang*

To achieve great things, we must live as though we were never going to die.
Vauvenargues

I am easily satisfied with the very best.   *Winston Churchill*

The more we realize our minuteness and our impotence in the face of cosmic forces, the more astonishing becomes what human beings have achieved.   *Bertrand Russell*

Don't be afraid to take a big step if one is indicated. You can't cross a chasm in two small jumps.   *David Lloyd George*

There is nothing so useless as doing efficiently that which should not be done at all.
Peter F. Drucker

Each morning sees some task begun
Each evening sees it close.
Something attempted, something done,
Has earned a night's repose.

Henry Wadsworth Longfellow

The reward of a thing well done, is to have done it.

Ralph Waldo Emerson

God will not look you over for medals, degrees or diplomas, but for scars.

Elbert Hubbard

There are two kinds of people: those who are always well and those who are always sick. Most of the evils of the world come from the first sort and most of the achievements from the second.

Louis Dudek

Absence

Greater things are believed of those who are absent.

Tacitus

Absences are a good influence in love and keep it bright and delicate.

Robert Louis Stevenson

The longest absence is less perilous to love than the terrible trials of incessant proximity.

Ouida

Failing to be there when a man wants her is a woman's greatest sin, except to be there when he doesn't want her.

Helen Rowland

Absence diminishes little passions and increases great ones just as the wind blows out a candle and fans a fire.

La Rochefoucauld

It takes time for the absent to assume their true shape in our thoughts. After death they take on a firmer outline and then cease to change.

Colette

Sometimes, when one person is missing, the whole world seems depopulated.

Alphonse de Lamartine

The absent are always wrong.

English proverb

Acting and the Theatre

A good drama critic is one who perceives what is happening in the theatre of his time. A great drama critic also perceives what is not happening.

Kenneth Tynan

A walking shadow, a poor player, that struts and frets his hour upon the stage and then is heard no more.

Shakespeare, 'Macbeth'

Acting is a question of absorbing other people's personalities and adding some of your own experience.

Paul Newman

An actor is a guy who, if you ain't talking about him ain't listening.
(often quoted by Marlon Brando but originated by George Glass)

An agent is a guy who is sore because an actor gets 90% of what he makes.
Alva Johnston

Bugs Bunny—the perfect employee. Never absent. Never late. Never changes the script. Doesn't have an agent. Never asks for a percent of the profit. Doesn't ask to have his relatives on the payroll.   *Anon.*

In music, the punctuation is absolutely strict, the bars and the rests are absolutely defined. But our punctuation cannot be quite strict because we have to relate it to the audience. In other words, we are continually changing the score. *Ralph Richardson*

Acting is the most public form of indecent exposure.   *Ruth Cracknell*

She was good at playing abstract confusion in the same way that a midget is good at being short.   *Clive James*

The best audience is intelligent, well-educated, and a little drunk.   *Alvin Barkley*

The play was a great success, but the audience was a disaster.   *Oscar Wilde*

The structure of a play is always the story of how the birds come home to roost.
Arthur Miller

When the characters are really alive before their author, the latter does nothing but follow them in their action, in their words, in the situations which they suggest to him.
Luigi Pirandello

Working in the theatre has a lot in common with unemployment.   *Arthur Gingold*

There are some great roles—mostly in Shakespeare's tragedies, which no one can play at full strength from beginning to end. One simply hopes that one can hit the peaks as often as one has the strength.   *Peggy Ashcroft*

Acting is not being emotional, but being able to express emotion.   *Kate Reid*

A good actor must never be in love with anyone but himself.   *Jean Anouilh*

Every actor in his heart believes everything bad that's printed about him.
Orson Welles

Actors are the only honest hypocrites.   *William Hazlitt*

Drama is life with the dull bits cut out.   *Alfred Hitchcock*

Film-making has become a kind of hysterical pregnancy.   *Richard Lester*

Not to go to the theatre is like making one's toilet without a mirror.
Arthur Schopenhauer

You can't automate in the arts. Since the sixteenth century there has been no change in the number of people necessary to produce *Hamlet*.   *William T. Wylie*

When actors begin to think, it is time for a change. They are not fitted for it.
Stephen Leacock

Opening night is the night before the play is ready to open.   *George Jean Nathan*

An actor is a sculptor who carves in snow.   *Edwin Booth*

The unencumbered stage encourages the truth operative in everyone. The less seen, the more heard. The eye is the enemy of the ear in real drama.   *Thornton Wilder*

Comedy is tragedy, plucked unripe.   *'Tom Collins' (Joseph Furphy)*

Acting is happy agony.   *Alec Guinness*

With the collapse of vaudeville new talent has no place to stink.   *George Burns*

When the audience knows you know better, it's satire, but when they think you can't do any better, it's corn.   *Spike Jones*

The person who wants to make it has to sweat. There are no short cuts. And you've got to have the guts to be hated.   *Bette Davis*

True tragedy may be defined as a dramatic work in which the outward failure of the principal personage is compensated for by the dignity and greatness of his character.
Joseph Wood Krutch

A fan club is a group of people who tell an actor he is not alone in the way he feels about himself.   *Jack Carson*

The real actor—like any real artist—has a direct line to the collective heart.
Bette Davis

The best actors do not let the wheels show.   *Henry Fonda*

A talent for drama is not a talent for writing, but is an ability to articulate human relationships.   *Gore Vidal*

Many plays, certainly mine, are like blank cheques. The actors and directors put their own signatures on them.   *Thornton Wilder*

You need three things in the theatre—the play, the actors and the audience—and each must give something.   *Kenneth Haigh*

From the point of view of the playwright, then, the essence of a tragedy, or even of a serious play, is the spiritual awakening, or regeneration, of his hero.
Maxwell Anderson

The trouble with nude dancing is that not everything stops when the music does.

Robert Helpmann

A film is never really good unless the camera is an eye in the head of a poet.

Orson Welles

The whole motivation for any performer is 'Look at me, Ma.'   *Lenny Bruce*

If you give audiences a chance they'll do half your acting for you.

Katharine Hepburn

Show business is like sex. When it's wonderful, it's wonderful. But when it isn't very good, it's still all right.   *Max Wall*

All the movies used to be 'colossal'. Now they're all 'frank'. I think I liked 'colossal' better.   *Beryl Pfizer*

Satire is what closes Saturday night.   *George S. Kaufman*

A play should give you something to think about. When I see a play and understand it the first time, then I know it can't be much good.   *T. S. Eliot*

By increasing the size of the keyhole, today's playwrights are in danger of doing away with the door.   *Peter Ustinov*

We do not go (to the theatre) like our ancestors, to escape from the pressure of reality, so much as to confirm our experience of it.   *Charles Lamb*

A play visibly represents pure existing.   *Thornton Wilder*

I sweat. If anything comes easy to me, I mistrust it.   *Lilli Palmer*

I sometimes wish they would swagger more now, buy bigger overcoats and wilder hats, and retain those traces of make-up that put them outside respectability and keep them rogues and vagabonds, which is what, at heart—bless 'em—they are.

J. B. Priestley

Actor-manager—one to whom the part is greater than the whole.   *Ronald Jeans*

I know it was wonderful, but I don't know how I did it.

Laurence Olivier (after a brilliant performance as 'Othello')

Very few people go to the doctor when they have a cold, they go to the theatre instead.

W. Boyd Gatewood

The unique thing about Margaret Rutherford is that she can act with her chin alone. Among its many moods I especially cherish the chin commanding, the chin in doubt, and the chin at bay.   *Kenneth Tynan*

There are five stages to an actor's career: who is Herschel Bernardi? get me Herschel Bernardi; get me a Herschel Bernardi type; get me a young Herschel Bernardi; and who is Herschel Bernardi?
Herschel Bernardi

On stage I make love to twenty-five thousand people; then I go home alone.
Janis Joplin

There is undoubtedly something about the theatre which suits the Australian genius. It is an exhibitionist art and the Australians are by nature exhibitionists.
John Douglas Pringle

Long experience has taught me that in England nobody goes to the theatre unless he or she has bronchitis.
James Agate

Playing Shakespeare is very tiring. You never get to sit down, unless you're a king.
Josephine Hull

Theatre is simply what cannot be expressed by any other means; a complexity of words, movements, gestures that convey a vision of the world inexpressible in any other way.
Eugene Ionesco

As an actor, he should be an extra in police line-ups.
Robert H. Gurney

Action

After all is said and done, more is said than done.
Anon.

Between saying and doing many a pair of shoes is worn out.
Italian proverb

But search the land of living men,
Where wilt thou find their like again.
Sir Walter Scott

Deliberation is the work of many men. Action, of one alone.
Charles de Gaulle

Go and wake up your cook.
Arabian proverb

The difference between a stupid man and a wise man is in the stupid man's inability to calculate the consequences of action.
Brian Penton

I want to see you shoot the way you shout.
Theodore Roosevelt

If you want something done right, get someone else to do it.
Marion Giacomini

Looking at small advantages prevents great affairs from being accomplished.
Confucius

Noble deeds and hot baths are the best cures for depression.
Dodie Smith

Play out the game, act well your part, and if the gods have blundered, we will not.
Ralph Waldo Emerson

The central problem of our age is how to act decisively in the absence of certainty.
Bertrand Russell

The fair request ought to be followed by the deed, in silence.   *Dante*

To knock a thing down, especially if it is cocked at an arrogant angle, is a deep delight
to the blood.   *George Santayana*

When written in Chinese, the word crisis is composed of two characters. One represents
danger and the other represents opportunity.   *John F. Kennedy*

Why, then the world's mine oyster
Which I with sword will open.   *Shakespeare 'The Merry Wives of Windsor'*

Through the picture, I see reality. Through the word, I understand it.   *Sven Lidman*

He who desires, but acts not, breeds pestilence.   *William Blake*

The frontiers are not east or west, north or south, but wherever a man fronts a fact.
Henry David Thoreau

If you want a thing done, go—if not, send.   *Benjamin Franklin*

All glory comes from daring to begin.   *Anon.*

Action is eloquence.   *Shakespeare, 'Coriolanus'*

From the moment of birth we are immersed in action, and can only fitfully guide it
by taking thought.   *Alfred North Whitehead*

The great end of life is not knowledge, but action.   *Thomas Fuller*

The men who act stand nearer to the mass of man than the men who write; and it is
in their hands that new thought gets its translation into the crude language of deeds.
Woodrow Wilson

We accept the verdict of the past until the need for change cries out loudly enough to
force upon us a choice between the comforts of further inertia and the irksomeness of
action.   *Learned Hand*

It is much easier to do and die than it is to reason why.   *G. A. Studdert-Kennedy*

'Mean to' don't pick no cotton.   *Anon.*

Everything comes to him who hustles while he waits.   *Thomas A. Edison*

It is only in marriage with the world that our ideals can bear fruit; divorced from it,
they remain barren.   *Bertrand Russell*

There are risks and costs to a program of action. But they are far less than the long-range risks and costs of comfortable inaction.   *John F. Kennedy*

Take time to deliberate; but when the time for action arrives, stop thinking and go in.
Andrew Jackson

You may be disappointed if you fail, but you are doomed if you don't try.
Beverly Sills

When you appeal to force, there's one thing you must never do—lose.
Dwight D. Eisenhower

In action, be primitive; in foresight, a strategist.   *René Char*

I am not built for academic writings. Action is my domain.   *Gandhi*

Trust only movement. Life happens at the level of events, not of words. Trust movement.   *Alfred Adler*

Let us act on what we have, since we have not what we wish.   *Cardinal Newman*

Nothing is often a good thing to do and always a good thing to say.   *Will Durant*

A = r + p (or Adventure equals risk plus purpose.)   *Robert McClure*

For purposes of action nothing is more useful than narrowness of thought combined with energy of will.   *Henri Frédéric Amiel*

I shall tell you a great secret, my friend. Do not wait for the last judgement, it takes place every day.   *Albert Camus*

Blessed is he who carries within himself a god and an ideal and who obeys it—an ideal of art, of science, or gospel virtues. Therein lie the springs of great thoughts and great actions.   *Louis Pasteur*

I learn by going where I have to go.   *Theodore Roethke*

He who is outside his door already has a hard part of his journey behind him.
Dutch proverb

The shortest answer is doing.   *English proverb*

Action is consolatory. It is the enemy of thought and the friend of flattering illusions.
Joseph Conrad

We will either find a way, or make one.   *Hannibal*

If you have anything to tell me of importance, for God's sake begin at the end.
Sara Jeannette Duncan

There are only two forces that unite men—fear and interest.   *Napoleon Bonaparte*

Adversity

An earthquake achieves what the law promises but does not in practice maintain—the equality of all men.
Ignazio Silone

When you are faced with an impasse you have got to crash through or you've got to crash.
Gough Whitlam

I have an inward treasure born within me, which can keep me alive if all the extraneous delights should be withheld; or offered only at a price I cannot afford.
Charlotte Brontë

Nothing is more desirable than to be released from an affliction, but nothing is more frightening than to be divested of a crutch.
James Baldwin

People don't ever seem to realize that doing what's right is no guarantee against misfortune.
William McFee

The struggle to the top is in itself enough to fulfill the human heart. Sisyphus should be regarded as happy.
Albert Camus

There are three modes of bearing the ills of life: by indifference, by philosophy and by religion.
Charles Caleb Colton

Only a loser finds it impossible to accept a temporary setback. A winner asks why.
Ita Buttrose

Night brings our troubles to the light rather than banishes them.
Seneca

Too much happens . . . Man performs, engenders so much more than he can or should have to bear. That's how he finds that he can bear anything.
William Faulkner

A great man does not lose his self-possession when he is afflicted; the ocean is not made muddy by the falling in of its banks.
Panchatantra

I've had an unhappy life, thank God.
Russell Baker

Do not show your wounded finger, for everything will knock up against it.
Baltasar Gracián

They sicken of the calm that know the storm.
Dorothy Parker

Trouble is only opportunity in work clothes.
Henry J. Kaiser

The man who is swimming against the stream knows the strength of it.
Woodrow Wilson

The ultimate measure of a man is not where he stands in moments of comfort and convenience, but where he stands at times of challenge and controversy.
Martin Luther King, Jr.

Great occasions do not make heroes or cowards; they simply unveil them to the eyes of men. Silently and imperceptibly, as we wake or sleep, we grow strong or weak; and at last some crisis shows what we have become.   *Brooke Foss Westcott*

What does not destroy me, makes me strong.   *Friedrich Nietzsche*

I long ago came to the conclusion that all life is six to five against. *Damon Runyon*

(Adversity is) the state in which a man most easily becomes acquainted with himself, being especially free from admirers then.   *Samuel Johnson*

Adversity has the same effect on a man that severe training has on the pugilist—it reduces him to his fighting weight.   *Josh Billings*

From a fallen tree, all make kindling.   *Spanish proverb*

The virtue of prosperity is temperance; the virtue of adversity is fortitude, which in morals is the heroical virtue.   *Francis Bacon*

The keenest sorrow is to recognize ourselves as the sole cause of all our adversities.
    Sophocles

No untroubled day has ever dawned for me.   *Seneca*

You can't have more bugs than a blanketful.   *Spanish proverb*

Even in the deepest sinking there is the hidden purpose of an ultimate rising. Thus it is for all men, from none is the source of light withheld unless he himself withdraws from it. Therefore the most important thing is not to despair.   *Hasidic saying*

Trouble will rain on those who are already wet.   *Anon.*

They say a reasonable amount o' fleas is good for a dog—it keeps him from broodin' over bein' a dog mebbe.   *Edward Noyes Westcott*

There is nothing the body suffers which the soul may not profit by.
    George Meredith

The burden is equal to the horse's strength.   *The Talmud*

Nothing befalls a man except what is in his nature to endure.   *Marcus Aurelius*

I am escaped by the skin of my teeth.   *Job 19:20*

Prosperity tries the fortunate; adversity the great.   *Pliny the Younger*

Be willing to have it so; acceptance of what has happened is the first step to overcoming the consequences of any misfortune.   *William James*

If all our misfortunes were laid in one common heap, whence every one must take an equal portion, most people would be content to take their own and depart.   *Solon*

I never knew any man in my life who could not bear another's misfortunes perfectly like a Christian.   *Alexander Pope*

When the world has once begun to use us ill, it afterwards continues the same treatment with less scruple or ceremony, as men do to a whore.   *Jonathan Swift*

Is there no balm in Gilead? Is there no physician there?   *Jeremiah 8:22*

Every difficulty slurred over will be a ghost to disturb your repose later on.
                                                                    Frédéric Chopin

Fire tries gold, misfortune men.   *Anon.*

The fiery trials through which we pass will light us down in honour or dishonour to the latest generation.   *Abraham Lincoln*

Thou hast shown thy people hard things: thou hast made us to drink the wine of astonishment.   *Psalms 60:3*

Advertising

The incessant witless repetition of advertisers' moron-fodder has become so much a part of life that if we are not careful, we forget to be insulted by it.
      The London Times (quoted in the Concise Columbia Dictionary of Quotations)

Advertising is the folk art of the twentieth century.   *John Romeril*

The advertisements in a newspaper are more full of knowledge in respect to what is going on in a state or community than the editorial columns are.
                                                                Henry Ward Beecher

If it doesn't sell, it isn't creative.   *David Ogilvy*

In advertising not to be different is virtually suicidal.   *Bill Bernback*

Advertising—a judicious mixture of flattery and threats.   *Northrop Frye*

Advertising may be described as the science of arresting the human intelligence long enough to get money from it.   *Stephen Leacock*

The best ad is a good product.   *Alan H. Meyer*

The philosophy behind much advertising is based on the old observation that every man is really two men—the man he is and the man he wants to be.
                                                                    William Feather

The number of agency people required to shoot a commercial on location is in direct proportion to the mean temperature of the location.   *Shelby Page*

Advertising is the most fun you can have with your clothes on. *Jerry Della Femina*

Buy me and you will overcome the anxieties I have just reminded you of.
Michael Schudson

Advertising men and politicians are dangerous if they are separated. Together they are diabolical. *Phillip Adams*

If I were starting life over again, I am inclined to think that I would go into the advertising business in preference to almost any other. The general raising of standards of modern civilization among all groups of people during the past half-century would have been impossible without that spreading of the knowledge of higher standards by means of advertising. *Franklin D. Roosevelt*

Promise, large promise, is the soul of an advertisement. *Samuel Johnson*

The deeper problems connected with advertising come less from the unscrupulousness of our 'deceivers' than from our pleasure in being deceived; less from the desire to seduce than from the desire to be seduced. *Daniel J. Boorstin*

Ads are the cave art of the twentieth century. *Marshall McLuhan*

The advertisement is one of the most interesting and difficult of modern literary forms.
Aldous Huxley

What kills a skunk is the publicity it gives itself. *Abraham Lincoln*

Few people at the beginning of the nineteenth century needed an adman to tell them what they wanted. *J. K. Galbraith*

The art of publicity is a black art. *Learned Hand*

Advertising is legalized lying. *H. G. Wells*

Advertising is what you do when you can't go to see somebody. That's all it is.
Fairfax Cone

The consumer is not a moron. She's your wife.
David Ogilvy (advice to advertising copywriters)

Advice

But one must know where one stands, and where the others wish to go. *Goethe*

No man ever listened himself out of a job. *Calvin Coolidge*

Never sing in chorus; if you do you won't be heard. *J. F. Archibald*

The proverb warns that, 'You should not bite the hand that feeds you.' But maybe you should, if it prevents you from feeding yourself.   *Thomas Szasz*

I remember my father telling me the story of the preacher delivering an exhortation to his flock, and as he reached the climax of his exhortation, a man in the front row got up and said, 'O Lord, use me. Use me, O Lord—in an advisory capacity!'
   Adlai Stevenson

Be frank and explicit. That is the right line to take when you wish to conceal your own mind and to confuse the minds of others.   *Benjamin Disraeli*

To make pleasure pleasant, shorten.   *Charles Buston*

Put all thine eggs in one basket and—watch that basket.   *Mark Twain*

It has seemed to be more necessary to have regard to the weight of words rather than to their number.   *Cicero*

Don't offer me advice, give me money.   *Spanish proverb*

If you aren't rich, you should always look useful.   *Louis-Ferdinand Céline*

He who can lick can bite.   *French proverb*

When a man comes to me for advice, I find out the kind of advice he wants, and I give it to him.   *Josh Billings*

We only make a dupe of the friend whose advice we ask, for we never tell him all; and it is usually what we have left unsaid that decides our conduct.
   Diane de Poitiers

I give myself, sometimes, admirable advice, but I am incapable of taking it.
   Mary Wortley Montagu

Advice is like snow; the softer it falls, the longer it dwells upon, and the deeper it sinks into, the mind.   *Samuel Taylor Coleridge*

The true secret of giving advice is, after you have honestly given it, to be perfectly indifferent whether it is taken or not and never persist in trying to set people right.
   Hannah Whitall Smith

'Be yourself!' is about the worst advice you can give to some people.   *Tom Masson*

Do not forget that in this wicked world people take you at your own valuation, so make a big noise. That is what men do!   *Jessie Street*

The advice of the elders to young men is very apt to be as unreal as a list of the hundred best books.   *Oliver Wendell Holmes, Jr.*

Fewer things are harder to put up with than the annoyance of a good example.
   Mark Twain

The only thing to do with good advice is to pass it on. It is never of any use to oneself.
Oscar Wilde

A good scare is worth more to a man than good advice.   *Edgar Watson Howe*

There is little serenity comparable to the serenity of the inexperienced giving advice
to the experienced.   *Anon.*

Advice is seldom welcome; and those who want it the most always like it the least.
Lord Chesterfield

It is well enough, when one is talking to a friend, to lodge in an odd word by way
of counsel now and then; but there is something mighty irksome in its staring upon
one in a letter, where one ought to see only kind words and friendly remembrances.
Mary Lamb

Men of much depth of mind can bear a great deal of counsel; for it does not easily
deface their own character, nor render their purposes indistinct.   *Arthur Helps*

Have more than thou showest,
Speak less than thou knowest.   *Shakespeare, 'King Lear'*

What you don't see with your eyes, don't invent with your tongue.   *Jewish proverb*

If you keep your mind sufficiently open, people will throw a lot of rubbish into it.
William A. Orton

Don't fight forces; use them.   *Buckminster Fuller*

Drink nothing without seeing it; sign nothing without reading it.   *Spanish proverb*

Expert advice is the very devil. You want at least 100 experts, then conduct a Gallup
Poll among them—then think out the answer for yourself.   *R. G. Menzies*

Simplicity, simplicity, simplicity. I say, let your affairs be as two or three, and not a
hundred or a thousand; instead of a million count half a dozen, and keep your accounts
on your thumbnail.   *Henry David Thoreau*

You must not think, sir, to catch old birds with chaff.   *Cervantes*

Aging and Old Age

Age and treachery will triumph over youth and skill.   *Anon.*

All the best sands of my life are somehow getting into the wrong end of the hourglass.
If I could only reverse it! Were it in my power to do so, would I?
Thomas Bailey Aldrich

All would live long, but none would be old.   *Benjamin Franklin*

An old man concludeth from his knowing mankind that they know him too, and that maketh him very wary.   *Marquis of Halifax (George Saville)*

An old man loved is Winter with flowers.   *German proverb*

An older author is constantly rediscovering himself in the more or less fossilized productions of his earlier years.   *Oliver Wendell Holmes*

Youth troubles over eternity; age grasps at a day and is satisfied to have even the day.
                    Mary Gilmore

Grow old with me!
The best is yet to be,
The last of life, for which the first was made:
Our times are in his hands
Who sayeth 'a whole I plant,
Youth shows but half;
Trust God; see all nor be afraid.'   *Robert Browning*

Growing old is like being increasingly penalized for a crime you have not committed.
                    Anthony Powell

Here's a new day. O Pendulum move slowly!   *Harold Munro*

I am 65 and I guess that puts me in with the geriatrics. But if there were 15 months in every year, I'd only be 48. That's the trouble with us. We number everything. Take women, for example, I think they deserve to have more than 12 years between the ages of 28 and 40.   *James Thurber*

I am just turning 40 and taking my time about it.   *Harold Lloyd (in his 70s)*

I haven't asked you to make me young again. All I want is to go on getting older.
                    Konrad Adenauer

I refuse to admit that I am more than 52, even if that makes my sons illegitimate.
                    Nancy Lady Astor

If I'd known I was gonna live this long (100 years), I'd have taken better care of myself.   *Ubie Blake (James Hubert Blake, 1883–1983)*

If the young only knew; if the old only could.   *French saying*

Is it not strange that desire should so many years outlive performance?
                    Shakespeare, 'King Henry VI, Part II'

Middle age snuffs out more talent than even wars or sudden deaths do.
                    Richard Hughes

Old age is the Outpatient's Dept of purgatory.   *Lord Cecil*

Old age takes away from us what we have inherited and gives us what we have earned.
Gerald Brenan

The difference between being an elder statesman
And posing successfully as an elder statesman
Is practically negligible. *T. S. Eliot*

The old repeat themselves and the young have nothing to say. The boredom is mutual.
Jacques Bainville

There is many a good tune played on an old fiddle. *Old saying*

Time goes by: reputation increases, ability declines. *Dag Hammarskjöld*

To keep the heart unwrinkled, to be hopeful, kindly, cheerful, reverent—that is to
triumph over old age. *Thomas Bailey Aldrich*

We do not die wholly at our deaths: we have moldered away gradually long before.
Faculty after faculty, interest after interest, attachment after attachment disappear: we
are torn from ourselves while living. *William Hazlitt*

Wrinkles—the service stripes of life. *Anon.*

To be seventy years young is sometimes far more cheerful and hopeful than to be forty
years old. *Oliver Wendell Holmes, Jr.*

One of the delights known to age, and beyond the grasp of youth, is that of 'not
going'! *J. B. Priestley*

A man of sixty has spent twenty years in bed and over three years in eating.
Arnold Bennett

Many young peole die of old age. *F. J. Mills*

Middle age: when you're sitting at home on Saturday night and the telephone rings
and you hope it isn't for you. *Ogden Nash*

No Spring, nor Summer beauty hath such grace,
As I have seen in one Autumnal face. *John Donne*

If you live long enough the venerability factor creeps in; you get accused of things
you never did and praised for virtues you never had. *I. F. Stone*

I advise you to go on living solely to enrage those who are paying your annuities. It
is the only pleasure I have left. *Voltaire*

Growing old is no more than a bad habit which a busy man has no time to form.
André Maurois

Old age is an island surrounded by death. *Juan Montalvo*

It is time to be old,
To take in sail.

Ralph Waldo Emerson

I feel age like an icicle down my back.

Dyson Carter

Old age is a time of humiliations, the most disagreeable of which, for me, is that I cannot work long at sustained high pressure with no leaks in concentration.

Igor Stravinsky

Dignity, high station, or great riches are in some sort necessary to old men, in order to keep the younger at a distance, who are otherwise too apt to insult them upon the score of their age.

Jonathan Swift

The young feel tired at the end of an action;
The old at the beginning.

T. S. Eliot

Old foxes want no tutors.

Thomas Fuller

Old birds are hard to pluck.

German proverb

A man of fifty looks as old as Santa Claus to a girl of twenty.

William Feather

How old would you be if you didn't know how old you are?

Satchell Paige

The young always have the same problem—how to rebel and conform at the same time. They have now solved this by defying their parents and copying one another.

Quentin Crisp

Before you contradict an old man, my fair friend, you should endeavour to understand him.

George Santayana

Zsa Zsa Gabor, when asked which of the Gabor women was the oldest, said 'She'll never admit it, but I believe it is Mama.'

When men grow virtuous in their old age, they only make a sacrifice to God of the devil's leavings.

Jonathan Swift

When you are forty, half of you belongs to the past . . . And when you are seventy, nearly all of you.

Jean Anouilh

To an old man any place that's warm is homeland.

Maxim Gorky

By the time a man gets well into his seventies his continued existence is a mere miracle.

Robert Louis Stevenson

One trouble with growing older is that it gets progressively tougher to find a famous historical figure who didn't amount to much when he was your age.   *Bill Vaughan*

Forty is the old age of youth; fifty is the youth of old age.

Victor Hugo

Middle age is youth without its levity,
And age without decay.   *Daniel Defoe*

And he (King David) died in a good old age, full of days, riches and honour.
                                                              1 Chronicles 29:28

I never dared be radical when young
For fear it would make me conservative when old.   *Robert Frost*

Old age is by nature rather talkative.   *Cicero*

Old age, especially an honoured old age, has so great authority, that this is of more
value than all the pleasures of youth.   *Cicero*

Age has a good mind and sorry shanks.   *Pietro Aretino*

To me, old age is always fifteen years older than I am.   *Bernard Baruch*

Few people know how to be old.   *La Rochefoucauld*

First you forget names, then you forget faces, then you forget to pull your zipper up,
then you forget to pull your zipper down.   *Leo Rosenberg*

I really believe that more harm is done by old men who cling to their influence than
by young men who anticipate it.   *Owen D. Young*

He had come to that time in his life (it varies for every man) when a human being
gives himself over to his demon or to his genius, according to a mysterious law which
orders him either to destroy or to surpass himself.   *Marguerite Yourcenar*

The individual succumbs, but he does not die if he has left something to mankind.
                                                              Will Durant

It is always in season for old men to learn.   *Aeschylus*

So, lively brisk old fellow, don't let age get you down. White hairs or not, you can
still be a lover.   *Goethe*

He that has seen both sides of fifty has lived to little purpose if he has no other views
of the world than he had when he was much younger.   *William Cowper*

Let us respect gray hairs, especially our own.   *J. P. Senn*

The spiritual eyesight improves as the physical eyesight declines.   *Plato*

A man over ninety is a great comfort to all his elderly neighbours: he is a picket-guard
at the extreme outpost: and the young folks of sixty and seventy feel that the enemy
must get by him before he can come near their camp.   *Oliver Wendell Holmes, Jr.*

An old codger, rampant, and still learning.   *Aldous Huxley*

A person is always startled when he hears himself seriously called an old man for the first time.   *Oliver Wendell Holmes, Jr.*

Many a man that couldn't direct ye to th' drug store on th' corner when he was thirty will get a respectful hearin' when age has further impaired his mind.

Finley Peter Dunne

The denunciation of the young is a necessary part of the hygiene of older people, and greatly assists the circulation of their blood.   *Logan Pearsall Smith*

Never have I enjoyed youth so thoroughly as I have in my old age. In writing *Dialogues in Limbo, The Last Puritan,* and now all these descriptions of the friends of my youth and the young friends of my middle age, I have drunk the pleasure of life more pure, more joyful than it ever was when mingled with all the hidden anxieties and little annoyances of actual living. Nothing is inherently and invincibly young except spirit. And spirit can enter a human being perhaps better in the quiet of old age and dwell there more undisturbed than in the turmoil of adventure.   *George Santayana*

The arctic loneliness of age.   *S. Weir Mitchell*

When pain ends, gain ends too.   *Robert Browning*

When you're young it's very hard to understand that old people feel exactly the same as they felt when they were young. Things get a little less acute, both in misery and in joy, and certainly in expectation. But otherwise, you're essentially the same person.

Dame Roma Mitchell

Longevity is having a chronic disease and taking care of it.

Oliver Wendell Holmes, Jr.

Age is a high price to pay for maturity.   *Tom Stoppard*

I'm very pleased with each advancing year. It stems back to when I was forty. I was a bit upset about reaching that milestone, but an older friend consoled me. 'Don't complain about growing old—many people don't have that privilege.'   *Earl Warren*

When I was very young, I was disgracefully intolerant but when I passed the thirty mark I prided myself on having learned the beautiful lesson that all things were good, and equally good. That, however, was really laziness. Now, thank goodness, I've sorted out what matters and what doesn't. And I'm beginning to be intolerant again.

G. B. Stern

It is the fear of being as dependent as a young child, while not being loved as a child is loved, but merely being kept alive against one's will.   *Malcolm Cowley*

Happy the man who gains sagacity in youth, but thrice happy he who retains the fervour of youth in age.   *Dagobert Runes*

Your old men shall dream dreams, your young men shall see visions.   *Joel 2:28*

I am long on ideas, but short on time. I expect to live only about a hundred years.
Thomas A. Edison

How beautifully the leaves grow old. How full of light and colour are their last days.
John Burroughs

In the last few years everything I'd done up to sixty or so has seemed very childish.
T. S. Eliot

What makes old age so sad is not that our joys but our hopes cease.
Jean Paul Richter

The young man knows the rules but the old man knows the exceptions.
Oliver Wendell Holmes

To know how to grow old is the master-work of wisdom, and one of the most difficult
chapters in the great art of living.   *Henri Frédéric Amiel*

When you reach your sixties, you have to decide whether you're going to be a sot or
an ascetic. In other words if you want to go on working after you're sixty, some degree
of asceticism is inevitable.   *Malcolm Muggeridge*

Yes, I'm 68, but when I was a boy I was too poor to smoke, so knock off ten years.
That makes me 58. And since I never developed the drinking habit, you can knock
off ten more years. So I'm 48—in the prime of my life. Retire? Retire to what?
W. A. C. Bennett

Life has got to be lived—that's all there is to it. At seventy, I would say the advantage
is that you take life more calmly. You know that 'this, too, shall pass!'
Eleanor Roosevelt

Senescence begins
And middle age ends,
The day your descendants
Outnumber your friends.   *Ogden Nash*

Time must needs call the tune and man must follow it.   *Alain*

On the day of his death, in his eightieth year, Elliot, 'the Apostle of the Indians,' was
found teaching an Indian child at his bedside. 'Why not to rest from your labours
now?' asked a friend. 'Because,' replied the venerable man, 'I have prayed God to
render me useful in my sphere, and he has heard my prayers; for now that I can no
longer preach, he leaves me strength enough to teach this poor child the alphabet.'
S. Chaplin

As the world is wearie of me so am I of it.   *John Knox*

Middle age is when you have a choice of two temptations and choose the one that
will get you home earlier.   *Anon.*

No wise man ever wished to be younger.   *Jonathan Swift*

Every man who has lived his life to the full should, by the time his senior years are reached, have established a reserve inventory of unfinished thinking.

Clarence Randall

For the unlearned, old age is winter; for the learned, it is the season of the harvest.

Hasidic saying

My opportunities were still there, nay, they multiplied tenfold; but the strength and youth to cope with them began to fail, and to need eking out with the shifty cunning of experience.   *George Bernard Shaw*

I must be getting absent-minded. Whenever I complain that things aren't what they used to be, I always forget to include myself.   *George Burns*

We grow neither better nor worse as we get old, but more like ourselves.

May Lamberton Becker

Golden lads and girls all must,
As chimney-sweepers, come to dust.   *Shakespeare, 'Cymbeline'*

It's never too late to have a fling
For autumn is just as nice as spring
And it's never too late to fall in love.   *Sandy Wilson*

Growing old—it's not nice, but it's interesting.   *August Strindberg*

If you think that I am going to bother myself again before I die about social improvement, or read any of those stinking upward and onwarders—you err—I mean to have some good out of being old.   *Oliver Wendell Holmes, Jr.*

They tell you that you'll lose your mind when you grow older. What they don't tell you is that you won't miss it very much.   *Malcolm Cowley*

I have learned little from the years that fly; but I have wrung the colour from the years.   *Frances Pollock*

America and Americans

There is nothing wrong with America that cannot be cured by what is right with America.   *President William F. Clinton*

The office of the president is such a bastardized thing, half royalty and half democracy, that nobody knows whether to genuflect or spit.   *Jimmy Breslin*

Part of the American dream is to live long and die young.   *Edgar Z. Friedenberg*

America is so vast that almost everything said about it is likely to be true, and the opposite is probably equally true.   *James T. Farrell*

American youth attributes much more importance to arriving at driver's license age than at voting age.   *Marshall McLuhan*

If ever there was an aviary overstocked with jays it is that Yaptown-on-the-Hudson called New York.   *O. Henry*

There are three things wrong with the Yanks: they're overpaid, oversexed and over here.   *Anonymous observation about GIs in Australia during World War II*

Let's talk sense to the American people. Let's tell them the truth, that there are no gains without pains.   *Adlai Stevenson*

Ours is the country where, in order to sell your product, you don't so much point out its merits as you first work like hell to sell yourself.   *Louis Kronenberger*

People who leave Washington D.C. do so by way of the box—ballot or coffin.
                                                                        Claiborne Pell

America is a collective work of the imagination whose making never ends.
                                                                        Robert Hughes

That strange blend of the commercial traveller, the missionary and the barbarian conqueror, which was the American abroad.   *Olaf Stapledon*

The faces in New York remind me of people who played a game ! and lost.
                                                                        Murray Kepton

The President spends most of his time kissing people on the cheek in order to get them to do what they ought to do without getting kissed.   *Harry S. Truman*

The real America that Whitman proclaimed and Thoreau decoded.   *Allen Ginsberg*

Thou, oh my country, hast thy foolish ways,
Too apt to purr at every stranger's praise.   *Oliver Wendell Holmes*

You can always get the truth from an American statesman after he has turned 70, or given up all hope of the Presidency.   *Wendell Phillips*

America is a willingness of the heart.   *F. Scott Fitzgerald*

(A country where) the young are always ready to give to those who are older than themselves the full benefits of their inexperience.   *Oscar Wilde*

We are now at the point where we must decide whether we are to honour the concept of a plural society which gains strength through diversity, or whether we are to have bitter fragmentation that will result in perpetual tension and strife.   *Earl Warren*

Nothing ever gets settled in this town (Washington). It's not like running a company or even a university. It's a seething debating society, in which the debate never stops; in which people never give up, including me, and that's the atmosphere in which you administer.   *Secretary of State, George P. Shultz*

The skyline of New York is a monument of a splendour that no pyramids or palaces will ever equal or approach.   *Ayn Rand*

Whoever wants to know the hearts and minds of America had better learn baseball.
Jacques Barzun

Americans are like a rich father who wishes he knew how to give his son the hardships that made him rich.   *Robert Frost*

America . . . an economic system prouder of the distribution of its products than of the products themselves.   *Murray Kempton*

The United States was born in the country and moved to the city in the nineteenth century.   *Anon.*

Delaware: a state that has three counties when the tide is out, and two when it is in.
J. J. Ingalls

Washington is an endless series of mock palaces clearly built for clerks.
Ada Louise Huxtable

The Americans believe they answered all first questions in 1776: since then they've just been hammering out the practical details.   *Ray Smith*

Our national flower is the concrete cloverleaf.   *Lewis Mumford*

Americans have a special horror of letting things happen their own way, without interference. They would like to jump down their stomachs, digest the food, and shovel the shit out.   *William Burroughs*

When asked by an anthropologist what the Indians called America before the white man came, an Indian said simply 'Ours.'   *Vine Deloria, Jr.*

In the United States 'First' and 'Second' class can't be painted on railroad cars, for all passengers, being Americans, are equal and it would be 'unAmerican.' But paint 'Pullman' on a car and everyone is satisfied.   *Owen Wister*

The true America is the Middle West, and Columbus discovered nothing at all except another Europe.   *W. L. George*

America once had the clarity of a pioneer axe.   *Robert Osborn*

In the United States there is more space where nobody is than where anybody is. This is what makes America what it is.   *Gertrude Stein*

You say to your soldier, 'Do this' and he does it. But I am obliged to say to the American, 'This is why you ought to do this' and then he does it.
Baron von Steuben

The greatest American superstition is belief in facts.   *Hermann Keyserling*

America should care more for its poor and reform itself in other ways; but even if it won't do those things, it remains the least constrained society on earth.

Robert M. Adams

Florida: God's waiting room.   *Glenn le Grice*

The Englishman is under no constitutional obligation to believe that all men are created equal. The American agony is therefore scarcely intelligible, like a saint's self-flagellation viewed by an atheist.   *John Updike*

There is nothing the matter with Americans except their ideals. The real American is all right; it is the ideal American who is all wrong.   *G. K. Chesterton*

Nobody ever went broke underestimating the taste of the American public.

H. L. Mencken

Good Americans, when they die, go to Paris.   *Thomas Gold Appleton*

The sorrows and disasters of Europe always brought fortune to America.

Stephen Leacock

The American's conversation is much like his courtship . . . He gives an inkling and watches for a reaction; if the weather looks fair, he inkles a little more. Wishing neither to intrude nor be intruded upon, he advances by stages of acceptance, by levels of agreement, by steps of concurrence.   *Donald Lloyd*

The central fact of North American history is that there were fifteen British Colonies before 1776. Thirteen rebelled and two did not.   *June Callwood*

A natural New Yorker is a native of the present tense.   *V. S. Pritchett*

New York is notoriously inhospitable to the past, disowning it whenever it can.

John D. Rosenberg

Why, if you're not in New York you are camping out.   *Thomas W. Dewing*

That enfabled rock, that ship of life, that swarming, million-footed, tower-masted, sky-soaring citadel that bears the magic name of the Island of Manhattan.

Thomas Wolfe

I don't like the life here in New York. There is no greenery. It would make a stone sick.   *Nikita Khrushchev*

New York, the nation's thyroid gland.   *Christopher Morley*

You will find the Americans much as the Greeks found the Romans: great, big, vulgar, bustling people more vigorous than we are and also more idle, with more unspoiled virtues but also more corrupt.   *Harold Macmillan*

As for what you're calling hard luck—well, we made New England out of it. That and codfish.   *Stephen Vincent Benét*

The lusts of the flesh can be gratified anywhere; it is not this sort of licence that distinguishes New York. It is, rather, a lust of the total ego for recognition, even for eminence. More than elsewhere, everybody here wants to be Somebody.

Sydney J. Harris

After twenty annual visits, I am still surprised each time I return to see this giant asparagus bed of alabaster and rose and green skyscrapers.   *Cecil Beaton*

He speaks English with the flawless imperfection of a New Yorker.

Gilbert Millstein

A town that has no ceiling price,
A town of double-talk;
A town so big men name her twice,
Like so: 'N'Yawk, N'Yawk.'   *Christopher Morley*

And this is good old Boston
The home of the bean and the cod—
Where the Lowells talk to the Cabots,
And the Cabots talk only to God.   *J. C. Bossidy*

New England is a finished place. Its destiny is that of Florence or Venice, not Milan, while the American empire careens onward toward its predicted end . . . it is the first American section to be finished, to achieve stability in the conditions of its life. It is the first old civilization, the first permanent civilization in America.

Bernard de Voto

A Bostonian—an American, broadly speaking.   *G. E. Woodberry*

The swaggering underemphasis of New England.   *Heywood Broun*

A well-established village in New England or the northern Middle-West could afford a town drunkard, a town atheist, and a few Democrats.   *D. W. Brogan*

I shall enter on no encomium upon Massachussets; she needs none. There she is. Behold her, and judge for yourselves.   *Daniel Webster*

The most serious charge which can be brought against New England is not Puritanism but February.   *Joseph Wood Krutch*

Boston is a moral and intellectual nursery always busy applying first principles to trifles.   *George Santayana*

America—the best poor man's country in the world.   *William Allen*

Chicago—a façade of skyscrapers facing a lake and behind the façade every type of dubiousness.   *E. M. Forster*

I'm from Indiana, the home of more first-rate second-class men than any other state in the union.   *Thomas R. Marshall*

Pennsylvania, the state that has produced two great men: Benjamin Franklin of Massachusetts, and Albert Gallatin of Switzerland. *J. J. Ingalls*

Stormy, husky, brawling,
City of the Big Shoulders. *Carl Sandburg, 'Chicago'*

I come from a state that raises corn and cotton and cockleburs and Democrats, and frothy eloquence neither convinces nor satisfies me. I am from Missouri. You have got to show me. *Willard D. Vandiver*

Washington is a place where men praise courage and act on elaborate personal cost-benefit calculations. *J. K. Galbraith*

I think that New York is not the cultural centre of America, but the business and administrative centre of American culture. *Saul Bellow*

Washington is a city of people doing badly what shouldn't be done at all.
Robert H. Gurney

America and its demons, Europe and its ghosts. *Le Monde*

Anger

Anger is one of the sinners of the soul. *Thomas Fuller*

It's my rule never to lose my temper until it would be detrimental to keep it.
Sean O'Casey

Never go to bed mad. Stay up and fight. *Phyllis Diller*

Never forget what a man says to you when he is angry. *Henry Ward Beecher*

Who can refute a sneer? *William Paley*

I never work better than when I am inspired by anger; for when I am angry, I can write, pray, and preach well, for then my whole temperament is quickened, my understanding sharpened, and all mundane vexations and temptations depart.
Martin Luther

There is no passion so much transports the sincerity of judgement as doth anger.
Montaigne

Don't get mad, get even. *Robert F. Kennedy*

Beware the fury of a patient man. *John Dryden*

I was angry with my friend:
I told my wrath, my wrath did end.
I was angry with my foe:
I told it not, my wrath did grow.

William Blake

A good indignation brings out all one's powers.

Ralph Waldo Emerson

Anger makes dull men witty, but it keeps them poor.

Attributed to Queen Elizabeth I

Heaven has no rage like love to hatred turned,
Nor hell a fury like a woman scorned.

William Congreve

Anger as soon as fed is dead—
'Tis starving makes it fat.

Emily Dickinson

Many people lose their tempers merely from seeing you keep yours.

Frank Moore Colby

Animals

Who could imagine a platypus?

Arthur C. Clarke

Whatever a bird is, is perfect in the bird.

Judith Wright

Cats, no less liquid than their shadows,
Offer no angles to the wind.
They slip, diminished,
Neat, through loopholes
Less than themselves.

A. S. J. Tessimond

Dogs come when they are called; cats take a message and get back to you.

Mary Bly

Hi, handsome hunting man
Fire your little gun
Bang! Now the animal
Is dead and dumb and done.
Nevermore to peep again, creep again, leap again
Eat or sleep or drink again.
Oh, what fun.

Walter de la Mare

I loathe people who keep dogs. They are cowards who haven't got the guts to bite
people themselves.

August Strindberg

If called by a panther
Don't anther.

Ogden Nash

Of all God's creatures there is only one that cannot be made the slave of the lash. That one is the cat. If man could be crossed with the cat, it would improve man, but it would deteriorate the cat.   *Mark Twain*

To hear the lark begin his flight,
And singing startle the dull night.
From his watchtower in the skies,
Til the dappled dawn doth rise.   *John Milton*

Wee, sleekit, cow'rin, timrous beastie
O what a panic's in thy breastie!
Wi' bickering brattle!   *Robert Burns*

The quizzical expression of the monkey at the zoo comes from his wondering whether he is his brother's keeper, or his keeper's brother.   *Evan Esar*

You have now learned to see
That cats are much like you and me
And other people whom we find
Possessed of various types of mind.   *T. S. Eliot*

No animal admires another animal.   *Blaise Pascal*

The great pleasure of a dog is that you may make a fool of yourself with him and not only will he not scold you, but he will make a fool of himself too.   *Samuel Butler*

All animals are equal, but some animals are more equal than others. *George Orwell*

To his dog, every man is Napoleon; hence the constant popularity of dogs.
                                                                  Aldous Huxley

Cats—a standing rebuke to behavioural scientists . . . least human of all creatures.
                                                                  Lewis Thomas

I'd rather have an inch of dog than miles of pedigree.   *Dana Burnet*

Cats seem to go on the principle that it never does any harm to ask for what you want.
                                                          Joseph Wood Krutch

Animals are such agreeable friends—they ask no questions, they pass no criticisms.
                                                                  George Eliot

I never saw a wild thing sorry for itself.   *D. H. Lawrence*

A robin redbreast in a cage
Sets all heaven in a rage.   *William Blake*

I think one reason we admire cats, those of us who do, is their proficiency in one-upmanship. They always seem to come out on top, no matter what they are doing—or pretend they do. Rarely do you see a cat discomfited. They have no conscience, and they never regret. Maybe we secretly envy them. *Barbara Webster*

There is only one place for a fur coat, and that is on the back of an animal.

Peter Singer

A fowl-run is very similar to a cocktail party.   *Glen McBride*

A squid, as you know of course, has ten testicles.

Graham Kerr, The Galloping Gourmet

The dog is the god of frolic.   *Henry Ward Beecher*

Anxiety and Worry

Nothing puzzles me more than time and space; yet nothing troubles me less.

Charles Lamb

Uncertainty and expectation are the joys of life. Security is an insipid thing, and the overtaking and possessing of a wish, discovers the folly of the chase.

William Congreve

When I lie down, I say, When shall I arise and the night be gone? And I am full of tossings to and fro unto the dawning of the day.   *Job 7:4*

The only effect the atomic age has had on man has been to give him an underlying sense of nervous apprehension, which must also have been felt during the Black Death, and by the Christians under Diocletian.   *Martin Boyd*

Trouble is the common denominator of living. It is the great equalizer. *Ann Landers*

Trouble is a part of your life, and if you don't share it, you don't give the person who loves you a chance to love you enough.   *Dinah Shore*

Anxiety is essential to the human condition. The confrontation with anxiety can relieve us from boredom, sharpen the sensitivity and assure the presence of tension that is necessary to preserve human existence.   *Rollo May*

We poison our lives with fear of burglary and shipwreck, and, ask anyone, the house is never burgled, and the ship never goes down.   *Jean Anouilh*

Neurosis is the way of avoiding non-being by avoiding being.   *Paul Tillich*

Anxiety is the dizziness of freedom.   *Søren Kierkegaard*

Anxiety is fear of one's self.   *Wilhelm Stekel*

Fear ringed by doubt is my eternal moon.   *Malcolm Lowry*

Worries go down better with soup than without.   *Jewish proverb*

Neurotic means he is not as sensible as I am, and psychotic means he's even worse than my brother-in-law. *Karl Menninger*

Anxiety is the interest paid on trouble before it is due. *Dean William R. Inge*

Anxiety is a thin stream of fear trickling through the mind. If encouraged, it cuts a channel into which all other thoughts are drained. *Arthur Somers Roche*

There is a difference between a psychopath and a neurotic. A psychopath thinks two and two are five. A neurotic knows that two and two are four, but he worries about it. *Anon*

Worrying helps you some. It seems as if you are doing something when you're worrying. *Lucy Maud Montgomery*

Everything great in the world comes from neurotics. They alone have founded our religions, and composed our masterpieces. Never will the world know all it owes to them, nor all they have suffered to enrich us. *Marcel Proust*

For what human ill does not dawn seem to be an alleviation. *Thornton Wilder*

Architects and Architecture

Architecture is a continuing dialogue between generations which creates an environment across time. *Vincent Scully*

Why can't we have those curves and arches that express feeling in design? What is wrong with them? Why has everything got to be vertical, straight, unbending, only at right angles—and functional? *Charles, Prince of Wales*

You have to give this much to the Luftwaffe—when it knocked down our buildings it did not replace them with anything more offensive than rubble. We did that. *Charles, Prince of Wales*

Real architects have always been and must be inventors, in mechanics, in form, in tone and colour. *Robin Boyd*

In architecture the pride of man, his triumph over gravitation, his will to power, assume a visible form. Architecture is a sort of oratory of power by means of forms. *Friedrich Nietzsche*

The materials of city planning are sky, space, trees, steel and cement in that order and in that hierarchy. *Le Corbusier*

Buildings should be good neighbours. *Paul Thiry*

Pictures deface walls oftener than they decorate them. *Frank Lloyd Wright*

Life is rich, always changing, always challenging, and we architects have the task of transmitting into wood, concrete, glass and steel, of transforming human aspirations into habitable and meaningful space.   *Arthur Erickson*

A building is a string of events belonging together.   *Chris Fawcett*

Good architecture is like a piece of beautifully composed music crystallized in space that elevates our spirits beyond the limitation of time.   *Tao Ho*

Architecture (is) a theatre stage setting where the leading actors are the people, and to dramatically direct the dialogue between these people and space is the technique of designing.   *Kisho Kurokawa*

I saw the bathroom fixtures as a kind of American Trinity.   *Claes Oldenberg*

Perspective is worth 80 I.Q. points.   *Alan Kay*

Architecture is the will of an epoch translated into space.   *Mies van der Rohe*

Buildings are the most subtle, accurate and enduring records of life—hence their problems are the problems of life and not problems of form; but through the form and material of buildings we can gain an insight into the life of the past.
                                                             Walter Burley Griffin

Light, God's eldest daughter, is a principal beauty in a building.   *Thomas Fuller*

No architecture can be truly noble which is not imperfect.   *John Ruskin*

Architecture is inhabited sculpture.   *Constantin Brancusi*

The flowering of geometry.   *Ralph Waldo Emerson*

Society needs a good image of itself. That is the job of the architect.
                                                                   Walter Gropius

Architecture begins when you place two bricks *carefully* together.
                                                              Mies van der Rohe

An arch never sleeps.   *Hindu proverb*

Develop an infallible technique and then place yourself at the mercy of inspiration.
                                                                   Ralph Rapson

The reality of the building does not consist in the roof and walls, but in the space within to be lived in.   *Lao-Tzu*

Good architecture lets nature in.   *Mario Pei*

Architecture should be dedicated to keeping the outside out and the inside in.
                                                                  Leonard Baskin

Early in life I had to choose between arrogance and hypocritical humility. I chose honest arrogance and have seen no occasion to change.   *Frank Lloyd Wright*

No house should ever be on a hill, or on anything. It should be of the hill. Hill and house should live together, each the happier for the other.   *Frank Lloyd Wright*

How can we expect our students to become bold and fearless in thought and action if we encase them in sentimental shrines feigning a culture which has long since disappeared?   *Walter Gropius*

The house does not frame the view: it projects the beholder into it.
Harwell Hamilton Harris

Architecture is space structured to serve man and to move him.   *Étienne Gaboury*

Take nothing for granted as beautiful or ugly, but take every building to pieces, and challenge every feature. Learn to distinguish the curious from the beautiful. Get the habit of analysis—analysis will in time enable synthesis to become your habit of mind. 'Think simples' as my old master used to say—meaning to reduce the whole of its parts into the simplest terms, getting back to first principles.   *Frank Lloyd Wright*

Always design a thing by considering it in its next larger context—a chair in a room, a room in a house, a house in an environment, an environment in a city plan.
Eero Saarinen

In speculative buildings, which is most of our business, there are really only three chances to make architecture: the lobby or entrance sequence, the top and the elevator cab.   *Chao-Ming Wu*

A house is a machine for living.   *Buckminster Fuller*

A doctor can bury his mistakes, but an architect can only advise his clients to plant vines.   *Frank Lloyd Wright*

Genius is personal, decided by fate, but it expresses itself by means of system. There is no work of art without system.   *Le Corbusier*

We shape our buildings; thereafter they shape us.   *Winston Churchill*

I call architecture 'petrified music'.   *Goethe*

Form ever follows function.   *Louis H. Sullivan*

Arguments and Quarrels

A man never tells you anything until you contradict him.   *George Bernard Shaw*

In a true tragedy, both parties must be right.   *Georg W. F. Hegel*

Some guy hit my fender the other day, and I said unto him, 'Be fruitful, and multiply.' But not in those words.   *Woody Allen*

We're eyeball to eyeball, and the other fellow just blinked.   *Dean Rusk*

A good life is more conclusive than a brilliant argument.
Archbishop Roger Bede Vaughan

There is no good arguing with the inevitable. The only argument available with an east wind is to put on your overcoat.   *James Russell Lowell*

It is not necessary to understand things in order to argue about them. *Beaumarchais*

I learned long ago never to wrestle with a pig. You get dirty, and besides, the pig likes it.   *Cyrus Ching*

The test of a man or woman's breeding is how they behave in a quarrel.
George Bernard Shaw

I have never in my life learned anything from any man who agreed with me.
Dudley Field Malone

Better be quarrelling than lonesome.   *Irish proverb*

Quarrels would not last long if the fault was only on one side.   *La Rochefoucauld*

When we quarrel, how we wish we had been blameless.   *Ralph Waldo Emerson*

The most savage controversies are those about matters as to which there is no good evidence either way.   *Bertrand Russell*

Every story has three sides to it—yours, mine and the facts.
Foster Meharny Russell

Art and the Artist

Vita brevis, ars longa. Life is short, art is long.   *Seneca*

A picture can become for us a highway between a particular thing and a universal feeling.   *Lawren Harris*

A work of art cannot be satisfied with being a representation; it should be a presentation.   *Jacques Reverdy*

An amateur is an artist who supports himself with outside jobs which enable him to paint. A professional is someone whose wife works to enable him to paint.
Ben Shahn

Art distills sensation and embodies it with enhanced meaning in memorable form—or else it is not art.   *Jacques Barzun*

Artistic temperament is a disease that afflicts amateurs.   *G. K. Chesterton*

Artists are the antennae of the race, but the bullet-headed many will never learn to trust the great artists.   *Ezra Pound*

Artists must be sacrificed to their art. Like bees, they must put their lives into the sting they give.   *Ralph Waldo Emerson*

Artists, by definition innocent, don't steal. But they do borrow without giving back.
                                                                    Ned Rorem

As a painter I shall never signify anything of importance. I feel it absolutely.
                                                             Vincent van Gogh

Classic means standard as opposed to Romantic: form before meaning as opposed to meaning before form. It grows from inside out, while Romantic grows from outside in.   *Ned Rorem*

Everything in nature is formed upon the sphere, the cone and the cylinder. One must learn to paint these simple figures and then one can do all that he may wish.
                                                                 Paul Cézanne

Fine art is that in which the hand, the head, and the heart of man go together.
                                                                  John Ruskin

Good artists exist simply in what they make, and consequently are perfectly uninteresting in what they are.   *Oscar Wilde*

Great art speaks a language which every intelligent person can understand. The people who call themselves modernists today speak a different language.   *R. G. Menzies*

I wonder whether Art has a higher function than to make me feel, appreciate, and enjoy natural objects for their art value?   *Bernard Berenson*

I've been 40 years discovering that the Queen of all colours is black.
                                                               Auguste Renoir

If artists and poets are unhappy, it is after all because happiness does not interest them.
                                                             George Santayana

Interpretation is the revenge of the intellect upon art.   *Susan Sontag*

One of the most difficult things to do is to paint darkness which nonetheless has light in it.   *Vincent van Gogh*

Painting is a faith, and it imposes the duty to disregard public opinion.
                                                             Vincent van Gogh

Painting is silent poetry, and poetry is painting with the gift of speech.   *Simonides*

Rembrandt painted about 700 pictures—of these, 3,000 are in existence.

Wilhelm Bode

Never believe what an artist says, only what he paints.   *Fred Williams*

Style, like the human body, is specially beautiful when the veins are not prominent and the bones cannot be counted.   *Tacitus*

The fingers must be educated, the thumb is born knowing.   *Marc Chagall*

The genuine artist is as much a dissatisfied person as the revolutionary, yet how diametrically opposed are the products each distills from his dissatisfaction.

Eric Hoffer

The object of art is to give life a shape.   *Jean Anouilh*

The scholar seeks, the artist finds.   *André Gide*

The song of the brush.   *Chinese saying about painting*

Theatre takes place all the time wherever one is and art simply facilitates persuading one this is the case.   *John Cage*

Two boys arrived yesterday with a pebble they said was the head of a dog until I pointed out that it was really a typewriter.   *Pablo Picasso*

We live in a rainbow of chaos.   *Paul Cézanne*

We must grant the artist his subject, his idea, his donnée: Our criticisms apply only to what he makes of it.   *Henry James*

When they asked Michelangelo how he made his statue of David he is reported to have said, 'It is easy. You just chip away the stone that doesn't look like David.'

Michelangelo

Works of Art are of an infinite loneliness.   *Rainer Maria Rilke*

Art is I, science is we.   *Claude Bernard*

The artist, like the God of the creation, remains within or behind or beyond or above his handiwork, invisible, refined, out of existence, indifferent, paring his fingernails.

James Joyce

An artist is something on two legs with a simple soul and a belief that he was made before God.   *Margaret Preston*

Children, like animals, use all their senses to discover the world. Then artists come along and discover it the same way all over again.   *Eudora Welty*

When power leads man toward arrogance, poetry reminds him of his limitations. When power narrows the areas of man's concern, poetry reminds him of the richness and diversity of his experience. When power corrupts, poetry cleanses. For art establishes the basic human truths which must serve as the touchstones of our judgement. The artist . . . faithful to his personal vision of reality, becomes the last champion of the individual mind and sensibility against an intrusive society and an offensive state.

John F. Kennedy

Art is the expression of an enormous preference.   *Wyndham Lewis*

Conception, my boy, fundamental brainwork, is what makes the difference in all art.

Dante Gabriel Rossetti

An artist may visit a museum but only a pedant can live there.   *George Santayana*

All profoundly original art looks ugly at first.   *Clement Greenberg*

Pioneers did not produce original works of art, because they were creating original human environments; they did not imagine utopias because they were shaping them.

George Woodcock

Art is a human activity, consisting in this, that one man consciously, by means of external signs, hands on to others feelings he has worked through, and other people are infected by these feelings and also experience them.   *Leo Tolstoy*

A picture lives by companionship. It dies by the same token. It is therefore risky to send it out into the world. How often it must be impaired by the eyes of the unfeeling.

Mark Rothko

Abstract art is uniquely modern. It is a fundamentally romantic response to modern life—rebellious, individualistic, unconventional, sensitive, irritable.

Robert Motherwell

Culture is something you cannot buy, something you cannot import, something you cannot learn or produce at will. A writer, an artist or musician cannot sit down and say 'Now I will produce culture.' Culture is something that evolves out of the simple, enduring elements of everyday life; elements most truthfully expressed in the folk arts and crafts of a nation.   *Thor Hansen*

Every aesthetic expression is dynamic and therefore involves distortion.

Margaret Preston

Art is not an end in itself, but a means of addressing humanity. *Modest Mussorgsky*

All art is a revolt against man's fate.   *André Malraux*

Art is a delayed echo.   *George Santayana*

Art is a kind of illness.   *Giacomo Puccini*

A work of art is a corner of creation seen through a temperament.   *Emile Zola*

Art washes away from the soul the dust of everyday life.   *Pablo Picasso*

The difference between the artist and the non-artist is that the artist is the one who does it.   *Helen Garner*

The new job of art is to sit on the wall and get more expensive.   *Robert Hughes*

What's an artist, but the dregs of his work—the human shambles that follows it around?   *William Gaddis*

Art has no other object than to set aside the symbols of practical utility, the generalities that are conventionally and socially accepted, everything in fact which masks reality from us, in order to set us face to face with reality itself.   *Henri Bergson*

Every artist preserves deep within him a single source from which, throughout his lifetime, he draws what he is and what he says and when the source dries up the work withers and crumbles.   *Albert Camus*

As an artist grows older, he has to fight disillusionment and learn to establish the same relation to nature as an adult as he had when a child.   *Charles Burchfield*

Perpetual modernness is the measure of merit in every work of art.   *Ralph Waldo Emerson*

Nothing can come out of an artist that is not in the man.   *H. L. Mencken*

It is not in life but in art that self-fulfillment is to be found.   *George Woodcock*

An artist never really finishes his work, he merely abandons it.   *Paul Valéry*

I am convinced it is a mistake to find an artist human outside his work. If you cannot find him human in and through his work, you are better not to know it when you come to formulate an opinion of his public value.   *Kenneth Winters*

One must work, nothing but work, and one must have patience.   *Auguste Rodin*

Art does not reproduce the visible; rather it makes it visible.   *Paul Klee*

The more horrifying this world becomes, the more art becomes abstract.   *Paul Klee*

One of the recognizable features of the authentic masterpiece is its capacity to renew itself, to endure the loss of some kinds of immediate relevance while still answering the most important questions men can ask, including new ones they are just learning how to frame.   *Arnold Stein*

Every child is an artist. The problem is how to remain an artist once he grows up.   *Pablo Picasso*

Art is man's nature; nature is God's art.   *P. J. Bailey*

With the pride of the artist, you must blow against the walls of every power that exists the small trumpet of your defiance.   *Norman Mailer*

All art is a kind of confession, more or less oblique. All artists, if they are to survive are forced, at last, to tell the whole story; to vomit the anguish up.   *James Baldwin*

History repeats itself, but the special call of an art which has passed away is never reproduced. It is utterly gone out of the world as the song of a destroyed wild bird.
                                                                 Joseph Conrad

If you ask me what I came to do in this world, I, an artist, will answer you: 'I am here to live out loud.'   *Emile Zola*

Illustrations have as much to say as the text. The trick is to say the same thing, but in a different way. It's no good being an illustrator who is saying a lot that is on his or her mind, if it has nothing to do with the text . . . the artist must override the story but he must also override his own ego for the sake of the story.   *Maurice Sendak*

In any evolutionary process, even in the arts, the search for novelty becomes corrupting
                                                               Kenneth Boulding

The cheap, no matter how charming, how immediate, does not wear so well. It has a way of telling its whole story the first time through.   *William Littler*

Art at its most significant is a Distant Early Warning System that can always be relied on to tell the old culture what is beginning to happen to it.   *Marshall McLuhan*

It is well with me only when I have a chisel in my hand.   *Michelangelo*

Art is based on order. The world is full of 'sloppy Bohemians' and their work betrays them.   *Eduard Weston*

Living is a form of not being sure, not knowing what next or how. The moment you know how, you begin to die a little. The artist never entirely knows. We guess. We may be wrong, but we take leap after leap in the dark.   *Agnes de Mille*

The artist, like the idiot, or clown, sits on the edge of the world, and a push may send him over it.   *Osbert Sitwell*

Art-speech is the only truth. An artist is usually a damned liar but his art, if it be art will tell you the truth of his day. And that is all that matters. Away with eternal truth The truth lives from day to day, and the marvelous Plato of yesterday is chiefly bosh today.   *D. H. Lawrence*

Art isn't something you marry, it's something you rape.   *Edgar Dégas*

It's not what you see that is art, art is the gap.   *Marcel Duchamp*

I always suspect an artist who is successful before he is dead. *John Murray Gibbon*

An artist has to take life as he finds it. Life by itself is formless wherever it is. Art must give it form.
Hugh MacLennan

Art upsets, science reassures.
Georges Braque

An artist has been defined as a neurotic who continually cures himself with his art.
Lee Simonson

Art is either plagiarism or revolution.
Paul Gauguin

The father of every good work is discontent, and its mother is diligence.
Lajos Kassak

A work should contain its total meaning within itself and should impress it on the spectator before he even knows the subject.
Henri Matisse

The terror of art lies in the representation of the hidden reality with its shattering effect.
Martin Greenburg

Drawing is speaking to the eye; talking is painting to the ear.
Joseph Joubert

We should comport ourselves with the masterpieces of art as with exalted personages—stand quietly before them and wait till they speak to us.
Arthur Schopenhauer

Be regular and orderly in your life like a bourgeois, so that you may be violent and original in your work.
Gustave Flaubert

The painting rises from the brushstrokes as a poem rises from the words. The meaning comes later.
Joan Miro

Caricature is rough truth.
George Meredith

A work of art is an exaggeration.
André Gide

Art not only imitates nature, but also completes its deficiencies.
Aristotle

When one admires an artist it is important not to know him personally.
Jacinto Benaventey Martinez

Australia and Australians

Australia is a lucky country run mainly by second-rate people who share its luck.
Donald Horne

What's Australia? A big, thirsty, hungry wilderness, with one or two cities for the convenience of foreign speculators, and a few collections of humpies, called towns—also for the convenience of foreign speculators, and populated mostly by mongrel sheep, and partly by fools.
Henry Lawson

This supposedly sophisticated country is still, alas, a colonial sheep-run.

Patrick White

Australia spent the first half of the century as a farm for the British. Now it looks as though we may spend the second half as a quarry for the Japanese. *Gough Whitlam*

Waiting for the Australian republic is like waiting for the other shoe to drop. We all know it is coming; according to one's convictions, the waiting is therefore either a sour and uncreative delaying operation or a sort of null interregnum in which all energies are frustrated. *Les Murray*

Everyone lives in his own Australia. It is the creation of the imagination working on the data of strictly personal experience. *John Hallows*

It is a continent of dreams we inhabit, a waiting continent. All who have set foot in its bush, its lonely places, know that silence. The continent is dreaming.

David Ireland, 'A Woman of the Future'

Where is Australia?

Brendan Behan

Australia is a large country with a small population, far from the rest of the world. No one goes there by chance, for it is not on the way to anywhere else. *Ian Bevan*

Australia, *n.* A country lying in the South Sea whose industrial and commercial development has been unspeakably retarded by an unfortunate dispute among geographers as to whether it is a continent or an island. *Ambrose Bierce*

It must be so pretty with all the dear little kangaroos flying about. Agatha has found it on the map. What a curious shape it is! Just like a large packing case. However, it is a very young country, isn't it? *Oscar Wilde, 'Lady Windermere's Fan'*

They call her a young country, but they lie:
She is the last of lands, the emptiest,
A woman beyond her change of life, a breast
Still tender, but within the womb is dry. *A. D. Hope*

The landscape is so unimpressive, like a face with little or no features, a dark face. It is so Aboriginal, out of our ken, and it hangs back so aloof. *D. H. Lawrence*

The surrealism of our landscape shimmers in the Australian mind. *David Campbell*

The fault of all Australian scenery is its monotony. *Anthony Trollope*

There is an infinity of landscape here, caused by the purity of the atmosphere. It has been said that there is a lack of colour. It is not so obvious as the greenness of England, but it is infinitely more varied and more delicate in tone. *Hans Heysen*

Australia is a singularity of nature. Her barren, stony surface exposes the history of half this planet's existence and the genesis of life itself. And yet she is bewilderingly hostile. *Eric Willmot*

The bush, which Australians still love to praise as 'the real Australia', though so few of them live there.   *John Douglas Pringle*

The mystery of the bush seems to recede from you as you advance, and then it is behind you if you look around.   *D. H. Lawrence*

It's so empty and featureless, like a newspaper that has been entirely censored. We used to drive for miles, always expecting that around the next corner there'd be something to look at, but there never was. That is the charm of Australia.
                                        Robert Morley

I'll tell you where the dead heart of Australia is. It's right back there in the cities. Not out in the sand and the mulga and the stones burning hot under the sun.
                                        David Ireland, 'Burn'

There's time enough for everything in the Never-Never.
                                        Jeannie Gunn, 'We of the Never-Never'

This would be a lovely country if one wanted to *withdraw* from the world.
                                        D. H. Lawrence

In a way Australia is like Catholicism. The company is sometimes questionable and the landscape is grotesque. But you always come back.   *Thomas Keneally*

Australian history is almost always picturesque; indeed it is so curious and strange that it is itself the chiefest novelty the country has to offer, and so it pushes the other novelties into second and third place. It does not read like history, but like the most beautiful lies; and all of a fresh new sort, no mouldy old stale ones. It is full of surprises and adventures, and incongruities and incredibilities; but they are all true, they all happened.   *Mark Twain*

This is the only land which has never enjoyed agrarian society. Our history is without peasants. We've had hunter-gatherers and then industrial civilisation. It means we've been either conservationists or developers, without appreciating the cultivated landscape. We've not made a permanent home, even using refrigeration to pretend we live somewhere else.   *Michael Symons*

Australia is not an innocent country. This nation's short history is shadowed, into the present day, by the fate of its native peoples, by forms of unyielding prejudice, by a strain of derision and unexamined violence, and by a persistent current of misogyny.
                                        Shirley Hazzard

The inhabitants of this country are the miserablest People in the world.
                                        William Dampier

They may appear to some to be the most wretched people on Earth, but in reality they are far more happier than we Europeans; being wholly unacquainted not only with the superfluous but the necessary Conveniences so much sought after in Europe, they are happy in not knowing the use of them.   *Captain James Cook*

While subsisting adequately but with little material comfort, Aborigines formulated a world view in which social bonding was firm and the individual lived in intimate relationship with his territory; men had more leisure to devote to art, myth and ceremonial than all but a few Western artists and composers. Women laboured to feed them, but for many fewer hours than women in peasant agrarian societies.

D. J. Mulvaney

Every fence in Australia encloses land that was once the sole or the shared possession of a particular group of Aborigines.   *W. E. H. Stanner*

We cannot own the land. We are but custodians of the land.

Oodjeroo Noonuccal (Kath Walker)

Fire, grass, kangaroos, and human inhabitants, seem all dependent on each other for existence in Australia; for any one of these things being wanting, the others could no longer continue.   *Sir Thomas Mitchell*

The Australian native can withstand all the reverses of nature, fiendish droughts and sweeping floods, horrors of thirst and enforced starvation—but he cannot withstand civilisation.   *Daisy Bates*

If Australia is The Lucky Country, the Aborigines must be the unluckiest people in the world.   *Frank Hardy*

We have survived forty thousand years. They tried to rape us, they tried to murder us, they tried to burn us out. They took our land, they took our kids, they tried to breed us out—the whole bang lot. We survived all that and we are still going to be here when they are gone. That's how I figure it. So we just have to hang in there.

Pat O'Shane

When the British invaded the continent of Australia in 1788 they did more than colonise a continent and its Aboriginal inhabitants. They also colonised an entire sex—the female sex.   *Anne Summers*

Australia is a country almost devoid of intimacy. There are few close horizons here, either environmentally or culturally.   *S. J. Baker*

To live in Australia permanently is rather like going to a party and dancing all night with one's mother. There's something a little bit unhealthy about it.

Barry Humphries

Australia will never acquire a national identity until individual Australians acquire identities of their own.   *Patrick White*

Australia's identity is a prematurely urbanised philistinism.   *Robin Boyd*

Australians are the most urbanised, suburbanised, mechanised and dependent people in the world.   *Edward Kynaston*

The suburb was the major element of Australian society.   *Robin Boyd*

The Australian preference for family life in private houses and gardens is probably intelligent. Instead of despising the suburbs we should work to improve them.

Hugh Stretton

You don't have to be a mindless conformist to choose suburban life. Most of the best poets and painters and inventors and protesters choose it too.   *Hugh Stretton*

Australia is a huge rest home, where no unwelcome news is ever wafted onto the pages of the worst newspaper in the world.   *Germaine Greer*

The immense cities lie basking on the beaches of the continent like whales that have taken to the land again.   *Arnold Toynbee*

Australians themselves have a saying that when a stranger arrives in Perth, the first question he is asked is, 'Where do you come from?'; in Adelaide, 'What Church do you belong to?'; in Melbourne, 'What school were you at?'; in Sydney, 'How much money have you got?'; while in Brisbane they merely say, 'Come and have a drink.'

John Douglas Pringle

In Adelaide they take you to their hearts; in Melbourne, to their homes; and in Sydney, to the races.   *Anonymous*

Sydney is one of those places which, when a man leaves it knowing that he will never return, he cannot leave without a pang and a tear. Such is its loveliness.

Anthony Trollope

Sydney? That's a strange name for a city. Why didn't they call it Fred?

Robert Morley

If Jesus wept over Jerusalem He must be heartbroken over Sydney.   *Rev. Fred Nile*

Balmain boys don't cry.   *Neville Wran*

Like all cities, Sydney is a Rorschach test, and your interpretation of it reveals yourself.

Ruth Park

Melbourne seems to have been ironed out by a celestial flat-iron determined to smooth out every crease and wrinkle for the sake of neatness.   *Charmian Clift*

Visiting Melbourne today is like entering the hushed bed chamber of a dying relative and telling him he looks great.   *Barry Humphries*

'On the Beach' is a story about the end of the world, and Melbourne sure is the right place to film it.   *Attributed to Ava Gardner*

For many people the advantage of living in Canberra is that their relatives are interstate.

Alan Fitzgerald

Tasmanians always refer to the rest of Australia as 'mainland' with an almost imperceptible lift of the nose.   *David Walker*

Queensland—Australia's Deep North.   *Anon.*

In the Deep North it is well known that a bloodthirsty socialist and, more than likely, a communist tries to hide behind every peanut and pumpkin scone.   *The Bulletin*

In the midst of life we are in Perth.   *Harry Hooton*

Above our writers—and other artists—looms the intimidating mass of Anglo-Saxon culture. Such a situation almost inevitably produces the characteristic Australian Cultural Cringe.   *A. A. Phillips*

You Australians absorb American culture as if you were made of blotting paper.
                                                                 Joan Ganz Cooney

As in all young countries, the culture of Australia is to a very small extent an integral part of the national life. It has not worked itself into the social fabric. It is something tacked on.   *Hartley Grattan*

I don't despair about the cultural scene in Australia because there isn't one here to despair about.   *Robert Helpmann*

It is almost impossible to assimilate an Australian into another culture.
                                                                    Sidney Nolan

It shows a lot about our culture that Rotarians sing *God Save The Queen* and then go on with American rituals about business.   *Frank Moorhouse*

Australia speaks with many voices. It becomes confusing which one to accept as serious or otherwise.   *Dr Mahathir*

Foreigners easily—too easily—assume that Australia is a crude habitat. They do not understand that, on the contrary, it is a subtle one, home of a subtle people.
                                                                    David Martin

There's no point in being subtle in Australia. I think the message is not heard.
                                                                    Paul Keating

In the Australian spirit there is an easy-going casualness, and there is also a pathos, not always expressed but lining the soul as a residue of sullenness.   *Ross Terrill*

'You feel free in Australia.' And so you do. There is a great relief in the atmosphere, a relief from tension, from pressure. An absence of control or will or form. The sky is open above you, and the air is open around you. Not the old closing-in of Europe.
                                                                    D. H. Lawrence

But nobody (in Australia) felt *better* than anybody else, or higher; only better off. And there is all the difference in the world between feeling *better* than your fellow man, and merely feeling *better-off*.   *D. H. Lawrence*

Australia is perhaps the last stronghold of egalitarian democracy.   *Hartley Grattan*

Australian democracy is genuinely benevolent, but is preoccupied with its own affairs. From time to time it remembers the primitive people it has dispossessed, and sheds over their predestined passing an economical tear. *W. K. Hancock*

The aggressive insistence on the worth and unique importance of the common man seems to me to be one of the fundamental Australian characteristics.
Hartley Grattan

The idea of a working man's paradise in Australia belongs to another century, as does the glitter of El Dorado. *Bruce Grant*

It is our historic task to show the world what can be created by a resolute pursuit of mediocrity . . . Our mediocrity is our saving grace. *John Passmore*

In Australia,
inter alia,
Mediocrities
Think they're Socrates. *Peter Porter*

Australia has, in fact, some of the characteristics of an adolescent or of an alcoholic. It is a country high on ego and low on self-esteem; its inhabitants can be unsure of themselves, yet also narcissistic and arrogant. *Kate Jennings*

In the area of understanding, thinking and responding as a nation we appear to be mildly retarded. *Barry O. Jones*

The Englishman has a natural respect for law and authority; the Australian resents authority and regards the policeman as his natural enemy. *John Douglas Pringle*

To be fair to Australians, they don't afford excessive respect to anybody. It's one of their virtues. *Malcolm Muggeridge*

(He) is a very nice fellow, certainly: nobody would ever guess he was born in Australia.
George Bernard Shaw, 'Major Barbara'

Like uncut opals, Australians are sometimes rough on the outside and are basically colourful and can be polished to a high brilliance. *Hayes Gordon*

Australians are too divided, too melancholy, too schizoid and too Irish to be imprisoned forever in the pragmatic. *Dorothy Hewett*

The system of government we have in Australia is socialism for the rich and free enterprise for the poor. *Bob Ellis*

And when people say they want to maintain 'the Australian way of life', it is usually pretty obvious that they mean *their particular privileges*. *John Anderson*

We are, to a large extent, the poor who got away. *Les A. Murray*

The Australian fiscal system which has evolved since World War II may then be seen as one which maximises the amount of political noise and minimises the degree of electoral accountability, financial responsibility, economic efficiency and effective policy choice. *Rae Else-Mitchell*

It is not dishonesty that brands the Australian politician. He is either brainless on matters of State because of lack of experience, or he is in the bondage of salary and party, and dare not use his brains if he possess any. *Jessie Ackermann*

The desire to enjoy the games of the rich became one of the most effectively expressed moods of Australian egalitarianism. *Donald Horne*

Sport is the ultimate Australian super-religion, the one thing every Australian believes in passionately. *Keith Dunstan*

Australia is an outdoor country. People only go inside to use the toilet. And that's only a recent development. *Barry Humphries*

It is only in sport that many Australians express those approaches to life that are un-Australian if expressed in any other connection. *Donald Horne*

Obviously Australia is a country which takes its sport seriously. Otherwise she would hardly have enshrined the heart of a racehorse in her national capital, and parked the hide of the same lovely beast in a famous museum. *Harry Gordon*

White Australian hedonism, which so alarms many visiting intellectuals and resident puritans, has its fullest expression in the life of Australians at the beach.
Geoffrey Dutton

Every Australian worships the Goddess of Sport with profound adoration, and there is no nation in the world which treats itself to so many holidays. *Edward Kinglake*

Australians have no sense of the religious, no sense of occasion, either. If the Apocalypse came they wouldn't know it, they'd probably think it was a public holiday.
Louis Nowra, 'Inside the Island'

In Anzac Day, Australians would create a holiday, not transplanted from elsewhere, not confined to one region, not an occasion for pleasure; commemorating the shedding of blood for nation and empire, and honouring heroes as nobody in Australia had ever been honoured before. *K. S. Inglis*

I am convinced that there are no troops in the world to equal the Australians in cool daring, courage and endurance. *Sir John Monash*

. . . the finest body of young men ever brought together in modern times. For physical beauty and nobility of bearing they surpassed any men I have ever seen; they walked and looked like kings in old poems.
John Masefield (on Australian soldiers at Gallipoli)

The Australians are undisciplined people . . . Life has been too easy for us.
Donald Rogers (John Curtin's secretary)

Life is not meant to be easy.   *Malcolm Fraser*

In their own country they may be unorthodox, or perhaps slovenly, in speech and costume . . . but morally and intellectually most of them strike me as quite desperately conformist.   *J. R. Darling*

Australians don't like to think there are class accents in their society because in general they don't like to think there are classes, but in both cases they are simply denying reality.   *Craig McGregor*

Australians are on the whole an inarticulate people. We convey a whole world of meanings by a grunt, or a lifting of the eyebrows.   *Manning Clark*

Australians swallow more syllables than any other single item of consumption.
                                                                          H. D. Black

It is one of the saddest things in my life that I've never been able to manage an Australian accent. But they tell me: 'Lean on something and don't open your mouth.'
                                                                          Joyce Grenfell

The standard expression on the face of the Australian male is the frown.
                                                                          Russell Braddon

Every now and then a shark eats an Australian. But every day Australians eat enormous numbers of sharks. The trade balance is very much in our favour.   *Cyril Pearl*

If it moves, shoot it; if it doesn't, chop it down ('national motto of Australia').
                                                                          Anon.

So many Australians equate driving with masculinity: pass them and they suffer instant emasculation.   *Ian Moffitt*

The Australian man loves sex and hates women.   *Alan Whicker*

We're a nation of punters and party-goers.   *Paul Hogan*

A 'typical Australian' could be a Maltese-born lesbian as much as an ocker male.
                                                                          Dennis Altman

They're a weird mob.   *'Nino Culotta' (John O'Grady)*

Beauty

And all the loveliest things there be
Come simply, so it seems to me.   *Edna St. Vincent Millay*

Beauty without expression tires.   *Ralph Waldo Emerson*

Provided a woman is beautiful, allowance will be made for all her shortcomings.
Miles Franklin, 'My Brilliant Career'

Remember that the most beautiful things in the world are the most useless, peacocks and lilies for instance.
John Ruskin

Beauty is unbearable, drives us to despair, offering us for a minute the glimpse of an eternity that we should like to stretch out over the whole of time.   *Albert Camus*

Beauty is potent but money is omnipotent.
Old saying

Beauty is truth—truth, beauty—that is all Ye know on earth, and all ye need to know.
John Keats

Ask a toad what is beauty? . . . a female with two great round eyes coming out of her little head, a large flat mouth, a yellow belly and a brown back.   *Voltaire*

Beauty may seek other expressions, complexities of light and nature, but its emblem must first be human beauty.
Norman Lindsay

Though we travel the world over to find the beautiful, we must carry it with us or we find it not.   *Ralph Waldo Emerson*

Beauty is an ecstasy; it is as simple as hunger. There is really nothing to be said about it.
W. Somerset Maugham

As a beauty I am not a star,
There are others more handsome by far,
But my face—I don't mind it
For I am behind it.
It's the people in front get the jar.
Anthony Euwer

Until I saw Chardin's painting, I never realized how much beauty lay around me in my parents' house, in the half-cleared table, in the corner of a tablecloth left awry, in the knife beside the empty oyster shell.   *Marcel Proust*

The beauty of the animal form is in exact proportion to the amount of moral and intellectual virtue expressed by it.   *John Ruskin*

Do you love me because I'm beautiful, or am I beautiful because you love me?
Oscar Hammerstein, II

Beauty is everlasting
And dust is for a time.
Marianne Moore

Beauty, more than bitterness
Makes the heart break.
Sara Teasdale

Things are beautiful if you love them.
Jean Anouilh

We ascribe beauty to that which is simple; which has no superfluous parts; which exactly answers its ends.   *Ralph Waldo Emerson*

Something wonderful and strange that the artist fashions out of the chaos of the world in the torment of his soul.   *W. Somerset Maugham*

Beauty is the purgation of superfluities.   *Michelangelo*

Beauty—the adjustment of all parts proportionately so that one cannot add or subtract or change without impairing the harmony of the whole.   *Leon Battista Alberti*

Underneath this stone doth lie
As much beauty as could die.   *Ben Jonson*

There is no excellent beauty that hath not some strangeness in the proportion.
                                                                        Francis Bacon

A very beautiful woman hardly ever leaves a clear-cut impression of features and shape in the memory: usually there remains only an aura of living colour. *William Bolitho*

The excellence of every art is its intensity, capable of making all disagreeables evaporate, from their being in close relationship with beauty and truth.   *John Keats*

It is amazing how complete is the delusion that beauty is goodness.   *Leo Tolstoy*

Exuberance is beauty.   *William Blake*

The Bible

Fear is the denomination of the Old Testament; belief is the denomination of the New.
                                                                        Benjamin Whichcote

The English of the Bible has a pithiness and raciness, a homely tang, a terse sententiousness, an idiomatic flavour which comes home to men's business and bosoms . . . a nobility of diction and . . . a rhythmic quality . . . unrivaled in its beauty.
                                                                        John Livingston Lowes

The next day John seeth Jesus coming unto him and saith. Behold the Lamb of God, which taketh away the sins of the world.   *John 1:29*

That kind of so-called housekeeping where they have six Bibles and no cork-screw.
                                                                        Mark Twain

The total absence of humour in the Bible is one of the most singular things in all literature.   *Alfred North Whitehead*

The Old and New Testaments are the Great Code of Art.   *William Blake*

The fathers have eaten a sour grape, and the children's teeth are set on edge.
Jeremiah 31:29

I have fought a good fight, I have finished my course, I have kept the faith.
2 Timothy 4:7

The whole head is sick, and the whole heart faint.   *Isaiah 1:5*

It is better to dwell in a corner of the housetop, than with a brawling woman in a wide house.
Proverbs 21:9

Oh my Father, if it be possible, let this cup pass from me: nevertheless, not as I will, but as thou wilt.
Matthew 26:39

A prophet is not without honour, save in his own country.   *Matthew 13:57*

Be not curious in unnecessary matters: for more things are shewed unto thee than men understand.
Ecclesiasticus 3:24-25

Seek not out the things that are too hard for thee, neither search the things that are above thy strength.
Ecclesiasticus 3:22

How beautiful upon the mountains are the feet of him that bringeth good tidings, that publisheth peace.
Isaiah 52:7

His countenance was like lightning, and his raiment white as snow.   *Matthew 28:3*

Be not deceived; God is not mocked: for whatsoever a man soweth, that shall he also reap.
Galatians 6:7

Watchman, what of the night?   *Isaiah 21:11*

Man goeth to his long home, and the mourners go about the streets.
Ecclesiastes 12:5

The letter killeth, but the spirit giveth life.   *2 Corinthians 3:6*

For if the trumpet give an uncertain sound, who shall prepare himself to the battle?
1 Corinthians 14:8

The wilderness and the solitary place shall be glad for them and the desert shall rejoice and blossom as the rose.
Isaiah 35:1

Entreat me not to leave thee, or to return from following after thee; for whither thou goest, I will go; and where thou lodgest, I will lodge; thy people shall be my people and thy God my God: where thou diest will I die, and there will I be buried; the Lord do so to me, and more also, if ought but death part thee and me.   *Ruth 1:16-17*

We have piped unto you, and ye have not danced; we have mourned to you, and ye have not wept.
Luke 7:32

I know thy works, that thou art neither cold nor hot: I would thou wert cold or hot.
Revelation 3:15

The Book of Revelation is purely psychedelic.   *Ted Noffs*

They are as stubble before the wind, and as chaff that the storm carrieth away.
Job 21:18

Neither do men light a candle and put it under a bushel, but on a candlestick; and it giveth light unto all that are in the house.   *Matthew 5:15*

Bone of my bones, and flesh of my flesh: she shall be called woman.   *Genesis 2:23*

To a practising politician I know of no document more disturbing than the Ten Commandments—unless it be the Sermon on the Mount.   *Sir Robert Menzies*

When caught reading the Bible, W.C. Fields said 'I'm looking for loop-holes.'

The Bible is nothing but a succession of civil rights struggles by the Jewish people against their oppressors.   *Jesse Jackson*

The Gospels are the purest Socialistic literature we have.
'Tom Collins' (Joseph Furphy)

Out of the mouths of babes and sucklings hast thou ordained strength.   *Psalms 8:2*

Unto everyone that hath shall be given, and he shall have abundance: but from him that hath not shall be taken away even that which he hath.   *Matthew 25:29*

He that is not with me is against me.   *Matthew 12:30*

Man is born unto trouble, as the sparks fly upward.   *Job 5:7*

For what is your life? It is even a vapour, that appeareth for a little time, and then vanisheth away.   *James 4:14*

My days are swifter than a weaver's shuttle.   *Job 7:6*

I know thy pride, and the naughtiness of thine heart.   *1 Samuel 17:28*

The bible should be taught so early and so thoroughly that it sinks straight to the bottom of the mind where everything that comes along can settle on it.
Northrop Frye

Birth

To be born is to be lucky.   *Kylie Tennant, 'Ride on Stranger'*

The egg it is the source of all
To everyone's ancestral hall.   *Clarence Day*

Being pregnant is a very boring six months. I am not particularly maternal. It's an occupational hazard of being a wife. *Princess Anne*

The government is concerned about the population explosion, and the population is concerned about the government explosion. *Ruth Rankin*

We have been God-like in our planned breeding of our domestic plants and animals, but rabbit-like in our unplanned breeding of ourselves. *Arnold Toynbee*

Some are born to sweet delight,
Some are born to endless night. *William Blake*

In my beginning is my end. *T. S. Eliot*

When I was born I did lament and cry
And now each day doth shew the reason why. *Richard Watkyns*

Where, unwilling, dies the rose,
Buds the new, another year. *Dorothy Parker*

Husbands don't really count . . . in the miracle of birth. *Doug Spettigue*

And when I was born, I drew in the common air, and fell upon the earth, which is of like nature, and the first voice which I uttered was crying, as all others do . . . For all men have one entrance into life. *The Apocrypha*

Monday's child is fair of face,
Tuesday's child is full of grace,
Wednesday's child is full of woe
Thursday's child has far to go
Friday's child is loving and giving,
Saturday's child works hard for a living,
But the child born on the Sabbath day
Is happy and wise and good and gay. *Anon.*

As the births of living creatures at first are ill-shapen, so are all innovations, which are the births of time. *Francis Bacon*

Books and Reading

A lexicographer, a writer of dictionaries, a harmless drudge. *Samuel Johnson*

All good books are alike in that they are truer than if they really happened and after you are finished reading one you feel that it all happened to you and after which it all belongs to you. *Ernest Hemingway*

All the glory of the world would be buried in oblivion, unless God had provided mortals with the remedy of books. *Richard De Bury*

Books are the most mannerly of companions, accessible at all times, in all moods, frankly declaring the author's mind, without offense.   *Amos Bronson Alcott*

Everyone who knows how to read has it in their power to magnify themselves, to multiply the ways in which they exist, to make their life full, significant, and interesting.   *Aldous Huxley*

Having your book turned into a movie is like seeing your oxen turned into bouillon cubes.   *John Le Carré*

He has only half learned the art of reading who has not added to it the even more refined accomplishments of skipping and skimming.   *Arthur Balfour*

If a book is worth reading at all, it is worth reading more than once. Suspense is the lowest of excitants, designed to take your breath away when the brain and heart crave to linger in nobler enjoyment. Suspense drags you on; appreciation causes you to linger.   *William Gerhardie*

If you would not be forgotten as soon as you are dead, either write things worth reading or do things worth writing.   *Benjamin Franklin*

Neither is a dictionary a bad book to read. There is no cant in it, no excess of explanation, and it is full of suggestions, the raw material of possible poems and histories.   *Ralph Waldo Emerson*

Nothing links man to man like the frequent passage from hand to hand of a good book.   *Walter Sickert*

Some books are undeservedly forgotten; none are undeservedly remembered.   *W. H. Auden*

The delight of opening a new pursuit, or a new course of reading, imparts the vivacity and novelty of youth even to old age.   *Benjamin Disraeli*

(Books) are the channels through which the influence flows that makes the difference between the wise, and well—the otherwise.   *E. W. Cole*

The fact of knowing how to read is nothing, the whole point is knowing what to read.   *Jacques Ellul*

The habit of reading is the only enjoyment in which there is no alloy; it lasts when all other pleasures fade.   *Anthony Trollope*

The possession of a book becomes a substitute for reading it.   *Anthony Burgess*

The responsibility of a dictionary is to record a language, not set its style.   *Phillip Babcock Gove (U.S. dictionary editor)*

To finish is both a relief and a release from an extraordinarily pleasant prison.   *Robert Burchfield (U.K. dictionary editor)*

What is reading but silent conversation?   *Walter Savage Landor*

'Sartor Resartus' is simply unreadable, and for me that always sort of spoils a book.
Harry S. Truman

You should read it, though there is much that is skip-worthy.   *Herbert Asquith*

The greatest masterpiece in literature is only a dictionary out of order.
Jean Cocteau

When you read a classic you do not see in the book more than you did before. You
see more in you than there was before.   *Clifton Fadiman*

Properly we should read for power. Man reading should be man intensely alive. The
book should be a ball of light in one's hand.   *Ezra Pound*

Best-sellerism is the star system of the book world. A (best-seller) is a celebrity among
books. It is a book known primarily (sometimes exclusively) for its well-knownness.
Daniel J. Boorstin

A book is as implacable as an unborn child, a rising day, inevitable in its demands.
M. Barnard Eldershaw

Reading after a certain (time) diverts the mind too much from its creative pursuits.
Any man who reads too much and uses his own brain too little falls into lazy habits
of thinking.   *Albert Einstein*

The most technologically efficient machine that man has ever invented is the book.
Northrop Frye

Literature is news that *stays* news.   *Ezra Pound*

Just the knowledge that a good book is awaiting one at the end of a long day makes
that day happier.   *Kathleen Norris*

Laws die, books never.   *Edward Bulwer-Lytton*

Master books, but do not let them master you. Read to live, not live to read.
Edward Bulwer-Lytton

A good book is the precious life-blood of a master spirit, embalmed and treasured up
on purpose to a life beyond life.   *John Milton*

Any book which is at all important should be re-read immediately.
Arthur Schopenhauer

Do give books—religious or otherwise—for Christmas. They're never fattening, seldom
sinful, and permanently personal.   *Lenore Hershey*

Never lend books—nobody ever returns them; the only books I have in my library are
those which people have lent me.   *Anatole France*

Discretion is not the better part of biography.   *Lytton Strachey*

A dictionary should be descriptive, not prescriptive.   *Phillip Babcock Gove*

Book lovers never go to bed alone.   *Anon.*

It circulated for five years, through the halls of fifteen publishers, and finally ended up with Vanguard Press, which as you can see is rather deep into the alphabet.
Patrick Dennis (Edward Everett Tanner) of his novel 'Auntie Mame'

The first book of the nation is the dictionary of its language.
Contanitin, Comte de Volney

A novel is a mirror carried along a main road.   *Stendhal*

I read part of it all the way through.   *Sam Goldwyn*

A successful book cannot afford to be more than ten percent new.
Marshall McLuhan

First publication is a pure, carnal leap into that dark which one dreams is life.
Hortense Calisher

Books give not wisdom where none was before. But where some is, there reading makes it more.   *John Harington*

A good book has no ending.   *R. D. Cumming*

Oh that my words were now written! Oh that they were printed in a book!
Job 19:23

What a sense of security in an old book which time has criticized for us!
James Russell Lowell

I hate books; they teach us only to talk about what we do not know.
Jean-Jacques Rousseau

'Tis the good reader that makes the good book.   *Ralph Waldo Emerson*

The telephone book is full of facts but it doesn't contain a single idea.
Mortimer J. Adler

In the case of good books, the point is not to see how many of them you can get through, but rather how many can get through to you.   *Mortimer J. Adler*

Books think for me.   *Charles Lamb*

Dictionaries are like watches. The worst is better than none at all and even the best cannot be expected to run quite true.   *Samuel Johnson*

Does it afflict you to find your books wearing out? I mean literally . . . the mortality of all inanimate things is terrible to me, but that of books most of all.

William Dean Howells

The true university of these days is a collection of books.   *Thomas Carlyle*

I keep my books at the British Museum and at Mudies.   *Samuel Butler*

One man is as good as another until he has written a book.   *Benjamin Jowett*

If a book is worth reading, it is worth buying.   *John Ruskin*

Reading is sometimes an ingenious device for avoiding thought.   *Arthur Helps*

The oldest books are still only just out to those who have not read them.

Samuel Butler

A book is a mirror: if an ass peers into it, you can't expect an apostle to look out.

G. C. Lichtenberg

The man who does not read good books has no advantage over the man who can't read them.   *Mark Twain*

Where is human nature so weak as in the bookstore?   *Henry Ward Beecher*

Ordinary people know little of the time and effort it takes to learn to read. I have been eighty years at it, and have not reached my goal.   *Goethe*

I am a part of all I have read.   *John Kieran*

Reading is the work of the alert mind, is demanding, and under ideal conditions produces finally a sort of ecstasy. This gives the experience of reading a sublimity and power unequalled by any other form of communication.   *E. B. White*

I do not know any reading more easy, more fascinating, more delightful than a catalogue.   *Anatole France*

To me the charm of an encyclopedia is that it knows—and I needn't.

Francis Yeats-Brown

A best-seller was a book which somehow sold well simply because it was selling well.

Daniel J. Boorstin

A good title is the title of a successful book.   *Raymond Chandler*

Books should be tried by a judge and jury as though they were crimes.

Samuel Butler

Reading, like prayer, remains one of our few private acts.   *William Jovanovich*

My education was the liberty I had to read indiscriminately and all the time, with my eyes hanging out. *Dylan Thomas*

A publisher is somebody looking for someone who has something to say.
Lorne Pierce

There are perhaps no days of our childhood we lived so fully as those we believe we left without having lived them: those we spent with a favourite book.
Marcel Proust

Some books are to be tasted, others to be swallowed, and some few to be chewed and digested. *Francis Bacon*

If you would understand your own age, read the works of fiction produced in it. People in disguise speak freely. *Arthur Helps*

Camerado, this is no book.
Who touches this, touches a man. *Walt Whitman*

A book is like a garden carried in the pocket. *Chinese proverb*

The walls of books around him, dense with the past, formed a kind of insulation against the present world and its disasters. *Ross MacDonald*

There are still a few of us booklovers around despite the awful warnings of Marshall McLuhan with his TV era and his pending farewell to Gutenberg. *Frank Davies*

Bores and Boredom

A healthy male adult bore consumes each year one and a half times his own weight in other people's patience. *John Updike*

He is an old bore; even the grave yawns for him. *Herbert Beerbohm Tree*

How is it that we remember the least triviality that happens to us, and yet not remember how often we have recounted it to the same person? *La Rochefoucauld*

We may be willing to tell a story twice, never to hear it more than once.
William Hazlitt

Some people can stay longer in an hour than others can in a week.
William Dean Howells

A bore is a man who deprives you of solitude without providing you with company.
Gian Vincenzo Cravina

A bore is a man who, when you ask him how he is, tells you. *Bert Leston Taylor*

The man who suspects his own tediousness has yet to be born.

Thomas Bailey Aldrich

Ennui has made more gamblers than avarice, more drunkards than thirst, and perhaps as many suicides as despair.   *Charles Caleb Colton*

The inexorable boredom that is at the core of life.   *Jacques-Bénigne Bossuet*

He has returned from Italy a greater bore than ever; he bores on architecture, painting, statuary and music.   *Sydney Smith*

O wad some power the giftie gie us to see some people before they see us.

Ethel Watts Mumford

The most costly disease is not cancer or coronaries. The most costly disease is boredom—costly for both individual and society.   *Norman Cousins*

The devil's name is dullness.   *Robert E. Lee*

The basic fact about human existence is not that it is a tragedy, but that it is a bore.

H. L. Mencken

His shortcoming is his long staying.   *Lewis L. Lewisohn*

Uncertainty and mystery are energies of life. Don't let them scare you unduly, for they keep boredom at bay and spark creativity.   *R. I. Fitzhenry*

Boredom is a vital problem for the moralist, since at least half the sins of mankind are caused by the fear of it.   *Bertrand Russell*

I grew up thinking there was one unpardonable sin—to be boring.   *Germaine Greer*

When people are bored, it is primarily with their own selves.   *Eric Hoffer*

A variety of nothing is superior to a monotony of something.   *Jean Paul Richter*

We often forgive those who bore us, but can't forgive those whom we bore.

La Rochefoucauld

A man can stand almost anything except a succession of ordinary days.   *Goethe*

Any idiot can face a crisis—it's this day-to-day living that wears you out.

Anton Chekhov

The secret of boring people lies in telling them everything.   *Voltaire*

Boredom turns a man to sex, a woman to shopping, and it drives newscasters berserk.

Bruce Herschensohn

Blessed is the man who, having nothing to say, refrains from giving wordy evidence of the fact.   *George Eliot*

Boredom is rage spread thin.   *Paul Tillich*

Almost all human affairs are tedious. Everything is too long. Visits, dinners, concerts, plays, speeches, pleadings, essays, sermons, are too long. Pleasure and business labour equally under this defect, or, as I should rather say, this fatal superabundance.
Arthur Helps

Business, Capitalism and Corporate Enterprise

You cannot strengthen the weak by weakening the strong. You cannot help the wage earner by pulling down the wage payer. You cannot help the poor by destroying the rich. You cannot help men permanently by doing for them what they could and should do for themselves.   *John Henry Boetcker*

Those who can, do; those who can't, teach; and those who can do neither, administer.
Collet Calverley

Anti-intellectualism has long been the anti-Semitism of the business man.
Arthur Schopenhauer

No-wher so bisy a man as he ther nas,
And yet he semed bisier than he was.   *Geoffrey Chaucer*

As one retiring chief executive said to his successor 'Yesterday was the last day you heard the truth from your subordinates.'   *Robert W. McMurry*

Commerce is greedy. Ideology is blood-thirsty.   *Mason Cooley*

Crime is a logical extension of the sort of behaviour that is often considered perfectly respectable in legitimate business.   *Robert Rice*

Entrepreneurship is the last refuge of the trouble-making individual.
James K. Glassman

The big print giveth and the fine print taketh away.   *Monsignor J. Fulton Sheen*

Expenditure rises to meet income.   *C. Northcote Parkinson*

I am a Millionaire. That is my religion.   *George Bernard Shaw*

If you fail to plan, you plan to fail.   *Old saying*

It is an economic axiom as old as the hills that goods and services can be paid for only with goods and services.   *Albert J. Nock*

Under capitalism, man exploits man. Under communism, it's just the opposite.
Russian saying

It might be termed the Law of Triviality. Briefly stated, it means that the time spent on any item of the agenda will be in adverse proportion to the sum involved.

Northcote Parkinson

It takes no more actual sagacity to carry on the everyday hawking and haggling of the world, or to ladle out its normal doses of bad medicine and worse law, than it takes to operate a taxi cab or fry a pan of fish. *H. L. Mencken*

Live together like brothers and do business like strangers. *Anon.*

Managers don't have to cook the books to manipulate earnings; they often have all the power they need in the leeway built into accounting rules. *Fred S. Worthy*

Mere parsimony is not economy . . . expense, and great expense, may be an essential part of true economy. *Edmund Burke*

Remember that when an employee enters your office, he is in a strange land.

Erwin H. Schell

The best way to destroy the capitalist system is to debauch the currency. By a continuing process of inflation, governments can confiscate, secretly and unobserved, an important part of the wealth of their citizens. *John Maynard Keynes*

Big companies and big unions have a similar tendency towards monopoly. The public company often has a monopoly of supplying goods and services and the union often has a monopoly of supplying labour, but both are reluctant to describe themselves as monopolies. *Geoffrey Blainey*

Monopoly is a terrible thing, till you have it. *Rupert Murdoch*

Luck is infatuated with the efficient. *Persian proverb*

The big-business mergers and the big-labour mergers have the appearance of dinosaurs mating. *John Naisbitt*

The corporation is an artificial being, invisible, intangible, and existing only in contemplation of law. *John Marshall*

The forces in a capitalist society, if left unchecked, tend to make the rich richer and the poor poorer. *Jawaharlal Nehru*

The manager with the in-basket problem does not yet understand that he must discipline himself to take care of activities that fail to excite him. *Priscilla Elfrey*

To business that we love we rise betime,
And go to it with delight. *Shakespeare, 'Antony and Cleopatra'*

The white man knows how to make everything, but he does not know how to distribute it. *Sitting Bull*

There are an enormous number of managers who have retired on the job.
Peter F. Drucker

There is only one social responsibility of business—to use its resources and engage in activities designed to increase its profits without deception or fraud.
Milton Friedman

I fully realise, as a good citizen, that private property is sacred and that no man should be robbed except by the proper business methods.   *Lennie Lower*

Things have to be made to happen in a way you want them to happen. Without management, without the intervention of organized willpower the desired result simply cannot be obtained.   *Robert Heller*

Today's sales should be better than yesterday's—and worse than tomorrow's.
Old saying

We have yet to find a significant case where the company did not move in the direction of the chief executive's home.   *Ken Patton*

You are never giving, nor can you ever give, enough service.   *James R. Cook*

In matters of commerce the fault of the Dutch
Is offering too little and asking too much.
The French are with equal advantage content,
So we clap on Dutch bottoms just 20%.   *George Canning*

Christmas is over, and Business is Business.   *Franklin Pierce Adams*

People of privilege will always risk their complete destruction rather than surrender any material part of their advantage.   *J. K. Galbraith*

Competition means decentralized planning by many separate persons.
Friedrich Hayek

All business sagacity reduces itself in the last analysis to a judicious use of sabotage.
Thorstein Veblen

Expansion means complexity and complexity decay.   *Northcote Parkinson*

One man's wage rise is another man's price increase.   *Harold Wilson*

Few have heard of Fra Luca Parioli, the inventor of double-entry bookkeeping, but he has probably had more influence on human life than has Dante or Michelangelo.
Herbert J. Muller

When you've got them by their wallets, their hearts and minds will follow.
Fern Naito

Chaplin is no businessman—all he knows is that he can't take anything less.
Sam Goldwyn

What kind of society isn't structured on greed? The problem of social organization is how to set up an arrangement under which greed will do the least harm; capitalism is that kind of a system.   *Milton Friedman*

Barbaric accuracy—whimpering humility.   *G. C. Lichtenberg*

Patience is a most necessary quality for business; many a man would rather you heard his story than grant his request.   *Lord Chesterfield*

A holding company is the people you give your money to while you're being searched.
Will Rogers

In economics, the majority is always wrong.   *J. K. Galbraith*

Whenever you see a successful business, someone once made a courageous decision.
Peter Drucker

Pounds are the sons, not of pounds, but of pence.   *Charles Buxton*

Business? It's quite simple. It's other people's money.
Alexandre Dumas the Younger

A man isn't a man until he has to meet a payroll.   *Ivan Shaffer*

As a rule, from what I've observed, the American Captain of Industry doesn't do anything out of business hours. When he has put the cat out and locked up the office for the night, he just relapses into a state of coma from which he emerges only to start being a Captain of Industry again.   *P. G. Wodehouse*

I don't believe in just ordering people to do things. You have to sort of grab an oar and row with them.   *Harold Geneen*

Executive ability is deciding quickly and getting somebody else to do the work.
J. C. Pollard

Capitalism in the United States has undergone profound modification, not just under the New Deal but through a consensus that continued to grow after the New Deal. Government in the U.S. today is a senior partner in every business in the country.
Norman Cousins

Going to work for a large company is like getting on a train. Are you going sixty miles an hour or is the train going sixty miles an hour and you're just sitting still?
Paul Getty

The happiest time in any man's life is when he is in red-hot pursuit of a dollar with a reasonable prospect of overtaking it.   *Josh Billings*

In a hierarchy every employee tends to rise to his level of incompetence.
Laurence J. Peter

What recommends commerce to me is its enterprise and bravery. It does not clasp its
hands and pray to Jupiter.   *Henry David Thoreau*

Business is a combination of war and sport.   *André Maurois*

Net—the biggest word in the language of business.   *Herbert Casson*

Big business is basic to the very life of this country; and yet many—perhaps
most—Americans have a deep-seated fear and an emotional repugnance to it. Here is
monumental contradiction.   *David Lilienthal*

The secret of business is to know something that nobody else knows.
                                                               Aristotle Onassis

Don't gamble; take all your savings and buy some good stock and hold it till it goes
up, then sell it. If it don't go up, don't buy it.   *Will Rogers*

Good management consists of showing average people how to do the work of superior
people.   *John D. Rockefeller*

All business proceeds on beliefs, on judgements of probabilities, and not on certainties.
                                                                 Charles W. Eliot

Corporations cannot commit treason, nor be outlawed, nor excommunicated, for they
have no souls.   *Edward Coke*

People of the same trade seldom meet together, even for merriment and diversion, but
the conversation ends in a conspiracy against the public, or in some contrivance to
raise prices.   *Adam Smith*

Capital is past savings accumulated for future production.   *Jackson Martindell*

The business of America is business.   *Calvin Coolidge*

Power over a man's subsistence amounts to a power over his will.
                                                               Alexander Hamilton

In the history of enterprise, most of the protagonists of major new products and
companies began their education—not in the classroom, where the old ways are taught,
but in the factories and labs where new ways are wrought . . . nothing has been so
rare in recent years as an Ivy League graduate who has made a significant innovation
in American enterprise.   *George Gilder*

If a cluttered desk is an indication of a cluttered mind, what is indicated by an empty
desk?   *Anon.*

A businessman is a hybrid of a dancer and a calculator.   *Paul Valéry*

Had there been a computer a hundred years ago, it would probably have predicted that
by now there would be so many horse-drawn vehicles it would be impossible to clear
up all the manure.   *K. William Kapp*

The Middle East is a region where oil is thicker than blood.   *James Holland*

All professions are conspiracies against the laity.   *George Bernard Shaw*

Labour is not a commodity, or a standard, or a means to an ulterior end, but an end in itself.   *George Brockway*

Without some dissimulation no business can be carried on at all.   *Lord Chesterfield*

Along this tree
From root to crown
Ideas flow up
And vetoes down.   *A senior executive, quoted by Peter Drucker*

A criminal is a person with predatory instincts who has not sufficient capital to form a corporation.   *Howard Scott*

Profitability is the sovereign criterion of the enterprise.   *Peter Drucker*

Business is more exciting than any game.   *Lord Beaverbrook*

A company is judged by the president it keeps.   *James Hulbert*

Inflation is defined as the quality that makes balloons larger and candy bars smaller.
General Features Corporation

I think that there is nothing, not even crime, more opposed to poetry, to philosophy, ay, to life itself than this incessant business.   *Henry David Thoreau*

It is not the employer who pays wages—he only handles the money. It is the product that pays wages.   *Henry Ford*

Business is really more agreeable than pleasure; it interests the whole mind . . . more deeply. But it does not look as if it did.   *Walter Bagehot*

The ability to deal with people is as purchasable a commodity as sugar or coffee. And I pay more for that ability than for any other under the sun.   *John D. Rockefeller*

In all modern depressions, recessions, or growth-correction, as variously they are called, we never miss the goods that are not produced. We miss only the opportunities for the labour—for the jobs—that are not provided.   *J. K. Galbraith*

The solid wealth of insurance companies and the success of those who organize gambling are some indication of the profits to be derived from the efficient use of chance.   *Edward de Bono*

To convert an hourly wage to an approximate yearly salary, double the wage and change the decimal to a comma.   *Don Tichnor*

After an eight-hour day, workers require three overtime hours to produce two regular hours of results.   *Illinois Institute of Technology*

Gross National Product is our Holy Grail.   *Stuart Udall*

When two men in business always agree, one of them is unnecessary.
William Wrigley, Jr.

Few great men could pass Personnel.   *Paul Goodman*

You build on cost and you borrow on value.   *Paul Reichmann*

By pursuing his own interest (the individual) frequently promotes that of the society more effectually than when he really intends to promote it. I have never known much good done by those who affected to trade for the public good.   *Adam Smith*

Management is now where the medical profession was when it decided that working in a drug store was not sufficient training to become a doctor.   *Lawrence Appley*

The Bell System is like a damn big dragon. You kick it in the tail, and two years later, it feels it in its head.
Frederick Kappel (when Chairman, American Telephone and Telegraph Co.)

Benefits should be granted little by little, so that they may be better enjoyed.
Niccolo Machiavelli

The price spoils the pleasure.   *French proverb*

Whose bread I eat, his song I sing.   *German proverb*

Buying and Selling

Everyone lives by selling something.   *Robert Louis Stevenson*

It is naught, it is naught; saith the buyer. But when he is gone his way, then he boasteth.
Proverbs 20:14

Piracy, n: commerce without its folly-swaddles—just as God made it.
Ambrose Bierce

A study of economics usually reveals that the best time to buy anything is last year.
Marty Allen

A consumer is a shopper who is sore about something.   *Harold Coffin*

Who buys has need of two eyes
But one's enough to sell the stuff.   *Anon.*

Bargain: something you can't use at a price you can't resist.   *Franklin P. Jones*

Don't buy the house; buy the neighborhood.   *Russian proverb*

A fair price for oil is whatever you can get plus ten to twenty per cent.   *Anon.*

Supermarkets stand condemned as symbols of man's inhumanity to women.
Phillip Adams

An extravagance is anything you buy that is of no earthly use to your wife.
Franklin P. Jones

What costs nothing is worth nothing.   *Anon.*

Keep thy shop and thy shop will keep thee.   *Ben Jonson*

Everything is worth what its purchaser will pay for it.   *Publilius Syrus*

There is hardly anything in the world that some man can't make a little worse and
sell a little cheaper, and the people who consider price only are this man's lawful prey.
John Ruskin

Cheat me in the price but not in the goods.   *Thomas Fuller*

When you buy, use your eyes and your mind, not your ears.
Czechoslovakian proverb

People will buy anything that's one to a customer.   *Sinclair Lewis*

Censorship

Nobody is competent to decide what the people of a country should read except the
people themselves.   *Frank Dalby Davison*

The dirtiest book of all is the expurgated book.   *Walt Whitman*

No member of a society has a right to teach any doctrine contrary to what society
holds to be true.   *Samuel Johnson*

If you're going to permit them to see and read everything, you've got to permit them
to do everything.   *Henry Bolte*

There is no such thing as a moral or an immoral book. Books are well written or badly
written.   *Oscar Wilde*

Knowledge cannot defile, nor consequently the books, if the will and conscience be
not defiled.   *John Milton*

We can never be sure that the opinion we are endeavouring to stifle is a false opinion;
and if we were sure, stifling it would be an evil still.   *John Stuart Mill*

No government ought to be without censors; and where the press is free, no one ever
will.   *Thomas Jefferson*

Censorship, like charity, should begin at home; but unlike charity, it should end there.
Clare Boothe Luce

Obscenity is whatever gives a judge an erection.   *Anonymous American Lawyer*

You cannot believe in the power of words . . . and simultaneously hold that anything can be said, at any time, by anyone.   *Clive James*

Chance and Fortune

I make the most of all that comes,
And the least of all that goes.   *Sarah Teasdale*

If you do not expect it, you will not find the unexpected, for it is hard to find and difficult.   *Heraclitus*

Two roads diverged in a wood and I—
I took the one less travelled by,
And that has made all the difference.   *Robert Frost*

Unless a man has trained himself for his chance, the chance will only make him ridiculous.   *W. Matthews*

Chance is always powerful. Let your hook be always cast. In the pool where you least expect it, will be a fish.   *Ovid*

Chance is the pseudonym of God when he did not want to sign.   *Anatole France*

The harder you work, the luckier you get.   *Gary Player*

I think we consider too much the good luck of the early bird and not enough the bad luck of the early worm.   *Franklin D. Roosevelt*

Fortune favours the bold.   *Terence*

The luck of having talent is not enough; one must also have a talent for luck.
Hector Berlioz

In the field of observation, chance favours the prepared mind.   *Louis Pasteur*

If you were born lucky, even your rooster will lay eggs.   *Russian proverb*

Depend on the rabbit's foot if you will, but remember it didn't work for the rabbit!
R. E. Shay

Those who mistake their good luck for their merit are inevitably bound for disaster.
J. Christopher Herold

Luck is being ready for the chance.   *J. Frank Dobie*

Every man, even the most blessed, needs a little more than average luck to survive this world.
Vance Bourjaily

With luck on your side you can do without brains.
Giordano Bruno

If fortune turns against you, even jelly breaks your tooth.
Persian proverb

Fortune brings in some boats that are not steered.
Shakespeare, 'Cymbeline'

I'm a great believer in luck. I find the harder I work, the more I have of it.
Stephen Leacock

Vexed sailors curse the rain
For which poor shepherds prayed in vain.
Edmund Waller

Change and Transience

A permanent state of transition is man's most noble condition. *Juan Ramon Jimenez*

Change is not made without inconvenience, even from worse to better.
Richard Hooker

All things are subject to change, and we change with them. (*Omnia mutantur, nos et mutamur in illis.*)
Anon.

If you want things to stay as they are, things will have to change.
Giuseppe di Lampedusa

The days come and go like muffled and veiled figures sent from a distant friendly party, but they say nothing, and if we do not use the gifts they bring, they carry them as silently away.
Ralph Waldo Emerson

The more things change, the more they stay the same. (Plus ça change, plus c'est la même chose.)
Alphonse Karr

There are three things which the public will always clamor for, sooner or later: namely, novelty, novelty, novelty.
Thomas Hood

There is only one certainty in life—it will change.
Dame Zara Bate

You can't step into the same river twice.
Heraclitus

What is actual is actual only for one time.
And only for one place.
T. S. Eliot

As one gets older, one discovers everything is going to be exactly the same with different hats on.
Noel Coward

All changes, even the most longed for, have their melancholy, for what we leave behind us is a part of ourselves; we must die to one life before we can enter into another.
Anatole France

When you get there, there isn't any there there.   *Gertrude Stein*

Change must be measured from a known base line.   *Evan Shute*

When you're on top of the world you should remember it turns over every twenty-four hours.   *Tamie Fraser*

All things must change to something new, to something strange.
Henry Wadsworth Longfellow

Every new adjustment is a crisis in self-esteem.   *Eric Hoffer*

I see gr-reat changes takin' place ivry day, but no change at all ivry fifty years.
Finley Peter Dunne

'Change' is scientific, 'progress' is ethical; change is indubitable, whereas progress is a matter of controversy.   *Bertrand Russell*

Turbulence is life force. It is opportunity. Let's love turbulence and use it for change.
Ramsay Clark

Would that life were like the shadow cast by a wall or a tree, but it is like the shadow of a bird in flight.   *The Talmud*

Character and Personality

Failure is God's steel mould of character.   *Furnley Maurice*

He was not of an age but for all time.   *Ben Jonson*

As time requireth, a man of marvellous mirth and past times, and sometimes of as sad gravity, as who say: a man for all seasons.   *Robert Whittington*

At every single moment of one's life, one is going to be no less than what one has been.   *Oscar Wilde*

Surely the world we live in is but the world that lives in us.   *Daisy Bates*

Don't compromise yourself. You are all you've got.   *Janis Joplin*

Evil be to him who evil thinks. *(Honi soit qui mal y pense.)*
Motto for ther Order of the Garter

Good breeding, a union of kindness and independence.   *Ralph Waldo Emerson*

If you can keep your head when all about you
   Are losing theirs and blaming it on you;
If you can trust yourself when all men doubt you,
   But make allowance for their doubting too;
If you can wait and not be tired by waiting,
   Or being lied about, don't deal in lies,
Or being hated, don't give away to hating
   And yet don't look too good nor talk too wise;
If you can dream—and not make dreams your master;
   If you can think—and not make thoughts your aim;
If you can meet with Triumph and Disaster,
   And treat those two imposters just the same; . . .
If you can make one heap of all your winnings
   And risk it on one turn of pitch-and-toss,
And lose, and start again at your beginnings
   And never breathe a word about your loss; . . .
If you can talk with crowds and keep your virtue,
   Or walk with Kings nor lose the common touch,
If neither foes nor loving friends can hurt you,
   If all men count with you, but none too much;
If you can fill the unforgiving minute
   With sixty seconds' worth of distance run,
Yours is the Earth and everything that's in it,
   And—which is more—you'll be a Man my son!
   Rudyard Kipling

Good, but not religious-good.
   Thomas Hardy

He has not a single redeeming defect.
   Benjamin Disraeli

His life was gentle, and the elements
So mixed in him that nature might stand up
And say to all the world, 'This was a man!'
   Shakespeare, 'Hamlet'

Humility is no substitute for a good personality.
   Fran Lebowitz

I am a deeply superficial person.
   Andy Warhol

I have always hated my personality—it's one of the most unfortunate I've ever encountered.
   Percy Grainger

I believe that this neglected, wounded, inner child of the past is the major source of human misery.
   John Bradshaw

I can't believe that out of 100,000 sperm, you were the quickest.
   Steven Pearl

I mean by this Sacrament an outward and visible sign of an inward and spiritual grace.
   Book of Common Prayer

I'm not hard, I'm frightfully soft. But I will not be hounded.
   Margaret Thatcher

Sufferers are seldom sweet-tempered.
   Henry Handel Richardson

If I try to be like him, who will be like me? *Yiddish proverb*

Individualism is rather like innocence; there must be something unconscious about it. *Louis Kronenberger*

It is thus with most of us; we are what other people say we are. We know ourselves chiefly by hearsay. *Eric Hoffer*

Lord Ronald said nothing; he flung himself from the room, flung himself upon his horse and rode madly off in all directions. *Stephen Leacock*

Oozing charm from every pore,
He oiled his way around the floor. *Alan Jay Lerner, 'My Fair Lady'*

Self-denial is not a virtue, it is only the effect of prudence on rascality. *George Bernard Shaw*

The first time you meet Winston (Churchill) you see all his faults and the rest of your life you spend in discovering his virtues. *Lady Constance Lytton*

The proper time to influence the character of a child is about 100 years before he is born. *Dean William R. Inge*

There is a secret person undamaged in every individual. *Paul Shepard*

They are proud in humility; proud that they are not proud. *Robert Burton*

We only become what we are by the radical and deep-seeded refusal of that which others have made of us. *Jean-Paul Sartre*

When they came to shoe the horses, the beetle stretched out his leg. *English proverb*

It is native personality, and that alone, that endows a man to stand before presidents or generals, or in any distinguished collection, with aplomb—and not culture, or any intellect whatever. *Walt Whitman*

Talents are best nurtured in solitude: character is best formed in the stormy billows of the world. *Goethe*

Style, personality—deliberately adopted and therefore a mask—is the only escape from the hot-faced bargainers and money-changers. *William Butler Yeats*

Show me a good and gracious loser, and I'll show you a failure. *Knute Rockne*

Everyone is a moon and has a dark side which he never shows to anybody. *Mark Twain*

I'd rather be strongly wrong than weakly right. *Tallulah Bankhead*

Altruism declares that any action taken for the benefit of others is good, and any action taken for one's own benefit is evil. Thus the beneficiary of an action is the only criterion of moral value—and so long as that beneficiary is anybody other than oneself, anything goes.   *Ayn Rand*

To enjoy the things we ought, and to hate the things we ought, has the greatest bearing on excellence of character.   *Aristotle*

Character building begins in our infancy, and continues until death.
Eleanor Roosevelt

Character is perfectly educated will.   *Novalis*

Character is long-standing habit.   *Plutarch*

I was born modest; not all over, but in spots.   *Mark Twain*

Moderation is an ostentatious proof of our strength of character.   *La Rochefoucauld*

If you think about what you ought to do for other people, your character will take care of itself.   *Woodrow Wilson*

You cannot dream yourself into a character; you must hammer and forge yourself one.
James A. Froude

A modest man is usually admired—if people ever hear of him. *Edgar Watson Howe*

The clock struck eleven with the respectful unobtrusiveness of one whose mission in life is to be ignored.   *Saki*

Some people approach every problem with an open mouth.   *Adlai Stevenson*

My specialty is detached malevolence.   *Alice Roosevelt Longworth*

Every one is as God made him and oftentimes a good deal worse.   *Cervantes*

Character is that which can do without success.   *Ralph Waldo Emerson*

Character is what God and the angels know of us; reputation is what men and women think of us.   *Horace Mann*

One can acquire everything in solitude except character.   *Stendhal*

Every man has three characters—that which he exhibits, that which he has, and that which he thinks he has.   *Alphonse Karr*

If I take care of my character, my reputation will take care of itself.   *D. L. Moody*

A wise and an understanding heart.   *1 Kings 3:12*

Everyone ought to bear patiently the results of his own conduct.   *Phaedrus*

Every man has his follies—and often they are the most interesting things he has got.
Josh Billings

Indecision is like a stepchild: if he doesn't wash his hands, he is called dirty; if he does, he is wasting the water.   *African proverb*

'Tis e'er the wont of simple folk to prize the deed and overlook the motive, and of learned folk to discount the deed and lay open the soul of the doer.   *John Barth*

Learn to say 'No'; it will be of more use to you than to be able to read Latin.
Charles Haddon Spurgeon

To dream of the person you would like to be is to waste the person you are.   *Anon.*

Character is like a tree, and reputation like its shadow. The shadow is what we think of it; the tree is the real thing.   *Anon.*

Every man in the world is better than some one else. And not as good as some one else.   *William Saroyan*

In Victorian times the purpose of life was to develop a personality once and for all and then stand on it.   *Ashley Montagu*

Charm is a way of getting the answer yes without having asked any clear question.
Albert Camus

Children and Childhood

An adolescent is both an impulsive child and a self-starting adult.   *Mason Cooley*

Beat your child once a day. If you don't know why, he does.   *Chinese proverb*

Children have no use for psychology. They detest sociology. They still believe in God, the family, angels, devils, witches, goblins, logic, clarity, punctuation, and other such obsolete stuff. When a book is boring, they yawn openly. They don't expect their writer to redeem humanity, but leave to adults such childish allusions.
Isaac Bashevis Singer

Juvenile appraisals of other juveniles make up in clarity what they lack in charity.
Edgar Z. Friedenberg

Of all animals, the boy is the most unmanageable.   *Plato*

For the spreading of rumours boys easily lead the world in a field which is full of competition.   *J.R. Darling, headmaster*

Childhood—a period of waiting for the moment when I could send everyone and everything connected with it to hell.   *Igor Stravinsky*

Childhood was a totalitarian regime from which I was very glad to escape.
Phillip Adams

The great cathedral space which was childhood. *Virginia Woolf*

A child thinks twenty shillings and twenty years can scarce ever be spent.
Benjamin Franklin

If children grew up according to early indications, we should have nothing but geniuses.
Goethe

What children expect from grownups is not to be 'understood', but only to be loved, even though this love may be expressed clumsily or in sternness. Intimacy does not exist between generations—only trust. *Carl Zucker*

Healthy children will not fear life if their elders have integrity enough not to fear death. *Erik Erikson*

William Blake really is important, my cornerstone. Nobody ever told me before he did that childhood was such a damned serious business. *Maurice Sendak*

Out of the mouths of babes and sucklings hast thou ordained strength. *Psalms 8:2*

When I was a child, I spake as a child, I understood as a child, I thought as a child; but when I became a man I put away childish things. *1 Corinthians 13:11*

Children have more need of models than of critics. *Joseph Joubert*

Children are remarkable for their intelligence and ardour, for their curiosity, their intolerance of shams, the clarity and ruthlessness of their vision. *Aldous Huxley*

The events of childhood do not pass but repeat themselves like seasons of the year.
Eleanor Farjeon

Children have never been very good at listening to their elders, but they have never failed to imitate them. *James Baldwin*

Ask your child what he wants for dinner only if he is buying. *Fran Lebowitz*

All children wear the sign: 'I want to be important NOW.' Many of our juvenile delinquency problems arise because nobody reads the sign. *Dan Pursuit*

If a child lives with approval, he learns to live with himself. *Dorothy Law Nolte*

What's done to children, they will do to society. *Karl Menninger*

The hardest job kids face today is learning good manners without seeing any.
Fred Astaire

Unlike grownups, children have little need to deceive themselves. *Goethe*

We've had bad luck with our kids—they've all grown up.   *Christopher Morley*

There are only two lasting bequests we can hope to give our children. One of these is roots, the other, wings.   *Hodding Carter*

Give me the children until they are seven and anyone may have them afterwards.
St. Francis Xavier

There are only two things a child will share willingly—communicable diseases and his mother's age.   *Benjamin Spock*

Do not mistake a child for his symptom.   *Erik Erikson*

Babies are such a nice way to start people.   *Don Herold*

Children need love, especially when they do not deserve it.   *Harold S. Hulbert*

If a child is to keep alive his inborn sense of wonder without any such gift from the fairies, he needs the companionship of at least one adult who can share it, rediscovering with him the joy, excitement and mystery of the world we live in.   *Rachel Carson*

Nothing has a stronger influence psychologically on their environment, and especially on their children, than the unlived lives of the parents.   *Carl Jung*

Christians and Christianity

Christianity, if false, is not important. If Christianity is true, however, it is of infinite importance. What it cannot be is moderately important.   *C. S. Lewis*

Organized religion is making Christianity political rather than making politics Christian.
Laurens Van der Post

The idea of Christ is much older than Christianity.   *George Santayana*

Unlike Christianity, which preached a peace that it never achieved, Islam unashamedly came with a sword.   *Stephen Runciman*

Why do born-again people so often make you wish they'd never been born the first time?   *Katherine Whitehorn*

I am one of those who would join a church if they could only find a Christian church to join.   *Walter Murdoch*

Christians have burned each other, quite persuaded
That all the apostles would have done as they did.   *Lord Byron*

Christian: one who believes that the New Testament is a divinely inspired book admirably suited to the spiritual needs of his neighbour.   *Ambrose Bierce*

Most people believe that the Christian commandments are intentionally a little too severe—like setting a clock half an hour ahead to make sure of not being late in the morning.
Søren Kierkegaard

I believe in Christianity as I believe that the sun has risen. Not only because I see it, but because I see everything by it.
C. S. Lewis

A Christian is a man who feels
Repentance on a Sunday
For what he did on Saturday
And is going to do on Monday.
Thomas R. Ybarra

Hatred of Judaism is at bottom hatred of Christianity.
Sigmund Freud

It is not by driving away our brother that we can be alone with God.
George Macdonald

God will forgive me. That's his business.
Heinrich Heine

People in general are equally horrified at hearing the Christian religion doubted, and at seeing it practised.
Samuel Butler

Christian life consists of faith and charity.
Martin Luther

Many a sober Christian would rather admit that a wafer is God than that God is a cruel and capricious tyrant.
Edward Gibbon

If you go to church, and like the singing better than the preaching, that's not orthodox.
Edgar Watson Howe

No clergyman can nowadays attain high office who has not first given solid and continuous proof that he is ga-ga.
Clive James

The City and the Country

A great city is not to be confounded with a populous one.
Aristotle

A hick town is one in which there is no place to go where you shouldn't be.
Alexander Woollcott

City life—millions of people being lonesome together.
Henry David Thoreau

The government of cities is as complicated and as conflict-ridden as the government of whole societies.
Hugh Stretton

The country has charms only for those not obliged to stay there.
Edouard Manet

Only in cities can one live in the daily expectation of the unprecedented.
Charmian Clift

A great city, a great solitude.   *Old proverb*

A great city is the place to escape the true drama of provincial life, and find solace
in fantasy.   *G. K. Chesterton*

In small settlements everyone knows your affairs. In the big city, everyone does
not—only those you choose to tell will know about you. This is one of the attributes
of cities that is precious to most city people.   *Jane Jacobs*

If you would be known, and not know, vegetate in a village; if you would know and
not be known, live in a city.   *Charles Caleb Colton*

Farmers worry only during the growing season, but town people worry all the time.
                                                                               Edgar Watson Howe

What is the city but the people?   *Shakespeare, 'Coriolanus'*

As a remedy to life in society, I would suggest the big city. Nowadays it is the only
desert within our reach.   *Albert Camus*

All cities are mad: but the madness is gallant. All cities are beautiful: but the beauty
is grim.   *Christopher Morley*

Cities are good for bushies to enjoy themselves in once in a while, but no good for
living in.   *Xavier Herbert*

Cities force growth and make men talkative and entertaining, but they make them
artificial.   *Ralph Waldo Emerson*

The city is a cultural invention enforcing on the citizen knowledge of his own nature.
And this we do not like. That we are aggressive beings, easily given to violence; that
we get along together because we must more than because we want to, and that the
brotherhood of man is about as far from reality today as it was two thousand years
ago; that reason's realm is small; that we never have been and never shall be created
equal; that if the human being is perfectible, he has so far exhibited few symptoms—all
are considerations of man from which space tends to protect us.   *Robert Ardrey*

There is nothing good to be had in the country, or, if there be, they will not let you
have it.   *William Hazlitt*

Anybody can be good in the country. There are no temptations there.   *Oscar Wilde*

The axis of the earth sticks out visibly through the centre of each and every town or
city.   *Oliver Wendell Holmes*

To say the least, a town life makes one more tolerant and liberal in one's judgement
of others.   *Henry Wadsworth Longfellow*

Commuters give the city its tidal restlessness, natives give it solidity and continuity,
but the settlers give it passion.   *E. B. White*

There is no solitude in the world like that of the big city.   *Kathleen Norris*

Civilization

Civilization is nothing more than the effort to reduce the use of force to the last resort.
José Ortega y Gasset

Each new generation is a fresh invasion of savages.   *Harvey Allen*

Respectability is the dickey on the bosom of civilization.   *Elbert Hubbard*

The human race has improved everything except the human race.   *Adlai Stevenson*

A civilized society is one that exhibits the five qualities of truth, beauty, adventure,
art and peace.   *Alfred North Whitehead*

There is such a thing as too much couth.   *S. J. Perelman*

We are in the first age since the dawn of civilization in which people have dared to
think it practicable to make the benefits of civilization available to the whole human
race.   *Arnold Toynbee*

Civilisation isn't natural. It's an art and a science.
M. Barnard Eldershaw, 'Tomorrow and Tomorrow and Tomorrow'

Any sufficiently advanced technology is indistinguishable from magic.
Arthur C. Clarke

Our lifetime may be the last that will be lived out in a technological society.
Isaac Asimov

To be able to fill leisure intelligently is the last product of civilization.
Arnold Toynbee

So I should say that civilizations begin with religion and stoicism: they end with
scepticism and unbelief, and the undisciplined pursuit of individual pleasure. A
civilization is born stoic and dies epicurean.   *Will Durant*

We are all afraid—for our confidence, for the future, for the world. That is the nature
of the human imagination. Yet every man, every civilization, has gone forward because
of its engagement with what it has set itself to do. The personal commitment and the
emotional commitment working together as one, has made the Ascent of Man.
Jacob Bronowski

Civilization is just a slow process of learning to be kind.   *Charles L. Lucas*

Civilization is a movement—not a condition; a voyage—not a harbour.
Arnold Toynbee

Civilisation is not synonymous with felicity.   *A. G. Stephens*

The aim of civilisation, as I see it, is not to prepare for a better world *beyond* this earth, but to prepare a better world *on* this earth.   *Griffith Taylor*

We sit by and watch the barbarian. We tolerate him in the long stretches of peace, we are not afraid. We are tickled by his irreverence; his comic inversion of our old certitudes and our fixed creed refreshes us; we laugh. But as we laugh we are watched by large and awful faces from beyond, and on these faces there are no smiles.
Hilaire Belloc

A race preserves its vigour so long as it harbours a real contrast between what has been and what may be, and so long as it is nerved by the vigour to adventure beyond the safeties of the past. Without adventure, civilization is in full decay.
Alfred North Whitehead

Civilizations die from philosophical calm, irony, and the sense of fair play quite as surely as they die of debauchery.   *Joseph Wood Krutch*

The three great elements of modern civilization, Gunpowder, Printing, and the Protestant Religion.   *Thomas Carlyle*

The three never-failing accompaniments of advancing civilisation are a racecourse, a public house and a goal.   *John Dunmore Lang*

This is the way the world ends
Not with a bang but a whimper.   *T. S. Eliot*

A tablecloth restaurant is still one of the great rewards of civilization.
Harry Golden

The end of the human race will be that it will eventually die of civilization.
Ralph Waldo Emerson

If you would civilize a man, begin with his grandmother.   *Victor Hugo*

To be a man is to feel that one's own stone contributes to building the edifice of the world.   *Antoine de Saint-Exupéry*

Committees, Clubs and Institutions

The ideal committee is one with me as chairman, and two other members in bed with flu.   *Lord Milverton*

If Moses had been a committee, the Israelites would still be in Egypt.   *J. B. Hughes*

A committee of one gets things done.   *Joe Ryan*

A camel is a horse designed by a committee.   *Anon.*

If Columbus had had an advisory committee he would probably still be at the dock.
Justice Arthur Goldberg

An institution is the lengthening shadow of one man. *Ralph Waldo Emerson*

I do not care to belong to a club that accepts people like me as members.

Groucho Marx

Those mausoleums of inactive masculinity are places for men who prefer armchairs to women. *V. S. Pritchett*

What is a committee? A group of the unwilling, picked from the unfit, to do the unnecessary. *Richard Harkness*

No grand idea was ever born in a conference, but a lot of foolish ideas have died there. *F. Scott Fitzgerald*

Conscience

Conscience is a mother-in-law whose visit never ends. *H. L. Mencken*

Conscience is a cur that will let you get past it but that you cannot keep from barking.

Anon.

Conscience is but a word that cowards use,
Devised at first to keep the strong in awe. *Shakespeare, 'Richard III'*

Conscience reigns but it does not govern. *Paul Valéry*

A man's vanity tells him what is honour; a man's conscience what is justice.

Walter Savage Landor

Conscience does make cowards of us all. *Shakespeare, 'Hamlet'*

Conscience is thoroughly well-bred, and soon leaves off talking to those who do not wish to hear it. *Samuel Butler*

Conscience is a coward, and those faults it has not strength enough to prevent, it seldom has justice enough to accuse. *Oliver Goldsmith*

I feel bad that I don't feel worse. *Michael Frayn*

Shame arises from the fear of man; conscience from the fear of God.

Samuel Johnson

Consistency

Inconsistency is the only thing in which men are consistent. *Horace Smith*

Nothing that is not a real crime makes a man appear so contemptible and little in the eyes of the world as inconsistency. *Joseph Addison*

Like all weak men he laid an exaggerated stress on not changing one's mind.

W. Somerset Maugham

A foolish consistency is the hobgoblin of little minds, adored by little statesmen and philosophers and divines. With consistency a great soul has simply nothing to do. He may as well concern himself with his shadow on the wall. Speak what you think now in hard words and tomorrow speak what tomorrow thinks in hard words again, though it contradict everything you said today.   *Ralph Waldo Emerson*

Consistency requires you to be as ignorant today as you were a year ago.

Bernard Berenson

Consistency is the last refuge of the unimaginative.   *Oscar Wilde*

Conservatism is the maintenance of conventions already in force.   *Thorstein Veblen*

There are those who would misteach us that to stick in a rut is consistency—and a virtue, and that to climb out of the rut is inconsistency—and a vice.   *Mark Twain*

People who honestly mean to be true, really contradict themselves much more rarely than those who try to be 'consistent'.   *Oliver Wendell Holmes*

How difficult it is to find consistency! And the worse thing about consistency is that when you do find it, it is extremely dull.   *John Shaw Neilson*

Conversation

Conversation is the fine art of mutual consideration and communication about matters of common interest that basically have some human importance.   *Ordway Tead*

Great talkers are trying to fill the gap between themselves and others, but only widen it.   *Mason Cooley*

Half the world is composed of people who have something to say and can't and the other half who have nothing to say and keep on saying it.   *Robert Frost*

Conversation is the fire of social life.   *Christina Stead, 'Seven Poor Men of Sydney'*

Speech is civilization itself.   *Thomas Mann*

The habit of common and continuous speech is a symptom of mental deficiency. It proceeds from not knowing what is going on in other people's minds.

Walter Bagehot

The time to stop talking is when the other person nods his head affirmatively but says nothing.   *Henry S. Haskins*

There is no such thing as conversation. It is an illusion. There are intersecting monologues. That is all.   *Rebecca West*

He was one of those men whose constitutional inability to make small talk forfeits all one's sympathy, and makes one think that social grace is sometimes a moral duty.

James Morris

He (Macaulay) has occasional flashes of silence that make his conversation perfectly delightful.

Sydney Smith

As I got warmed up, and felt perfectly at home in talk, I heard myself boasting, lying, exaggerating. Oh, not deliberately, far from it. It would be unconvivial and dull to stop and arrest the flow of talk, and speak only after carefully considering whether I was telling the truth.

Bernard Berenson

Men always talk about the most important things to perfect strangers.

G. K. Chesterton

Not a sentence or a word is independent of the circumstances under which it is uttered.

Alfred North Whitehead

Communication is and should be hell fire and sparks as well as sweetness and light.

Aman Vivian Rakoff

The really important things are said over cocktails and are never done.

Peter F. Drucker

You never say a word of yourself, dear Lady Grey. You have that dreadful sin of anti-egotism.

Sydney Smith

The real art of conversation is not only to say the right thing in the right place but to leave unsaid the wrong thing at the tempting moment.

Dorothy Nevill

Listen or thy tongue will keep thee deaf.

American Indian proverb

People love to talk but hate to listen. Listening is not merely not talking, though even that is beyond most of our powers; it means taking a vigorous, human interest in what is being told us. You can listen like a blank wall or like a splendid auditorium where every sound comes back fuller and richer.

Alice Duer Miller

A man who listens because he has nothing to say can hardly be a source of inspiration. The only listening that counts is that of the talker who alternately absorbs and expresses ideas.

Agnes Repplier

When I think over what I have said, I envy dumb people.

Seneca

That is the happiest conversation where there is no competition, no vanity, but a calm quiet interchange of sentiments.

Samuel Johnson

John Wesley's conversation is good, but he is never at leisure. He is always obliged to go at a certain hour. This is very disagreeable to a man who loves to fold his legs and have his talk out as I do.

Samuel Johnson

She had lost the art of conversation, but not, unfortunately, the power of speech.
George Bernard Shaw

Too much agreement kills a chat.   *Eldridge Cleaver*

You can never hope to become a skilled conversationalist until you learn how to put your foot tactfully through the television set.   *M. Dale Baughman*

Some persons talk simply because they think sound is more manageable than silence.
Margaret Halsey

While the right to talk may be the beginning of freedom, the necessity of listening is what makes the right important.   *Walter Lippmann*

Listening is a magnetic and strange thing, a creative force. The friends who listen to us are the ones we move toward, and we want to sit in their radius. When we are listened to, it creates us, makes us unfold and expand.   *Karl Menninger*

A ceremony of self-wastage—good talkers are miserable, they know that they have betrayed themselves, that they have taken material which should have a life of its own, to disperse it in noises upon the air.   *Cyril Connolly*

Wit is the salt of conversation, not the food.   *William Hazlitt*

Conviction and Belief

A conservative believes nothing should be done for the first time.
Lynwood L. Giacomini

Now faith is the substance of things hoped for, the evidence of things not seen.
Hebrews 11:1

Genuine blasphemy, genuine in spirit and not purely verbal, is the product of partial belief, and is as impossible to the complete atheist as to the perfect Christian.
T. S. Eliot

I believe in the gods. Or rather, I believe that I believe in the gods. But I don't believe that they are great brooding presences watching over us; I believe they are completely absent-minded.   *Jean Giraudoux*

I believe and have always believed that life is totally meaningless and that we have no destiny, no purpose, no author.   *Phillip Adams*

I think that a society cannot live without a certain number of irrational beliefs. They are protected from criticism and analysis because they are irrational.
Claude Levi-Strauss

It is a perplexing and unpleasant truth that when men already have 'something worth fighting for', they do not feel like fighting.   *Eric Hoffer*

Martyrdom has always been a proof of the intensity, never of the correctness of a belief.   *Arthur Schnitzler*

Belief is better than anything else, and it is best when rapt—above paying its respects to anybody's doubt whatsoever.   *Robert Frost*

The peak of tolerance is most readily achieved by those who are not burdened with convictions.   *Alexander Chase*

A belief is not merely an idea the mind possesses; it is an idea that possesses the mind.   *Robert Bolton*

Every man who attacks my belief diminishes in some degree my confidence in it, and therefore makes me uneasy, and I am angry with him who makes me uneasy.
Samuel Johnson

Penetrating so many secrets, we cease to believe in the unknowable. But there it sits nevertheless, calmly licking its chops.   *H. L. Mencken*

Believe not your own brother—believe, instead, your own blind eye.
Russian proverb

Whether you are really right or not doesn't matter; it's the belief that counts.
Robertson Davies

I love an opposition that has convictions.   *Frederick the Great*

Every man, wherever he goes, is encompassed by a cloud of comforting convictions, which move with him like flies on a summer day.   *Bertrand Russell*

Convictions are the mainsprings of action, the driving powers of life. What a man lives are his convictions.   *Bishop Francis Kelly*

The best lack all conviction, while the worst
Are full of passionate intensity.   *William Butler Yeats*

(Conviction) is possible only in a world more primitive than ours can be perceived to be. A man can achieve a simply gnomic conviction only by ignoring the radical describers of his environment, or by hating them, as convinced men have hated, say, Darwin and Freud, as agents of some devil.   *John Ciardi*

Those who serve a cause are not those who love that cause. They are those who love the life which has to be led in order to serve it—except in the case of the very purest, and they are rare.   *Simone Weil*

The great thing in this world is not so much where we stand, as in what direction we are moving.   *Oliver Wendell Holmes*

Orthodoxy is my doxy—heterodoxy is another man's doxy.   *William Warburton*

Every dogma has its day.   *Abraham Rotstein*

A man can believe in a considerable deal of rubbish, and yet go about his daily work in a rational and cheerful manner. *Norman Douglas*

Every life is a possession of faith, and exercises an inevitable and silent propaganda. *Henri Frédéric Amiel*

Soon after a hard decision something inevitably occurs to cast doubt. Holding steady against that doubt usually proves the decision. *R. I. Fitzhenry*

I may have faults but being wrong ain't one of them. *Jimmy Hoffa*

Courage and Bravery

In Chinese, the word for crisis is *wei ji*, composed of the character *wei*, which means danger, and *ji*, which means opportunity. *Jan Wong*

My advice to you, if you should ever be in a hold up, is to line up with the cowards and save your bravery for an occasion when it may be of some benefit to you. *O. Henry*

It is easy enough to praise men for the courage of their convictions. I wish I could teach the sad young of this mealy generation the courage of their confusions. *John Ciardi*

Were all men with true courage fired,
Mere warriors would be less admired. *Charles Harpur*

Growth demands a temporary surrender of security. *Gail Sheehy*

Life shrinks or expands in proportion to one's courage. *Anaïs Nin*

No one provokes me with impunity. (*Nemo me impune lacessit.*) *Motto of Scotland*

Neither have they hearts to stay,
Nor wit enough to run away. *Samuel Butler*

Until the day of his death, no man can be sure of his courage. *Jean Anouilh*

There is no such thing as bravery; only degrees of fear. *John Wainwright*

'Why not' is a slogan for an interesting life. *Mason Cooley*

You don't learn to hold your own in the world by standing on guard, but by attacking, and getting well hammered yourself. *George Bernard Shaw*

Here I stand. I can do no other. God help me. Amen. *Martin Luther*

Many become brave when brought to bay. *Norwegian proverb*

O God, give us serenity to accept what cannot be changed; courage to change what should be changed; and wisdom to distinguish the one from the other.

Reinhold Niebuhr

The first virtue in a soldier is endurance of fatigue; courage is only the second virtue.

Napoleon Bonaparte

Courage is fear holding on a minute longer.

George S. Patton

We could be cowards, if we had courage enough.

Thomas Fuller

Cowardice, as distinguished from panic, is almost always simply a lack of ability to suspend the functioning of the imagination.

Ernest Hemingway

Showing up is eighty percent of life.

Woody Allen

A high station in life is earned by the gallantry with which appalling experiences are survived with grace.

Tennessee Williams

A decline in courage may be the most striking feature which an outside observer notices in the West in our days. The Western world has lost its civic courage, both as a whole and separately, in each country, in each government, in each political party, and, of course, in the United Nations. Such a decline in courage is particularly noticeable among the ruling groups and the intellectual elite, causing an impression that the loss of courage extends to the entire society.

Aleksandr Solzhenitsyn

Courage is doing what you're afraid to do. There can be no courage unless you're scared.

Eddie Rickenbacker

One man with courage makes a majority.

Andrew Jackson

If one is forever cautious, can one remain a human being?

Aleksandr Solzhenitsyn

Never let your head hang down. Never give up and sit down and grieve. Find another way. And don't pray when it rains if you don't pray when the sun shines.

Satchel Paige

The Ancient Mariner said to Neptune during a great storm, 'O God, you will save me if you wish, but I am going to go on holding my tiller straight.'

Montaigne

Fight on, my merry men all,
I'm a little wounded, but I am not slain;
I will lay me down for to bleed a while,
Then I'll rise and fight with you again.

John Dryden

The paradox of courage is that a man must be a little careless of his life even in order to keep it.

G. K. Chesterton

The last thing a woman will consent to discover in a man whom she loves, or on whom she simply depends, is want of courage.

Joseph Conrad

Please understand there is no depression in this house and we are not interested in the possibilities of defeat. They do not exist.   *Victoria, Queen of England*

Now the trumpet summons us again—not as a call to bear arms, though arms we need; not as a call to battle, though embattled we are; but a call to bear the burden of a long twilight struggle, year in and year out, 'rejoicing in hope, patient in tribulation', a struggle against the common enemies of man: tyranny, poverty, disease and war itself.   *John F. Kennedy*

To be brave one short instant is no easy matter; it is easier to die for a cause than to live for it.   *Comtesse Diane (Marie de Beausacq)*

The courage we desire and prize is not the courage to die decently, but to live manfully.
                    Thomas Carlyle

Have the courage to act instead of react.   *Earlene Larson Jenks*

Courage! I have shown it for years; think you I shall lose it at the moment when my sufferings are to end?   *Marie Antoinette on the way to the guillotine*

Necessity does the work of courage.   *George Eliot*

Courage is a quality so necessary for maintaining virtue that it is always respected, even when it is associated with vice.   *Samuel Johnson*

The courage of life is often a less dramatic spectacle than the courage of a final moment; but it is no less a magnificent mixture of triumph and tragedy. A man does what he must—in spite of personal consequences, in spite of obstacles and dangers and pressures—and that is the basis of all morality.   *John F. Kennedy*

He was a bold man that first ate an oyster.   *Jonathan Swift*

Unless one says goodbye to what one loves, and unless one travels to completely new territories, one can expect merely a long wearing away of oneself.   *Jean Dubuffet*

A decent boldness ever meets with friends.   *Homer*

Courage is resistance to fear, mastery of fear, not absence of fear.   *Mark Twain*

One doesn't discover new lands without consenting to lose sight of the shore for a very long time.   *André Gide*

The fly ought to be used as the symbol of impertinence and audacity; for whilst all other animals shun man more than anything else, and run away even before he comes near them, the fly lights upon his very nose.   *Arthur Schopenhauer*

Valour lies just halfway between rashness and cowardice.   *Cervantes*

Never undertake anything for which you wouldn't have the courage to ask the blessings of heaven.   *G. C. Lichtenberg*

As to moral courage, I have very rarely met with the two o'clock in the morning kind. I mean unprepared courage, that which is necessary on an unexpected occasion, and which, in spite of the most unforeseen events, leaves full freedom of judgement and decision.
Napoleon Bonaparte

The guts carry the feet, not the feet the guts.
Cervantes

Clothes and courage have much to do with each other.
Sara Jeannette Duncan

A great part of courage is the courage of having done the thing before.
Ralph Waldo Emerson

Courage—fear that has said its prayers.
Dorothy Bernard

Courage is rightly esteemed the first of human qualities because it is the quality which guarantees all others.
Winston Churchill

Constant exposure to dangers will breed contempt for them.
Seneca

(Courage) a perfect sensibility of the measure of danger, and a mental willingness to endure it.
William T. Sherman

Not simply one of the virtues but the form of every virtue at the testing point, which means at the point of highest reality.
C. S. Lewis

At the bottom of a good deal of the bravery that appears in the world there lurks a miserable cowardice. Men will face powder and steel because they cannot face public opinion.
E. H. Chapin

Whether it be to failure or success, the first need of being is endurance—to endure with gladness if we can, with fortitude in any event.
Bliss Carman

Creation and Creativity

Whenever man comes up with a better mousetrap, nature immediately comes up with a better mouse.
James Carswell

Musical comedies aren't written, they are re-written.
Stephen Sondheim

I see the playwright as a lay preacher peddling the ideas of his time in popular form.
August Strindberg

The art of creation is older than the art of killing.
Andrei Voznesensky

Human Salvation lies in the hands of the creatively maladjusted.
Martin Luther King, Jr.

In the creative state a man is taken out of himself. He lets down as it were a bucket into his subconscious, and draws up something which is normally beyond his reach. He mixes this thing with his normal experiences and out of the mixture he makes a work of art.   *E. M. Forster*

I do not seek. I find.   *Pablo Picasso*

The creation of a thousand forests is in one acorn.   *Ralph Waldo Emerson*

The life of the creative man is led, directed and controlled by boredom. Avoiding boredom is one of our most important purposes.   *Saul Steinberg*

An artist is a creature driven by demons. He doesn't know why they choose him and he's usually too busy to wonder why.   *William Faulkner*

No artist is ahead of his time. He is his time. It is just that others are behind the time.
                                                                                                                                                     Martha Graham

Doodling is the brooding of the hand.   *Saul Steinberg*

I am a choreographer. A choreographer is a poet. I do not create. God creates. I assemble, and I will steal from everywhere to do it.   *George Balanchine*

Creators are the sacrificial objects of a bored society.
                                                                                David Williamson, 'A Handful of Friends'

You lose it if you talk about it.   *Ernest Hemingway*

In creating, the only hard thing's to begin;
A grass-blade's no easier to make than an oak.   *James Russell Lowell*

I can always be distracted by love, but eventually I get horny for my creativity.
                                                                                                                                                       Gilda Radner

The End of every maker is himself.   *St. Thomas Aquinas*

Now I really make the little idea from clay, and I hold it in my hand. I can turn it, look at it from underneath, see it from one view, hold it against the sky, imagine it any size I like, and really be in control, almost like God creating something.
                                                                                                                                                       Henry Moore

No matter how old you get, if you can keep the desire to be creative, you're keeping the man-child alive.   *John Cassavetes*

What is originality? Undetected plagiarism.   *Dean William R. Inge*

Originality is nothing but judicious imitation.   *Voltaire*

A hunch is creativity trying to tell you something.   *Frank Capra*

Style is a simple way of saying complicated things.   *Jean Cocteau*

What another would have done as well as you, do not do it. What another would have said as well as you, do not say it. What another would have written as well, do not write it. Be faithful to that which exists nowhere but in yourself—and thus make yourself indispensable.   *André Gide*

It seems that the creative faculty and the critical faculty cannot exist together in their highest perfection.   *Thomas Babington Macaulay*

I must create a system or be enslaved by another man's.
I will not reason and compare;
My business is to create.   *William Blake*

Crime and Punishment

A small demerit extinguishes a long service.   *Thomas Fuller*

To call (war) a crime against mankind is to miss at least half its significance; it is also the punishment of a crime.   *Frederic Manning*

Jupiter is slow looking into his notebook, but he always looks.   *Zenobius*

The number of malefactors authorizes not the crime.   *Thomas Fuller*

No one is entirely useless. Even the worst of us can serve as horrible examples.
                                                            Anonymous prisoner (State Prison, Salt Lake City)

The faults of the burglar are the qualities of the financier.   *George Bernard Shaw*

He who excuses himself accuses himself. (*Qui s'excuse, s'accuse.*)   *Anon.*

The study of crime begins with the knowledge of oneself.   *Henry Miller*

Fear succeeds crime—it is its punishment.   *Voltaire*

All punishment is mischief. All punishment in itself is evil.   *Jeremy Bentham*

Speaking generally, punishment hardens and numbs, it produces concentration, it sharpens the consciousness of alienation, it strengthens the power of resistance.
                                                                                                             Friedrich Nietzsche

He only may chastise who loves.   *Rabindranath Tagore*

If England treats her criminals the way she has treated me, she doesn't deserve to have any.   *Oscar Wilde*

It is fairly obvious that those who are in favour of the death penalty have more affinity with assassins than those who are not.   *Remy de Gourmont*

Prisons don't rehabilitate, they don't punish, they don't protect, so what the hell do they do?   *Jerry Brown*

Capital punishment is as fundamentally wrong as a cure for crime as charity is wrong as a cure for poverty.   *Henry Ford*

The reformative effect of punishment is a belief that dies hard, chiefly, I think, because it is so satisfying to our sadistic impulses.   *Bertrand Russell*

Much as he is opposed to lawbreaking, he is not bigoted about it.   *Damon Runyon*

Crime, like virtue, has its degrees.   *Racine*

Critics and Criticism

A guest sees more in an hour than the host in a year.   *Polish proverb*

Asking a working writer what he thinks about critics is like asking a lamp-post how it feels about dogs.   *Christopher Hampton*

Book reviewers are little old ladies of both sexes.   *John O'Hara*

Constant, indiscriminate approval devalues because it is so predictable.   *Kit Reed*

Critics are biased, and so are readers. (Indeed, a critic is a bundle of biases held loosely together by a sense of taste.) But intelligent readers soon discover how to allow for the windage of their own and a critic's prejudices.   *Whitney Balliett*

Don't judge any man until you have walked two moons in his moccasins.
American Indian saying

All criticism is self-criticism.   *Harry Hooton*

Self-criticism is a luxury all politicians should indulge in, but it is best done in private.
Malcolm Fraser

It is easy—terribly easy—to shake a man's faith in himself. To take advantage of that, to break a man's spirit is devil's work.   *George Bernard Shaw*

The critic is an overgoer with pen-envy.   *Geoffrey Hartman*

Two and two continue to make four, in spite of the whine of the amateur for three, or the cry of the critic for five.   *James McNeill Whistler*

He has a right to criticize, who has a heart to help.   *Abraham Lincoln*

More and more people think of the critic as an indispensable middle man between writer and reader, and would no more read a book alone, if they could help it, than have a baby alone.   *Randall Jarrell*

It is not expected of critics that they should help us to make sense of our lives; they are bound only to attempt the lesser feat of making sense of the ways we try to make sense of our lives.   *Frank Kermode*

Analysis kills spontaneity. The grain once ground into flour springs and germinates no more.   *Henri Frédéric Amiel*

His words leap across rivers and mountains, but his thoughts are still only six inches long.   *E. B. White*

When critics disagree, the artist is in accord with himself.   *Oscar Wilde*

My aim was to destroy; my argument, the real painters will always survive, the others should think twice before submitting their work to critical appraisal.
                                                    Paul Haefliger, art critic

To many people dramatic criticism must seem like an attempt to tattoo soap bubbles.
                                                    John Mason Brown

The test of a good critic is whether he knows when and how to believe on insufficient evidence.   *Samuel Butler*

Reprove not a scorner, lest he hate thee; rebuke a wise man and he will love thee.
                                                    Proverbs 9:8

In judging others, folks will work overtime for no pay.   *Charles Edwin Carruthers*

A critic is a man who knows the way but can't drive the car.   *Kenneth Tynan*

If you are willing to take the punishment, you're halfway through the battle. That the issues may be trivial, the battle ugly, is another point.   *Lillian Hellman*

A critic is a legless man who teaches running.   *Channing Pollock*

Vilify! Vilify! Some of it will always stick.   *Beaumarchais*

Always bring money along with your complaints.   *Plautus*

Nature fits all her children with something to do
He who would write and can't write, can surely review.   *James Russell Lowell*

Nature, when she invented, manufactured and patented her authors, contrived to make critics out of the chips that were left.   *Oliver Wendell Holmes*

To escape criticism—do nothing, say nothing, be nothing.   *Elbert Hubbard*

Any fool can criticize, and many of them do.   *Archbishop C. Garbett*

Critics are like eunuchs in a harem: they know how it's done, they've seen it done every day, but they're unable to do it themselves.   *Brendan Behan*

I am sitting in the smallest room in my house. I have your review in front of me. Soon it will be behind me.   *Max Reger*

The good critic is he who narrates the adventures of his soul among masterpieces. *Anatole France*

Of all the cants which are canted in this canting world, tho' the cant of hypocrites may be the worst, the cant of criticism is the most tormenting.   *Laurence Sterne*

The critic is the duenna in the passionate affair between playwrights, actors and audiences—a figure dreaded, and occasionally comic, but never welcome, never loved. *Robertson Davies*

A critic at best is a waiter at the great table of literature.   *Louis Dudek*

Crowds and the Masses

In Heaven an angel is nobody in particular.   *George Bernard Shaw*

The mob has many heads but no brains.   *Thomas Fuller*

Talk-back radio is a device by which the stupid are allowed to reinforce the stupid in their stupidity. It is a device for arrogant, bigoted, limited, self-centred people to proselytise their cause and to create a vast social force of like-minded bird-brains. *Max Harris*

Insanity in individuals is rare—but in groups, parties, nations, and epochs, it is the rule.   *Friedrich Nietzsche*

Every crowd has a silver lining.   *P. T. Barnum*

When a hundred men stand together, each of them loses his mind and gets another one.   *Friedrich Nietzsche*

Wherever there is a crowd there is untruth.   *Søren Kierkegaard*

The time when, most of all, you should withdraw into yourself is when you are forced to be in a crowd.   *Epicurus*

You cannot make a man by standing a sheep on its hind legs. But by standing a flock of sheep in that position you can make a crowd of men.   *Max Beerbohm*

The average man's opinions are much less foolish than they would be if he thought for himself.   *Bertrand Russell*

Custom, Habit and Tradition

A precedent embalms a principle.
Benjamin Disraeli

Contemporary man has rationalized the myths, but he has not been able to destroy them.
Octavio Paz

Custom is second nature, and no less powerful.
Michel Eyquem Montaigne

Custom reconciles us to everything.
Edmund Burke

Few people have ever seriously wished to be exclusively rational. The good life which most desire is a life warmed by passions and touched with that ceremonial grace which is impossible without some affectionate loyalty to traditional forms and ceremonies.
Joseph Wood Krutch

Habit is a great deadener.
Samuel Beckett

Habit is habit, and not to be thrown out of the window by any man, but coaxed downstairs a step at a time.
Mark Twain

Have a place for everything and keep the things somewheres else. That is not advice, it is merely custom.
Mark Twain

He who does anything because it is the custom, makes no choice.   *John Stuart Mill*

In some remote regions of Islam it is said, a woman caught unveiled by a stranger will raise her skirt to cover her face.
Raymond Mortimer

Innumerable are the illusions and legerdemain tricks of custom: but of all these, perhaps the cleverest is her knack of persuading us that the miraculous by simple repetition ceases to be miraculous.
Thomas Carlyle

It is well to lie fallow for a while.
Martin F. Tupper

She always says she dislikes the abnormal, it is so obvious. She says the normal is so much more simply complicated and interesting.
Gertrude Stein

The despotism of custom is everywhere standing up to human advancement.
John Stuart Mill

The way of the world is to praise dead saints and persecute living ones.
Nathaniel Howe

There is nothing sacred about convention; there is nothing sacred about primitive passions or whims; but the fact that a convention exists indicates that a way of living has been devised capable of maintaining itself.
George Santayana

Tradition does not mean that the living are dead, it means that the dead are living.
Harold Macmillan

Tradition is a guide and not a jailer.   *W. Somerset Maugham*

Custom, that unwritten law,
By which the people keep even kings in awe.   *Charles Davenport*

Habit is stronger than reason.   *George Santayana*

Laws are never as effective as habits.   *Adlai Stevenson*

Habituation is a falling asleep or fatiguing of the sense of time, which explains why
young years pass slowly, while later life flings itself faster and faster upon its course.
Thomas Mann

The gnarled fidelity of an old habit.   *Rainer Maria Rilke*

The one thing more difficult than following a regimen is not imposing it on others.
Marcel Proust

Charlotte, having seen his body borne before her on a shutter, like a well conducted
person, went on cutting bread and butter.   *William Makepeace Thackeray*

We do not really mean, we do not really mean, that what we are going to say is true.
Usual beginning, Ashanti folktales

What thou lovest well remains, the rest is dross.   *Ezra Pound*

The most unendurable thing, to be sure, the really terrible thing, would be a life without
habits, a life which continually required improvisation.   *Friedrich Nietzsche*

Historic continuity with the past is not a duty, it is only a necessity.
Oliver Wendell Holmes, Jr.

Tradition means giving votes to the most obscure of all classes—our ancestors. It is
the democracy of the dead. Tradition refuses to submit to the small and arrogant
oligarchy of those who merely happen to be walking around.   *G. K. Chesterton*

What an enormous magnifier is tradition! How a thing grows in the human memory
and in the human imagination, when love, worship, and all that lies in the human
heart, is there to encourage it.   *Thomas Carlyle*

The trouble with the traditionalists is that they are traditionalists, and have lost the
sense of forward movement. They follow the tracks of the pioneers—and they thereby
deny the spirit of the pioneers, who followed no man's tracks.   *A. A. Phillips*

It seems, in fact, as though the second half of a man's life is made up of nothing but
the habits he has accumulated during the first half.   *Fyodor Dostoevsky*

To renew ties with the past need not always be daydreaming; it may be tapping old
sources of strength for new tasks.   *Simeon Strunsky*

I have not been afraid of excess: excess on occasion is exhilarating. It prevents moderation from acquiring the deadening effect of a habit.   *W. Somerset Maugham*

Habit is the enormous flywheel of society, its most precious conservative agent. There is no more miserable human being than one in whom nothing is habitual but indecision Full half the time of such a man goes to the deciding, or regretting, of matters which ought to be so ingrained in him as practically not to exist for his consciousness at all
William James

Chaos often breeds life, when order breeds habit.   *Henry Adams*

The main dangers in this life are the people who want to change everything—or nothing.   *Lady Astor*

The chains of habit are too weak to be felt until they are too strong to be broken.
Samuel Johnson

When you are accustomed to anything, you are estranged from it.
George Cabot Lodge

Cynicism

A cynic is not merely one who reads bitter lessons from the past; he is one who is prematurely disappointed in the future.   *Sidney J. Harris*

Cynicism is humour in ill health.   *H. G. Wells*

Cynicism such as one finds very frequently among the most highly educated young men and women of the West, results from the combination of comfort and powerlessness.   *Bertrand Russell*

A cynic is a man who, when he smells flowers, looks around for a coffin.
H. L. Mencken

Cynicism—the intellectual cripple's substitute for intelligence.   *Russell Lynes*

Cynicism is that blackguard defect of vision which compels us to see the world as it is, instead of as it should be.   *Ambrose Bierce*

Cynicism is intellectual dandyism, without the coxcomb's feathers. *George Meredith*

There is nothing to which men, while they have food and drink, cannot reconcile themselves.   *George Santayana*

It's not that the Irish are cynical. It's rather that they have a wonderful lack of respect for everything and everybody.   *Brendan Behan*

Watch what people are cynical about, and one can often discover what they lack.
Harry Emerson Fosdick

What is a cynic? A man who knows the price of everything and the value of nothing.
Oscar Wilde

A cynic can chill and dishearten with a single word.   *Ralph Waldo Emerson*

We can destroy ourselves by cynicism and disillusion just as effectively as by bombs.
Kenneth Clark

Cynicism is an unpleasant way of saying the truth.   *Lillian Hellman*

Death and Dying

Death twitches my ear. 'Live,' he says, 'I am coming'.
Virgil (quoted by Justice Oliver Wendell Holmes on his 90th birthday)

To die is a debt we must all of us discharge.   *Euripides*

Here lies Jack Williams. He done his damndest.
Harry S. Truman asked to be remembered by his favourite epitaph, seen in Tombstone, Arizona.

As long as I have a want, I have a reason for living. Satisfaction is death.
George Bernard Shaw

For death begins with life's first breath
And life begins at touch of death.   *John Oxenham*

As men, we are all equal in the presence of death.   *Publilius Syrus*

At last God caught his eye.   *Harry Secombe (epitaph for a waiter)*

Death—the last voyage, the longest, the best.   *Thomas Wolfe*

Death is a delightful hiding-place for weary men.   *Herodotus*

Death is just a distant rumour to the young.   *Andy Rooney*

For three days after death, hair and fingernails continue to grow but phone calls taper off.   *Johnny Carson*

He mourns the dead who lives as they desire.   *Edward Young*

He that dies pays all debts.   *Shakespeare, 'The Tempest'*

Honest listening is one of the best medicines we can offer the dying and the bereaved.
Jean Cameron (dying of cancer in 1982)

I believe that the struggle against death, the unconditional and self-willed determination to live, is the mode of power behind the lives and activities of all outstanding men.

Hermann Hesse

I care not; a man can die but once; we owe God a death.

Shakespeare, 'Henry IV', Part I

I had a lover's quarrel with the world.

Robert Frost

Death is, perhaps, the only commonplace thing that we do not feel to be so.

William Sutherland

In Spain, the dead are more alive than the dead of any other country in the world.

Fédérico Garcia Lorce

It is a far, far better thing that I do, than anything I have ever done; it is a far, far better rest that I go to, than I have ever known.

Charles Dickens

Man comes and tills the field and lies beneath,
And after many a summer dieth the swan.

Alfred Lord Tennyson

It may be that we have all lived before and died, and this is Hell.

A. L. Prusice

If there is another world, he lives in bliss.
If there is none, he made the best of this.

Robert Burns

Most persons have died before they expired—died to all earthly longings, so that the last breath is only, as it were, the locking of the door of the already deserted mansion.

Oliver Wendell Holmes

One short sleep past will wake eternally
And death shall be no more;
Death thou shalt die.

John Donne

Rather suffer than die is man's motto.

Jean de la Fontaine

The art of living well and the art of dying well are one.

Epicurus

The only truly dead are those who have been forgotten.

Jewish saying

The question is whether suicide is the way out, or the way in.

Ralph Waldo Emerson

When you have told anyone you have left him a legacy, the only decent thing to do is to die at once.

Samuel Butler

The dead, I believe, are our minders.

Manning Clark

It is . . . less difficult to die than to watch the dying.

Patrick White, 'The Tree of Man'

Do not go gentle into that good night
Old age should burn and rave at close of day;
Rage, rage against the dying of the light.
Dylan Thomas

The stroke of death is as a lover's pinch,
Which hurts and is desired.
Shakespeare, 'Antony and Cleopatra'

Nothing in his life
Became him like the leaving it.
Shakespeare, 'Macbeth'

Things have a terrible permanence when people die.
Joyce Kilmer

A solemn funeral is inconceivable to the Chinese mind.
Lin Yutang

At its most basic root, the death or disintegration of one's parents is a harsh reminder
of one's own mortality.
Janet Harris

I don't want to achieve immortality through my work. I want to achieve immortality
through not dying.
Woody Allen

Mausoleum, n: the final and funniest folly of the rich.
Ambrose Bierce

No, 'tis not so deep as a well, nor so wide as a church door; but 'tis enough, 'twill
serve: ask for me tomorrow, and you shall find me a grave man. I am peppered, I
warrant, for this world.
Shakespeare, 'Romeo and Juliet'

Epitaph, n: an inscription on a tomb showing that virtues acquired by death have a
retroactive effect.
Ambrose Bierce

Human life consists in mutual service. No grief, pain, misfortune, or 'broken heart' is
excuse for cutting off one's life while any power of service remains. But when all
usefulness is over, when one is assured of an unavoidable and imminent death, it is
the simplest of human rights to choose a quick and easy death in place of a slow and
horrible one.
Suicide note, Charlotte Perkins Gilman

Poisons pain you;
Rivers are damp;
Acid stains you;
And drugs cause cramp.
Guns aren't lawful;
Nooses give;
Gas smells awful;
You might as well live.
Dorothy Parker

Dying is a wild night and a new road.
Emily Dickinson

The reports of my death are greatly exaggerated.
Mark Twain

And I looked, and behold, a pale horse: and his name that sat on him was Death.
Revelation 6:8

There is no man so blessed that some who stand by his deathbed won't hail the occasion with delight.   *Marcus Aurelius*

There may be little or much beyond the grave,
But the strong are saying nothing until they see.   *Robert Frost*

All human things are subject to decay
And when fate summons, monarchs must obey.   *John Dryden*

The most gratifying feature about death is that you won't have to get up in the morning.
The Lone Hand

On his death bed Disraeli declined a visit from Queen Victoria. 'No, it is better not', he said, 'she would only ask me to take a message to Albert.'

I am a broken machine. I am ready to go.   *Woodrow Wilson's last words*

Let the tent be struck.   *Robert E. Lee's last words*

You can lose a man like that by your own death, but not by his.
George Bernard Shaw (of William Morris)

Because I could not stop for Death
He kindly stopped for me—
The carriage held but just ourselves
And Immortality.   *Emily Dickinson*

When a man dies, he does not just die of the disease he has: he dies of his whole life.
Charles Péguy

The long habit of living indisposeth us for dying.   *Thomas Browne*

Most people would die sooner than think; in fact, they do.   *Bertrand Russell*

One should be ever booted and spurred and ready to depart.   *Montaigne*

He who must die must die in the dark, even though he sells candles.
Colombian proverb

A dead man
Who never caused others to die
Seldom rates a statue.   *Anon.*

Nothing you can lose by dying is half so precious as the readiness to die, which is man's charter of nobility.   *George Santayana*

Death be not proud, though some have called Thee
Mighty and dreadful, for thou art not so.   *John Donne*

Toward the person who has died we adopt a special attitude: something like admiration for someone who has accomplished a very difficult task.   *Sigmund Freud*

You have to learn to do everything, even to die.   *Gertrude Stein*

I'm not afraid to die. I just don't want to be there when it happens.   *Woody Allen*

Oh death, you can wait; keep your distance.   *André Chenier*

Body and mind, like man and wife, do not always agree to die together.
Charles Caleb Colton

The undiscovered country from whose bourn no traveller returns.
Shakespeare, 'Hamlet'

A thousand goodbyes come after death—the first six months of bereavement.
Alan Gregg

You don't die in the United States, you underachieve.   *Jerzy Kosinski*

Life is a great surprise. I do not see why death should not be an even greater one.
Vladimir Nabokov

If life must not be taken too seriously—then so neither must death.   *Samuel Butler*

Death is terrible to Cicero, desirable to Cato, and indifferent to Socrates.   *Anon.*

In nature, there is less death and destruction than death and transmutation.
Edwin Way Teale

A man's dying is more the survivors' affair than his own.   *Thomas Mann*

I hate funerals, and would not attend my own if it could be avoided, but it is well for
every man to stop once in a while to think of what sort of a collection of mourners
he is training for his final event.   *Robert T. Morris*

If this is dying, I don't think much of it.   *Lytton Strachey*

Men use one another to assure their personal victory over death.   *Ernest Becker*

Any man's death diminishes me, because I am involved in mankind; and therefore
never send to know for whom the bell tolls; it tolls for thee.   *John Donne*

A belief in hell and the knowledge that every ambition is doomed to frustration at the
hands of a skeleton have never prevented the majority of human beings from behaving
as though death were no more than an unfounded rumour, and survival a thing not
beyond the bounds of possibility.   *Aldous Huxley*

I cannot forgive my friends for dying: I do not find these vanishing acts of theirs at
all amusing.   *Logan Pearsall Smith*

Make sure to send a lazy man for the Angel of Death.   *Jewish proverb*

It cost me never a stab nor squirm
To tread by chance upon a worm.
'Aha, my little dear' I say,
'Your clan will pay me back one day.'   *Dorothy Parker*

While you live, live in clover,
For when you're dead,
You're dead all over.   *Squizzy Taylor (who was shot dead in a gunfight)*

There is no such thing as death,
In nature, nothing dies:
From each sad moment of decay
Some forms of life arise.   *Charles Mackay*

I am going to seek a great Perhaps.   *François Rabelais' dying words*

Deception

Hood an ass with reverend purple. So you can hide his two ambitious ears, and he shall pass for a cathedral doctor.   *Ben Jonson*

Proportion is almost impossible to human beings. There is no one who does not exaggerate.   *Ralph Waldo Emerson*

Everything that deceives may be said to enchant.   *Plato*

We are never deceived; we deceive ourselves.   *Goethe*

All charming people have something to conceal, usually their total dependence on the appreciation of others.   *Cyril Connolly*

You k'n hide de fier, but what you guine do wid de smoke?   *Joel Chandler Harris*

Deep versed in books and shallow in himself.   *John Milton*

Half the work that is done in the world is to make things appear what they are not.
                                                    E. R. Beadle

If you are given the privilege of having your name in the papers every day, deception and self-aggrandisement are easy arts to practise.
                              George Johnston, 'My Brother Jack'

If the world will be gulled, let it be gulled.   *Robert Burton*

I give you bitter pills in sugar coating. The pills are harmless: the poison is in the sugar.   *Stanislaw Lec*

I have known a vast quantity of nonsense talked about bad men not looking you in the face. Don't trust that conventional idea. Dishonesty will stare honesty out of countenance, any day in the week, if there is anything to be got by it.

Charles Dickens

One should seek for the salutary in the unpleasant: if it is there, it is after all nectar. One should seek for the deceitful in the pleasant: if it is there it is after all poison.

Panchatantra

Deceive not thy physician, confessor, nor lawyer.   *George Herbert*

Frank and explicit—this is the right line to take when you wish to conceal your own mind and to confuse the mind of others.   *Benjamin Disraeli*

Defeat

Do not be afraid of defeat. You are never so near to victory as when defeated in a good cause.   *Henry Ward Beecher*

To lose
Is to learn.   *Anon.*

We have fought this fight as long, and as well as we know how. We have been defeated. For us, as a Christian people, there is now but one course to pursue. We must accept the situation.   *Robert E. Lee*

It is better to be defeated on principle than to win on lies.   *Arthur Calwell*

What is defeat? Nothing but education, nothing but the first step toward something better.   *Wendell Phillips*

Who, apart
From ourselves, can see any difference between
Our victories and our defeats?   *Christopher Fry*

They were never defeated, they were only killed.
(said of the French Foreign Legion)

The mountain remains unmoved at seeming defeat by the mist.
Rabindranath Tagore

Democracy

Democracy is based upon the conviction that there are extraordinary possibilities in ordinary people.   *Harry Emerson Fosdick*

In a democracy, the opposition is not only tolerated as constitutional, but must be maintained because it is indispensable.   *Walter Lippmann*

It has been said that Democracy is the worst form of government except all those other forms that have been tried from time to time.   *Winston Churchill*

Unless the democratic movement makes people better—more intelligent, conscientious and human—it is not worth support.   *Joseph Furphy*

Without the long view democracy becomes a mere squabble for bread and circuses; statesmanship disappears, and the adroit manoeuvres of evanescent politics prevail.
                    R. G. Menzies

Democracy is a small hard core of common agreement, surrounded by a rich variety of individual differences.   *James Bryant Conant*

People often say that, in a democracy, decisions are made by a majority of the people. Of course, that is not true. Decisions are made by a majority of those who make themselves heard and who vote—a very different thing.   *Walter H. Judd*

Democracy means government by the uneducated, while aristocracy means government by the badly educated.   *G. K. Chesterton*

Equality is a meaningless abstraction unless it is founded on economic security and economic strength.   *Mary Gaudron*

The essence of democracy is respect for minorities, not rule by majorities.
                    Sir John Latham

The greatest blessing of our democracy is freedom. But in the last analysis, our only freedom is the freedom to discipline ourselves.   *Bernard Baruch*

Democracy is the recurrent suspicion that more than half of the people are right more than half of the time.   *E. B. White*

The worst form of inequality is to try to make unequal things equal.   *Aristotle*

What men value in the world is not rights, but privileges.   *H. L. Mencken*

As I would not be a slave, so I would not be a master. This expresses my idea of democracy.   *Abraham Lincoln*

Democracy is a festival of mediocrity.   *E. M. Cioran*

The job of a citizen is to keep his mouth open.   *Gunter Grass*

Drink, Drinking and Drinkers

A torch-light procession marching down your throat.   *John L. O'Sullivan*

First you take a drink, then the drink takes a drink, then the drink takes you.
                    F. Scott FitzGerald

For when the wine is in, the wit is out.   *Thomas Becon*

He neither drank, smoked, nor rode a bicycle. Living frugally, saving his money, he died early, surrounded by greedy relatives. It was a great lesson to me.

John Barrymore

He who drinks a little too much drinks much too much.   *Old saying*

I am only a beer teetotaller, not a champagne teetotaller.   *George Bernard Shaw*

The worst thing about some men is that when they are not drunk they are sober.

William Butler Yeats

I have never been drunk, but I've often been overserved.   *George Gobel*

In vino veritas. (In wine there is truth.)   *Pliny the Elder*

They talk of my drinking but never my thirst.   *Old saying*

What, when drunk, one sees in other women, one sees in Garbo sober.

Kenneth Tynan

You are not drunk if you can lie on the floor without holding on.   *Dean Martin*

I like liquor—its taste and its effects—and that is just the reason why I never drink it.   *Thomas (Stonewall) Jackson*

The Persians are very fond of wine . . . It is also their general practice to deliberate upon affairs of weight when they are drunk; and then in the morning, when they are sober, the decision to which they came the night before is put before them by the master of the house in which it was made; and if it is then approved they act on it; if not, they set it aside. Sometimes, however, they are sober at their first deliberations, but in this case they always reconsider the matter under the influence of wine.

Herodotus

Drunkenness is temporary suicide: the happiness that it brings is merely negative, a momentary cessation of unhappiness.   *Bertrand Russell*

Bacchus has drowned more men than Neptune.   *Guiseppe Garibaldi*

Temperance is the control of all the functions of our bodies. The man who refuses liquor, goes in for apple pie and develops a paunch, is no ethical leader for me.

John Erskine

Nothing ever tasted any better than a cold beer on a beautiful afternoon with nothing to look forward to but more of the same.   *Hugh Hood*

Beer makes you feel the way you ought to feel without beer.

Attributed to Henry Lawson

Abstinence is as easy for me as temperance would be difficult.   *Samuel Johnson*

I drink to make other people interesting.   *George Jean Nathan*

One of the disadvantages of wine is that is makes a man mistake words for thoughts.
Samuel Johnson

The innkeeper loves the drunkard, but not for a son-in-law.   *Jewish proverb*

Whisky drowns some troubles and floats a lot more.   *Robert C. Edwards*

Malt does more than Milton can
To justify God's ways to man.   *A. E. Housman*

A man hath no better thing under the sun, than to eat, and to drink, and to be merry.
Ecclesiastes 8:15

Drink not the third glass—which thou can'st not tame when once it is within thee.
George Herbert

An Irish queer: a fellow who prefers women to drink.   *Sean O'Faolain*

Bundaberg rum, overproof rum,
will tan your insides and grow hair on your bum.   *Bill Scott*

Eat bread at pleasure, drink wine by measure.   *Randle Cotgrave*

We frequently hear of people dying from too much drinking. That this happens is a matter of record. But the blame almost always is placed on whisky. Why this should be I never could understand. You can die from drinking too much of anything—coffee, water, milk, soft drinks and all such stuff as that. And so long as the presence of death lurks with anyone who goes through the simple act of swallowing, I will make mine whisky.   *W. C. Fields*

It's a naive domestic burgundy without any breeding, but I think you'll be amused by its presumption.   *James Thurber*

Drunkenness is nothing but voluntary madness.   *Seneca*

There are more old drunkards than old physicians.   *Rabelais*

He is . . . like many other geniuses, a greater friend to the bottle, than the bottle is to him.   *William Lyon Mackenzie*

Boys should abstain from all use of wine until their eighteenth year, for it is wrong to add fire to fire.   *Plato*

I always keep a supply of stimulant handy in case I see a snake—which I also keep handy.   *W. C. Fields*

We had gone out there to pass the beautiful day of high summer like true Irishmen—locked in the dark Snug of a public house.   *Brendan Behan*

The whole world is about three drinks behind.   *Humphrey Bogart*

It's the drink I have when I'm not having a drink.

Advertisement for Clayton's Tonic

Education

A gentleman need not know Latin, but he should at least have forgotten it.

Brander Matthews

A one-book man is either a slow learner or an ill-equipped teacher.

Robert Wm. Burke

Arrogance, pedantry, and dogmatism are the occupational diseases of those who spend their lives directing the intellects of the young.   *Henry S. Canby*

Creatures whose main spring is curiosity will enjoy the accumulating of fact, far more than the pausing at times to reflect on those facts.   *Clarence Day*

Good teaching is 1/4th preparation and 3/4ths theatre.   *Gail Godwin*

He who would learn to fly one day must first learn to stand and walk and run and climb and dance; one cannot fly into flying.   *Friedrich Nietzsche*

Learning makes a man fit company for himself.   *Thomas Fuller*

I forget what I was taught. I only remember what I have learnt.   *Patrick White*

I pay the School Master, but 'tis the school boys that educate my son.

Ralph Waldo Emerson

If you educate a man you educate a person, but if you educate a woman, you educate a family.   *Rudy Manikan*

If you hit a pony over the nose at the outset of your acquaintance, he may not love you but he will take a deep interest in your movements ever afterwards.

Rudyard Kipling

On many American campuses the only qualification for admission was the ability actually to find the campus and then discover a parking space.   *Malcolm Bradbury*

One could get a first-class education from a shelf of books five feet long.

Charles William Eliot (when President of Harvard University)

One father is more than 100 schoolmasters.   *George Herbert*

One looks back with appreciation to the brilliant teachers, but with gratitude to those who touched our human feelings. The curriculum is so much necessary raw material, but warmth is a vital element for the growing plant and for the soul of the child.

Carl Jung

Pedantry crams our heads with learned lumber and takes out brains to make room for it. *Charles Caleb Colton*

Tell me and I'll forget. Show me, and I may not remember. Involve me, and I ll understand. *Native American saying*

The average PhD thesis is nothing but a transference of bones from one graveyard to another. *J. Frank Dobie*

The true teacher defends his pupils against his own personal influence. *A. B. Alcott*

Education properly understood is liberal; it implies the most thoroughgoing democracy, the rejection alike of privileged ideas and of privileged persons. *John Anderson*

Education should be gentle and stern, not cold and lax. *Joseph Joubert*

Universities are the cathedrals of the modern age. They shouldn't have to justify their existence by utilitarian criteria. *David Lodge*

We should not value education as a means to prosperity, but prosperity as a means to education. Only then will our priorities be right. For education, unlike prosperity is an end in itself. . . power and influence come through the acquisition of useless knowledge. . . irrelevant subjects bring understanding of the human condition, by forcing the student to stand back from it. *Roger Scruton*

When there are two PhD's in a developing country, one is Head of State and the other is in exile. *Lord Samuel*

You don't understand anything until you learn it more than one way.

Marvin Minsky

The schools ain't what they used to be and never was. *Will Rogers*

The things taught in schools are not an education but the means of an education.

Ralph Waldo Emerson

The university is the last remaining platform for national dissent. *Leon Eisenberg*

Education, to be of any value at all, must be useless in the first place.

Nettie Palmer

Surely the shortest commencement address in history—and for me one of the most memorable—was that of Dr. Harold E. Hyde, President of New Hampshire's Plymouth State College. He reduced his message to the graduating class to these three ideals: 'Know yourself—Socrates. Control yourself—Cicero; Give yourself—Christ.'

Walter T. Tatara

There is that indescribable freshness and unconsciousness about an illiterate person that humbles and mocks the power of the noblest expressive genius.   *Walt Whitman*

Intelligence appears to be the thing that enables a man to get along without education. Education appears to be the thing that enables a man to get along without the use of his intelligence.   *A. E. Wiggan*

By learning you will teach; by teaching you will learn.   *Latin proverb*

Most men of education are more superstitious than they admit—nay, than they think.
G. C. Lichtenberg

A university is what a college becomes when the faculty loses interest in students.
John Ciardi

Education is indoctrination, if you're white—subjugation if you're black.
James Baldwin

The investigation of the meaning of words is the beginning of education.
Antisthenes

Learning to learn is to know how to navigate in a forest of facts, ideas and theories, a proliferation of constantly changing items of knowledge. Learning to learn is to know what to ignore but at the same time not rejecting innovation and research.
Raymond Queneau

A good education should leave much to be desired.   *Alan Gregg*

'Whom are you?' he asked, for he had been to night school.   *George Ade*

Education with inert ideas is not only useless; it is above all things harmful.
Alfred North Whitehead

Schoolmasters and parents exist to be grown out of.   *John Wolfenden*

A child educated only at school is an uneducated child.   *George Santayana*

No one can become really educated without having pursued some study in which he took no interest. For it is part of education to interest ourselves in subjects for which we have no aptitude.   *T. S. Eliot*

It is in fact a part of the function of education to help us to escape, not from our own time—for we are bound by that—but from the intellectual and emotional limitations of our time.   *T. S. Eliot*

Nothing in education is so astonishing as the amount of ignorance it accumulates in the form of inert facts.   *Henry Adams*

You can lead a man up to the university, but you can't make him think.
Finley Peter Dunne

If you think education is expensive—try ignorance. *Derek Bok*

It is a greater work to educate a child, in the true and larger sense of the word, than to rule a state. *William Ellery Channing*

There is less flogging in our great schools than formerly, but then less is learned there; so that what the boys get at one end they lose at the other. *Samuel Johnson*

Education is not the filling of a pail, but the lighting of a fire. *William Butler Yeats*

Perhaps the most valuable result of all education is the ability to make yourself do the thing you have to do, when it ought to be done, whether you like it or not; it is the first lesson that ought to be learned, and however early a man's training begins, it is probably the last lesson that he learns thoroughly. *Thomas Huxley*

Some men are graduated from college *cum laude*, some are graduated *summa cum laude*, and some are graduated *mirabile dictu*. *William Howard Taft*

Education is the ability to listen to almost anything without losing your temper or your self-confidence. *Robert Frost*

We must reject that most dismal and fatuous notion that education is a preparation for life. *Northrop Frye*

Soon learnt, soon forgotten. *Anon.*

It is of interest to note that while some dolphins are reported to have learned English—up to fifty words used in correct context—no human being has been reported to have learned dolphinese. *Carl Sagan*

And if the student finds that this is not to his taste, well, that is regrettable. Most regrettable. His taste should not be consulted; it is being formed.
Flannery O'Connor

Education, n: that which discloses to the wise and disguises from the foolish their lack of understanding. *Ambrose Bierce*

The Romans would never have had time to conquer the world if they had been obliged to learn Latin first of all. *Heinrich Heine*

The antithesis between a technical and a liberal education is fallacious. There can be no adequate technical education which is not liberal, and no liberal education which is not technical. *Alfred North Whitehead*

John Milton called his school, Christ College, 'a stony-hearted step-mother'.

The ultimate goal of the educational system is to shift to the individual the burden of pursuing his education. *John W. Gardner*

To make your children capable of honesty is the beginning of education.
John Ruskin

Creative minds have always been known to survive any kind of bad training.
Anna Freud

Fathers send their sons to college either because they went to college, or because they didn't.
L. L. Hendren

Education today, more than ever before, must see clearly the dual objectives: education for living and educating for making a living.
James Mason Wood

The test and the use of man's education is that he finds pleasure in the exercise of his mind.
Jacques Barzun

The Jews have always been students, and their greatest study is themselves.
Albert Goldman

Whenever I'm asked what college I attended, I'm tempted to reply, 'Thornton Wilder'.
Garson Kanin

Let the schools teach the nobility of labour and the beauty of human service: but the superstitions of ages past? Never!
Peter Cooper

Education is what survives when what has been learnt has been forgotten.
B. F. Skinner

If a man empties his purse into his head, no one can take it from him.
Benjamin Franklin

I find the three major administrative problems on a campus are sex for the students, athletics for the alumni and parking for the faculty.
Clark Kerr, President, University of California

All learning has an emotional base.
Plato

Whatever is good to know is difficult to learn.
Greek proverb

Thus education forms the common mind;
Just as the twig is bent, the tree's inclined.
Alexander Pope

Enemies

The truth is forced upon us, very quickly, by a foe.
Aristophanes

We need our enemies to teach us
what friends in kindness never show.
Gwen Harwood

A wise man gets more use from his enemies than a fool from his friends.
Baltasar Gracián

He hasn't an enemy in the world, and none of his friends like him.
Oscar Wilde, of Bernard Shaw

Don't think there are no crocodiles because the water is calm.   *Malayan proverb*

The enemies of the future are always the very nicest people.   *Christopher Morley*

A man cannot be too careful in the choice of his enemies.   *Oscar Wilde*

You can discover what your enemy fears most by observing the means he uses to frighten you.
Eric Hoffer

There is no man so friendless but what he can find a friend sincere enough to tell him disagreeable truths.
Edward Bulwer-Lytton

Enemies could become the best companions. Companionship is based on a common interest, and the greater the interest the closer the companionship. What makes enemies of people, if not the eagerness, the passion for the same thing?   *Bernard Berenson*

Whoever has his foe at his mercy, and does not kill him, is his own enemy.   *Sa'di*

The little foxes that spoil the vines.   *Song of Solomon 2:15*

We have met the enemy, and he is us.   *Walt Kelly*

The Lacedemonians do not inquire how many the enemy are, but where they are.
Agis

The space in a needle's eye is sufficient for two friends, but the whole world is scarcely big enough to hold two enemies.   *Solomon ibn Gabirol*

Whoso sheddeth man's blood, by man shall his blood be shed.   *Genesis 9.6*

If we could read the secret history of our enemies, we should find in each man's life, sorrow and suffering enough to disarm all hostility.   *Henry Wadsworth Longfellow*

Those who hate you don't win unless you hate them—and then you destroy yourself.
Richard Nixon

There's nothing like the sight of an old enemy down on his luck.   *Euripides*

The enemy of my enemy is my friend.   *Arabic proverb*

England . . . and Britain

England is a nation of voyeurs.   *Nigel Newton*

Every man has a House of Lords in his own head. Fears, prejudices, misconceptions—those are the peers and they are hereditary.   *David Lloyd George*

George III
Ought never to have occurred.
One can only wonder
At so grotesque a blunder.   *Edmund Clerihew Bentley*

God save our Gracious King,
Long live our Noble King,
God save the King.
Send Him victorious
Happy and Glorious
Long to rule over us
God save the King.   *Henry Carey*

Great Britain has lost an empire and has not yet found a role.   *Dean Acheson*

His Majesty's dominions, on which the sun never sets.   *Christopher North*

I have been trying all my life to like Scotchmen, and am obliged to desist from the
experiment in despair.   *Charles Lamb*

If I should die, think only this of me,
that there's some corner of a foreign field
that is for ever England.   *Rupert Brooke*

It is impossible for an Englishman to open his mouth without making some other
Englishman despise him.   *George Bernard Shaw*

Land of hope and glory, Mother of the Free
How shall we extol thee, who are borne of thee?
Wider still and wider shall thy bounds be set;
God who made thee mighty, make thee mightier yet.   *A. C. Benson*

London is a roost for every bird.   *Benjamin Disraeli*

Remember that you are an Englishman and consequently have won first prize in the
lottery of life.   *Cecil Rhodes*

Rule Britannia, Britannia, rule the waves;
Britains never will be slaves.   *James Thomson*

Snobbery—the 'pox Britannica'.   *Anthony Sampson*

The difference between the vanity of a Frenchman and an Englishman seems to be
this: The one thinks everything right that is French, the other thinks everything wrong
that is not English.   *William Hazlitt*

The English woman is so refined
She has no bosom and no behind.   *Stevie (Florence Margaret) Smith*

The House of Lords is a model of how to care for the elderly.   *Frank Field*

The House of Lords is like a glass of champagne that has stood for 5 days.

Clement Attlee

The most dangerous thing in the world is to make a friend of an Englishman, because he'll come sleep in your closet rather than spend 10 shillings on a hotel.

Truman Capote

The young Cambridge group, the group that stood for 'freedom' and flannel trousers and flannel shirts open at the neck, and a well-bred sort of emotional anarchy, and a whispering, murmuring, sort of voice, and an ultra-sensitive sort of manner.

D. H. Lawrence

There will always be an England
While there's a country lane
Wherever there's a cottage small
Beside a field of grain.

Clark Ross Parker

Without class differences, England would cease to be the living theatre it is.

Anthony Burgess

You must not miss Whitehall. At one end you'll find a statue of one of our kings who was beheaded; at the other, the monument to the man who did it. This is just an example of our attempts to be fair to everybody.

Thomas Appleton (on Charles I and Cromwell)

Though I love my country, I do not love my countrymen.   *Lord Byron*

England has forty-two religions and only two sauces.   *Voltaire*

England and America are two countries separated by the same language.

George Bernard Shaw

In England I would rather be a man, a horse, a dog or a woman, in that order. In America I think the order would be reversed.   *Bruce Gould*

England is the paradise of individuality, eccentricity, heresy, anomalies, hobbies and humours.   *George Santayana*

Not only England, but every Englishman is an island.   *Novalis*

The English instinctively admire any man who has no talent and is modest about it.

James Agate

In the end it may well be that Britain will be more honoured by the historians for the way she disposed of an empire than for the way in which she acquired it.

David Ormsby Gore

Oh, it's a snug little island!
A right little, tight little island!   *Thomas Dibdin*

I regard England as my wife and America as my mistress.   *Cedric Hardwicke*

The Englishman respects your opinions, but he never thinks of your feelings.

Wilfrid Laurier

The Englishman has all the qualities of a poker except its occasional warmth.

Daniel O'Connell

The English never draw a line without blurring it.   *Winston Churchill*

Socialism has been preached for so long, the British people no longer have any sense of personal responsibility.   *Lord Thomson of Fleet*

Britain's best bulwarks are her wooden walls.   *T. Augustine Arne*

Queen Victoria—a mixture of national landlady and actress.   *V. S. Pritchett*

I think the British have the distinction above all other nations of being able to put new wine into old bottles without bursting them.   *Clement Attlee*

Whatever the rest of the world thinks of the English gentleman, the English lady regards him apprehensively as something between God and a goat and equally formidable on both scores.   *Margaret Halsey*

Deploring change is the unchangeable habit of all Englishmen. If you find any important figures who really like change, such as Bernard Shaw, Keir Hardie, Lloyd George, Selfridge or Disraeli, you will find that they are not really English at all, but Irish, Scotch, Welsh, American or Jewish. Englishmen make changes, sometimes great changes. But, secretly or openly, they always deplore them.   *Raymond Postgate*

Where there is one Englishman there is a garden. Where there are two Englishmen there will be a club. But this does not mean any falling off in the number of gardens. There will be three. The club will have one too.   *A. W. Smith*

What should they know of England, who only England know?   *Rudyard Kipling*

I had been told by Jimmy Edmond in Australia that there were only three things against living in Britain: the place, the climate and the people.   *David Low*

No one can be as calculatedly rude as the British, which amazes Americans, who do not understand studied insult and can only offer abuse as a substitute.   *Paul Gallico*

The English have an extraordinary ability for flying into a great calm.

Alexander Woollcott

We are articulate, but we are not particularly conversational. An Englishman won't talk for the sake of talking. He doesn't mind silence. But after the silence, he sometimes says something.   *Robert Morley*

The nice sense of measure is certainly not one of Nature's gifts to her English children . . . we have all of us yielded to infatuation at some moment of our lives.

Matthew Arnold

I find the Englishman to be him of all men who stands firmest in his shoes.
Ralph Waldo Emerson

It seems to me that you can go sauntering along for a certain period, telling the English some interesting things about themselves, and then all at once it feels as if you had stepped on the prongs of a rake.   *Patrick Campbell*

One matter Englishmen don't think in the least funny is their happy consciousness of possessing a deep sense of humour.   *Marshall McLuhan*

The English may not like music, but they absolutely love the noise it makes.
Thomas Beecham

That typically English characteristic for which there is no English name—esprit de corps.   *Frank Adcock*

The British are just as keen to make money as the Americans, but they prefer hypocrisy to a blatantly commercial attitude.   *Wendy Michener*

Nothing unites the English like war. Nothing divides them like Picasso. *Hugh Mills*

The British love permanence more than they love beauty.   *Hugh Casson*

An Englishman thinks he is moral when he is only uncomfortable.
George Bernard Shaw

The British are terribly lazy about fighting. They like to get it over and done with and then set up a game of cricket.   *Stephen Leacock*

A Scotch mist may wet an Englishman to the skin.   *English proverb*

Enjoyment and Pleasure

A person buying ordinary products in a supermarket is in touch with his deepest emotions.   *J. K. Galbraith*

A tavern chair is the throne of human felicity.   *Samuel Johnson*

After pleasant scratching comes unpleasant smarting.   *Danish proverb*

Danger and delight grow on one stalk.   *Old saying*

Leisure is being allowed to do nothing.   *G. K. Chesterton*

Pleasure for an hour, a bottle of wine; pleasure for a year, marriage; pleasure for a lifetime, a garden.   *Chinese saying*

The test of pleasure is the memory it leaves behind. (*Die Probe eines Genusses ist seine Erinnerung.*)   *Jean Paul Richter*

The true spirit of delight, the exultation, the sense of being more than Man which is the touchstone of the highest excellence, is to be found in mathematics as surely as in poetry.   *Bertrand Russell*

We must like what we have when we don't have what we like.
Roger de Bussy-Rabutin
(Similar to the old saying, 'When you don't have
what you want, you must want what you have.')

What the mass media offer is not popular art, but entertainment which is intended to be consumed like food, forgotten, and replaced by a new dish.   *W. H. Auden*

Speed provides the one genuinely modern pleasure.   *Aldous Huxley*

To be able to use leisure intelligently will be the last product of an intelligent civilization.   *Bertrand Russell*

There are two things to aim at in life: first, to get what you want, and after that to enjoy it.   *Logan Pearsall Smith*

That man is richest whose pleasures are the cheapest.   *Henry David Thoreau*

All the great pleasures in life are silent.   *Georges Clemenceau*

The only way to entertain some folks is to listen to them.   *Kin Hubbard*

Enthusiasm is the greatest asset in the world. It beats money and power and influence.   *Henry Chester*

Danger and delight grow on one stalk.   *English proverb*

Every luxury must be paid for, and everything is a luxury, starting with being in the world.   *Cesare Pavese*

Enjoyment is not a goal, it is a feeling that accompanies important ongoing activity.   *Paul Goodman*

Most of the luxuries, and many of the so-called comforts, of life are not only not indispensable, but positive hindrances to the elevation of mankind.   *Henry David Thoreau*

To really enjoy the better things in life, one must first have experienced the things they are better than.   *Oscar Homolka*

If you resolve to give up smoking, drinking and loving, you don't actually live longer; it just seems longer.   *Clement Freud*

We act as though comfort and luxury were the chief requirements of life, when all that we need to make us really happy is something to be enthusiastic about.   *Charles Kingsley*

No one in this world needs a mink coat but a mink. *Anon.*

One's first book, kiss, home run is always the best. *Clifton Fadiman*

Let us have Wine and Women, Mirth and Laughter
Sermons and soda-water the day after. *Lord Byron*

1. If your stomach disputes you, lie down and pacify it with cool thoughts. 2. Keep the juices flowing by jangling around gently as you move. 3. Go very lightly on the vices such as carrying on in society. The social ramble ain't restful. *Satchell Paige*

Love, and do what you like. *St. Augustine*

Every good thing that comes is accompanied by trouble. *Maxwell Perkins*

All the things I really like to do are either immoral, illegal or fattening.
Alexander Woollcott

The physically fit can enjoy their vices. *Lloyd Percival*

The superfluous is very necessary. *Voltaire*

There are three ingredients in the good life; learning, earning and yearning.
Christopher Morley

A sense of wrongdoing is an enhancement of pleasure. *Oliver Wendell Holmes, Jr.*

From desire I plunge to its fulfilment, where I long once more for desire. *Goethe*

Unsatisfied desire is in itself more desirable than any other satisfaction. *C. S. Lewis*

Luxury is more deadly than any foe. *Juvenal*

Environment

California is a fine place to live—if you happen to be an orange. *Fred Allen*

I asked a coughing friend of mine why he doesn't stop smoking. 'In this town it wouldn't do any good,' he explained. 'I happen to be a chain breather.'
Robert Sylvester

Population growth is the primary source of environmental damage.
Jacques Cousteau

A moment's insight is sometimes worth a life's experience. *Oliver Wendell Holmes*

Ecologists with a socialist perspective and socialists with an ecological perspective must form a coalition to tackle the wide-ranging problems relating to human survival. Such survival is based on a way of living in harmony with the rest of nature. My dream, and that of millions of others, might then come true: a socialist world with a human face, an ecological heart and an egalitarian body.   *Jack Mundey*

The environment is everything that isn't me.   *Albert Einstein*

The most important thing about Spaceship Earth—an instruction book didn't come with it.   *Buckminster Fuller*

For the first time in the history of the world, every human being is now subjected to contact with dangerous chemicals, from the moment of conception until death.
    Rachel Carson

Conservation is not worth having if it merely shifts hardships from rich to poor, or from later to now. Growth is not worth having if it merely speeds up the rate at which the rich can guzzle resources which the poor need both now and later.
    Hugh Stretton

Air pollution is turning Mother Nature prematurely gray.   *Irv Kupcinet*

The first law of ecology is that everything is related to everything else.
    Barry Commoner

The sun, moon and stars would have disappeared long ago had they been within the reach of predatory human hands.   *Havelock Ellis*

Hurt not the earth, neither the sea, nor the trees.   *Revelation 7:3*

Pity the meek for they shall inherit the earth.   *Don Marquis*

We have forgotten how to be good guests, how to walk lightly on the earth as other creatures do.   *1972 Only One Earth Conference*

Experience

Do not be too timid and squeamish about your actions. All life is an experience.
    Ralph Waldo Emerson

Let weakness learn meekness.   *A. C. Swinburne*

Experience has two things to teach: The first is that we must correct a great deal; the second that we must not correct too much.   *Eugène Delacroix*

Experience is in the fingers and the head. The heart is inexperienced.
    Henry David Thoreau

God will not look you over for medals, degrees or diplomas, but for scars!
Elbert Hubbard

I embrace emerging experience. I participate in discovery. I am a butterfly. I am not a butterfly collector. I want the experience of the butterfly. *William Stafford*

Many of the insights of the saint stem from his experience as a sinner. *Eric Hoffer*

Deep experience is never peaceful. *Henry James*

Experience is the name so many people give to their mistakes. *Oscar Wilde*

Experience, which destroys innocence, also leads one back to it. *James Baldwin*

To most men, experience is like the stern lights of a ship, which illumine only the track it has passed. *Samuel Taylor Coleridge*

The life of the law has not been logic, it has been experience.
Oliver Wendell Holmes, Jr.

A proverb is no proverb to you till life has illustrated it. *John Keats*

Today is yesterday's pupil. *Thomas Fuller*

All that I know I learned after I was thirty. *Georges Clemenceau*

Life is like playing a violin solo in public, and learning the instrument as one goes on. *Samuel Butler*

What you really value is what you miss, not what you have. *Jorge Luis Borges*

Everything happens to everybody sooner or later if there is time enough.
George Bernard Shaw

Men are wise in proportion, not to their experience, but to their capacity for experience.
George Bernard Shaw

Experience is not what happens to a man. It is what a man does with what happens to him. *Aldous Huxley*

To a great experience one thing is essential—an experiencing nature.
Walter Bagehot

Good judgement comes from experience, and experience—well, that comes from poor judgement. *Anon.*

When choosing between two evils, I always like to take the one I've never tried before.
Mae West

Age is only a number, a cipher for the records. A man can't retire his experience. He must use it. Experience achieves more with less energy and time. *Bernard Baruch*

Experience enables you to recognize a mistake when you make it again.
Franklin P. Jones

Experience is the worst teacher; it gives the test before presenting the lesson.
Vernon Law

From error to error one discovers the entire truth.   *Sigmund Freud*

There's no one more possessive of bad experiences than a writer.   *Aviva Layton*

Any man worth his salt has by the time he is forty-five accumulated a crown of thorns, and the problem is to learn to wear it over one ear.   *Christopher Morley*

Experience teaches only the teachable.   *Aldous Huxley*

Not to transmit an experience is to betray it.   *Elie Wiesel*

Motives and purposes are in the brain and heart of man. Consequences are in the world of fact.   *Henry Geaye*

Experience is a good teacher, but she sends in terrific bills.   *Minna Antrim*

Fame and Celebrities

Fame is as ephemeral as fairy floss. Like spun sugar melting in the mouth it melts in the mind.   *Phillip Adams*

Glory is fleeting, but obscurity is forever.   *Napoleon Bonaparte*

Have regard for your name, since it will remain for you longer than a great store of gold.   *Ecclesiasticus 42:12*

I have touch'd the highest point of all my greatness, And from that full meridian of my glory I haste now to my setting.   *Shakespeare, 'Henry VIII'*

There has always been fame. It's a human weakness. No other kind of living creature knows anything about fame, not even the peacock, who certainly craves attention but lacks the brain to know why.   *Clive James*

One of the drawbacks of Fame is that one can never escape from it.   *Nellie Melba*

Popularity is a crime from the moment it is sought; it is only a virtue where men have it whether they will or not.   *Sir George Savile*

Mistrust popularity, the rock on which many a good man has wrecked his soul.
Walter Murdoch

The only man who wasn't spoilt by being lionized was Daniel.
Herbert Beerbohm Tree

The ordinary man casts a shadow in a way we do not quite understand. The man of genius casts light.
George Steiner

Though familiarity may not breed contempt, it takes off the edge of admiration.
William Hazlitt

When I pass my name in such large letters I blush, but at the same time instinctively raise my hat.
Herbert Beerbohm Tree

Fame is the sum of the misunderstanding that gathers about a new name.
Rainer Maria Rilke

What a heavy burden is a name that has become too famous.
Voltaire

Now when I bore people at a party, they think it's their fault.
Henry Kissinger

One must choose between Obscurity with Efficiency, and Fame with its inevitable collateral of Bluff.
William McFee

One lives in the hope of becoming a memory.
Antonio Porchia

After I am dead, I would rather have men ask why Cato has no monument than why he had one.
Cato the Elder

Fame often comes to those who are thinking about something else, whereas celebrity comes to those who think about nothing else.
Phillip Adams

The greatest monarch on the proudest throne is obliged to sit upon his own arse.
Benjamin Franklin

All celebrated people lose dignity on a close view.
Napoleon Bonaparte

A celebrity is a person known for his well-knownness. Celebrities intensify their celebrity images simply by being well known for relations among themselves. By a kind of symbiosis, celebrities live off each other.
Daniel J. Boorstin

Before such a prodigious career, judgement is torn between blame an admiration.
Charles de Gaulle on Napoleon

Famous remarks are very seldom quoted correctly.
Simeon Strunsky

It is strange how the memory of a man may float to posterity on what he would have himself regarded as the most trifling of his works.
William Osler

To be somebody you must last.
Ruth Gordon

The world, like an accomplished hostess, pays most attention to those whom it will soonest forget.
John Churton Collins

Public opinion: a vulgar, impertinent, anonymous tyrant who deliberately makes life unpleasant for any one of us who is not content to be the average man.

Dean William R. Inge

Man's attitude toward great qualities in others is often the same as toward high mountains—he admires them but he prefers to walk around them.   *Moritz Saphir*

All the fame I look for in life is to have lived it quietly.   *Montaigne*

A celebrity is one who is known to many persons he is glad he doesn't know.

H. L. Mencken

Fame is a bee
It has a song—
It has a sting—
Ah, too, it has a wing.   *Emily Dickinson*

A sign of a celebrity is often that his name is worth more than his services.

Daniel J. Boorstin

Martyrdom is the only way a man can become famous without ability.

George Bernard Shaw

He that hath the name to be an early riser may sleep till noon.   *James Howell*

Some day each of us will be famous for fifteen minutes.   *Andy Warhol*

Family and Ancestry

He who has daughters is always a shepherd.   *Old saying*

I am married to Beatrice Salkeld, a painter. We have no children, except me.

Brendan Behan

I don't know who my grandfather was; I am much more concerned to know what his grandson will be.   *Abraham Lincoln*

I have called the principle, by which each slight variation, if useful, is preserved by the term of Natural Selection.   *Charles Darwin*

My father was frightened by his mother. I was frightened by my father, and I'm damned well going to make sure that my children are frightened of me.   *George V*

There are no illegitimate children—only illegitimate parents.   *Leon R. Yankwich*

All happy families resemble one another; every unhappy family is unhappy in its own way.   *Leo Tolstoy*

The dark, uneasy world of family life—where the greatest can fail and the humblest succeed.

Randall Jarrell

As a general thing, when a woman wears the pants in a family, she has a good right to them.

Josh Billings

Of all my wife's relations I like myself the best.

Joe Cook

Mothers-in-law are ladies who have daughters. A mother-in-law may be considered as the beard on the matrimonial oyster.

Marcus Clark

There is nothing like staying at home for real comfort.

Jane Austen

After all, blood is thicker than water. But then so is soup.

Lennie Lower, 'Here's Luck'

When family relations are no longer harmonious, we have filial children and devoted parents.

R. D. Laing

The family is the American fascism.

Paul Goodman

The thing that impresses me most about North America is the way parents obey their children.

Edward, Duke of Windsor

Who of us is mature enough for offspring before the offspring themselves arrive? The value of marriage is not that adults produce children but that children produce adults.

Peter de Vries

Absence is one of the most useful ingredients of family life, and to do it rightly is an art like any other.

Freya Stark

No matter how many communes anybody invents, the family always creeps back.

Margaret Mead

There are fathers who do not love their children; there is no grandfather who does not adore his grandson.

Victor Hugo

The most important thing a father can do for his children is to love their mother.

Theodore Hesburgh

Today, while the titular head of the family may still be the father, everyone knows that he is little more than chairman, at most, of the entertainment committee.

Ashley Montagu

Fashion

A love of fashion makes the economy go round.

Liz Tilberis

A pious man is one who would be an atheist if the king were.

Jean de la Bruyére

Every generation laughs at the old fashions but religiously follows the new.

Henry David Thoreau

Nothing is so hideous as an obsolete fashion.   *Stendhal*

'The tradition of the new.' Yesterday's avant-garde-experiment is today's chic and tomorrow's cliché.   *Richard Hofstadter*

Art produces ugly things which frequently become beautiful with time. Fashion, on the other hand, produces beautiful things which always become ugly with time.

Jean Cocteau

Be not the first by whom the new are tried,
Nor yet the last to lay the old aside.   *Alexander Pope*

Fashion can be bought. Style one must possess.   *Edna Woolman Chase*

Fashion, which elevates the bad to the level of the good, subsequently turns its back on bad and good alike.   *Eric Bentley*

Even knowledge has to be in fashion and where it is not it is wise to affect ignorance.

Baltasar Gracián

The fashion wears out more apparel than the man.

Shakespeare, Much Ado About Nothing

Fashions, after all, are only induced epidemics.   *George Bernard Shaw*

When a man is once in fashion, all he does is right.   *Lord Chesterfield*

I have heard with admiring submission the experience of the lady who declared that the sense of being well-dressed gives a feeling of inward tranquility, which religion is powerless to bestow.   *Ralph Waldo Emerson*

Fashion condemns us to many follies; the greatest is to make oneself its slave.

Napoleon Bonaparte

Conformism is so hot on the heels of the mass-produced avant-garde that the 'ins' and the 'outs' change places with the speed of mach 3.   *Igor Stravinsky*

In the defiance of fashion is the beginning of character.   *Les A. Murray*

Fashions fade—style is eternal.   *Yves Saint Laurent*

And by my grave you'd pray to have me back
So I could see how well you look in black.   *Marco Carson*

A man of eighty has outlived probably three new schools of painting, two of architecture and poetry, and a hundred in dress.   *Joyce Carey*

Fate and Destiny

Certainty generally is illusion and repose is not the destiny of man.
Oliver Wendell Holmes, Jr

How many roads must a man walk down
Before you call him a man? *Bob Dylan*

Heaven is the place where the donkey finally catches up with his carrot: hell is the eternity while he waits for it. *Russell Green*

Continuous effort—not strength or intelligence—is the key to unlocking our potential. *Liane Cardes*

That that is is. *Shakespeare, 'Twelfth Night'*

Everything passes; everything wears out; everything breaks.(*Tout passe, tout lasse, tout casse.*) *French proverb*

Whatso'er we perpetrate
We do but row, we are steered by fate. *Samuel Butler*

Whatever limits us we call Fate. *Ralph Waldo Emerson*

Whatever the universal nature assigns to any man at any time is for the good of that man at that time. *Marcus Aurelius*

Certain signs precede certain events. *Cicero*

See how the Fates their gifts allot.
For A is happy—B is not.
Yet B is worthy, I dare say,
Of more prosperity than A. *W. S. Gilbert*

Destiny, n: a tyrant's authority for crime and a fool's excuse for failure.
Ambrose Bierce

Fate rules the affairs of mankind with no recognizable order. *Seneca*

He who does not desire or fear the uncertain day or capricious fate, is equal to the gods above and loftier than mortals. *Justus Lipsius*

The worst is not always certain but it's very likely. *French proverb*

It is a long road from conception to completion. *Molière*

Our ends are shaped by a casual and unknowing fate. *M. Barnard Eldershaw*

Fortune is fickle and soon asks back what he has given. *Latin proverb*

Destiny is what you are supposed to do in life. Fate is what kicks you in the ass to make you do it.   *Henry Miller*

That which God writes on thy forehead, thou wilt come to it.   *The Koran*

When its time has come, the prey goes to the hunter.   *Persian proverb*

Fear

Fear is the parent of cruelty.   *James A. Froude*

We must travel in the direction of our fear.   *John Berryman*

Once men are caught up in an event they cease to be afraid. Only the unknown frightens men.   *Antoine de St. Exupéry*

People wish to learn to swim and at the same time to keep one foot on the ground.
                                                                    Marcel Proust

Fear is not an unknown emotion to us.   *Neil Armstrong*

So let me assert my firm belief that the only thing we have to fear is fear itself— nameless, unreasoning, unjustified terror which paralyzes needed efforts to convert retreat into advance.   *Franklin D. Roosevelt*

Freedom from fear can never be separated from freedom from want.   *H. V. Evatt*

I will show you fear in a handful of dust.   *T. S. Eliot*

Fear of losing is what makes competitors so great. Show me a gracious loser and I'll show you a perennial loser.   *O. J. Simpson*

Nothing in life is to be feared. It is only to be understood.   *Marie Curie*

There's nothing I'm afraid of like scared people.   *Robert Frost*

Nothing is more despicable than respect based on fear.   *Albert Camus*

Just as courage imperils life, fear protects it.   *Leonardo da Vinci*

Fear comes from uncertainty. When we are absolutely certain, whether of our worth or worthlessness, we are almost impervious to fear. Thus a feeling of utter unworthiness can be a source of courage.   *Eric Hoffer*

Where no hope is left, is left no fear.   *John Milton*

The human race is a race of cowards; and I am not only marching in that procession but carrying a banner.   *Mark Twain*

Men hesitate less to injure a man who makes himself loved than to injure one who makes himself feared, for their love is held by a chain of obligation which, because of men's wickedness, is broken on every occasion for the sake of selfish profit; but their fear is secured by a dread of punishment.   *Niccolo Machiavell*

I, a stranger and afraid
In a world I never made.   *A. E. Housman*

Fear has a smell, as Love does.   *Margaret Atwood*

Fear can be headier than whisky, once man has acquired a taste for it.
                                                        Donald Downe.

The suspense is terrible. I hope it will last.   *Oscar Wilde*

A good scare is worth more to a man than good advice.   *Edgar Watson Howe*

How does one kill fear, I wonder? How do you shoot a spectre through the heart, slash off its spectral head, take it by the spectral throat?   *Joseph Conrad*

In grief we know the worst of what we feel,
But who can tell the end of what we fear?   *Hannah More*

The only way to get rid of my fears is to make films about them. *Alfred Hitchcock*

I would often be a coward, but for the shame of it.   *Ralph Connor*

Horror is a feeling that cannot last long; human nature is incapable of supporting it.
                                                        James de Mille

Food

At the end of every diet, the path curves back toward the trough.   *Mason Cooley*

Food is an important part of a balanced diet.   *Fran Lebowitz*

It's a very odd thing
As odd as can be
That whatever Miss T. eats
Turns into Miss T.   *Walter de la Mare*

Never eat more than you can lift.   *Miss Piggy*

There is no love sincerer than the love of food.   *George Bernard Shaw*

Kissing don't last: cookery do.   *George Meredith*

Hunger is not debatable.   *Harry Hopkins*

To eat well in England you should have breakfast three times a day.

W. Somerset Maugham

To get the best results, you must talk to your vegetables.   *Charles, Prince of Wales*

Toots Shore's restaurant is so crowded nobody goes there anymore.   *Yogi Berra*

It would kill a brown dog.
Senator R. C. Elstob, commenting on the food in the dining room of the Australian Parliament

Dinner, a time when . . . one should eat wisely but not too well, and talk well but not too wisely.   *W. Somerset Maugham*

There is no such thing as a little garlic.   *Anon.*

Even were a cook to cook a fly, he would keep the breast for himself.

Polish proverb

No man is lonely while eating spaghetti—it requires so much attention.

Christopher Morley

A hungry man is not a free man.   *Adlai Stevenson*

A great step toward independence is a good-humoured stomach.   *Seneca*

I feel a recipe is only a theme, which an intelligent cook can play each time with a variation.   *Madame Benoit*

All happiness depends on a leisurely breakfast.   *John Gunther*

Cheese—milk's leap toward immortality.   *Clifton Fadiman*

A gourmet is just a glutton with brains.   *Philip W. Haberman, Jr.*

Vegetarianism is harmless enough, though it is apt to fill a man with wind and self-righteousness.   *Sir Robert Hutchinson*

If you wish to grow thinner, diminish your dinner.   *H. S. Leigh*

To a man with an empty stomach, food is god.   *Gandhi*

Hunger is the best sauce.   *Proverb*

A man is in general better pleased when he has a good dinner upon his table, than when his wife talks Greek.   *Samuel Johnson*

If you ask the hungry man how much is two and two, he replies four loaves.

Hindu proverb

A good meal makes a man feel more charitable toward the whole world than any sermon. *Arthur Pendenys*

More die in the United States of too much food than of too little.   *J. K. Galbraith*

A good meal ought to begin with hunger. *French proverb*

It is a hard matter, my fellow citizens, to argue with the belly, since it has no ears. *Plutarch*

A smiling face is half the meal. *Latvian proverb*

There is no such thing as a pretty good omelette. *French proverb*

Fish, to taste right, must swim three times—in water, in butter and in wine. *Polish proverb*

Fools and Foolishness

A fool's head never whitens. *Old saying*

For ye suffer fools gladly, seeing ye yourselves are wise.   *Corinthians II, 11:19*

Many have been the wise speeches of fools, though not so many as the foolish speeches of wise men. *Thomas Fuller*

Men trip not on mountains, they stumble on stones. *Old saying*

There are bearded fools. *Old saying*

Every man is a damn fool for at least five minutes every day; wisdom consists in not exceeding the limit. *Elbert Hubbard*

Nothing is more like a wise man than a fool who holds his tongue. *St. Francis de Sales*

If fifty million people say a foolish thing, it is still a foolish thing.   *Anatole France*

There are two kinds of fools: one says, 'This is old, therefore it is good'; the other says, 'This is new, therefore it is better.' *Dean William R. Inge*

A fool must now and then be right by chance. *William Cowper*

Let us be thankful for the fools. But for them the rest of us could not succeed. *Mark Twain*

Here cometh April again, and as far as I can see the world hath more fools in it than ever. *Charles Lamb*

A busy fool is fitter to be shut up than a downright madman. *George, Lord Halifax*

With stupidity the gods themselves struggle in vain.   *Friedrich von Schiller*

There are some people that if they don't know, you can't tell 'em. *Louis Armstrong*

A fellow who is always declaring he's no fool usually has his suspicions.

Wilson Mizner

Stupidity is an elemental force for which no earthquake is a match.   *Karl Kraus*

Every inch that is not fool is rogue.   *John Dryden*

A little nonsense now and then is relished by the wisest men.   *Anon.*

He who lives without folly is not as wise as he thinks.   *La Rochefoucauld*

No new thing under the sun:
The virtuous who prefer the dark;
Fools knighted; the brave undone.   *Vincent Buckley*

None but a fool worries about things he cannot influence.   *Samuel Johnson*

Nature never makes any blunders; when she makes a fool she means it.

Josh Billings

It is said that a wise man who stands firm is a statesman, and a foolish man who stands firm is a catastrophe.   *Adlai Stevenson*

It is hard to free fools from the chains they revere.   *Voltaire*

Hain't we got all the fools in town on our side? And ain't that a big enough majority for any town?   *Mark Twain*

For God's sake give me the young man who has brains enough to make a fool of himself.   *Robert Louis Stevenson*

Who loves not women, wine and song,
Remains a fool his whole life long.   *Attributed to Martin Luther*

What is life but a series of inspired follies? The difficulty is to find them to do.
George Bernard Shaw

There is no chance for old fools.   *Cree Indian proverb*

Friends and Friendship

A hedge between keeps friendship green.   *German proverb*

A man, Sir, should keep his friendship in constant repair.   *Samuel Johnson*

Be a friend to thyself, and others will be so too.   *Thomas Fuller*

Friendship admits of differences of character, as love does that of sex.   *Anon.*

Friendship is love minus sex and plus reason. Love is friendship plus sex and minus reason.   *Mason Cooley*

It is one of the blessings of old friends that you can afford to be stupid with them.
                                                        Ralph Waldo Emerson

You shall judge of a man by his foes as well as by his friends.   *Joseph Conrad*

There are formalities between the closest of friends.   *Japanese proverb*

If you press me to say why I loved him, I can say no more than it was because he was he, and I was I.   *Montaigne*

Of my friends I am the only one I have left.   *Terence*

Anybody amuses me for once. A new acquaintance is like a new book. I prefer it, even if bad, to a classic.   *Benjamin Disraeli*

Friendship is tested in the thick years of success rather than in the thin years of struggle.
                                                        Barry Humphries

There are three faithful friends: an old wife, an old dog, and ready money.
                                                        Benjamin Franklin

He makes no friend who never made a foe.   *Alfred, Lord Tennyson*

Give me the avowed, the erect, and manly foe,
Bold I can meet, perhaps may turn the blow;
But of all plagues, good Heaven, thy wrath can send,
Save, save, oh save me from the candid friend!   *George Canning*

It is not enough to succeed, a friend must fail.   *La Rochefoucauld*

A friend in power is a friend lost.   *Henry Adams*

Do not rely completely on any other human being, however dear. We meet all life's greatest tests alone.   *Agnes Macphail*

You cannot be friends upon any other terms than upon the terms of equality.
                                                        Woodrow Wilson

How often we find ourselves turning our backs on our actual friends, that we may go and meet their ideal cousins.   *Henry David Thoreau*

We make our friends; we make our enemies; but God makes our next-door neighbour.
                                                        G. K. Chesterton

She is such a good friend that she would throw all her acquaintances into the water for the pleasure of fishing them out.   *Talleyrand of Mme. de Staël*

I was such an outcast I could have had a meeting of all my friends and supporters in a telephone booth.   *Sir Arthur Fadden*

A friend is one before whom I may think aloud.   *Ralph Waldo Emerson*

Without friends no one would choose to live, though he had all other goods.
          Aristotle

The more we love our friends, the less we flatter them; it is by excusing nothing that pure love shows itself.   *Molière*

It's important to our friends to believe that we are unreservedly frank with them, and important to friendship that we are not.   *Mignon McLaughlin*

In life it is difficult to say who do you the most mischief, enemies with the worst intentions, or friends with the best.   *Edward Bulwer-Lytton*

It is better to be deceived by one's friends than to deceive them.   *Goethe*

We need new friends. Some of us are cannibals who have eaten their old friends up; others must have ever-renewed audiences before whom to re-enact an ideal version of their lives.   *Logan Pearsall Smith*

Friendship needs a certain parallelism of life, a community of thought, a rivalry of aim.   *Henry Adams*

When my friends lack an eye, I look at them in profile.   *Joseph Joubert*

As in political, so in literary action, a man wins friends for himself mostly by the passion of his prejudices.   *Joseph Conrad*

God save me from my friends—I can protect myself from my enemies.
          Marshall de Villars

Never exaggerate your faults; your friends will attend to that.   *Robert C. Edwards*

Don't tell your friends their social faults; they will cure the fault and never forgive you.   *Logan Pearsall Smith*

Iron sharpeneth man; so a man sharpeneth the countenance of his friend.
          Proverbs 27:17

Love demands infinitely less than friendship.   *George Jean Nathan*

Friendship is almost always the union of a part of one mind with a part of another; people are friends in spots.   *George Santayana*

Who friendship with a knave hath made,
Is judged a partner in the trade.
John Ga?

Chance makes our parents, but choice makes our friends.
Jacques Delille

If we were all given by magic the power to read each other's thoughts, I suppose the first effect would be to dissolve all friendships.
Bertrand Russel?

There is a magnet in your heart that will attract true friends. That magnet is unselfishness, thinking of others first . . . when you learn to live for others, they will live for you.
Paramahansa Yoganandc

Never join with your friend when he abuses his horse or his wife unless the one is tc be sold, and the other to be buried.
Charles Caleb Coltor

The Future

People are afraid of the future, of the unknown. If a man faces up to it, and takes the dare of the future, he can have some control over his destiny. That's an exciting idea to me, better than waiting with everybody else to see what's going to happen.
John H. Glenn, Jr.

Tomorrow is the most important thing in life. Comes in to us at midnight very clean. It's perfect when it arrives and it puts itself in our hands and hopes we've learnt something from yesterday.
John Wayne

If some of us were granted a glimpse of the future, most of us would remain asleep indefinitely.
Lennie Lower, 'Here's Luck?

Nothing in the world can one imagine beforehand, not the least thing. Everything is made up of so many unique particulars that cannot be foreseen. *Rainer Maria Rilke*

You can never plan the future by the past.
Edmund Burke

One must care about a world one will not see.
Bertrand Russell

If you can look into the seeds of time and say, which grain will grow, and which will not, speak then to me.
Shakespeare, 'Macbeth'

The future is something which every one reaches at the rate of sixty miles an hour, whatever he does, whoever he is.
C. S. Lewis

My interest is in the future because I am going to spend the rest of my life there.
Charles F. Kettering

Tomorrow is a satire on today,
And shows its weakness.
Edward Young

The future comes one day at a time.
Dean Acheson

Never let the future disturb you. You will meet it, if you have to, with the same weapons of reason which today arm you against the present.   *Marcus Aurelius*

What we look for does not come to pass.
God finds a way for what none foresaw.   *Euripides*

With high hope for the future, no prediction is ventured.   *Abraham Lincoln*

We can pay our debt to the past by putting the future in debt to ourselves.
John Buchan

The future is not a gift—it is an achievement.   *Harry Lauder*

The world is full of people whose notion of a satisfactory future is, in fact, a return to the idealized past.   *Robertson Davies*

That which is escaped now is pain to come.   *Proverb*

Light tomorrow with today!   *Elizabeth Barrett Browning*

If tomorrow were never to come, it would not be worth living today.
Dagobert Runes

The afternoon knows what the morning never suspected.   *Swedish proverb*

The future is purchased by the present.   *Samuel Johnson*

I never think of the future. It comes soon enough.   *Albert Einstein*

Life is an irreversible process and for that reason its future can never be a repetition of the past.   *Walter Lippman*

I believe the future is only the past again, entered through another gate.
Arthur Wing Pinero

The world will be saved by one or two people.   *André Gide*

Genius

The difference between genius and stupidity is that genius has its limits.   *Anon.*

The genius of Einstein leads to Hiroshima.   *Pablo Picasso*

Genius, in truth, means little more than the faculty of perceiving in an unhabitual way.
William James

Genius as such can neither be explained nor treated away; only, at times, its delay and inhibition and its perversion to destructive or self-destructive ends.   *Erik Erikson*

To believe your own thought, to believe that what is true for you in your private heart is true for all men—that is genius. *Ralph Waldo Emerson*

Doing easily what others find is difficult is talent; doing what is impossible for talent is genius. *Henri Frédéric Amiel*

It takes immense genius to represent, simply and sincerely, what we see in front of us. *Edmond Duranty*

There is no moral virtue in being endowed with genius rather than talent: it is a gift of the gods, or the luck of the genes. *Dorothy Green*

Every man of genius is considerably helped by being dead. *Robert S. Lund*

In the republic of mediocrity, genius is dangerous. *Robert G. Ingersoll*

We define genius as the capacity for productive reaction against one's training. *Bernard Berenson*

Before I was a genius I was a drudge. *Ignace Jan Paderewski*

In every work of genius we recognize our own rejected thoughts; they come back to us with a certain alienated majesty. *Ralph Waldo Emerson*

Genius develops in quiet places, character out in the full current of human life. *Goethe*

Men of genius are the worst possible models for men of talent. *Murray D. Edwards*

The public is wonderfully tolerant. It forgives everything except genius. *Oscar Wilde*

When a true genius appears in the world you may know him by this sign, that the dunces are all in confederacy against him. *Jonathan Swift*

Talent is that which is in a man's power; genius is that in whose power a man is. *James Russell Lowell*

There is a thin line between genius and insanity. I have erased this line. *Oscar Levant*

Improvement makes straight roads; but the crooked roads without improvement are roads of genius. *William Blake*

Geniuses are the luckiest of mortals because what they must do is the same as what they most want to do. *W. H. Auden*

Everyone is a genius at least once a year; a real genius has his original ideas closer together. *G. C. Lichtenberg*

The true genius is a mind of large general powers, accidentally determined to some particular direction.   *Samuel Johnson*

The mark of genius is an incessant activity of mind. Genius is a spiritual greed.
                                                                    V. S. Pritchett

Genius is an African who dreams up snow.   *Vladimir Nabokov*

Sometimes men come by the name of genius in the same way that certain insects come by the name of centipede—not because they have a hundred feet, but because most people can't count above fourteen.   *G. C. Lichtenberg*

Too often we forget that genius . . . depends upon the data within its reach, that Archimedes could not have devised Edison's inventions.   *Ernest Dimnet*

Goals and Ambition

The significance of a man is not in what he attains but rather in what he longs to attain.   *Kahlil Gibran*

Once you say you're going to settle for second, that's what happens to you in life, I find.   *John F. Kennedy*

A successful individual typically sets his next goal somewhat but not too much above his last achievement. In this way he steadily raises his level of aspiration.
                                                                    Kurt Lewin

The most absurd and reckless aspirations have sometimes led to extraordinary success.
                                                                    Vauvenargues

All rising to great places is by a winding stair.   *Francis Bacon*

It's only when you abandon your ambitions that they become possible.
                                                                    Thomas Keneally

Every ceiling, when reached, becomes a floor, upon which one walks as a matter of course and prescriptive right.   *Aldous Huxley*

We can always redeem the man who aspires and strives.   *Goethe*

The world stands aside to let anyone pass who knows where he is going.
                                                                    David Starr Jordan

I have learned to have very modest goals for society and myself, things like clean air, green grass, children with bright eyes, not being pushed around, useful work that suits one's abilities, plain tasty food, and the occasional satisfying nookie.
                                                                    Paul Goodman

If you would hit the mark, you must aim a little above it:
Every arrow that flies feels the attraction of earth.   *Henry Wadsworth Longfellow*

Ah, but a man's reach should exceed his grasp, or what's a heaven for?
Robert Browning

Before we set our hearts too much upon anything, let us examine how happy they are,
who already possess it.   *La Rochefoucauld*

It is not given us very often to have what we want at the height of desire.
Frank Dalby Davison

Ours is a world where people don't know what they want and are willing to go through
hell to get it.   *Don Marquis*

Accept the place the divine providence has found for you, the society of your
contemporaries, the connection of events.   *Ralph Waldo Emerson*

Those who aim at great deeds must also suffer greatly.   *Plutarch*

It is a mistake to look too far ahead. Only one link in the chain of destiny can be
handled at a time.   *Winston Churchill*

Do not wish to be anything but what you are, and try to be that perfectly.
St. Francis de Sales

This one thing I do, forgetting those things which are behind, and reaching forth unto
those things which are before, I press toward the mark!   *Philippians 3:13*

Winning isn't everything, but wanting to win is.   *Vince Lombardi*

It is no longer clear which way is up even if one wants to rise.   *David Riesman*

Ambition is pitiless. Any merit that it cannot use it finds despicable.
Joseph Joubert

Every man is said to have his peculiar ambition.   *Abraham Lincoln*

Well is it known that ambition can creep as well as soar.   *Edmund Burke*

Make no little plans; they have no magic to stir men's blood . . . Make big plans, aim
high in hope and work.   *Daniel H. Burnham*

God

How to make God laugh.
Tell him your future plans.   *Woody Allen*

God enters by a private door into every individual.   *Ralph Waldo Emerson*

God gives the milk but not the pail.   *English proverb*

God Himself is not secure, having given man dominion over His work.
Helen Keller

God is a circle whose centre is everywhere and circumference nowhere.
Voltaire (quoting Timaeus of Locris)

God is not dead but alive and well and working on a much less ambitious project.
Graffiti

If the God who is said to be love exists in the imagination of men it is because they
have created him.   *Germaine Greer*

God seems to have the receiver off the hook.   *Arthur Koestler*

God uses lust to impel men to marry, ambition to office, avarice to earning, and fear
to faith. God led me like an old blind goat.   *Martin Luther*

God will provide—if only God would provide until he provides.   *Yiddish proverb*

God, when he makes the prophet, does not unmake the man.   *John Locke*

He maketh his sun to rise on the evil and on the good, and sendeth rain on the just
and on the unjust.   *Jesus Christ*

I wouldn't put it past God to arrange a virgin birth if he wanted to, but I very much
doubt if he would because it seems to be contrary to the way in which he deals with
persons and brings his wonders out of natural personal relationships.
Right Rev. David Jenkins

If Jesus was Jewish, how come he has a Mexican name?   *Anon.*

In the faces of men and women I see God and in my own face in the glass, I find
letters from God dropt in the street, and every one is signed by God's name, and I
leave them where they are, for I know that wheresoever I go others will punctually
come for ever and ever.   *Walt Whitman*

The glory of God is in man fully alive.   *St. Irenaeus*

When God is no longer cruel many questions will be answered.
Patrick White, 'The Vivisector'

The worst that you can say about him (God) is that basically he's an underachiever.
Woody Allen

Though the mills of God grind slowly, yet they grind exceeding small; Though with
patience He stands waiting, with exactness grinds he all.   *Friedrich von Logau*

Try thyself first, and after call in God. For to the worker God himself lends aid.
Euripides

By night an atheist half-believes in God. *Edward Young*

Father expected a good deal of God. He didn't actually accuse God of inefficiency, but when he prayed his tone was loud and angry, like that of a dissatisfied guest in a carelessly managed hotel. *Clarence Day*

Lord, who art always the same, give that I know myself, give that I know Thee.
St. Augustine

We have no choice but to be guilty
God is unthinkable if we are innocent. *Archibald MacLeish*

Man appoints, and God disappoints. *Cervantes*

I am afraid I shall not find Him, but I shall still look for Him. If He exists, He may be appreciative of my efforts. *Jules Renard*

God is not a cosmic bellboy for whom we can press a button to get things done.
Harry Emerson Fosdick

God is usually on the side of big squadrons and against little ones.
Roger de Bussy-Rabutin

The more of himself man attributes to God, the less he has left in himself.
Karl Marx

God tempers the wind to the shorn lamb. *Laurence Sterne*

God is a comedian whose audience is afraid to laugh. *H. L. Mencken*

Every man thinks God is on his side. The rich and powerful know he is.
Jean Anouilh

I could prove God statistically. *George Gallup*

Man is a dog's ideal of what God should be. *André Malraux*

Christ—an anarchist who succeeded. *Axel Munthe*

An honest God is the noblest work of man. *Robert G. Ingersoll*

It is left only to God and to the angels to be lookers on. *Francis Bacon*

God is really another artist. He invented the giraffe, the elephant and the cat. He has no real style. He just goes on trying other things. *Pablo Picasso*

The nearer the church, the further from God. *Bishop Lancelot Andrewes*

God'll send the bill to you. *James Russell Lowell*

I believe there is no god but Allah alone and Muhammed is his prophet.

Muslim Creed

The world is more exacting than God himself.   *Yiddish proverb*

Give God time.   *The Koran*

God will be present, whether asked or not.   *Latin proverb*

If God did not exist, it would be necessary to invent him.   *Voltaire*

We trust, sir, that God is on our side. It is more important to know that we are on God's side.   *Abraham Lincoln*

The abdomen is the reason why man does not easily take himself for a god.

Friedrich Nietzsche

Beware of the man whose God is in the skies.   *George Bernard Shaw*

I can't believe that God plays dice with the universe.   *Albert Einstein*

One on God's side is a majority.   *Wendell Phillips*

If triangles had a God, he would have three sides.   *Montesquieu*

God does not pay weekly, but he pays at the end.   *Dutch proverb*

The finding of God is the coming to one's own self.   *Meher Baba*

God moves in a mysterious way
His wonders to perform;
He plants his footsteps in the sea
And rides upon the storm.   *William Cowper*

Man proposes; God disposes.   *Thomas à Kempis*

God doth not need
Either man's work or his own gifts; who best
Bear His mild yoke, they serve Him best; His state
Is kingly; thousands at His bidding speed
And post o'er land and ocean without rest—
They also serve who only stand and wait.   *John Milton*

If God made us in his image, we have certainly returned the compliment.   *Voltaire*

God does not die on the day when we cease to believe in a personal deity, but we die on the day when our lives cease to be illuminated by the steady radiance, renewed daily, of a wonder, the source of which is beyond all reason.   *Dag Hammarskjöld*

Goodness and Giving

Bad is never good until worse happens.   *Danish proverb*

Good and evil lie close together. Seek no artistic unity in character.   *Lord Acton*

Gifts are hooks.   *Martial*

Good things, when short, are twice as good.   *Baltasar Gracián*

If I can in any way contribute to the Diversion or Improvement of the Country in which I live, I shall leave it, when I am summoned out of it, with the secret Satisfaction of thinking that I have not lived in vain.   *Joseph Addison*

In nature, nothing can be given, all things are sold.   *Ralph Waldo Emerson*

Teach us to give and not to count the cost.   *Ignatius Loyola*

The meaning of good and bad, of better and worse, is simply helping or hurting.
                                                                 Ralph Waldo Emerson

Unto whomsoever much is given, of him shall much be required.   *Luke 12: 48*

If a man wants to be of the greatest possible value to his fellow-creatures, let him begin the long, solitary task of perfecting himself.   *Robertson Davies*

We'd all like a reputation for generosity and we'd all like to buy it cheap.
                                                                 Mignon McLaughlin

He who would do good to another, must do it in minute particulars.   *Anon.*

General good is the plea of the scoundrel, hypocite, flatterer.   *William Blake*

The word 'good' has many meanings. For example, if a man were to shoot his grandmother at a range of five hundred yards, I should call him a good shot, but not *necessarily* a good man.   *G. K. Chesterton*

I expect to pass though this world but once. Any good therefore that I can do, or any kindness that I can show to my fellow-creature, let me do it now. Let me not defer or neglect it, for I shall not pass this way again.   *Attributed to Stephen Grellet*

Pity costs nothin' and ain't worth nothin'.   *Josh Billings*

That best portion of a good man's life,
His little, nameless, unremembered acts
Of kindness and of love.

                                                                 William Wordsworth

There is no man so good, who, were he to submit all his thoughts and actions to the laws, would not deserve hanging ten times in his life.   *Montaigne*

Should not the giver be thankful that the receiver received? Is not giving a need? Is not receiving, mercy?   *Friedrich Nietzsche*

When thou doest alms, do not let thy left hand know what thy right hand doeth.
Matthew 6:3

No good deed ever goes unpunished.   *Brooks Thomas*

Be good, sweet maid, and let who can be clever.   *Charles Kingsley*

Charity begins at home, and seems nowadays to end there.   *Marcus Clarke*

Charity is a hateful thing because it is created by poverty.   *Frank Hardy*

Good things are not done in a hurry.   *German proverb*

Be charitable and indulgent to every one but thyself.   *Joseph Joubert*

We are all here on earth to help others; what on earth the others are here for I don't know.   *W. H. Auden*

Why is it that when people have no capacity for private usefulness they should be so anxious to serve the public?   *Sara Jeannette Duncan*

I have found men more kind than I expected, and less just.   *Samuel Johnson*

Is not a patron one who looks with unconcern on a man struggling for life in the water, and, when he has reached ground, encumbers him with help?
Samuel Johnson

There is so much good in the worst of us and so much bad in the best of us, that it's rather hard to tell which of us ought to reform the rest of us.
Sign in Springdale, Connecticut

Good men need no recommendation and bad men it wouldn't help.   *Jewish proverb*

Real unselfishness consists in sharing the interests of others.   *George Santayana*

I hate the giving of the hand unless the whole man accompanies it.
Ralph Waldo Emerson

If you're naturally kind, you attract a lot of people you don't like.   *William Feather*

The good should be grateful to the bad—for providing the world with a basis for comparison.   *Sven Halla*

All strangers and beggars are from Zeus, and a gift, though small, is precious.
Homer

Behold! I do not give lectures on a little charity.
When I give, I give myself.   *Walt Whitman*

If a friend is in trouble, don't annoy him by asking if there is anything you can do. Think up something appropriate and do it. *Edgar Watson Howe*

The greatest pleasure I know is to do a good action by stealth, and to have it found out by accident. *Charles Lamb*

As Charles Lamb says, there is nothing so nice as doing good by stealth and being found out by accident, so I now say it is even nicer to make heroic decisions and to be prevented by 'circumstances beyond your control' from ever trying to execute them. *William James*

Giving is the highest expression of potency. *Erich Fromm*

If I knew . . . that a man was coming to my house with the conscious design of doing me good, I should run for my life. *Henry David Thoreau*

If I've learned anything in my seventy years it's that nothing's as good or as bad as it appears. *Bushrod H. Campbell*

The Devil himself is good when he is pleased. *Thomas Fuller*

Wise men appreciate all men, for they see the good in each and know how hard it is to make anything good. *Baltasar Gracián*

The only gift is a portion of thyself. *Ralph Waldo Emerson*

Take egotism out, and you would castrate the benefactor. *Ralph Waldo Emerson*

It is one of the beautiful compensations of this life that no one can sincerely try to help another without helping himself. *Charles Dudley Warner*

No man deserves to be praised for his goodness unless he has the strength of character to be wicked. All other goodness is generally nothing but indolence or impotence of will. *La Rochefoucauld*

We know the good, we apprehend it clearly. But we can't bring it to achievement. *Euripides*

Generosity is the vanity of giving. *La Rochefoucauld*

My only policy is to profess evil and do good. *George Bernard Shaw*

For an inheritance to be really great, the hand of the defunct must not be seen. *René Cha-*

Fearful is the seductive power of goodness. *Bertolt Brecht*

There are bad people who would be less dangerous if they were quite devoid of goodness. *La Rochefoucauld*

The age of strong belief is over, the good is no longer always very good.

D. L. Coles

When you cease to make a contribution you begin to die.   *Eleanor Roosevelt*

Gossip and Gossips

And all who told it added something new,
And all who heard it made enlargements too.   *Alexander Pope*

Biography is higher gossip.   *Robert Winder*

Even doubtful accusations leave a stain behind them.   *Thomas Fuller*

Rumour prefers a scandal when in doubt.   *James McAuley*

No one gossips about other people's secret virtues.   *Bertrand Russell*

Gossip is when you hear something you like about someone you don't. *Earl Wilson*

Confession, when not launched as amusing details of gossip, can become embarrassing.
Patrick White, 'The Eye of the Storm'

Another good thing about gossip is that it is within everybody's reach,
And it is much more interesting than any other form of speech.   *Ogden Nash*

Hating anything in the way of ill-natured gossip ourselves, we are always grateful to
those who do it for us and do it well.   *Saki*

No gossip ever dies away entirely, if many people voice it: it, too, is a kind of divinity.
Hesiod

Gossip is vice enjoyed vicariously—the sweet, subtle satisfaction without the risk.
Kin Hubbard

The best-loved man or maid in the town would perish with anguish could they hear
all that their friends say in the course of a day.   *John Hay*

If you can't say something good about someone, sit right here by me.
Attributed to Alice Roosevelt Longworth

What some invent, the rest enlarge.   *Jonathan Swift*

What people say behind your back is your standing in the community.
Edgar Watson Howe

Whoever gossips to you will gossip of you.   *Spanish proverb*

A little public scandal is good once in a while—takes the tension out of the news.
Beryl Pfizer

Gossip is the art of saying nothing in a way that leaves practically nothing unsaid.
Walter Winchell

Government and Rule

When, in the course of human events, it becomes necessary for one people to dissolve the political bands which have connected them with another, and to assume among the powers of the earth the separate and equal station to which the laws of nature and of nature's God entitle them, a decent respect to the opinions of mankind requires that they should declare the causes which impel them to the separation. We hold these truths to be self-evident; that all men are created equal; that they are endowed by their creator with certain unalienable rights; that among these are life, liberty, and the pursuit of happiness; that to secure these rights, governments are instituted among men, deriving their just powers from the consent of the governed; that whenever any form of government becomes destructive to these ends, it is the right of the people to alter or to abolish it, and to institute new government, laying its foundation on such principles, and organizing its powers in such form, as to them shall seem most likely to effect their safety and happiness. *Thomas Jefferson*
First part of the Declaration of Independence [July 4, 1776]

A difficulty for every solution. *(Viscount) Herbert Samuel*

A good government remains the greatest of human blessings, and no nation has ever enjoyed it. *Dean William R. Inge*

A government which robs Peter to pay Paul can always depend on the support of Paul.
George Bernard Shaw

Bureaucrats are the only people in the world who can say absolutely nothing and mean it. *Hugh Sidey*

Egypt: Where the Israelites would still be if Moses had been a bureaucrat.
Laurence J. Peter

At certain times of grave national stress, when that rag-bag called the British Constitution is in grave danger of coming unstuck, thank heaven for the big safety-pin at the top that keeps it together. *Anonymous comment on the British monarchy*

Never trust governments absolutely, and always do what you can to prevent them from doing too much harm. *John Passmore*

The road to democracy is not a freeway. It is a toll road on which we pay by accepting and carrying out our civic responsibilities. *Lucius D. Clay*

I believe the greatest asset a Head of State can have is the ability to get a good night's sleep. *Harold Wilson*

In the Conservative view, you have 10 premiers and the Prime Minister as a kind of head waiter to take their orders. *Pierre Elliott Trudeau*

It is the duty of Her Majesty's Government neither to flap nor to falter. *Harold Macmillan*

It is useless for the sheep to pass resolutions in favour of vegetarianism while the wolf remains of a different opinion. *Dean William R. Inge*

It would be desirable if every government, when it comes to power, should have its old speeches burnt. *Philip Snowden*

Man's capacity for evil makes democracy necessary and man's capacity for good makes democracy possible. *Reinhold Niebuhr*

No man is good enough to govern another man without that other's consent. *Abraham Lincoln*

One can present people with opportunities. One cannot make them equal to them. *Rosamond Lehmann*

Parliament is the longest running farce in the West End. *Cyril Smith*

States, like men, have their growth, their manhood, their decrepitude, their decay. *Walter Savage Landor*

The enemies of Freedom do not argue; they shout and they shoot. *Dean William R. Inge*

The entire civil service is like a fortress, made of papers, forms and red tape. *Alexander Ostrovsky*

The king reigns, but does not govern. *Jan Zamoyski*

The point to remember is that what the Government gives it must first take away. *John S. Caldwell*

There's no place for the state in the bedrooms of the nation. *Pierre Elliott Trudeau*

Tyranny is always better organized than freedom. *Charles Péguy*

We have a tried and tested system of government that, in being so flexible, exists as a great ghost that no one has dared to conjure into flesh. *J. M. Parkin*

When the freedom they wished for most was the freedom from responsibility, then Athens ceased to be free and never was free again. *Edith Hamilton*

Wherever you have an efficient government you have a dictatorship. *Harry S. Truman*

While the people retain their virtue and vigilance, no administration, by any extreme of wickedness or folly, can very seriously injure the government in the short space of four years.
Abraham Lincoln

Any people anywhere, being inclined and having the power, have the right to rise up and shake off the existing government and form a new one. This is a most valuable and sacred right—a right which we hope and believe is to liberate the world.
Abraham Lincoln

No man should be in public office who can't make more money in private life.
Thomas E. Dewey

Government is the only institution that can take a valuable commodity like paper, and make it worthless by applying ink.
Ludwig van Moses

The poorest man may in his cottage bid defiance to all the force of the crown. It may be frail—its roof may shake—the wind may blow through it—the storm may enter—the rain may enter—but the King of England cannot enter!—all his force dares not cross the threshhold of the ruined tenement!
William Pitt the Elder

The art of government is the organization of idolatry.
George Bernard Shaw

Every government is run by liars and nothing they say should be believed.
I. F. Stone

The more the world is specialized the more it will be run by generalists.
Marcel Masse

We are under a Constitution, but the Constitution is what the judges say it is.
Charles Evans Hughes

A friend of mine says that every man who takes office in Washington either grows or swells, and when I give a man an office, I watch him carefully to see whether he is swelling or growing.
Woodrow Wilson

The majority is the best way, because it is visible, and has strength to make itself obeyed. Yet it is the opinion of the least able.
Blaise Pascal

The best government is a benevolent tyranny tempered by an occasional assassination.
Voltaire

No man ever saw a government. I live in the midst of the Government of the United States, but I never saw the Government of the United States.
Woodrow Wilson

The State, that cawing rookery of committees and subcommittees.
V. S. Pritchett

The weak have one weapon—the errors of those who think they are strong.
Georges Bidault

Government in the last analysis is organised opinion. Where there is little or no public opinion, there is likely to be bad government, which sooner or later becomes autocratic government.   *William Lyon Mackenzie King*

Under democracy, one party always devotes its chief energies to trying to prove that the other party is unfit to rule—and both commonly succeed, and are right.
H. L. Mencken

Inflation is one form of taxation that can be imposed without legislation.
Milton Friedman

Doing what's right isn't the problem. It's knowing what's right.   *Lyndon B. Johnson*

It is the aim of good government to stimulate production, of bad government to encourage consumption.   *Jean Baptiste Say*

Bureaucracy, the rule of no one, has become the modern form of despotism.
Mary McCarthy

Be thankful we're not getting all the government we're paying for.   *Will Rogers*

A government that is big enough to give you all you want is big enough to take it all away.   *Barry Goldwater*

Government is the political representative of a natural equilibrium, of custom, of inertia; it is by no means a representative of reason.   *George Santayana*

The best reason why monarchy is a strong government is that it is an intelligible government: the mass of mankind understand it, and they hardly anywhere in the world understand any other.   *Walter Bagehot*

The world is ruled only by consideration of advantages.   *Friedrich von Schiller*

Must a government of necessity be too strong for the liberties of its people or too weak to maintain its own existence?   *Abraham Lincoln*

As I get older . . . I become more convinced that good government is not a substitute for self-government.   *Dwight Morrow*

Every man wishes to pursue his occupation and to enjoy the fruits of his labours and the produce of his property in peace and safety, and with the least possible expense. When these things are accomplished, all the objects for which government ought to be established are answered.   *Thomas Jefferson*

A monarchy is a merchantman, which sails well, but will sometimes strike on a rock and go to the bottom, whilst a republic is a raft which will never sink, but then your feet are always in water.   *Fisher Ames*

The state, it cannot too often be repeated, does nothing, and can give nothing, which it does not take from somebody.   *Henry George*

Government, even in its best state, is but a necessary evil; in its worst state, an intolerable one.   *Thomas Paine*

Government is not reason, it is not eloquence—it is force.   *George Washington*

Bureaucracy is a giant mechanism operated by pygmies.   *Honoré de Balzac*

Whenever by an unfortunate occurrence of circumstances an opposition is compelled to support the government, the support should be given with a kick and not a caress and should be withdrawn at the first available moment.   *Randolph Churchill*

To govern is to choose.   *Pierre Mendès-France*

For a country to have a great writer is to have another government.
Aleksandr Solzhenitsyn

Republics are brought to their ends by luxury; monarchies by poverty.   *Montesquieu*

The foremost art of kings is the power to endure hatred.   *Seneca*

Governments don't like to be caught in the act of changing their minds.
Bill Hayden

In the long run every government is the exact symbol of its people, with their wisdom and unwisdom.   *Thomas Carlyle*

The art of governing consists in not letting men grow old in their jobs.
Napoleon Bonaparte

The worst thing in this world, next to anarchy, is government.   *Henry Ward Beecher*

Anarchy is against the law.   *Graffiti*

The legitimate object of government is to do for a community of people, whatever they need to have done, but cannot do at all, or cannot so well do for themselves, in their separate and individual capacities.   *Abraham Lincoln*

That government is best which governs the least, because its people discipline themselves.   *Thomas Jefferson*

How can you govern a country with two hundred and forty-six varieties of cheese?
Charles de Gaulle

The proper end of government is to order things rather than men.   *Brian Fitzpatrick*

The illegal we do immediately. The unconstitutional takes a little longer.
Henry Kissinger

The average man that I encounter all over the country regards government as a sort of great milk cow, with its head in the clouds eating air, and growing a full teat for everybody on earth.   *Clarence C. Manion*

To make certain that crime does not pay, the government should take it over and try to run it. *G. Norman Collie*

The art of putting the right men in the right places is first in the science of government; but that of finding places for the discontented is the most difficult. *Talleyrand*

The Governor-General should be put in his proper place—as a ceremonial figure on leave from *The Merry Widow*. *Bill Hayden*

It is common sense to take a method and try it. If it fails, admit it frankly and try another, but above all, try something. *Franklin D. Roosevelt*

The government is becoming the family of last resort. *Jerry Brown*

All this will not be finished in the first one hundred days. Nor will it be finished in the first one thousand days, nor in the life of this administration, nor even perhaps in our lifetime on this planet. *John F. Kennedy*

Governments last as long as the undertaxed can defend themselves against the overtaxed. *Bernard Berenson*

The impersonal hand of government can never replace the helping hand of a neighbour. *Hubert Humphrey*

Too bad that all the people who know how to run the country are busy driving taxicabs and cutting hair. *George Burns*

When we got into office, the thing that surprised me most was to find that things were just as bad as we'd been saying they were. *John F. Kennedy*

No government can be long secure without a formidable opposition. *Benjamin Disraeli*

The dogmas of the quiet past are inadequate to the stormy present. The occasion is piled high with difficulty and we must rise with the occasion. As our case is new, so we must think anew and act anew. We must disenthrall ourselves, and then we shall save our country. *Abraham Lincoln*

When I am abroad, I always make it a rule never to criticize or attack the government of my own country. I make up for lost time when I come home. *Winston Churchill*

The people's right to change what does not work is one of the greatest principles of our system of government. *Richard Nixon*

No intelligence system can predict what a government will do if it doesn't know itself. *J. K. Galbraith*

The U.S. Senate—an old scow which doesn't move very fast, but never sinks. *Everett Dirksen*

The supply of government exceeds the demand. *Lewis H. Lapham*

Tyranny is yielding to the lust of governing. *Lord Moulton*

Greatness

A great man stands on God. A small man stands on a great man.

Ralph Waldo Emerson

The heights by men reached and kept
Were not attained by sudden flight,
But they, while their companions slept,
Were toiling upward in the night.   *Henry Wadsworth Longfellow*

Calmness is always Godlike.   *Ralph Waldo Emerson*

Every generation revolts against its fathers and makes friends with its grandfathers.

Lewis Mumford

He (Winston Churchill) mobilized the English language and sent it into battle to steady
his fellow countrymen . . .   *Anon.*

We are all worms, but I do believe that I am a glow-worm.   *Winston Churchill*

To do great things is difficult, but to command great things is more difficult.

Friedrich Nietzsche

Greatness is a zigzag streak of lightning in the brain.   *Herbert Asquith*

If you want to know your true opinion of someone, watch the effect produced in you
by the first sight of a letter from him.   *Arthur Schopenhauer*

Few great men could pass Personnel.   *Paul Goodman*

Clever men are impressed in their differences from their fellows. Wise men are
conscious of their resemblance to them.   *R. H. Tawney*

His eminence was due to the flatness of the surrounding landscape.

John Stuart Mill

One can build the Empire State Building, discipline the Prussian army, make a state
hierarchy mightier than God, yet fail to overcome the unaccountable superiority of
certain human beings.   *Aleksandr Solzhenitsyn*

Each honest calling, each walk of life, has its own elite, its own aristocracy based on
excellence of performance.   *James Bryant Conant*

Only great men may have great faults.   *French proverb*

The world knows nothing of its greatest men.   *Henry Taylor*

Every age needs men who will redeem the time by living with a vision of things that
are to be.   *Adlai Stevenson*

Not a day passes over the earth, but men and women of no note do great deeds, speak great words and suffer noble sorrows.   *Charles Reade*

Some are born great, some achieve greatness, and some hire public relations officers.
                                                                    Daniel J. Boorstin

Do continue to believe that with your feeling and your work you are taking part in the greatest; the more strongly you cultivate in yourself this belief, the more will reality and the world go forth from it.   *Rainer Maria Rilke*

It is not the strength, but the duration, of great sentiments that makes great men.
                                                                    Friedrich Nietzsche

Greatness is a road leading towards the unknown.   *Charles de Gaulle*

A great ship asks deep water.   *George Herbert*

Great men too often have greater faults than little men can find room for.
                                                                    Walter Savage Landor

The highest and most lofty trees have the most reason to dread the thunder.
                                                                    Charles Rollin

Great and good are seldom the same man.   *Thomas Fuller*

Born of the sun they travelled a short while towards the sun
And left the vivid air signed with their honour.   *Stephen Spender*

If I am a great man, then a good many of the great men of history are frauds.
                                                                    Bonar Law

You cannot fly like an eagle with the wings of a wren.   *William Henry Hudson*

Great men hallow a whole people, and lift up all who live in their time.
                                                                    Sydney Smith

The greatest truths are the simplest, and so are the greatest men.
                                                                    J. C. and A . W. Hare

The dullard's envy of brilliant men is always assuaged by the suspicion that they will come to a bad end.   *Max Beerbohm*

The perfection preached in the Gospels never yet built up an Empire. Every man of action has a strong dose of optimism, pride, hardness and cunning. But all these things will be forgiven him, indeed they will be regarded as high qualities, if he can make of them the means to achieve great ends.   *Charles de Gaulle*

The banalities of a great man pass for wit.   *Alexander Chase*

When you're as great as I am, it's hard to be humble.   *Muhammad Ali*

No sadder proof can be given by a man of his own littleness, than disbelief in great men. *Thomas Carlyle*

A tomb now suffices him for whom the whole world was not sufficient.
Anonymous epitaph for Alexander the Great

If my theory of relativity is proven successful, Germany will claim me as a German, and France will declare that I am a citizen of the world. Should my theory prove untrue, France will say that I am a German, and Germany will declare that I am a Jew. *Albert Einstein*

Most of the trouble in the world is caused by people wanting to be important.
T. S. Eliot

What makes a nation great is not primarily its great men, but the stature of its innumerable mediocre ones. *José Ortega y Gasset*

The mind reaches great heights only by spurts. *Vauvenargues*

The biggest dog has been a pup. *Joaquin Miller*

There's a pinch of the madman in every great man. *French proverb*

It is unavoidable that if we learn more about a great man's life, we shall also hear of occasions on which he has done no better than we, and has in fact come nearer to us as a human being. *Sigmund Freud*

None think the great unhappy, but the great. *Edward Young*

Happiness

Back of tranquility lies always captured unhappiness. *David Grazin*

Eden is that old-fashioned House
We dwell in every day
Without suspecting our abode
Until we drive away. *Emily Dickinson*

Happiness is a mystery like religion, and it should never be rationalized.
G. K. Chesterton

He that is of a merry heart hath a continual feast. *Proverbs 15:15*

Man is preceded by forest followed by desert. *French graffiti*

Man needs, for his happiness, not only the enjoyment of this or that, but hope and enterprise and change. *Bertrand Russell*

Servitude debases men to the point where they end up liking it. *Vauvenargues*

The greatest happiness of the greatest number is the foundation of morals and legislation. *Jeremy Bentham*

When one door of happiness closes, another opens; but often we look so long at the closed door that we do not see the one which has been opened for us. *Helen Keller*

We are never so happy nor so unhappy as we imagine. *La Rochefoucauld*

We have no more right to consume happiness without producing it than to consume wealth without producing it. *George Bernard Shaw*

Man's real life is happy, chiefly because he is ever expecting that it soon will be so. *Edgar Allan Poe*

Unquestionably, it is possible to do without happiness, it is done involuntarily by nineteen-twentieths of mankind. *John Stuart Mill*

Many persons have a wrong idea of what constitutes true happiness. It is not attained through self-gratification but through fidelity to a worthy purpose. *Helen Keller*

A man should always consider how much he has more than he wants, and how much more unhappy he might be than he really is. *Joseph Addison*

If a man has important work, and enough leisure and income to enable him to do it properly, he is in possession of as much happiness as is good for any of the children of Adam. *R. H. Tawney*

The greatest happiness you can have is knowing that you do not necessarily require happiness. *William Saroyan*

Existence is a strange bargain. Life owes us little; we owe it everything. The only true happiness comes from squandering ourselves for a purpose. *William Cowper*

Even if we can't be happy, we must always be cheerful. *Irving Kristol*

New Year's Day is every man's birthday. *Charles Lamb*

Happiness is the perpetual possession of being well deceived. *Lytton Strachey*

To be without some of the things you want is an indispensable part of happiness. *Bertrand Russell*

For the rational, psychologically healthy man, the desire for pleasure is the desire to celebrate his control over reality. For the neurotic, the desire for pleasure is the desire to escape from reality. *Nathaniel Branden*

It has never been given to a man to attain at once his happiness and his salvation. *Charles Péguy*

If thou workest at that which is before thee, following right reason seriously, vigorously, calmly, without allowing anything else to distract thee, but keeping thy divine part pure, as if thou shouldst be bound to give it back immediately; if thou holdest to this, expecting nothing, fearing nothing, but satisfied with thy present activity according to Nature, and with heroic truth in every word and sound which thou utterest, thou wilt live happy. And there is no man who is able to prevent this.   *Marcus Aurelius*

We act as though comfort and luxury were the chief requirements of life, when all that we need to make us really happy is something to be enthusiastic about.

Charles Kingsley

One thing I know: the only ones among you who will be really happy are those who will have sought and found how to serve.   *Albert Schweitzer*

Happiness is the light on the water. The water is cold and dark and deep.

William Maxwell

There is no duty we so much underrate as the duty of being happy.

Robert Louis Stevenson

Happiness: a good bank account, a good cook and a good digestion.

Jean-Jacques Rousseau

Knowledge of what is possible is the beginning of happiness.   *George Santayana*

Happiness is the interval between periods of unhappiness.   *Don Marquis*

Weeping may endure for a night, but joy cometh in the morning.   *Psalms 30:5*

Behold, we count them happy which endure. Ye have heard of the patience of Job.

James 5:3

The will of man is his happiness.   *Friedrich von Schiller*

Man's happiness springs mainly from moderate troubles, which afford the mind a healthful stimulus, and are followed by a reaction which produces a cheerful flow of spirits.   *E. Wigglesworth*

There is only one way to happiness and that is to cease worrying about things which are beyond the power of our will.   *Epictetus*

It is nonsense to speak of 'higher' and 'lower' pleasures. To a hungry man it is, rightly, more important that he eat than that he philosophize.   *W. H. Auden*

The secret of happiness is not in doing what one likes, but in liking what one has to do.   *James M. Barrie*

True happiness is of a retired nature and an enemy to pomp and noise; it arises, in the first place, from the enjoyment of one's self; and, in the next, from the friendship and conversations of a few select companions.   *Joseph Addison*

I have known some quite good people who were unhappy, but never an interested person who was unhappy. *A. C. Benson*

My creed is that:
Happiness is the only good.
The place to be happy is here.
The time to be happy is now.
The way to be happy is to make others so. *Robert G. Ingersoll*

My life has no purpose, no direction, no aim, no meaning, and yet I'm happy. I can't figure it out. What am I doing right? *Charles M. Schulz*

Happiness to a dog is what lies on the other side of a door. *Charleton Ogburn, Jr.*

Happiness comes fleetingly now and then,
To those who have learned to do without it
And to them only. *Don Marquis*

I believe in the possibility of happiness, if one cultivates intuition and outlives the grosser passions, including optimism. *George Santayana*

Happiness is brief
It will not stay.
God batters at its sails. *Euripides*

To be happy, we must not be too concerned with others. *Albert Camus*

. . . the little hills rejoice on every side. The pastures are clothed with flocks; the valleys also are covered over with corn; they shout for joy, they also sing.
Psalms 65:12 and 13

For each ecstatic instant
We must an anguish pay
In keen and quivering ratio
To the ecstasy. *Emily Dickinson*

At rare moments in history, by a series of accidents never to be repeated, arise flower societies in which the cult of happiness is paramount, hedonistic, mindless, intent upon the glorious physical instant. *Colm MacInnes*

Man is that he might have joy. *Joseph Smith*

The formula for complete happiness is to be very busy with the unimportant.
A. Edward Newton

Make happy those who are near, and those who are far will come. *Chinese proverb*

Remember that happiness is a way of travel—not a destination. *Roy M. Goodman*

If we cannot live so as to be happy, let us at least live so as to deserve it.
Immanuel Hermann von Fichte

I never admired another's fortune so much that I became dissatisfied with my own.
Cicero

Happiness is essentially a state of going somewhere, wholeheartedly, one-directionally, without regret or reservation. *William H. Sheldon*

Happiness? That's nothing more than health and a poor memory. *Albert Schweitzer*

Happiness is the only sanction of life; where happiness fails, existence remains a mad and lamentable experiment. *George Santayana*

Happiness makes up in height for what it lacks in length. *Robert Frost*

It is not easy to find happiness in ourselves, and it is not possible to find it elsewhere.
Agnes Repplier

Happiness depends, as Nature shows,
Less on exterior things than most suppose. *William Cowper*

Happiness is a small and unworthy goal for something as big and fancy as a whole lifetime, and should be taken in small doses. *Russell Baker*

Hatred

Few people can be happy unless they hate some other person, nation, or creed.
Bertrand Russell

It's a sign of your own worth sometimes if you are hated by the right people.
Miles Franklin, 'My Career Goes Bung'

Hatred is the coward's revenge for being intimidated. *George Bernard Shaw*

Hatred comes from the heart; contempt from the head; and neither feeling is quite within our control. *Arthur Schopenhauer*

Hatred seems to operate on the same glands as love; it even produces the same actions. If we had not been taught how to interpret the story of the Passion, would we have been able to say from their actions alone whether it was the jealous Judas or the cowardly Peter who loved Christ? *Graham Greene*

As every experienced politician knows, it is better to be vigorously hated than to be tepidly admired. *Sir Robert Menzies*

Psychiatrists today . . . see the irrational hostility that people everywhere vent upon one another as chiefly projected self-hate. *Bonaro Overstreet*

Don't hate, it's too big a burden to bear. *Martin Luther King, Sr.*

A hateful act is the transference to others of the degradation we bear in ourselves.

Simone Weil

The worst, the least curable hatred is that which has superseded deep love.

Euripides

Hatred is settled anger.   *Cicero*

Passionate hatred can give meaning and purpose to an empty life.   *Eric Hoffer*

Hate is the consequence of fear; we fear something before we hate it; a child who fears noises becomes a man who hates noise.   *Cyril Connolly*

Hatred is self-punishment.   *Hosea Ballou*

Hatreds are the cinders of affection.   *Walter Raleigh*

I never hated a man enough to give him his diamonds back.   *Zsa Zsa Gabor*

It does not matter much what a man hates, provided he hates something.

Samuel Butler

Whom they have injured, they also hate.   *Seneca*

We love without reason, and without reason we hate.   *Jean-François Regnard*

If you hate a person, you hate something in him that is part of yourself. What isn't part of ourselves doesn't disturb us.   *Hermann Hesse*

Hate is such a luxurious emotion, it can only be spent on one we love.

Bob Udkoff

Hell and the Devil

The devil gets up to the belfry by the vicar's skirts.   *Thomas Fuller*

The safest road to Hell is the gradual one—the gentle slope, soft underfoot, without sudden turnings, without milestones, without signposts.   *C. S. Lewis*

A perpetual holiday is a good working definition of hell.   *George Bernard Shaw*

The Devil's boots don't creak.   *Scottish proverb*

Man can hardly even recognize the devils of his own creation.   *Albert Schweitzer*

What is hell? I maintain that it is the suffering of being unable to love.

Fyodor Dostoevsky

Hell, madame, is to love no longer.   *Georges Bernanos*

Isn't it a wonder men didn't make the devil a woman?   *Louisa Lawson*

Hell is truth seen too late.   *Anon.*

Be sober, be vigilant; because your adversary the devil, as a roaring lion, walketh
about, seeking whom he may devour.   *I Peter 5:8*

Heaven for climate, hell for company.   *James M. Barrie*

We may not pay Satan reverence, for that would be indiscreet, but we can at least
respect his talents.   *Mark Twain*

An apology for the Devil—it must be remembered that we have only heard one side
of the case. God has written all the books.   *Samuel Butler*

When you first learn to love hell, you will be in heaven.   *Thaddeus Golas*

The devil's name is Dullness.   *Robert E. Lee*

Hell is indefinite.   *Charles Williams*

It has been more wittily than charitably said that hell is paved with good intentions.
They have their place in heaven also.   *Robert Southey*

Heredity

A man finds room in a few square inches of his face for the traits of all his ancestors;
for the expression of all his history, and his wants.   *Ralph Waldo Emerson*

Every man is the son of his own works.   *Cervantes*

Heredity is nothing but stored environment.   *Luther Burbank*

One of the best things people could do for their descendants would be to sharply limit
the number of them.   *Olin Miller*

A man's rootage is more important than his leafage.   *Woodrow Wilson*

Nothing is so soothing to our self-esteem as to find our bad traits in our forebears. It
seems to absolve us.   *Van Wyck Brooks*

Heredity is an omnibus in which all our ancestors ride, and every now and then one
of them puts his head out and embarrasses us.   *Oliver Wendell Holmes*

It is indeed a desirable thing to be well descended, but the glory belongs to our
ancestors.   *Plutarch*

With him for a sire, and her for a dam
What should I be, but just what I am?   *Edna St. Vincent Millay*

The child is father to the man.   *William Wordsworth*

Gentility is what is left over from rich ancestors after the money is gone.
                                                                        John Ciardi

Whoever serves his country well has no need of ancestors.   *Voltaire*

The best blood will sometimes get into a fool or a mosquito.   *Austin O'Malley*

The man who has not anything to boast of but his illustrious ancestors is like a potato—the only good belonging to him is underground.   *Thomas Overbury*

A genealogist is one who traces your family back as far as your money will go.
                                                                          Anon.

The pedigree of honey
Does not concern the bee;
A clover, anytime, to him
Is aristocracy.   *Emily Dickinson*

A hen is only an egg's way of making another egg.   *Samuel Butler*

When I want a peerage, I shall buy one like an honest man.   *Lord Northcliffe*

Heroes and Heroism

If a man hasn't discovered something that he will die for, he isn't fit to live.
                                                                Martin Luther King

Martyrdom—the only way in which a man can become famous without ability.
                                                                George Bernard Shaw

Every hero becomes a bore at last.   *Ralph Waldo Emerson*

Play the man, Master Ridley; we shall this day light such a candle, by God's grace, in England, as I trust shall never be put out.
                                            Bishop Hugh Latimer (before his execution)

Being a hero is about the shortest-lived profession on earth.   *Will Rogers*

Heroes are created by popular demand, sometimes out of the scantiest materials . . . such as the apple that William Tell never shot, the ride that Paul Revere never finished, the flag that Barbara Frietchie never waved.   *Gerald Johnson*

A hero is a man who stands up manfully against his father and in the end victoriously overcomes him.   *Sigmund Freud*

When the heroes go off the stage, the clowns come on.   *Heinrich Heine*

A hero is no braver than an ordinary man, but he is brave five minutes longer.

Ralph Waldo Emerson

One of the forms of psychological heroism is the willingness to tolerate anxiety and uncertainty in the pursuit of our values—whether these values be work goals, the love of another human being, the raising of a family or personal growth.

Samuel Branden

Don't be so humble. You're not that great.

Golda Meir

Nothing proceeds nobly like a classical tragedy.
Heroes must be prepared to be undignified.

Geoffrey Dutton

All these were honoured in their generations and were the glory of their times.

Ecclesiasticus 44:7

This thing of being a hero, about the main thing to it is to know when to die.

Will Rogers

One murder makes a villain, millions a hero.

Bishop Beilby Porteus

The savage bows down to idols of wood and stone, the civilized man to idols of flesh and blood.

George Bernard Shaw

An efficiency-regime cannot be run without a few heroes stuck about it to carry off the dullness—much as plums have to be put into a bad pudding to make it palatable.

E. M. Forster

In a truly heroic life there is no peradventure. It is always doing or dying.

R. D. Hitchcock

It is said that no man is a hero to his valet. That is because a hero can be recognized only by a hero.

Goethe

History and Historians

History is a vast early warning system.

Norman Cousins

History is simply a piece of paper covered with print; the main thing is still to make history, not to write it.

Otto von Bismarck

History is the devil's scripture.

Lord Byron

History is the essence of innumerable biographies.

Thomas Carlyle

History, like poetry, music, painting, sculpture and dancing, is one of the great comforters which men have put between themselves and death—to make their living and their dying more bearable.

Manning Clark

In essence, the Renaissance is simply the green end of one of civilization's hardest winters.
John Fowles

Man is a history-making creature who can neither repeat his past nor leave it behind.
W. H. Auden

That men do not learn very much from the lessons of history is the most important of all the lessons that History has to teach.
Aldous Huxley

The effect of boredom on a large scale in history is underestimated. It is a main cause of revolutions, and would soon bring to an end all the static Utopias and the farmyard civilization of the Fabians.
Dean William R. Inge

The game of History is usually played by the best and the worst over the heads of the majority in the middle.
Eric Hoffer

The importance of an historical event lies not in what happened but in what later generations believed to have happened.
Gough Whitlam

When the historian Charles A. Beard was asked about the lessons from history, he said there were four:
1. The bee fertilizes the flower it robs.
2. Whom the gods would destroy, they first make mad with power.
3. The mills of God grind slowly, but they grind exceeding small.
4. When it is dark enough, you can see the stars.

History doesn't pass the dishes again.
Louis-Ferdinand Céline

The past is a foreign country; they do things differently there.
Anon.

Very few things happen at the right time, and the rest do not happen at all; the conscientious historian will correct these defects.
Herodotus

Most history is a record of the triumphs, disasters and follies of top people. The black hole in it is the way of life of mute, inglorious men and women who made no nuisance of themselves in the world.
Philip Howard

Nostalgia is a seductive liar.
George W. Ball

It has been said that though God cannot alter the past, historians can—it is perhaps because they can be useful to Him in this respect that He tolerates their existence.
Samuel Butler

It is pleasant to be transferred from an office where one is afraid of a sergeant-major into an office where one can intimidate generals, and perhaps this is why history is so attractive to the more timid among us.
E. M. Forster

History never looks like history when you are living through it. It always looks confusing and messy, and it always feels uncomfortable.
John W. Gardner

History is philosophy learned from examples.
Dionysius of Halicarnassus

History teaches us that men and nations behave wisely once they have exhausted all other alternatives. *Abba Eban*

Noble acts and momentous events happen in the same way and produce the same impression as the ordinary facts. *Roberto Rossellini*

Don't brood on what's past, but never forget it either. *Thomas H. Raddall*

Those who cannot remember the past are condemned to repeat it.
George Santayana

Most of us spend too much time on the last twenty-four hours and too little on the last six thousand years. *Will Durant*

I never realized that there was history, close at hand, beside my very own home. I did not realize that the old grave that stood among the brambles at the foot of our farm was *history*. *Stephen Leacock*

All history is but the lengthened shadow of a great man. *Ralph Waldo Emerson*

The history of the world is the record of a man in quest of his daily bread and butter.
Hendrik Willem van Loon

The historian looks backward. In the end he also believes backward.
Friedrich Nietzsche

Biography is history seen through the prism of a person. *Louis Fischer*

The past is a work of art, free of irrelevancies and loose ends. *Max Beerbohm*

Any event, once it has occurred, can be made to appear inevitable by a competent historian. *Lee Simonson*

History is not another name for the past, as many people imply. It is the name for stories about the past. *A. J. P. Taylor*

History is:
    Fables agreed upon—*Voltaire*
    The biography of a few stout and earnest persons—*Ralph Waldo Emerson*
    A vast Mississippi of falsehood—*Matthew Arnold*
    A confused heap of facts—*Lord Chesterfield*
    A cyclic poem written by time upon the memories of man—*Percy Bysshe Shelley*

Men make their own history more wisely when they know what that history has been about. *Manning Clark*

Give the historians something to write about. *Propertius*

Societies that do not eat people are fascinated by those that do. *Ronald Wright*

War makes rattling good history; but Peace is poor reading. *Thomas Hardy*

The history of almost every civilization furnishes examples of geographical expansion coinciding with deterioration in quality.   *Arnold Toynbee*

History is past politics; and politics present history.   *John Seeley*

Every time history repeats itself, the price goes up.   *Old saying*

The first duty of an historian is to be on his guard against his own sympathies.   *J. A. Froude*

The first qualification for a historian is to have no ability to invent.   *Stendhal*

One of the lessons of history is that nothing is often a good thing to do and always a clever thing to say.   *Will Durant*

When great changes occur in history, when great principles are involved, as a rule the majority are wrong.   *Eugene V. Debs*

More history's made by secret handshakes than by battles, bills and proclamations.   *John Barth*

History, n: an account mostly false, of events, mostly unimportant, which are brought about by rulers, mostly knaves, and soldiers, mostly fools.   *Ambrose Bierce*

The historical sense involves a perception, not only of the pastness of the past, but of its presence.   *T. S. Eliot*

Truth is the only merit that gives dignity and worth to history.   *Lord Acton*

History is more or less bunk.   *Henry Ford*

I have no history but the length of my bones.   *Robin Skelton*

History is a pact between the dead, the living, and the yet unborn.   *Edmund Burke*

A people without history is like wind on the buffalo grass.   *Sioux proverb*

The function of posterity is to look after itself.   *Dylan Thomas*

The world's history is constant, like the laws of nature, and simple, like the souls of men. The same conditions continually produce the same results.   *Friedrich von Schiller*

History is just the portrayal of crimes and misfortunes.   *Voltaire*

All history is a little false.   *Martin Boyd, 'The Cardboard Crown'*

The history of mankind is written by the victors.   *Manning Clark*

The memories of men are too frail a thread to hang history from.   *John Still*

The rich experience of history teaches that up to now not a single class has voluntarily made way for another class.

Joseph Stalin

When the history of this century is written, its reality will be seen as the era during which the eternal hopes of humanity were begun to be realised.

Humphrey McQueen

The Home

A house may draw visitors, but it is the possessor alone that can detain them.

Charles Caleb Colton

A man's home is his wife's castle.

Alexander Chase

I want a house that has got over all its troubles; I don't want to spend the rest of my life bringing up a young and inexperienced house.

Jerome K. Jerome

The great advantage of a hotel is that it's a refuge from home life.

George Bernard Shaw

Home is not where you live but where they understand you.   *Christian Morgenstern*

Where thou art, that, is Home.

Emily Dickinson

Home is the place where, when you have to go there,
They have to take you in.

Robert Frost

A man builds a fine house; and now he has a master, and a task for life is to furnish watch, show it, and keep it in repair the rest of his life.   *Ralph Waldo Emerson*

The strength of a nation, especially of a republican nation, is in the intelligent and well-ordered homes of the people.

Lydia Sigourney

Justice was born outside the home and a long way from it; and it has never been adopted there.

Walter Cronkite

The home of everyone is to him his castle and fortress, as well for his defence against injury and violence, as for his repose.

Edward Coke

Pride, avarice and envy are in every home.

Thornton Wilder

Of all modern notions, the worst is this: that domesticity is dull. Inside the home, they say, is dead decorum and routine; outside is adventure and variety. But the truth is that the home is the only place of liberty, the only spot on earth where a man can alter arrangements suddenly, make an experiment or indulge in a whim. The home is not the one tame place in a world of adventure; it is the one wild place in a world of rules and set tasks.

G. K. Chesterton

I have come back again to where I belong; not an enchanted place, but the walls are strong.
Dorothy H. Rath

To mankind in general Macbeth and Lady Macbeth stand out as the supreme type of all that a host and hostess should not be.
Max Beerbohm

The fellow that owns his own home is always just coming out of a hardware store.
Kin Hubbard

I never lived in a house yet without there was something wrong with it. Gimme a good tent.
Henry Lawson, 'The Ghostly Door'

Homo Sapiens

I am mortal, born to love and to suffer.
Friedrich Hölderlin

I am a man; nothing human is alien to me.
Terence

Few men are of one plain, decided colour, most are mixed, shaded, and blended; and vary as much, from different situations as changeable silks do from different lights.
Lord Chesterfield

I often marvel how it is that though each man loves himself beyond all else, he should yet value his own opinion of himself less than that of others.   *Marcus Aurelius*

Every man is ultimately the prisoner of his formative years.   *A. A. Phillips*

It is when we try to grapple with another man's intimate need that we perceive how incomprehensible, wavering and misty are the beings that share with us the sight of the stars and the warmth of the sun.   *Joseph Conrad*

Man is at the bottom an animal, midway, a citizen, and at the top, divine. But the climate of this world is such that few ripen at the top.   *Henry Ward Beecher*

Man is physically as well as metaphysically a thing of shreds and patches, borrowed unequally from good and bad ancestors, and a misfit from the start.
Ralph Waldo Emerson

Being human is a hideous burden.   *Thea Astley, 'The Acolyte'*

Man partly is and wholly hopes to be.   *Robert Browning*

Man, as we know him, is a poor creature; but he is halfway between an ape and a god and he is travelling in the right direction.   *Dean William R. Inge*

Mankind is an unco squad
And muckle he may grieve thee.
Robert Burns

Many people believe they are attracted by God, or by Nature when they are only repelled by Man.
Dean William R. Inge

Most human beings have an absolute and infinite capacity for taking things for granted.
Aldous Huxley

The cultivated man, wise to know and bold to perform, is the end to which nature works.
Ralph Waldo Emerson

The middle class prefers comfort to pleasure, convenience to liberty, and a pleasant temperature to the deathly inner consuming fire.
Hermann Hesse

The question is this: Is man an ape or an angel? I, my lords, am on the side of the angels.
Benjamin Disraeli

There are 193 living species of monkeys and apes. 192 of them are covered with hair. The exception is a naked ape, self-named Homo Sapiens.
Desmond Morris

There is nothing but the human
Touch can heal the human woe.
Victor Daley

We should expect the best and the worst from mankind, as from the weather.
Vauvenargues

Whosoever would be a man must be a non-conformist.
Ralph Waldo Emerson

Every man is to be respected as an absolute end in himself: and it is a crime against the dignity that belongs to him as a human being, to use him as a mere means for some external purpose.
Immanuel Kant

The race of man, while sheep in credulity, are wolves for conformity.
Carl van Doren

Men are cruel, but man is kind.
Rabindranath Tagore

In this world, a man must either be anvil or hammer. *Henry Wadsworth Longfellow*

I believe I've found the missing link between animal and civilized man. It is us.
Konrad Lorenz

When man is truly humbled, when he has learnt that he is not God, then he is nearest to becoming so. In the end, he may ascend.
Patrick White, 'Voss

He was a man, take him for all in all, I shall not look upon his like again.
Shakespeare, 'Hamlet

I am a member of the rabble in good standing.
Westbrook Pegler

The strongest human instinct is to impart information, the second strongest is to resist it.
Kenneth Grahame

Who is wise? He that learns from everyone.
Who is powerful? He that governs his passions.
Who is rich? He that is content.
Who is that? Nobody.   *Benjamin Franklin*

God made him, and therefore let him pass for a man.
                              Shakespeare, 'The Merchant of Venice'

Darwinian Man, though well-behaved,
At best is only a monkey shaved!   *W. S. Gilbert*

Each man is his own absolute lawgiver and dispenser of glory or gloom to himself,
the maker of his life, his reward, his punishment.   *Anon.*

Man is the only animal whose desires increase as they are fed; the only animal that
is never satisfied.   *Henry George*

Most people in action are not worth very much; and yet every human being is an
unprecedented miracle.   *James Baldwin*

People are too durable, that's their main trouble. They can do too much to themselves,
they last too long.   *Bertolt Brecht*

I believe that man will not merely endure: he will prevail. He is immortal, not because
he alone among creatures has an inexhaustible voice, but because he has a soul, a
spirit capable of compassion and sacrifice and endurance.   *William Faulkner*

A man is a kind of inverted thermometer, the bulb uppermost, and the column of
self-valuation is all the time going up and down.   *Oliver Wendell Holmes*

To be reborn is a constantly recurring human need.   *Henry Hewes*

Man's most valuable trait
Is a judicious sense of what not to believe.   *Euripides*

The natural man has only two primal passions: to get and to beget.   *William Osler*

A humanist is anyone who rejects the attempt to describe or account for man wholly
on the basis of physics, chemistry or animal behaviour.   *Joseph Wood Krutch*

Mankind may be divided into two races, those who acquiesce and those who growl.
I am on the side of the growlers, always and everywhere; because I remember what
I owe to them.   *Walter Murdoch*

The forgotten man. He is the clean, quiet, virtuous domestic citizen who pays his debts
and his taxes and is never heard of outside his little circle . . . He works, he votes,
generally he prays, but his chief business in life is to pay.   *William Graham Sumner*

Limited in his nature, infinite in his desires, man is a fallen god who remembers
heaven.   *Alphonse de Lamartine*

Man is a make-believe animal—he is never so truly himself as when he is acting a part.   *William Hazlitt*

Men must endure their going hence, even as their coming hither; ripeness is all.
                                                                Shakespeare, 'King Lear'

Every man in the world is better than someone else and not as good as someone else.
                                                                William Saroyan

The voice is a second signature.   *R. I. Fitzhenry*

It would hardly be possible to exaggerate man's wretchedness if it were not so easy to overestimate his sensibility.   *George Santayana*

Know then thyself, presume not God to scan:
The proper study of mankind is man.   *Alexander Pope*

Man, an animal that makes bargains.   *Adam Smith*

Man is a reasoning, rather than a reasonable animal.   *Robert B. Hamilton*

Man will ever stand in need of man.   *Theocritus*

We are members one of another.   *Ephesians 4:25*

Man is only a reed, the weakest thing in nature, but he is a thinking reed.
                                                                  Blaise Pascal

Man is the only animal that laughs and weeps; for he is the only animal that is struck by the difference between what things are and what they might have been.
                                                                William Hazlitt

To her fair works did Nature link
The human soul that through me ran;
And much it grieved my heart to think
What Man has made of Man.   *William Wordsworth*

Admire, exult, despise, laugh, weep—for here
There is such matter for all feelings:—Man!
Thou pendulum betwixt a smile and tear.   *Lord Byron*

The dignity of man lies in his ability to face reality in all its meaninglessness.
                                                                  Martin Esslin

If heaven made him, earth can find some use for him.   *Chinese proverb*

Everything in space obeys the laws of physics. If you know these laws, and obey them, space will treat you kindly. And don't tell me man doesn't belong out there. Man belongs wherever he wants to go—and he'll do plenty well when he gets there.
                                                              Wernher von Braun

An unlearned carpenter of my acquaintance once said in my hearing: 'There is very little difference between one man and another, but what there is is *very important.'*

William James

One of the laws of paleontology is that an animal which must protect itself with thick armour is degenerate. It is usually a sign that the species is on the road to extinction.

John Steinbeck

The Family of Man is more than three billion strong. It lives in more than one hundred nations. Most of its members are not white. Most of them are not Christians. Most of them know nothing about free enterprise, or due process of law, or the Australian ballot.   *John F. Kennedy*

Man is as full of potentiality as he is of impotence.   *George Santayana*

That man is an aggressive creature will hardly be disputed. With the exception of certain rodents, no other vertebrate habitually destroys members of its own species.

Anthony Storr

Every man is more than just himself; he also represents the unique, the very special and always significant and remarkable point at which the world's phenomena intersect, only once in this way, and never again.   *Hermann Hesse*

Man is a gaming animal. He must be always trying to get the better in something or other.   *Charles Lamb*

Man makes holy what he believes, as he makes beautiful what he loves.

Ernest Renan

Man is an abyss, and I turn giddy when I look down into it.   *Georg Büchner*

Honesty

What comes from the heart, goes to the heart.   *Samuel Taylor Coleridge*

It's better to be quotable than to be honest.   *Tom Stoppard*

Amid a world of sceptred sham,
  Be this my humble aim, at least;
To seem the sort of beast I am,
  And not some other sort of beast.   *Walter Murdoch*

Of all feats of skill, the most difficult is that of being honest.
          Comtesse Diane (Marie de Beausacq)

To be honest, one must be inconsistent.   *H. G. Wells*

He that resolves to deal with none but honest men, must leave off dealing.
          Thomas Fuller

'Tis my opinion every man cheats in his way, and he is only honest who is not discovered.
Susannah Centlivre

There is one way to find out if a man is honest—ask him. If he says 'yes', you know he is crooked.
Groucho Marx

The honester the man, the worse luck.
John Ray

Let none of us delude himself by supposing that honesty is always the best policy. It is not.
Dean William R. Inge

Barring that natural expression of villainy which we all have, the man looked honest enough.
Mark Twain

Honesty's praised, then left to freeze.
Juvenal

Wealth makes everything easy—honesty most of all.
Comtesse Diane (Marie de Beausacq)

Honesty is as rare as a man without self-pity.
Stephen Vincent Benét

Every man has his fault, and honesty is his.
Shakespeare, 'Timon of Athens'

One must not cheat anybody, not even the world of one's triumph.
Franz Kafka

People who are brutally honest get more satisfaction out of the brutality than out of the honesty.
Richard J. Needham

Anger cannot be dishonest.
George R. Bach

I'm frank, brutally frank. And even when I'm not frank, I look frank.
Lord Thomson of Fleet

The young man turned to him with a disarming candour, which instantly put him on his guard.
Saki

A man should be careful never to tell tales of himself to his own disadvantage. People may be amused at the time, but they will be remembered, and brought out against him upon some subsequent occasion.
Samuel Johnson

Being entirely honest with oneself is a good exercise.
Sigmund Freud

Honour

And they were offended in him. But Jesus said unto them, 'A prophet is not without honour, save in his own country, and in his own house.'
Matthew 13:57

No person was ever honoured for what he received. Honour has been the reward for what he gave.
Calvin Coolidge

It is better to deserve honours and not have them than to have them and not deserve them.   *Mark Twain*

A man has honour if he holds himself to an ideal of conduct though it is inconvenient, unprofitable or dangerous to do so.   *Walter Lippmann*

The louder he talked of his honour, the faster we counted our spoons.
                                                         Ralph Waldo Emerson

Honour follows those who flee it.   *Anon.*

God sells knowledge for labour—honour for risk.   *Arabic proverb*

Fame is something which must be won; honour is something which must not be lost.
                                                        Arthur Schopenhauer

Dignity does not consist in possessing honours, but in deserving them.   *Aristotle*

I could not love thee, dear, so much
Loved I not honour more.   *Richard Lovelace*

Honour pricks me on. Yea, but how if honour prick me off when I come on? How then? Can honour set to a leg? No. Or an arm? No. Or take away the grief of a wound? No. Honour hath no skill in surgery, then? No. What is honour? A word.
                                                 Shakespeare, 'Henry IV' Part I

Would that . . . a sense of the true aim of life might elevate the tone of politics and trade till public and private honour become identical.   *Margaret Fuller*

No revenge is more honorable than the one not taken.   *Spanish proverb*

Hope

An act of God was defined as something which no reasonable man could have expected.
                                                              A. P. Herbert

It is a long lane that has no turning.   *Old saying*

Everyone who has ever built anywhere a 'new heaven' first found the power thereto in his own hell.   *Friedrich Nietzsche*

Hope is a pleasant acquaintance, but an unsafe friend. *Thomas Chandler Haliburton*

We do not really feel grateful toward those who make our dreams come true; they ruin our dreams.   *Eric Hoffer*

When you get to the end of your rope, tie a knot and hang on.   *Anon.*

For what human ill does not dawn seem to be an alleviation?   *Thornton Wilder*

Hope is itself a species of happiness, and, perhaps, the chief happiness which this world affords.
Samuel Johnson

Hope, deceitful as it is, serves at least to lead us to the end of life along an agreeable road.
La Rochefoucauld

One need not hope in order to undertake; nor succeed in order to persevere.
William the Silent

Hope! of all ills that men endure
The only cheap and universal cure.
Abraham Cowley

Hope is the poor man's bread.
George Herbert

Hope springs eternal in the human breast;
Man never is, but always *to be* blest.
Alexander Pope

I suppose it can be truthfully said that hope is the only universal liar who never loses his reputation for veracity.
Robert G. Ingersoll

Every thing that is done in the world is done by hope.
Martin Luther

Hope is a good breakfast, but it is a bad supper.
Francis Bacon

Man's many desires are like the small metal coins he carries about in his pocket. The more he has the more they weight him down.
Satya Sai Baba

One of the best safeguards of our hopes, I have suggested, is to be able to mark off the areas of hopelessness and to acknowledge them, to face them directly, not with despair but with the creative intent of keeping them from polluting all the areas of possibility.
William F. Lynch

The human body experiences a powerful gravitational pull in the direction of hope. That is why the patient's hopes are the physician's secret weapon. They are the hidden ingredients in any prescription.
Norman Cousins

Some one once said to me, 'Reverend Schuller, I hope you live to see all your dreams fulfilled.' I replied, 'I hope not, because if I live and all my dreams are fulfilled, I'm dead.' It's unfulfilled dreams that keep you alive.
Robert Schuller

The slow compromise, or even surrender, of our fondest hopes is a regular feature of normal human life.
Leston L. Havens

Hope is an illusion for squares.
Colin Johnson, 'Wild Cat Falling'

'Hope' is the thing with feathers
That perches in the soul—
And sings the tune without words
And never stops—at all.
Emily Dickinson

Human Relations

A sudden, bold, and unexpected question doth many times surprise a man and lay him open.   *Francis Bacon*

Charity is injurious unless it helps the recipient to become independent of it.   *John D. Rockefeller*

Diplomacy is the art of saying 'nice doggie' until you can find a rock.   *Will Rogers*

I present myself to you in a form suitable to the relationship I wish to achieve with you.   *Luigi Pirandello*

I respect only those who resist me, but cannot tolerate them.   *Charles de Gaulle*

I wish everybody would go back into the closet.   *Josefa Heifetz*

It is in vain to hope to please all alike. Let a man stand with his face in what direction he will, he must necessarily turn his back on one half of the world.   *George Dennison Prentice*

Modern dancers give a sinister portent about our times. The dancers don't even look at one another. They are just a lot of isolated individuals jiggling in a kind of self-hypnosis and dancing with others only to remind themselves that we are not completely alone in this world.   *Agnes de Mille*

One kind word can warm three winter months.   *Japanese saying*

Outside, among your fellows, among strangers, you must preserve appearances, 100 things you cannot do; but inside, the terrible freedom!   *Ralph Waldo Emerson*

The easiest kind of relationship for me is with 10,000 people. The hardest is with one.   *Joan Baez*

The opinions which we hold of one another, our relations with friends and kinsfolk are in no sense permanent, save in appearance, but are as eternally fluid as the sea itself.   *Marcel Proust*

The ultimate indignity is to be given a bedpan by a stranger who calls you by your first name.   *Maggie Kuhn*

There is no society or conversation to be kept up in the world without good nature, or something which must bear its appearance and supply its place. For this reason, mankind have been forced to invent a kind of artificial humanity, which is what we express by the words Good Breeding.   *Joseph Addison*

When the man is at home, his standing in society is well known and quietly taken; but when he is abroad, it is problematical, and is dependent on the success of his manners.   *Ralph Waldo Emerson*

The adoption of an adult and independent outlook is marked by a refusal to be protected for one's own good; and, in harmony with this position, we should refuse to protect others for their own good.   *John Anderson*

Almost all of our relationships begin, and most of them continue, as forms of mutual exploitation, a mental or physical barter, to be terminated when one or both parties run out of goods.   *W. H. Auden*

When you meet anyone in the flesh you realize immediately that he is a human being and not a sort of caricature embodying certain ideas. It is partly for this reason that I don't mix much in literary circles, because I know from experience that once I have met and spoken to anyone I shall never again be able to feel any intellectual brutality towards him, even when I feel I ought to—like the Labour M.P.s who get patted on the back by dukes and are lost forever more.   *George Orwell*

The wisest man I have ever known once said to me: 'Nine out of every ten people improve on acquaintance,' and I have found his words true.   *Frank Swinnerton*

I am a part of all that I have met.   *Alfred, Lord Tennyson*

At the heart of our friendly or purely social relations, there lurks a hostility momentarily cured but recurring in fits and starts.   *Marcel Proust*

The worst sin towards our fellow creatures is not to hate them, but to be indifferent to them; that's the essence of inhumanity.   *George Bernard Shaw*

We rarely confide in those who are better than we are.   *Albert Camus*

A sense of duty is useful in work, but offensive in personal relations. People wish to be liked, not be endured with patient resignation.   *Bertrand Russell*

The fact is that the possession of a highly social conscience about large-scale issues is no guarantee whatever of reasonable conduct in private relations.   *Lewis Hastings*

With three or more people there is something bold in the air: direct things get said which would frighten two people alone and conscious of each inch of their nearness to one another. To be three is to be in public—you feel safe.   *Elizabeth Bowen*

Acquaintance, n: a person whom we know well enough to borrow from, but not well enough to lend to.   *Ambrose Bierce*

The largest quantity of willing human cooperation occurs within and between households; cooperation there is the pattern, and has to be the continuing basis, for cooperation anywhere else.   *Hugh Stretton*

Make yourself necessary to somebody.   *Ralph Waldo Emerson*

Only the person who has faith in himself is able to be faithful to others.
                                                      Erich Fromm

We accept every person in the world as that for which he gives himself out; only he must give himself out for something. We can put up with the unpleasant more easily than we can endure the insignificant.   *Goethe*

Each of us keeps, battened down inside himself, a sort of lunatic giant—impossible socially, but full-scale. It's the knockings and batterings we sometimes hear in each other that keep our intercourse from utter banality.   *Elizabeth Bowen*

We wander through this life together in a semi-darkness in which none of us can distinguish exactly the features of his neighbour. Only from time to time, through some experience that we have of our companion, or through some remark that he passes, he stands for a moment close to us, as though illuminated by a flash of lightning. Then we see him as he really is.   *Albert Schweitzer*

A loving person lives in a loving world. A hostile person lives in a hostile world: everyone you meet is your mirror.   *Ken Keyes, Jr.*

It is always safe to assume that people are more subtle and less sensitive than they seem.   *Eric Hoffer*

I was born modest; not all over, but in spots.   *Mark Twain*

A modest man is usually admired—if people ever hear of him. *Edgar Watson Howe*

When the Quaker Penn kept his hat on in the royal presence, Charles (King Charles II) politely removed his, explaining that it was the custom in that place for only one person at a time to remain covered.   *Arthur Bryant*

If you treat men the way they are you never improve them. If you treat them the way you want them to be, you do.   *Goethe*

See everything: overlook a great deal: correct a little.   *Pope John XXIII*

The more you let yourself go, the less others let you go.   *Friedrich Nietzsche*

A hundred times every day I remind myself that my inner and outer life depend on the labours of other men, living and dead, and that I must exert myself in order to give in the same measure as I have received.   *Albert Einstein*

Respect is the term by which you describe your feelings towards the people who don't attract you very much.   *The Lone Hand*

I reckon there's as much human nature in some folks as there is in others, if not more.
                                                          Edward Noyes Westcott

If only there were evil people somewhere, insidiously committing evil deeds, and it were necessary only to separate them from the rest of us and destroy them. But the line dividing good and evil cuts through the heart of every human being. And who is willing to destroy a piece of his own heart?   *Aleksandr Solzhenitsyn*

Science may have found a cure for most evils: but it has found no remedy for the worst of them all—the apathy of human beings.   *Helen Keller*

The go-between wears out a thousand sandals.   *Japanese proverb*

Life is livable because we know that wherever we go most of the people we meet will be restrained in their actions toward us by an almost instinctive network of taboos.
Havelock Ellis

I was taught when I was young that if people would only love one another, all would be well with the world. This seemed simple and very nice; but I found when I tried to put it in practice not only that other people were seldom lovable, but that I was not very lovable myself.   *George Bernard Shaw*

Depend on it, you and I are both laughed at by those who know us best. What we must hope for is that some of them may laugh with affection rather than with rancour.
Walter Murdoch

Humour and Humorists

Humour is the first of the gifts to perish in a foreign tongue.   *Virginia Woolf*

The difficulty with humourists is that they will mix what they believe with what they don't; whichever seems likelier to win an effect.   *John Updike*

The teller of a mirthful tale has latitude allowed him. We are content with less than absolute truth.   *Charles Lamb*

He that jokes confesses.   *Italian proverb*

There are things of deadly earnest that can only be safely mentioned under cover of a joke.   *J. J. Procter*

Humour is the only test of gravity, and gravity of humour, for a subject which will not bear raillery is suspicious, and a jest which will not bear serious examination is false wit.   *Aristotle*

Everything is funny as long as it is happening to somebody else.   *Will Rogers*

A satirist is a man who discovers unpleasant things about himself and then says them about other people.   *Peter McArthur*

Humour is emotional chaos remembered in tranquillity.   *James Thurber*

The best definition of humour I know is: humour may be defined as the kindly contemplation of the incongruities of life, and the artistic expression thereof. I think this is the best I know because I wrote it myself.   *Stephen Leacock*

A humorist is a man who feels bad but who feels good about it.   *Don Herold*

Humour plays close to the big, hot fire, which is the truth, and the reader feels the heat.   *E. B. White*

Wit is the only wall
Between us and the dark.   *Mark Van Doren*

Look at Jewish history. Unrelieved lamenting would be intolerable. So, for every ten Jews beating their breasts, God designated one to be crazy and amuse the breast-beaters. By the time I was five I knew I was that one.   *Mel Brooks*

Mirthfulness is in the mind and you cannot get it out. It is just as good in its place as conscience or veneration.   *Henry Ward Beecher*

Novelist Peter de Vries, like Adlai Stevenson and Mark Twain, has suffered from the American assumption that anyone with a sense of humour is not to be taken seriously.
Timothy Foote

Humour can be dissected, as a frog can, but the thing dies in the process.
E. B. White

Humour is the contemplation of the finite from the point of view of the infinite.
Christian Morgenstern

The total absence of humour from the Bible is one of the most singular things in all literature.   *Alfred North Whitehead*

Laughter is the closest thing to the grace of God.   *Karl Barth*

Humour is richly rewarding to the person who employs it. It has some value in gaining and holding attention. But it has no persuasive value at all.   *J. K. Galbraith*

Humour is the most engaging cowardice. With it myself I have been able to hold some of my enemy in play far out of gunshot.   *Robert Frost*

A comedian is a fellow who finds other comedians too humorous to mention.
Jack Herbert

If it's sanity you're after
There's no recipe like
Laughter.
Laugh it off.   *Henry Rutherford Elliot*

Humour is an affirmation of dignity, a declaration of man's superiority to all that befalls him.   *Romain Gary*

Comedy is simply a funny way of being serious.   *Peter Ustinov*

Comedy is tragedy—plus time.   *Carol Burnett*

Caricature: putting the face of a joke upon the body of a truth.   *Joseph Conrad*

The ability to laugh at life is right at the top, with love and communication, in the hierarchy of our needs. Humour has much to do with pain; it exaggerates the anxieties and absurdities we feel, so that we gain distance and through laughter, relief.

Sara Davidson

He deserves paradise who makes his companions laugh.   *The Koran*

I was only joking . . . are the four saddest words in the world.

Jessica Anderson, 'Tirra Lirra by the River'

You encourage a comic man too much, and he gets silly.   *Stephen Leacock*

Any man will admit if need be that his sight is not good, or that he cannot swim or shoots badly with a rifle, but to touch upon his sense of humour is to give him mortal affront.   *Stephen Leacock*

Anything awful makes me laugh. I misbehaved once at a funeral.   *Charles Lamb*

Wit is far more often a shield than a lance.   *Anon.*

If there's anything I hate it's the word humorist—I feel like countering with the word seriousist.   *Peter de Vries*

A jest's prosperity lies in the ear
Of him that hears it, never in the tongue
Of him that makes it.   *Shakespeare, 'Love's Labour's Lost'*

Nonsense is an assertion of man's spiritual freedom in spite of all the oppressions of circumstance.   *Aldous Huxley*

Humour is just another defence against the universe.   *Mel Brooks*

The great humorist forgets himself in his delighted contemplation of other people.

Douglas Bush

The role of a comedian is to make the audience laugh, at a minimum of once every fifteen seconds.   *Lenny Bruce*

Laughter is the sensation of feeling good all over, and showing it principally in one spot.   *Josh Billings*

He who laughs, lasts.   *Anon.*

We are all here for a spell, get all the good laughs you can.   *Will Rogers*

No one is more profoundly sad than he who laughs too much.   *Jean Paul Richter*

A joke is an epigram on the death of a feeling.   *Friedrich Nietzsche*

One loses so many laughs by not laughing at oneself.   *Sara Jeannette Duncan*

You can pretend to be serious, but you can't pretend to be witty.   *Sacha Guitry*

Charles Dickens' creation of Mr. Pickwick did more for the elevation of the human race—I say it in all seriousness—than Cardinal Newman's *Lead Kindly Light Amid the Encircling Gloom*. Newman only cried out for light in the gloom of a sad world. Dickens gave it.   *Stephen Leacock*

The love of truth lies at the root of much humour.   *Robertson Davies*

Hypocrisy

Man is the only animal that can remain on friendly terms with the victims he intends to eat until he eats them.   *Samuel Butler*

Hypocrisy is the homage which vice pays to virtue.   *La Rochefoucauld*

He that hath the name to be an early riser may sleep till noon.   *James Howell*

We are not hypocrites in our sleep.   *William Hazlitt*

No man is a hypocrite in his pleasures.   *Samuel Johnson*

The wolf was sick, he vowed a monk to be—
But when he got well, a wolf once more was he.   *Walter Bower*

Remember this: If you work for a man, in Heaven's name, work for him. If he pays you wages which supply you bread and butter, work for him; speak well of him; stand by the institution he represents. If put to a pinch, an ounce of loyalty is worth a pound of cleverness. If you must vilify, condemn and eternally disparage—resign your position, and when you are on the outside, damn to your heart's content, but as long as you are part of the institution do not condemn it.   *Elbert Hubbard*

For neither man nor angel can discern hypocrisy, the only evil that walks invisible.
    John Milton

The teeth are smiling, but is the heart?   *Congo proverb*

Affectation is a greater enemy to the face than smallpox.   *English proverb*

It is a trick among the dishonest to offer sacrifices that are not needed, or not possible, to avoid making those that are required.   *Ivan Goncharov*

When you say that you agree to a thing in principle, you mean that you have not the slightest intention of carrying it out.   *Otto von Bismarck*

An appeaser is one who feeds a crocodile—hoping it will eat him last.
    Winston Churchill

There is luxury in self-reproach. When we blame ourselves we feel that no one else has the right to blame us. *Oscar Wilde*

Extremes meet, and there is no better example than the naughtiness of humility. *Ralph Waldo Emerson*

Hypocrite—mouth one way, belly 'nother way. *Australian Aboriginal proverb*

When the fox preaches, look to your geese. *German proverb*

I hope you have not been leading a double life, pretending to be wicked and being really good all the time. That would be hypocrisy. *Oscar Wilde*

Reasons are whores. *Leonard Michaels*

Ideas

For parlour use, the vague generality is a lifesaver. *George Ade*

If anyone has a new idea in this country, there are twice as many people who keep putting a man with a red flag in front of it. *Prince Philip*

If you are possessed by an idea, you find it expressed everywhere, you even smell it. *Thomas Mann*

In a war of ideas it is people who get killed. *Stanislaw Lec*

To say that an idea is fashionable is to say, I think, that it has been adulterated to a point where it is hardly an idea at all. *Murray Kempton*

You cannot put a rope around the neck of an idea: you cannot put an idea up against a barrack-square wall and riddle it with bullets: you cannot confine it in the strongest prison cell that your slaves could ever build. *Sean O'Casey*

Great ideas are not charitable. *Henry de Montherlant*

For an idea ever to be fashionable is ominous, since it must afterwards be always old-fashioned. *George Santayana*

Every man with an idea has at least two or three followers. *Brooks Atkinson*

An idea is a feat of association, and the height of it is a good metaphor. *Robert Frost*

Every time a man puts a new idea across he finds ten men who thought of it before he did—but they only thought of it. *Anon.*

There is no adequate defence, except stupidity, against the impact of a new idea. *Percy W. Bridgman*

No army can withstand the strength of an idea whose time has come.   *Victor Hugo*

Man's mind stretched to a new idea never goes back to its original dimensions.
Oliver Wendell Holmes

Ideas won't keep: something must be done about them.   *Alfred North Whitehead*

Ideas, as distinguished from events, are never unprecedented.   *Hannah Arendt*

The obstacle is often the departure point for inspiration.   *Clive James*

A cold in the head causes less suffering than an idea.   *Jules Renard*

Very simple ideas lie within the reach only of complex minds.   *Rémy de Gourmont*

An idea is salvation by imagination.   *Frank Lloyd Wright*

Only the wise possess ideas; the greater part of mankind are possessed by them.
Samuel Taylor Coleridge

Big ideas are so hard to recognize, so fragile, so easy to kill. Don't forget that, all of you who don't have them.   *John Elliott, Jr.*

Idleness

A perpetual holiday is a good working definition of Hell.   *George Bernard Shaw*

A physician can sometimes bury the scythe of death, but he has no power over the sand in the hourglass.   *Hester Lynch Thrale*

Life is a zoo in a jungle.   *Peter de Vries*

More free time means more time to waste. The worker who used to have only a little time in which to get drunk and beat his wife now has time to get drunk, beat his wife—and watch TV.   *Robert M. Hutchins*

It is no rest to be idle.   *Paul Peel*

It is impossible to enjoy idling thoroughly unless one has plenty of work to do.
Jerome K. Jerome

There is less leisure now than in the Middle Ages, when one third of the year consisted of holidays and festivals.   *Ralph Borsodi*

Any fool can be fussy and rid himself of energy all over the place, but a man has to have something in him before he can settle down to do nothing.   *J. B. Priestley*

Extreme busyness, whether at school, or college, kirk or market, is a symptom of deficient vitality; and a faculty for idleness implies a catholic appetite and a strong sense of personal identity. *Robert Louis Stevenson*

The hardest work is to go idle. *Jewish proverb*

Of all our faults, the one that we excuse most easily is idleness. *La Rochefoucauld*

Idleness, like kisses, to be sweet must be stolen. *Jerome K. Jerome*

With enough 'ifs' we could put Paris into a bottle. *French proverb*

We are lazier in our minds than in our bodies. *La Rochefoucauld*

Nothing is so intolerable to man as being fully at rest, without passion, without business, without entertainment, without care. It is then that he recognizes that he is empty, insufficient, dependent, ineffectual. From the depths of his soul now comes at once boredom, gloom, sorrow, chagrin, resentment and despair. *Blaise Pascal*

He is idle that might be better employed. *Thomas Fuller*

Nine-tenths of the miseries and vices of mankind proceed from idleness. *Thomas Carlyle*

Even if a farmer intends to loaf, he gets up in time to get an early start. *Edgar Watson Howe*

Did nothing in particular, and did it very well. *W. S. Gilbert*

If a soldier or labourer complains of the hardship of his lot, set him to do nothing. *Blaise Pascal*

How beautiful it is to do nothing, and then rest afterward. *Spanish proverb*

Ignorance

Against stupidity the very gods
Themselves contend in vain. *Friedrich von Schiller*

The uniformed and reckless are always ready to denounce any work which they cannot comprehend. *Sir Henry Parkes*

If I cannot brag of knowing something, then I brag of not knowing it, at any rate, brag. *Ralph Waldo Emerson*

Nothing sways the stupid more than arguments they can't understand. *Cardinal de Retz*

The empty vessel giveth a greater sound than the full barrel. *John Lyly*

There is more stupidity around than hydrogen and it has longer shelf life.

Frank Zappa (Rock star)

To be ignorant of one's ignorance is the malady of the ignorant.

Amos Bronson Alcott

The trouble ain't that people are ignorant: it's that they know so much that ain't so.

Josh Billings

There is nothing more frightening than ignorance in action.   *Goethe*

When an idea is wanting, a word can always be found to take its place.   *Goethe*

If ignorance is indeed bliss, it is a very low grade of the article.   *Tehyi Hsieh*

Not ignorance, but ignorance of ignorance is the death of knowledge.

Alfred North Whitehead

Ignoramus: a person unacquainted with certain kinds of knowledge familiar to yourself, and having certain other kinds that you know nothing about.   *Ambrose Bierce*

Ignorance is no excuse, it's the real thing.   *Irene Peter*

The good Lord set definite limits on man's wisdom, but set no limits on his stupidity—and that's just not fair.   *Konrad Adenauer*

Everybody is ignorant, only on different subjects.   *Will Rogers*

A weak mind does not accumulate force enough to hurt itself; stupidity often saves a man from going mad.   *Oliver Wendell Holmes*

Little wit in the head makes much work for the feet.   *Anon.*

I am not ashamed to confess that I am ignorant of what I do not know.   *Cicero*

all ignorance toboggans into know
and trudges up to ignorance again.

e. e. cummings

The little I know, I owe to my ignorance.   *Sacha Guitry*

It is a blind goose that cometh to the fox's sermon.   *John Lyly*

And here, poor fool, with all my lore
I stand no wiser than before.   *Goethe*

Illusion

Magic lives in curves, not angles.   *Mason Cooley*

Nothing is more sad than the death of an illusion.   *Arthur Koestler*

As I was going up the stair
I met a man who wasn't there.
He wasn't there again today.
I wish, I wish, he'd stay away.   *Hughes Mearns*

The task of the real intellectual consists of analyzing illusions in order to discover
their causes.   *Arthur Miller*

An illusion which makes me happy is worth a verity which drags me to the ground.
                                                   Christoph Martin-Wieland

We must select the illusion which appeals to our temperament, and embrace it with
passion, if we want to be happy.   *Cyril Connolly*

At the end of life illusion falls away.   *Douglas Stewart*

Reputation is an idle and most false imposition; oft got without merit, and lost without
deserving.   *Shakespeare, 'Othello'*

Every real object must cease to be what it seemed and none could ever be what the
whole soul desired.   *George Santayana*

Aspects are within us, and who seems most kingly is king.   *Thomas Hardy*

Those who lose dreaming are lost.   *Australian Aboriginal proverb*

It is dangerous to let the public behind the scenes. They are easily disillusioned and
then they are angry with you, for it was the illusion they loved.
                                                   W. Somerset Maugham

Imagination

A rock pile ceases to be a rock pile the moment a single man contemplates it, bearing
within him the image of a cathedral.   *Antoine de Saint-Exupéry*

Ever let the Fancy roam,
Pleasure never is at home.   *John Keats*

Fools act on imagination without knowledge, pedants act on knowledge without
imagination.   *Alfred North Whitehead*

From ghoulies and ghosties and long-leggedy beasties
And things that go bump in the night, good Lord, deliver us!   *Anon.*

I admit that twice two makes four is an excellent thing, but if we are to give everything
its due, twice two makes five is sometimes a very charming thing too.
                                                   Fyodor Dostoevsky

Inspiration could be called inhaling the memory of an act never experienced.

Ned Rorem

It was a year when Frankie thought about the world. And she did not see it as a round school globe, with the countries neat and different-coloured. She thought of the world as huge and cracked and loose and turning a thousand miles an hour.

Carson McCullers

Saddle your dreams afore you ride 'em.   *Mary Webb*

The eyes are not responsible when the mind does the seeing.   *Publilius Syrus*

Were it not for imagination, a man would be as happy in the arms of a chambermaid as of a duchess.   *Samuel Johnson*

Imagination grows by exercise, and contrary to common belief, is more powerful in the mature than in the young.   *W. Somerset Maugham*

The imagination of a boy is healthy, and the mature imagination of a man is healthy, but there is a space of life between, in which the soul is in ferment, the character undecided, the way of life uncertain.   *John Keats*

His imagination resembled the wings of an ostrich. It enabled him to run, though not to soar.   *Thomas Babington Macaulay (of John Dryden)*

Imagination is the eye of the soul.   *Joseph Joubert*

Imagination is a poor substitute for experience.   *Havelock Ellis*

Imagination frames events unknown,
In wild, fantastic shapes of hideous ruin,
And what it fears, creates.   *Hannah More*

Reason respects the differences, and imagination the similitudes of things.

Percy Bysshe Shelley

The sky is the daily bread of the eyes.   *Ralph Waldo Emerson*

Let us leave pretty women to men without imagination.   *Marcel Proust*

Where does the imagination start
but from primeval images
in man's barbaric heart?   *Roland Robinson*

The value of a sentiment is the amount of sacrifice you are prepared to make for it.

John Galsworthy

It is good to know the truth, but it is better to speak of palm trees.

Arabic proverb

Imitation

Most people go on living their everyday life: frightened, half indifferent, they behold the ghostly tragi-comedy that has been performed on the international stage before the eyes and ears of the world.   *Albert Einstein*

We are, in truth, more than a half of what we are by imitation.   *Lord Chesterfield*

When people are free to do as they please, they usually imitate each other.
Eric Hoffer

Almost all absurdity of conduct arises from the imitation of those whom we cannot resemble.   *Samuel Johnson*

There is a difference between imitating a good man and counterfeiting him.
Benjamin Franklin

Every man is a borrower and a mimic; life is theatrical and literature a quotation.
Ralph Waldo Emerson

We do not imitate, but are a model to others.   *Pericles*

The crow that mimics a cormorant gets drowned.   *Japanese proverb*

We love in others what we lack ourselves, and would be everything but what we are.
R. H. Stoddard

Immature poets imitate: mature poets steal.   *Philip Massinger*

Agesilaus, the Spartan king, was once invited to hear a mimic imitate the nightingale, but declined with the comment that he had heard the nightingale itself.   *Plutarch*

Fewer things are harder to put up with than the annoyance of a good example.
Mark Twain

Indifference and Apathy

There is nothing harder than the softness of indifference.   *Juan Montalvo*

Communists have committed great crimes, but at least they have not stood aside, like an established society, and been indifferent. I would rather have blood on my hands than water, like Pilate.   *Graham Greene*

Hate is not the opposite of love; apathy is.   *Rollo May*

What makes life dreary is want of motive.   *George Eliot*

The hottest places in hell are reserved for those who, in time of great moral crisis, maintain their neutrality.   *Dante*

Once conform, once do what others do because they do it, and a kind of lethargy steals over all the finer senses of the soul.   *Montaigne*

Not to he who is offensive to us are we most unfair, but to he who does not concern us at all.   *Friedrich Nietzsche*

Most of us have no real loves and no real hatreds. Blessed is love, less blessed is hatred, but thrice accursed is that indifference which is neither one nor the other.
     Mark Rutherford

The only menace is inertia.   *St. John Perse*

Tolerance is a tremendous virtue, but the immediate neighbours of tolerance are apathy and weakness.   *Sir James Goldsmith*

The true opposite of love is not hate but indifference. Hate, bad as it is, at least treats the neighbour as a thou, whereas indifference turns the neighbour into an it, a thing. This is why we may say that there is actually one thing worse than evil itself and that is indifference to evil. In human relations the nadir of morality, the lowest point as far as Christian ethics is concerned, is manifest in the phrase, 'I couldn't care less.'
     Joseph Fletcher

I wonder would the apathy of wealthy men endure
Were all their windows level with the faces of the Poor?   *Henry Lawson*

If moderation is a fault, then indifference is a crime.   *G. C. Lichtenberg*

Indifference may not wreck a man's life at any one turn, but it will destroy him with a kind of dry-rot in the long run.   *Bliss Carman*

Innocence

When Pilate saw that he could prevail nothing but that rather a tumult was made, he took water, and washed his hands before the multitude, saying 'I am innocent of the blood of this just person: See to it.' Then answered all the people, and said 'His blood be on us, and on our children.'   *Matthew 27:24–25*

The truly innocent are those who not only are guiltless themselves, but who think others are.   *Josh Billings*

The innocent is the person who explains nothing.   *Albert Camus*

Whoever blushes is already guilty; true innocence is ashamed of nothing.
     Jean-Jacques Rousseau

Through our own recovered innocence we discern the innocence of our neighbours.
     Henry David Thoreau

As innocent as a new-laid egg.   *W. S. Gilbert*

Had laws not been, we never had been blam'd; For not to know we sinn'd is innocence.
William Davenant

Good is when I steal other people's wives and cattle; bad is when they steal mine.
Hottentot proverb

Insults and Calumny

I hope all yer chooks turn into emus and kick yer dunny down.   *Anon*

Injuries may be forgiven, but not forgotten.   *Aesop*

It seldom pays to be rude. It never pays to be only half-rude.   *Norman Douglas*

Lloyd George could not see a belt without hitting below it.   *Margot Asquith*

Be thou as chaste as ice, as pure as snow, thou shalt not escape calumny.
Shakespeare, 'Hamlet

A fly, Sir, may sting a stately horse and make him wince; but one is but an insect and the other a horse still.   *Samuel Johnson*

Calumny is only the noise of madmen.   *Diogenes*

To persevere in one's duty and be silent, is the best answer to calumny.
George Washington

Woe unto you, when all men shall speak well of you.   *Luke 6:26*

Young men soon give, and soon forget affronts,
Old age is slow in both.   *Joseph Addison*

As long as there are readers to be delighted with calumny, there will be found reviewers to calumniate.   *Samuel Taylor Coleridge*

He that flings dirt at another dirtieth himself most.   *Thomas Fuller*

It takes your enemy and your friend, working together to hurt you to the heart; the one to slander you and the other to get the news to you.   *Mark Twain*

What did you say to this gentleman,
   While the altercation lasted?
Did you insult the man in any way?
   I called him a worship, you bastard.   *Denis Kevans, the Poet Lorikeet*

Calumny requires no proof. The throwing out of malicious imputations against any character leaves a stain which no after-refutation can wipe out. To create an unfavourable impression, it is not necessary that certain things should be true, but that they have been said.   *William Hazlitt*

It is often better not to see an insult, than to avenge it.   *Seneca*

Abuse a man unjustly, and you will make friends for him.   *Edgar Watson Howe*

One of the surest signs of the Philistine is his reverence for the superior tastes of those who put him down.   *Pauline Kael*

Intellect

Here's a good rule of thumb
Too clever, is dumb.   *Ogden Nash*

We should take care not to make the intellect our god; it has, of course, powerful muscles, but no personality.   *Albert Einstein*

The intellect is always fooled by the heart.   *La Rochefoucauld*

The job of intellectuals is to come up with ideas, and all we've been producing is footnotes.   *Theodore H. White*

Intellect arrives without the aid of education and culture.   *Norman Lindsay*

All zeal runs down. What replaces it? Intellectualism.   *Arthur R. M. Lower*

Will and intellect are one and the same thing.   *Spinoza*

The highest intellects, like the tops of mountains, are the first to catch and to reflect the dawn.   *Thomas Babington Macaulay*

An intellectual is someone whose mind watches itself.   *Albert Camus*

I hate intellectuals. They are from the top down. I am from the bottom up.
            Frank Lloyd Wright

Think sideways!   *Edward de Bono*

A conclusion is the place where you got tired of thinking.   *Arthur Bloch*

The world holds nothing more precious or beautiful than the cultivated intellect of a man enlightened by faith.   *Cardinal Moran*

My body has certainly wandered a good deal, but I have an uneasy suspicion that my mind has not wandered enough.   *Noel Coward*

There are innumerable instances suggesting that modern intellectuals do not believe themselves, that they don't really believe what they say, that they say certain things only in order to assure themselves that they possess opinions and ideas that are different from those that are entertained by the common herd of men.   *John Lukacs*

Intuition is a spiritual faculty and does not explain, but simply points the way.

Florence Scovel Shinn

The intellect of man is forced to choose
Perfection of the life or of the work.

William Butler Yeats

An intellectual is a man who takes more words than necessary to tell more than he knows.

Dwight D. Eisenhower

The common sense is that which judges the things given to it by other senses.

Leonardo da Vinci

Intelligence

Intelligence is quickness to apprehend as distinct from ability, which is capacity to act wisely on the thing apprehended.

Alfred N. Whitehead

Intuition becomes increasingly valuable in the new information society precisely because there is so much data.

John Naisbitt

The unluckiest insolvent in the world is the man whose expenditure is too great for his income of ideas.

Christopher Morley

To the good listener half a word is enough.

Spanish proverb

Time has a way of demonstrating . . . the most stubborn are the most intelligent.

Yevgeny Yevtushenko

Intelligence must follow faith, never precede it, and never destroy it.

Thomas à Kempis

Intelligence is derived from two words—inter and legere—inter meaning 'between' and legere meaning 'to choose'. An intelligent person, therefore, is one who has learned 'to choose between'. He knows that good is better than evil, that confidence should supersede fear, that love is superior to hate, that gentleness is better than cruelty, forbearance than intolerance, compassion than arrogance, and that truth has more virtue than ignorance.

J. Martin Klotsche

One of the functions of intelligence is to take account of the dangers that come from trusting solely to the intelligence.

Lewis Mumford

The intelligent man who is proud of his intelligence is like the condemned man who is proud of his large cell.

Simone Weil

The sign of an intelligent people is their ability to control emotions by the application of reason.

Marya Mannes

Never tell people how to do things. Tell them what to do and they will surprise you with their ingenuity.

George S. Patton

I not only use all the brains I have, but all I can borrow.   *Woodrow Wilson*

Intelligence is not all that important in the exercise of power and is often, in point of fact, useless. Just as a leader doesn't need intelligence, a man in my job doesn't need too much of it either.   *Henry Kissinger*

The cuckoo who is on to himself is halfway out of the clock.   *Wilson Mizner*

I've had a lot of experience with people smarter than I am.   *Gerald Ford*

Justice

It is always wise, as it is also fair, to test a man by the standards of his own day, and not by those of another.   *Odell Shepard*

The strictest justice is sometimes the greatest injustice.   *Terence*

You have a pretty good case, Mr. Pitkin. How much justice can you afford?
    New Yorker cartoon

Injustice is relatively easy to bear; what stings is justice.   *H. L. Mencken*

Justice and humanity demand interference whenever the weak are being crushed by the strong.   *James Scullin*

A fox should not be on the jury at a goose's trial.   *Thomas Fuller*

Thwackum was for doing justice, and leaving mercy to heaven.   *Henry Fielding*

The Court's authority—possessed of neither the purse nor the sword—ultimately rests on substantial public confidence in its moral sanctions.   *Felix Frankfurter*

Charity is no substitute for justice withheld.   *St. Augustine*

I would remind you that extremism in the defence of liberty is no vice. And let me remind you also that moderation in the pursuit of justice is no virtue.
    Barry Goldwater

Ne'er of the living can the living judge—
Too blind the affection, or too fresh the grudge.   *Anon.*

There never was such a thing as justice in the English laws but any amount of injustice to be had.   *Ned Kelly*

This is a court of law, young man, not a court of justice.
    Oliver Wendell Holmes, Jr.

The whole history of the world is summed up in the fact that, when nations are strong, they are not always just, and when they wish to be just, they are no longer strong.

Winston Churchill

Nobody is poor unless he stand in need of justice.   *Lactantius*

In England, justice is open to all—like the Ritz Hotel.   *Sir James Mathew*

The hungry judges soon the sentence sign,
And wretches hang that jurymen may dine.   *Alexander Pope*

There is no such thing as justice—in or out of court.   *Clarence Darrow*

Justice is too good for some people, and not good enough for the rest.

Norman Douglas

Injustice never rules forever.   *Seneca*

Acquittal of the guilty damns the judge.   *Horace*

Knowledge

All men by nature desire to know.   *Aristotle*

I am not young enough to know everything.   *Oscar Wilde*

I have tried to know absolutely nothing about a great many things, and I have succeeded fairly well.   *Robert Benchley*

Little minds are interested in the extraordinary; great minds in the commonplace.

Elbert Hubbard

Our knowledge can only be finite, while our ignorance must necessarily be infinite.

Karl Popper

Pocket all your knowledge with your watch and never pull it out in company unless desired.   *Lord Chesterfield*

President Reagan didn't always know what he knew.   *Lt. Col. Oliver North*

Ten lands are sooner known than one man.   *Old saying*

The public do not know enough to be experts, yet know enough to decide between them.   *Samuel Butler*

There are times I think I am not sure of something which I absolutely know.

Mongkut, King of Siam

There are two kinds of statistics, the kind you look up and the kind you make up.

Rex Stout

There was never an age in which useless knowledge was more important than in our own.   *Cyril Joad*

We're drowning in information and starving for knowledge.   *Rutherford D. Rogers*

You never know what is enough unless you know what is more than enough.

William Blake

Zeal without knowledge is fire without light.   *Thomas Fuller*

Our knowledge is a receding mirage in an expanding desert of ignorance.

Will Durant

Knowledge is of two kinds; we know a subject ourselves, or we know where we can find information upon it.   *Samuel Johnson*

As we acquire more knowledge, things do not become more comprehensible, but more mysterious.   *Albert Schweitzer*

A man must carry knowledge with him, if he would bring home knowledge.

Samuel Johnson

Grace is given of God, but knowledge is bought in the market.

Arthur Hugh Clough

If a little knowledge is dangerous—where is the man who has so much as to be out of danger?   *Thomas Huxley*

We owe almost all our knowledge not to those who have agreed, but to those who have differed.   *Charles Caleb Colton*

Sit down before fact as a little child, be prepared to give up every preconceived notion, follow humbly wherever and to whatever abyss nature leads, or you shall learn nothing.

Thomas Huxley

The learned is happy, nature to explore,
The fool is happy, that he knows no more.   *Alexander Pope*

One of the greatest joys known to man is to take a flight into ignorance in search of knowledge.   *Robert Lynd*

I do not pretend to know what many ignorant men are sure of.   *Clarence Darrow*

A man only understands what is akin to something already existing in himself.

Henri Frédéric Amiel

Everybody gets so much common information all day long that they lose their common sense.   *Gertrude Stein*

Anyone who stops learning is old, whether at twenty or eighty. Anyone who keeps learning stays young. The greatest thing in life is to keep your mind young.

Henry Ford

The first problem for all of us, men and women, is not to learn, but to unlearn.

Gloria Steinem

We should live and learn; but by the time we've learned, it's too late to live.

Carolyn Wells

The specialist is a man who fears the other subjects. *Martin H. Fisher*

All that men really understand is confined to a very small compass; to their daily affairs and experience; to what they have an opportunity to know; and motives to study or practise. The rest is affectation and imposture. *William Hazlitt*

There is much pleasure to be gained from useless knowledge. *Bertrand Russell*

Every great advance in natural knowledge has involved the absolute rejection of authority. *Thomas Huxley*

It isn't what we don't know that gives us trouble, it's what we know that ain't so.

Will Rogers

In all affairs, love, religion, politics or business, it's a healthy idea, now and then, to hang a question mark on things you have long taken for granted. *Bertrand Russell*

Knowledge is power. *Francis Bacon*

Man is not weak—knowledge is more than equivalent to force. The master of mechanics laughs at strength. *Samuel Johnson*

To know that we know what we know, and that we do not know what we do not know, that is true knowledge. *Henry David Thoreau*

No-one is ever too old to know better. *Margaret Preston*

They know enough who know how to learn. *Henry Adams*

Law and Lawyers

Appeal in law: to put the dice into the box for another throw. *Ambrose Bierce*

Divorce is a game played by lawyers. *Cary Grant*

Far more has been accomplished for the welfare and progress of mankind by preventing bad actions than by doing good ones. *William Lyon Mackenzie King*

It is as if the ordinary language we use every day has a hidden set of signals, a kind of secret code. *William Stafford*

It usually takes 100 years to make a law, and then, after it's done its work, it usually takes 100 years to be rid of it. *Henry Ward Beecher*

Law is the witness and external deposit of our moral life. Its history is the history of the moral development of the race. *Oliver Wendell Holmes*

Laws are the spider's webs which, if anything small falls into them they ensnare it, but large things break through and escape. *Solon*

Lawyers are the only persons in whom ignorance of the law is not punished. *Jeremy Bentham*

Lawyers spend a great deal of time shovelling smoke. *Oliver Wendell Holmes, Jr.*

Revenge is a kind of wild justice, which the more man's nature runs to, the more ought law to weed it out. *Francis Bacon*

That is the beauty of the Common Law, it is a maze and not a motorway. *Lord Diplock*

The law of England is a very strange one; it cannot compel anyone to tell the truth. . . . But what the law can do is to give you seven years for not telling the truth. *Lord Darling*

A community that endures a contemptible law is itself contemptible. *A.G. Stephens*

When the 30–year-old lawyer died he said to St. Peter, 'How can you do this to me?—a heart attack at my age? I'm only 30.'
Replied St. Peter: 'When we looked at your total hours billed we figured you were 95.' *Anon.*

You are remembered for the rules you break. *Douglas MacArthur*

Law . . . begins when someone takes to doing something someone else does not like. *Karl Llewellyn*

Any fool can make a rule, and every fool will mind it. *Anon.*

Show me the man and I'll show you the law. *David Ferguson*

A man may as well open an oyster without a knife, as a lawyer's mouth without a fee. *Barten Holyday*

The law is the greatest threat to democracy. *Evan Whitton*

When you have no basis for an argument, abuse the plaintiff. *Cicero*

The adversary system is a kind of warfare in mufti. *R. I. Fitzhenry*

A jury consists of twelve persons chosen to decide who has the better lawyer.
Robert Frost

Lawyers are men who hire out their words and anger.   *Martial*

Litigant: a person about to give up his skin for the hope of retaining his bone.
Ambrose Bierce

In America, an acquittal doesn't mean you're innocent, it means you beat the rap. My clients lose even when they win.   *F. Lee Bailey*

Law and order is one of the steps taken to maintain injustice.   *Edward Bond*

Whatever is enforced by command is more imputed to him who exacts than to him who performs.   *Montaigne*

The life of the law has not been logic: it has been experience.
Oliver Wendell Holmes, Jr

Every new time will give its law.   *Maxim Gorky*

Lawyers and painters can soon change white to black.   *Danish proverb*

No man is above the law and no man is below it: nor do we ask any man's permission when we ask him to obey it.   *Theodore Roosevelt*

Fragile as reason is and limited as law is as the institutionalized medium of reason that's all we have standing between us and the tyranny of mere will and the cruelty of unbridled, undisciplined feeling.   *Felix Frankfurter*

A lawyer's dream of heaven—every man reclaimed his property at the resurrection and each tried to recover it from all his forefathers.   *Samuel Butler*

A vague uneasiness; the police. It's like when you suddenly understand you have to undress in front of the doctor.   *Ugo Betti*

A successful lawsuit is the one worn by a policeman.   *Robert Frost*

Those who are too lazy and comfortable to think for themselves and be their own judges obey the laws. Others sense their own laws within them.   *Hermann Hesse*

Every skilled person is to be believed with reference to his own art.   *Legal maxim*

An excess of law inescapably weakens the rule of law.   *Laurence H. Tribe*

A judge is a law student who marks his own examination papers.   *H. L. Mencken*

I understand you undertake to overthrow my undertaking.   *Gertrude Stein*

The law locks up both man and woman
Who steals the goose from off the common,
But lets the great felon loose
Who steals the common from the goose.   *Anon.*

I know of no method to secure the repeal of bad or obnoxious laws so effective as
their stringent execution.   *Ulysses S. Grant*

Law school taught me one thing: how to take two situations that are exactly the same
and show how they are different.   *Hart Pomerantz*

To some lawyers, all facts are created equal.   *Felix Frankfurter*

And whether you're an honest man, or whether you're a thief,
Depends on whose solicitor has given me my brief.   *W. S. Gilbert*

The law, in its majestic equality, forbids the rich as well as the poor to sleep under
bridges, to beg in the streets, and to steal bread.   *Anatole France*

In cross-examination, as in fishing, nothing is more ungainly than a fisherman pulled
into the water by his catch.   *Louis Nizer*

Well, I don't know as I want a lawyer to tell me what I cannot do. I hire him to tell
me how to do what I want to do.   *J. P. Morgan*

The law must be stable and yet it must not stand still.   *Roscoe Pound*

An appeal is when ye ask wan court to show its contempt for another court.
                    Finley Peter Dunne

Law is nothing unless close behind it stands a warm, living public opinion.
                    Wendell Phillips

If there were no bad people, there would be no good lawyers.   *Charles Dickens*

The aim of law is the maximum gratification of the nervous system of man.
                    Learned Hand

Laws, like the spider's web, catch the fly and let the hawk go free.
                    Spanish proverb

Laziness

He has a head that is for rent unfurnished.   *Anon.*

The lust for comfort, that stealthy thing that enters the house a guest and then becomes
a host, and then a master.   *Kahlil Gibran*

The lazy man gets round the sun as quickly as the busy one.   *R. T. Wombat*

It is the just doom of laziness and a gluttony to be inactive without ease, and drowsy without tranquillity.   *Samuel Johnson*

Tomorrow is often the busiest day of the year.   *Spanish proverb*

The lazy are always wanting to do something.   *Vauvenargues*

Some folks can look so busy doing nothin' that they seem indispensable.
Kin Hubbard

Indolence is a delightful but distressing state. We must be doing something to be happy.
William Hazlitt

Failure is not our only punishment for laziness: there is also the success of others.
Jules Renard

Leaders and Leadership

He who would rule must hear and be deaf, see and be blind.   *German proverb*

I know I have the body of a weak and feeble woman, but I have the heart and stomach of a King, and of a King of England too.   *Elizabeth I*

It is a characteristic of all movements and crusades that the psychopathic element rises to the top.   *Robert Lindner*

It is much safer to obey than to rule.   *Thomas à Kempis*

It is said that Mr. Gladstone could persuade most people of most things, and himself of anything.   *Dean William R. Inge*

It is the characteristic excellence of the strong man that he can bring momentous issues to the fore and make a decision about them. The weak are always forced to decide between alternatives they have not chosen themselves.   *Dietrich Bonhoeffer*

Nothing is more difficult, and therefore more precious, than to be able to decide.
Napoleon Bonaparte

There are two levers for moving men—interest and fear.   *Napoleon Bonaparte*

To get others to come into our ways of thinking, we must go over to theirs; and it is necessary to follow, in order to lead.   *William Hazlitt*

With a good conscience our only sure reward, with history the final judge of our deeds, let us go forth to lead the land we love asking His blessing and His help, but knowing that here on earth God's work must truly be our own.   *John F. Kennedy*

Achilles absent, was Achilles still.   *Homer*

To lead the people, walk behind them.   *Lao-Tzu*

I suppose leadership at one time meant muscles; but today it means getting along with people.   *Indira Gandhi*

When you come into the presence of a leader of men, you know that you have come into the presence of fire—that it is best not uncautiously to touch that man—that there is something that makes it dangerous to cross him.   *Woodrow Wilson*

I've got to follow them—I am their leader.   *Alexandre Ledru-Rollin*

The reward of a general is not a bigger tent—but command.
                                                    Oliver Wendell Holmes, Jr.

A leader may symbolize and express what is best in his people, like Pericles, or what is worst, like Hitler, but he cannot successfully express what is only in his heart and not in theirs.   *Charles Yost*

After 15 years of work I have achieved, as a common German soldier and merely with my fanatical willpower, the unity of the German nation, and have freed it from the death sentence of Versailles.   *Adolf Hitler*

A true leader always keeps an element of surprise up his sleeve, which others cannot grasp but which keeps his public excited and breathless.   *Charles de Gaulle*

If I advance, follow me! If I retreat, kill me! If I die, avenge me!   *La Rochejaquelin*

If I advance, follow me! If I retreat, cut me down! If I die, avenge me!   *Mussolini*

Follow me, if I advance; kill me if I retreat; revenge me if I die!
                                    Ngo Dinh Diem (on becoming President of Vietnam)

A frightened captain makes a frightened crew.   *Lister Sinclair*

As for the best leaders, the people do not notice their existence. The next best, the people honour and praise. The next, the people fear, and the next the people hate. When the best leader's work is done, the people say, 'we did it ourselves!' *Lao-Tzu*

The slave begins by demanding justice and ends by wanting to wear a crown. He must dominate in his turn.   *Albert Camus*

A leader is a dealer in hope.   *Napoleon Bonaparte*

To lead means to direct and to exact, and no man dares do either—he might be unpopular. What authority we are given now is a trinity: the grin, the generality, and God (the Word).   *Marya Mannes*

Dictators are rulers who always look good until the last ten minutes.   *Jan Masaryk*

A chief is a man who assumes responsibility. He says, 'I was beaten'; he does not say 'My men were beaten.'   *Antoine de Saint-Exupéry*

Every man of action has a strong dose of egotism, pride, hardness and cunning. But all those things will be forgiven him, indeed, they will be regarded as high qualities, if he can make them the means to achieve great ends. *Charles de Gaulle*

Dictators ride to and fro upon tigers from which they dare not dismount. *Hindu proverb*

A Prime Minister exercises his greatest public influence by creating a public impression of himself, hoping all the time that the people will be generous rather than just. *R. G. Menzies*

It is better to have a lion at the head of an army of sheep, than a sheep at the head of an army of lions. *Daniel Defoe*

Where there are no tigers, a wildcat is very self-important. *Korean proverb*

I always tell my staff, 'I don't care a damn for your loyalty when you think I am right. The time I want it is when you think I am wrong.' *Sir John Monash*

I really believe my greatest service is in the many unwise steps I prevent. *William Lyon Mackenzie King*

I have nothing to offer but blood, toil, tears and sweat. *Winston Churchill*

I have never accepted what many people have kindly said, namely that I have inspired the nation. It was the nation and the race dwelling all around the globe that had the lion heart. I had the luck to be called upon to give the roar. *Winston Churchill*

Winston has written four volumes about himself and called it 'World Crisis'. *Arthur Balfour*

Winston Churchill—fifty per cent genius, fifty per cent bloody fool. *Clement Attlee*

If you shoot at a king you must kill him. *Ralph Waldo Emerson*

The final test of a leader is that he leaves behind in other men the conviction and the will to carry on. *Walter Lippmann*

Flexibility in pursuit of the nation's interests must never be allowed to degenerate into expediency. *Malcolm Fraser*

Every woman's man, and every man's woman. *Said to be the elder Curio's description of Julius Caesar*

In America, any boy may become president, and I suppose it's just one of the risks he takes. *Adlai Stevenson*

Liars and Lying

Travellers from afar can lie with impunity.   *French proverb*

Truth is the safest lie.   *Jewish proverb*

All men are born truthful, and die liars.   *Vauvenargues*

The lie is a condition of life.   *Friedrich Nietzsche*

It takes a wise man to handle a lie. A fool had better remain honest.
Norman Douglas

We pay a person the compliment of acknowledging his superiority whenever we lie
to him.   *Samuel Butler*

Who lies for you will lie against you.   *Bosnian proverb*

Lying commends itself to the juvenile mind as being easy, inexpensive and convenient;
and in course of time the habit becomes fixed. In fact, mankind may be broadly divided
into two classes—perpetual liars and intermittent liars.
'Tom Collins' (Joseph Furphy)

I deny the lawfulness of telling a lie to a sick man for fear of alarming him; you have
no business with consequences, you are to tell the truth.   *Samuel Johnson*

There are frequently no larger or more deceptive lies than those which are based on
truth.   *F. J. Mills*

I do not mind lying, but I hate inaccuracy.   *Samuel Butler*

A little inaccuracy sometimes saves tons of explanations.   *Saki*

A half-truth is a whole lie.   *Jewish proverb*

A liar should have a good memory.   *Quintilian*

Oh, don't tell me of facts—I never believe in facts; you know Canning said nothing
was so fallacious as facts, except figures.   *Sydney Smith*

Liberty and Human Rights

I am not so much concerned with the right of everyone to say anything he pleases as
I am about our need as self-governing people to hear everything relevant.
John F. Kennedy

Liberty is always unfinished business.   *American Civil Liberties Union*

Rights that do not flow from duty well performed are not worth having.   *Gandhi*

So free we seem, so fettered fast we are!   *Robert Browning*

The liberty of the individual must be thus far limited; he must not make himself a
nuisance to other people.   *John Stuart Mill*

We look forward to a world founded upon four essential human freedoms. The first
is freedom of speech and expression—everywhere in the world. The second is freedom
of every person to worship God in his own way everywhere in the world. The third
is freedom from want...everywhere in the world. The fourth is freedom from fear . . .
anywhere in the world.   *Franklin D. Roosevelt*

Yes, 'n' how many years can some people exist
Before they're allowed to be free?
Yes, 'n' how many times can a man turn his head
Pretending he just doesn't see?
The answer, my friend is blowin' in the wind.   *Bob Dylan*

These are the times that try men's souls. The summer soldier and the sunshine patriot
will, in this crisis, shrink from the service of their country, but he that stands it now,
deserves the love and thanks of man and woman. Tyranny, like hell, is not easily
conquered; yet we have this consolation with us, that the harder the conflict, the more
glorious the triumph.   *Thomas Paine*

It is a fair summary of history to say that the safeguards of liberty have frequently
been forged in cases involving not very nice people.   *Felix Frankfurter*

The spirit of liberty is the spirit which is not too sure that it is right.   *Learned Hand*

Liberty is always dangerous—but it is the safest thing we have.
                                                                                   Harry Emerson Fosdick

And so, my fellow Americans, ask not what your country can do for you—ask what
you can do for your country. My fellow citizens of the world: ask not what America
will do for you, but what together we can do for the freedom of man.
                                                   John F. Kennedy (Inaugural Address, January 1961)

None can love freedom heartily, but good men—the rest love not freedom, but licence.
                                                                                   John Milton

One should never put on one's best trousers to go out to battle for freedom and truth.
                                                                                   Henrik Ibsen

I understand by 'freedom of spirit' something quite definite—the unconditional will to
say No, where it is dangerous to say No.   *Friedrich Nietzsche*

Man was born free and everywhere he is in shackles.   *Jean-Jacques Rousseau*

Liberty means responsibility. That is why most men dread it.   *George Bernard Shaw*

My definition of a free society is a society where it is safe to be unpopular.
                                                                                   Adlai Stevenson

For two decades the state has been taking liberties, and these liberties were once ours.
E. P. Thompson

By physical liberty I mean the right to do anything which does not interfere with the happiness of another. By intellectual liberty I mean the right to think wrong.
Robert G. Ingersoll

There can be no real freedom without the freedom to fail.   *Eric Hoffer*

Liberty, as it is conceived by current opinion, has nothing inherent about it; it is a sort of gift or trust bestowed on the individual by the state pending good behaviour.
Mary McCarthy

The right to be heard does not automatically include the right to be taken seriously.
Hubert Humphrey

If liberty has any meaning it means freedom to improve.   *Philip Wylie*

Those who expect to reap the blessings of freedom must, like men, undergo the fatigue of supporting it.   *Thomas Paine*

Let every nation know, whether it wishes us well or ill, that we shall pay any price, bear any burden, meet any hardship, support any friend, oppose any foe, in order to assure the survival and the success of liberty.   *John F. Kennedy*

The measure of freedom in any community is the extent of opposition to the ruling order, of criticism of the ruling ideas; and beliefs in established freedom, or in State-guaranteed 'benefits', is a mark of the abandonment of liberty.   *John Anderson*

To be truly free, it takes more determination, courage, introspection and restraint than to be in shackles.   *Pietro Bellusch*

Equality of opportunity is an equal opportunity to prove unequal talents.
Viscount Samuel

The greatest right in the world is the right to be wrong.   *Harry Weinberger*

We who lived in concentration camps can remember the men who walked through the huts comforting others, giving away their last piece of bread. They may have been few in number, but they offer sufficient proof that everything can be taken from a man but one thing: the last of human freedoms—to choose one's attitude in any given set of circumstances—to choose one's own way.   *Viktor Frankl*

The world must be made safe for democracy. Its peace must be planted upon the tested foundations of political liberty. We have no selfish ends to serve. We desire no conquest, no domination. We seek no indemnities for ourselves, no material compensation for the sacrifices we shall freely give. We are but one of the champions of the rights of mankind. We shall be satisfied when those rights have been made as secure as the faith and freedom of nations can make them.   *Woodrow Wilson*

A free man is as jealous of his responsibilities as he is of his liberties.   *Cyril James*

All free men, wherever they may live, are citizens of Berlin. And therefore, as a free man, I take pride in the words 'Ich bin ein Berliner.' *John F. Kennedy*

Liberty is the right to do what the law permits. *Montesquieu*

Once freedom lights its beacon in a man's heart, the gods are powerless against him. *Jean-Paul Sartre*

Equality is the result of human organization. We are not born equal. *Hannah Arendt*

When you have robbed a man of everything, he is no longer in your power. He is free again. *Aleksandr Solzhenitsyn*

The effect of liberty on individuals is that they may do what they please: we ought to see what it will please them to do, before we risk congratulations. *Edmund Burke*

We are in bondage to the law in order that we may be free. *Cicero*

The most certain test by which we judge whether a country is really free is the amount of security enjoyed by minorities. *John, Lord Acton*

People hardly ever make use of the freedom they have, for example, freedom of thought; instead they demand freedom of speech as a compensation. *Søren Kierkegaard*

Life

The world is a beautiful place
to be born into
if you don't mind some people dying
all the time
or maybe only starving
some of the time
which isn't half so bad
if it isn't you.

Laurence Ferlinghetti
'Pictures of the Gone World'

A tragedy means always a man's struggle with that which is stronger than man. *G. K. Chesterton*

After the game, the king and pawn go into the same box. *Italian proverb*

All I want is a little more than I'll ever get. *©Ashleigh Brilliant*

All men should strive to learn before they die
What they are running from, and to, and why. *James Thurber*

And how am I to face the odds
Of man's bedevilment and God's?
I, a stranger and afraid
In a world I never made.   *A. E. Housman*

Before I knew the best part of my life had come, it had gone.
                                        ©*Epitaph by Ashleigh Brilliant*

I like life. It's something to do. Somewhere on this globe every 10 seconds, there is
a woman giving birth to a child. She must be found and stopped.   *Sam Levinson*

Cats and monkeys—monkeys and cats—all human life is there.   *Henry James*

Don't do things to not die, do things to enjoy living.
The by-product may be not dying.   *Bernie S. Siegel, M.D.*

Every man's road in life is marked by the graves of his personal likings.
                                        Alexander Smith

Give me neither poverty nor riches; feed me with food convenient for me.
                                        Proverbs 30:8

I haven't heard of anybody who wants to stop living on account of the cost.
                                        F. McKinney Hubbard

If there is another world, he lives in bliss
If there is none, he made the best of this.   *Robert Burns*

If way to the Better there be, it exacts a full look at the Worst.   *Thomas Hardy*

If you won't be better tomorrow than you were today, then what do you need tomorrow
for?   *Rabbi Nahman of Bratslav*

In the morning a man walks with his whole body; in the evening, only with his legs.
                                        Ralph Waldo Emerson

Is not this the true romantic feeling—not to desire to escape life, but to prevent life
from escaping you.   *Thomas Wolfe*

Life is a handful of short stories, pretending to be a novel.   *Anon.*

Life is a long lesson in humility.   *Sir James M. Barrie*

Life is all memory, except for the one present moment that goes by you so quickly
you hardly catch it going.   *Tennessee Williams*

Life is better than death, I believe, if only because it is less boring and because it has
fresh peaches in it.   *Thomas Walker*

Life is for each man a solitary cell whose walls are mirrors.   *Eugene O'Neill*

Life is like a game of cards. The hand that is dealt you represents determinism; the way you play it is free will. *Jawaharlal Nehru*

Life is not having been told that the man has just waxed the floor. *Ogden Nash*

Life is the art of drawing sufficient conclusions from insufficient premises. *Samuel Butler*

Life is the only art that we are required to practise without preparation, and without being allowed the preliminary trials, the failures and botches, that are essential for the training of a mere beginner. *Lewis Mumford*

Magnificently unprepared
For the long littleness of life. *Frances Cornford*

Man arrives as a novice at each age of his life. *Sebastien Chamfort*

Man wants but little here below
Nor wants that little long. *Oliver Goldsmith*

Oh for a life of sensations rather than of thoughts. *John Keats*

Our insignificance is often the cause of our safety. *Aesop*

Population, when unchecked, increases in a geometrical ratio. Subsistence only increases in an arithmetical ratio. *Thomas Robert Malthus*

Real life is to most men, a long second best, a perpetual compromise between the ideal and the possible. *Bertrand Russell*

Sometimes I wish life had a fast-forward button. *Dan Chopin*

St. Teresa of Avila described our life in this world as like a night at a second-class hotel. *Malcolm Muggeridge*

The character of human life, like the character of the human condition, like the character of all life, is 'ambiguity': the inseparable mixture of good and evil, the true and false, the creative and destructive forces—both individual and social. *Paul Tillich*

The closing years of life are like the end of a masquerade party, when the masks are dropped. *Arthur Schopenhauer*

The flower is the poetry of reproduction. It is the example of the eternal seductiveness of life. *Jean Giraudoux*

The great business of life is to be, to do, to do without and to depart. *John Morley*

The Indian Summer of life should be a little sunny and a little sad, like the season, and infinite in wealth and depth of tone—but never hustled. *Henry Adams*

The real reason for not committing suicide is because you always know how swell life gets again after the hell is over.   *Ernest Hemingway*

The trouble with the rat race is that even if you win, you're still a rat.   *Lily Tomlin*

The vanity of human life is like a river, constantly passing away, and yet constantly coming on.   *Alexander Pope*

The world is made up of people who never quite get into the first team and who just miss the prizes at the flower show.   *Jacob Bronowski*

There are days when it takes all you've got just to keep up with the losers.
Robert Orpen

This is the true joy in life, the being used for a purpose recognized by yourself as a mighty one; the being thoroughly worn out before you are thrown on the scrap heap.
George Bernard Shaw

We live in what is, but we find 1,000 ways not to face it. Great theatre strengthens our faculty to face it.   *Thornton Wilder*

When the world has once begun to use us ill, and afterwards continues the same treatment with less scruple or ceremony, as men do to a whore.   *Jonathan Swift*

Without duty, life is soft and boneless; it cannot hold itself together.   *Joseph Joubert*

Life only demands from the strength you possess. Only one feat is possible—not to have run away.   *Dag Hammarskjöld*

In three words I can sum up everything I've learned about life. It goes on.
Robert Frost

Life is ours to be spent, not to be saved.   *D. H. Lawrence*

Life is a luminous halo, a semi-transparent envelope surrounding us from the beginning.
Virginia Woolf

Life is mostly froth and bubble,
  Two things stand like stone,
Kindness in another's trouble,
  Courage in your own.   *Adam Lindsay Gordon*

Life would be infinitely happier if we could only be born at the age of eighty and gradually approach eighteen.   *Mark Twain*

Living is only made bearable by a succession of miracles.   *John Shaw Neilson*

The first half of our lives is ruined by our parents and the second half by our children.
Clarence Darrow

The great pleasure in life is doing what people say you cannot do.   *Walter Bagehot*

Life consists in what a man is thinking of all day. *Ralph Waldo Emerson*

Life is action and passion; therefore, it is required of a man that he should share the passion and action of the time, at peril of being judged not to have lived.
Oliver Wendell Holmes, Jr.

I have measured out my life with coffee spoons. *T. S. Eliot*

If there is a sin against life, it consists perhaps not so much in despairing of life as in hoping for another, and in eluding the implacable grandeur of this life.
Albert Camus

Life can only be understood backwards; but it must be lived forwards.
Søren Kierkegaard

The joy of life is variety; the tenderest love requires to be renewed by intervals of absence. *Samuel Johnson*

O Life! thou art a galling load,
Along a rough, a weary road,
To wretches such as I. *Robert Burns*

I am on the side of the unregenerate who affirm the worth of life as an end in itself, as against the saints who deny it. *Oliver Wendell Holmes, Jr.*

The natural rhythm of human life is routine punctuated by orgies. *Aldous Huxley*

Were the offer made true, I would engage to run again, from beginning to end, the same career of life. All I would ask should be the privilege of an author, to correct, in a second edition, certain errors of the first. *Benjamin Franklin*

Life is what happens to us while we are making other plans. *Thomas la Mance*

The man who has no inner life is the slave of his surroundings.
Henri Frédéric Amiel

People in the West are always getting ready to live. *Chinese proverb*

You've got to keep fighting—you've got to risk your life every six months to stay alive. *Elia Kazan*

Unless you can find some sort of loyalty, you cannot find unity and peace in your active living. *Josiah Royce*

Life, as it is called, is for most of us one long postponement. *Henry Miller*

Life is a progress from want to want, not from enjoyment to enjoyment.
Samuel Johnson

Life as we find it is too hard for us; it entails too much pain, too many disappointments, impossible tasks. We cannot do without palliative remedies. *Sigmund Freud*

Be intent upon the perfection of the present day.   *William Law*

Life is a long preparation for something that never happens.   *William Butler Yeats*

You only live once—but if you work it right, once is enough.   *Joe E. Lewis*

Growth is the only evidence of life.   *Cardinal Newman*

Life is a stranger's sojourn, a night at an inn.   *Marcus Aurelius*

Most people get a fair amount of fun out of their lives, but on balance life is suffering and only the very sound or the very foolish imagine otherwise.   *George Orwell*

The whole of what we know is a system of compensations. Each suffering is rewarded; each sacrifice is made up; every debt is paid.   *Ralph Waldo Emerson*

The truth that many people never understand, until it is too late, is that the more you try to avoid suffering the more you suffer because smaller and more insignificant things begin to torture you in proportion to your fear of being hurt.   *Thomas Merton*

The tragedy of life is not so much what men suffer, but rather what they miss.
Thomas Carlyle

He who despairs of the human condition is a coward, but he who has hope for it is a fool.   *Albert Camus*

Basically, I'm interested in friendship, sex and death.   *Sharon Riis*

Such as we are made of, such we be.   *Shakespeare*

Measurement of life should be proportioned rather to the intensity of the experience than to its actual length.   *Thomas Hardy*

Life is seldom as unendurable as, to judge by the facts, it logically ought to be.
Brooks Atkinson

Birth, copulation and death. That's all the facts when you come to brass tacks.
T. S. Eliot

Life is an offensive, directed against the repetitious mechanism of the universe.
Alfred North Whitehead

There is no cure for birth and death, save to enjoy the interval.   *George Santayana*

The art of living is more like that of wrestling than of dancing. The main thing is to stand firm and be ready for an unforeseen attack.   *Marcus Aurelius*

We never live, but we are always in the expectation of living.   *Voltaire*

Life, we learn too late, is in the living, in the tissue of every day and hour.
Stephen Leacock

There is time for work. And time for love. That leaves no other time. *Coco Chanel*

It is not the years in your life but the life in your years that counts.

Adlai Stevenson

A single event can awaken within us a stranger totally unknown to us. To live is to be slowly born. *Antoine de Saint-Exupéry*

One hour of life, crowded to the full with glorious action, and filled with noble risks, is worth whole years of those mean observances of paltry decorum. *Walter Scott*

The good life, as I conceive it, is a happy life. I do not mean that if you are good you will be happy—I mean that if you are happy you will be good.

Bertrand Russell

One man in his time plays many parts. *Shakespeare, 'As You Like It'*

He alone deserves liberty and life who daily must win them anew. *Goethe*

One returns to the place one came from. *Jean de la Fontaine*

The true meaning of life is to plant trees, under whose shade you do not expect to sit.

Nelson Henderson

It is now life and not art that requires the willing suspension of disbelief.

Lionel Trilling

The great use of life is to spend it for something that will outlast it. *William James*

Life is painting a picture, not doing a sum. *Oliver Wendell Holmes, Jr.*

Go placidly amid the noise and the haste, and remember what peace there may be in silence. As far as possible without surrender, be on good terms with all persons. Speak your truth quietly and clearly, and listen to others, even the dull and ignorant; they too have their story. Be yourself. Especially do not feign affection. Neither be cynical about love—for in the face of all aridity and disenchantment it is as perennial as the grass. Take kindly the counsel of the years, gracefully surrendering the things of youth. Nurture strength of spirit to shield you in sudden misfortune. But do not distress yourself with imaginings. Many fears are born of fatigue and loneliness. Beyond a wholesome discipline, be gentle with yourself. You are a child of the universe no less than the trees and the stars; you have a right to be here. And whether or not it is clear to you, no doubt the universe is unfolding as it should. Therefore be at peace with God, whatever you conceive Him to be, and whatever your labours and aspirations, in the noisy confusion of life keep peace with your soul. With all its sham, drudgery and broken dreams, it is still a beautiful world. *From the works of Max Ehrmann*

At any given moment life is completely senseless. But viewed over a period, it seems to reveal itself as an organism existing in time, having a purpose, tending in a certain direction. *Aldous Huxley*

Without a measureless and perpetual uncertainty, the drama of human life would be destroyed.
Winston Churchill

Life begins on the other side of despair.
Jean-Paul Sartre

For he who lives more lives than one,
More deaths than one must die.
Oscar Wilde

It is better to wear out than to rust out.
George Whitefield

My advice to those who are about to begin, in earnest, the journey of life, is to take their heart in one hand and a club in the other.
Josh Billings

One must choose in life between boredom and suffering.
Madame de Staël

All of life is more or less what the French would call *s'imposer*—to be able to create one's own terms for what one does.
Kenneth Tynan

The power of habit and the charm of novelty are the two adverse forces which explain the follies of mankind.
Comtesse Diane (Marie de Beausacq)

Real life seems to have no plots.
Ivy Compton-Burnett

There are two ways to slide easily through life; to believe everything or doubt everything. Both ways save us from thinking.
Alfred Korzybski

Life is one long process of getting tired.
Samuel Butler

He who has a why to live can bear with almost any how.
Friedrich Nietzsche

Oh, how daily life is. (*Ah, que la vie est quotidienne.*)
Jules Laforgue

Death and taxes and childbirth. There's never any convenient time for any of them.
Margaret Mitchell

We're all in this together—by ourselves.
Lily Tomlin

Normal day, let me be aware of the treasure you are. Let me learn from you, love you, savour you, bless you before you depart. Let me not pass you by in quest of some rare and perfect tomorrow. Let me hold you while I may, for it will not always be so. One day I shall dig my nails into the earth, or bury my face in the pillow, or stretch myself taut, or raise my hands to the sky, and want, more than all the world, your return.
Mary Jean Irion

A proverb is no proverb to you till life has illustrated it.
John Keats

Ah well, I suppose it has come to this! . . . Such is Life.
Ned Kelly

It is not true that life is one damn thing after another—it's one damn thing over and over.
Edna St. Vincent Millay

Literature

I am never long, even in the society of her I love, without yearning for the company of my lamp and my library.   *Lord Byron*

The walls are the publishers of the poor.   *Eduardo Galearo*

A novel is a static thing that one moves through; a play is a dynamic thing that moves past one.   *Kenneth Tyncn*

Chaucer, I confess, is a rough diamond; and must be polished e'er he shines.
John Dryden

I can find my biography in every fable that I read.   *Ralph Waldo Emerscn*

Literature is mostly about sex and not much about having children; and life is the other way around.   *David Lodge*

Literature is my utopia.   *Helen Keller*

Literature is the art of writing something that will be read twice; journalism what will be grasped at once.   *Cyril Connolty*

Literature was formerly an art and finance a trade: today it is the reverse.
Joseph Roux

Great literature is like moral leadership; everyone deplores the lack of it, but there is a tendency to prefer it from the safely dead.   *Shirley Hazzard*

The first thing to be done by a biographer in estimating character is to examine the stubs of the victim's cheque books.   *Silas W. Mitchell*

The llama is a woolly sort of fleecy hairy goat,
With an indolent expression and an undulating throat
Like an unsuccessful literary man.   *Hilaire Belloc*

The universe is made up of stories, not of atoms.   *Muriel Rukeyser*

Those expressions are omitted which cannot with propriety be read aloud in the family.
Dr. Thomas Bowdler

What is a diary as a rule? A document useful to the person who keeps it, dull to the contemporary who reads it and invaluable to the student, centuries afterwards, who treasures it!   *Helen Terry*

When a man can observe himself suffering and is able, later, to describe what he's gone through, it means he was born for literature.   *Edouard Bourdet*

When I read Shakespeare I am struck with wonder
That such trivial people should muse and thunder
In such lovely language.   *D. H. Lawrence*

Style can no more exist apart from thought than the outside of a wall can exist apart
from the inside.   *Sir Mungo MacCallum*

Literature is the effort of man to indemnify himself for the wrongs of his condition.
Walter Savage Landor

The short story is the art form that deals with the individual when there is no longer
a society to absorb him, and when he is compelled to exist, as it were, by his own
inner light.   *Frank O'Connor*

A novel is a mirror carried along a main road.   *Stendhal*

A novel is never anything but a philosophy put into images.   *Albert Camus*

Biographies are but the clothes and buttons of the man—the biography of the man
himself cannot be written.   *Mark Twain*

What is an epigram? A dwarfish whole,
Its body brevity, and wit its soul.   *Samuel Taylor Coleridge*

A literary movement consists of five or six people who live in the same town and hate
each other cordially.   *George Moore*

Literature is a power to be possessed, not a body of objects to be studied.   *Anon.*

Fiction reveals truth that reality obscures.   *Jessamyn West*

A perfect judge will read each word of wit with the same spirit that its author writ.
Alexander Pope

In literary history, generation follows generation in a rage.   *Annie Dillard*

To be a good diarist, one must have a little snouty, sneaky mind.   *Harold Nicolson*

Published memoirs indicate the end of a man's activity, and that he acknowledges the
end.   *George Meredith*

It has come to be practically a sort of rule in literature that a man, having once shown
himself capable of original writing, is entitled thenceforth to steal from the writings
of others at discretion.   *Ralph Waldo Emerson*

The novel is a prose narrative of some length that has something wrong with it.
Randall Jarrell

All that non-fiction can do is answer questions. It's fiction's business to ask them.
Richard Hughes

Contemporary literature can be classified under three headings: the neurotic, the erotic and the tommy-rotic.   *W. Giese*

Literature is the orchestration of platitudes.   *Thornton Wilder*

Medicine is my lawful wife. Literature is my mistress.   *Anton Chekhov*

One hears about life all the time from different people with very different narrative gifts.   *Anthony Powell*

The essay is a literary device for saying almost everything about almost anything.
Aldous Huxley

The answers you get from literature depend upon the questions you pose.
Margaret Atwood

The classics are only primitive literature. They belong to the same class as primitive machinery and primitive music and primitive medicine.   *Stephen Leacock*

Biography is one of the new terrors of death.   *John Arbuthnot*

A biography is considered complete if it merely accounts for six or seven selves, whereas a person may well have as many as a thousand.   *Virginia Woolf*

In literature as in love we are astounded by what is chosen by others.
André Maurois

Good children's literature appeals not only to the child in the adult, but to the adult in the child.   *Anon.*

Literature flourishes best when it is half a trade and half an art.
Dean William R. Inge

Loneliness

Loneliness is never more cruel when it is felt in close propinquity with someone who has ceased to communicate.   *Germaine Greer*

To be adult is to be alone (*être adulte, c'est être seul*).   *Jean Rostand*

What loneliness is more lonely than distrust.   *George Eliot*

Loneliness is and always has been the central and inevitable experience of every man.
Thomas Wolfe

One may have a blazing hearth in one's soul, and yet no one ever comes to sit by it.
Vincent van Gogh

So lonely 'twas that God himself
Scarce seemed there to be.   *Samuel Taylor Coleridge*

The lonely one offers his hand too quickly to whomever he encounters.

Friedrich Nietszche

Man's loneliness is but his fear of life.   *Eugene O'Neill*

No man is an Island intire of it self; every man is a peece of the Continent, a part of
the maine; if a Clod be washed away by the sea, Europe is the lesse, as well as if a
Promontorie were, as well as if a manor of thy friends or thine own were. Any man's
death diminishes me because I am involved in Mankinde, and therefore never send to
know for whom the bell tolls; it tolls for thee.   *John Donne*

Who knows what true loneliness is—not the conventional word but the naked terror?
To the lonely themselves it wears a mask. The most miserable outcast hugs some
memory or some illusion.   *Joseph Conrad*

Little do men perceive what solitude is, and how far it extendeth. For a crowd is not
company, and faces are but a gallery of pictures, and talk but a tinkling cymbal, where
there is no love.   *Francis Bacon*

Where you used to be, there is a hole in the world, which I find myself constantly
walking around in the daytime, and falling into at night. I miss you like hell.

Edna St. Vincent Millay

The eternal quest of the individual human being is to shatter his loneliness.

Norman Cousins

Language has created the word 'loneliness' to express the pain of being alone, and the
word 'solitude' to express the glory of being alone.   *Paul Tillich*

Those who deny their distinctiveness can only pool their loneliness.   *Peter Steele*

Loneliness and the feeling of being unwanted is the most terrible poverty.

Mother Teresa

Love

'Tis not love's going hurts my days,
But that it went in little ways.   *Edna St. Vincent Millay*

After all, my erstwhile dear,
My no longer cherished,
Need we say it was no love,
Just because it perished?   *Edna St. Vincent Millay*

Alas!, how light a cause may move
Dissention between hearts that love!   *Thomas More*

Every theory of love, from Plato down, teaches that each individual loves in the other sex what he lacks in himself.

G. Stanley Hall

Love is the music of imperfection.

Geoffrey Dutton

Immature love says 'I love you because I need you.' Mature love says 'I need you because I love you.'

Erich Fromm

Love doesn't grow on the trees like apples in Eden—it's something you have to make and you must use your imagination to make it too, just like anything else. It's all work, work.

Joyce Carey

Love is a kind of military service.

Latin proverb

The best love affairs are those we never had.

Norman Lindsay

Love is not love
Which alters when it alteration finds.

Shakespeare, Sonnet CXVI

Love is the delusion that one woman differs from another.

H. L. Mencken

Love is the irresistible desire to be desired irresistibly.

Louis Ginsberg

Love makes the time pass. Time makes love pass.

French proverb

Love rules without rules. (*Amore regge senza legge.*)

Italian proverb

Love, the itch, and a cough cannot be hid.

Thomas Fuller

What we call love is the desire to awaken and to keep awake in another's body, heart and mind, the responsibility of flattering, in our place, the self of which we are not very certain.

Paul Geraldy

When one loves somebody, everything is clear—where to go, what to do—it all takes care of itself and one doesn't have to ask anybody about anything.

Maxim Gorky

Where love rules, there is no will to power and where power predominates, love is lacking. The one is the shadow of the other.

Carl G. Jung

Where there is love, there is pain.

Spanish proverb

Love consists in this, that two solitudes protect and touch and greet each other.

Rainer Maria Rilke

No one has ever loved anyone the way everyone wants to be loved.

Mignon McLaughlin

We always deceive ourselves twice about the people we love—first to their advantage, then to their disadvantage.

Albert Camus

Human love is often but the encounter of two weaknesses.

François Mauriac

I am two fools, I know, for loving, and saying so.   *John Donne*

The supreme happiness of life is the conviction that we are loved.   *Victor Hugo*

What dire offence from am'rous causes springs.
What mighty contests rise from trivial things.   *Alexander Pope*

Love is what makes the world go round—that and clichés.   *Michael Symons*

He who loves the more is the inferior and must suffer.   *Thomas Mann*

Love, you know, seeks to make happy rather than to be happy.   *Ralph Connor*

Love is a spendthrift, leaves its arithmetic at home, is always 'in the red'.
Paul Scherer

The loving are the daring.   *Bayard Taylor*

In love, as *in* pain, *in* shock, *in* trouble.   *Germaine Greer*

Little privations are easily endured when the heart is better treated than the body.
Jean-Jacques Rousseau

No love, no friendship can cross the path of our destiny without leaving some mark
on it forever.   *François Mauriac*

There is no fear in love; but perfect love casteth out fear.   *1 John 4:18*

Love, in order to exist, must first be imagined.   *David Foster, 'Testostero'*

You can always get someone to love you—even if you have to do it yourself.
Tom Masson

You've got to love what's lovable, and hate what's hateable. It takes brains to see the
difference.   *Robert Frost*

Romance without finance is no good.   *Willie 'The Lion' Smith*

To live is like to love—all reason is against it, and all healthy instinct for it.
Samuel Butler

People who throw kisses are hopelessly lazy.   *Bob Hope*

Wine comes in at the mouth
And love comes in at the eye;
That's all we shall know for truth
Before we grow old and die.   *William Butler Yeats*

Love lives on propinquity, but dies on contact.   *Thomas Hardy*

The heart that has truly loved never forgets
But as truly loves on to the close.

Thomas More

When the satisfaction or the security of another person becomes as significant to one as one's own satisfaction or security, then the state of love exists.

Henry Stack Sullivan

At the end of what is called the 'sexual life' the only love which has lasted is the love which has everything, every disappointment, every failure and every betrayal, which has accepted even the sad fact that in the end there is no desire so deep as the simple desire for companionship.

Graham Greene

When love and skill work together expect a masterpiece.

John Ruskin

The greater love is a mother's; then comes a dog's; then a sweetheart's.

Polish proverb

Selfishness is one of the qualities apt to inspire love.

Nathaniel Hawthorne

There can be no peace of mind in love, since the advantage one has secured is never anything but a fresh starting-point for further desires.

Marcel Proust

Love does not consist in gazing at each other, but in looking together in the same direction.

Antoine de Saint-Exupéry

The magic of first love is our ignorance that it can ever end.

Benjamin Disraeli

What we can do for another is the test of powers; what we can suffer is the test of love.

Brooke Foss Westcott

They gave each other a smile with a future in it.

Ring Lardner

Many a man in love with a dimple makes the mistake of marrying the whole girl.

Stephen Leacock

There is one who kisses, and the other who offers a cheek.

French proverb

The irony of love is that it guarantees some degree of anger, fear and criticism.

Harold H. Bloomfield

It has been wisely said that we cannot really love anybody at whom we never laugh.

Agnes Repplier

The entire sum of existence is the magic of being needed by just one person.

Vi Putnam

A lady of forty-seven who has been married twenty-seven years and has six children knows what love really is and once described it for me like this: 'Love is what you've been through with somebody.'

James Thurber

And if I loved you Wednesday,
Well, what is that to you?
I do not love you Thursday—
So much is true.   *Edna St. Vincent Millay*

Happiness comes more from loving than being loved; and often when our affection
seems wounded it is only our vanity bleeding. To love, and to be hurt often, and to
love again—this is the brave and happy life.   *J. E. Buckrose*

If you cannot inspire a woman with love of you, fill her above the brim with love of
herself; all that runs over will be yours.   *Charles Caleb Colton*

No one can do me any good by loving me; I have more love than I need or could do
any good with; but people do me good by making me love them—which isn't easy.
                                                       John Ruskin

Love is a gross exaggeration of the difference between one person and everybody else.
                                                   George Bernard Shaw

Respect is love in plain clothes.   *Frankie Byrne*

A man is only as good as what he loves.   *Saul Bellow*

In the act of loving someone you arm them against you.   *Anon.*

If you want to be loved, be lovable.   *Ovid*

The one thing we can never get enough of is love. And the one thing we never give
enough of is love.   *Henry Miller*

Love makes of the wisest man a fool, and of the most foolish woman, a sage.
                                                   Moritz G. Saphir

In how many lives does Love really play a dominant part? The average taxpayer is
no more capable of a 'grand passion' than of a grand opera.   *Israel Zangwill*

Love, all love of other sights controls.
And makes one little room an everywhere.   *John Donne*

If we are to judge of love by its consequences, it more nearly resembles hatred than
friendship.   *La Rochefoucauld*

Love cannot accept what it is. Everywhere on earth it cries out against kindness,
compassion, intelligence, everything that leads to compromise. Love demands the
impossible, the absolute, the sky on fire, inexhaustible springtime, life after death, and
death itself transfigured into eternal life.   *Albert Camus*

unlove's the heavenless hell and homeless home . . . lovers alone wear sunlight.
                                                       e. e. cummings

Marriage

A husband is what is left of a lover, after the nerve has been extracted.
Helen Rowland

A rich widow weeps with one eye and signals with the other.   *Portuguese proverb*

A wise woman will always let her husband have her way.
Richard Brinsley Sheridan

Bigamy is having one husband too many. Monogamy is the same.   *Erica Jong*

Conrad Hilton was very generous to me in the divorce settlement. He gave me 5,000 Gideon Bibles.   *Zsa Zsa Gabor*

In my conscience I believe the baggage loves me, for she never speaks well of me herself, nor suffers anybody else to rail at me.   *William Congreve*

It destroys one's nerves to be amiable every day to the same human being.
Benjamin Disraeli

Marriage has many pains, but celibacy has no pleasures.   *Samuel Johnson*

Married women are kept women, and they are beginning to find it out.
Logan Pearsall Smith

Marriage is nothing more than the protest of woman against the non-unionist.
Billy Hughes

The calmest husbands make the stormiest wives.
Isaac Disraeli (father of Benjamin)

The only thing that holds a marriage together is the husband being big enough to step back and see where the wife was wrong.   *Archie Bunker*

There is nothing like living together for blinding people to each other.
Ivy Compton-Burnett

There is so little difference between husbands you might as well keep the first.
Adela Rogers St. John

When a man opens the car door for his wife, it's either a new car or a new wife.
Prince Philip

You can bear your own faults, and why not a fault in your wife?
Benjamin Franklin

Whoso findeth a wife findeth a good thing.   *Proverbs 18:22*

Marriage is our last, best chance to grow up.   *Joseph Barth*

As a general thing, people marry most happily with their own kind. The trouble lies in the fact that people usually marry at an age when they do not really know what their own kind is.   *Robertson Davies*

Often the difference between a successful marriage and a mediocre one consists of leaving about three or four things a day unsaid.   *Harlan Miller*

Marriage is the deep, deep peace of the double bed after the hurly-burly of the chaise longue.   *Mrs. Patrick Campbell*

A good marriage is that in which each appoints the other guardian of his solitude. Once the realization is accepted that even between the closest human beings infinite distances continue to exist, a wonderful living side by side can grow up, if they succeed in loving the distance between them which makes it possible for each to see the other whole and against a wide sky.   *Rainer Maria Rilke*

Nothing flatters a man as much as the happiness of his wife; he is always proud of himself as the source of it.   *Samuel Johnson*

Pains do not hold a marriage together. It is threads, hundreds of tiny threads which sew people together through the years. That's what makes a marriage last—more than passion or even sex.   *Simone Signoret*

Marriage: a job. Happiness or unhappiness has nothing to do with it.
Kathleen Norris

Matrimony: friendship under difficult circumstances.   *Rose Scott*

A wife encourages her husband's egoism in order to exercise her own.
Russell Green

A man and a woman marry because both of them don't know what to do with themselves.   *Anton Chekhov*

Marriage is neither heaven nor hell; it is simply purgatory.   *Abraham Lincoln*

Every marriage tends to consist of an aristocrat and a peasant, of a teacher and a learner.   *John Updike*

Marriage is one long conversation checkered by disputes.   *Robert Louis Stevenson*

Husband and wife come to look alike at last.   *Oliver Wendell Holmes*

There is a radicalism in all getting, and a conservatism in all keeping. Lovemaking is radical, while marriage is conservative.   *Eric Hoffer*

The young man who wants to marry happily should pick out a good mother and marry one of her daughters—any one will do.   *J. Ogden Armour*

His designs were strictly honourable, as the phrase is: that is, to rob a lady of her fortune by way of marriage.   *Henry Fielding*

If thee marries for money, thee surely will earn it.   *Ezra Bowen*

Only two things are necessary to keep one's wife happy. One is to let her think she is having her own way, and the other, to let her have it.   *Lyndon B. Johnson*

Henry VIII had so many wives because his dynastic sense was very strong whenever he saw a maid of honour.   *Will Cuppy*

A simple enough pleasure, surely, to have breakfast alone with one's husband, but how seldom married people in the midst of life achieve it.   *Anne Morrow Lindbergh*

Marriages would in general be as happy, and often more so, if they were all made by the Lord Chancellor.   *Samuel Johnson*

No man is regular in his attendance at the House of Commons until he is married.
                                                        Benjamin Disraeli

Love is a fever which marriage puts to bed and cures.   *Richard J. Needham*

An ideal wife is one who remains faithful to you but tries to be just as if she weren't.
                                                        Sacha Guitry

No labourer in the world is expected to work for room, board, and love—except the housewife.   *Letty Cottin Pogrebin*

What is instinct? It is the natural tendency in one when filled with dismay to turn to his wife.   *Finley Peter Dunne*

A husband always prefers his wife's mother-in-law to his own.   *Anon.*

Woe to the house where the hen crows and the rooster keeps still.   *Spanish proverb*

Married couples who love each other tell each other a thousand things without talking.
                                                        Chinese proverb

Marriage is not a finished affair. No matter to what age you live, love must be continuously consolidated. Being considerate, thoughtful and respectful without ulterior motives is the key to a satisfactory marriage.
                        Pamphlet from Chinese Family Planning Centre

Seldom, or perhaps never, does a marriage develop into an individual relationship smoothly and without crises; there is no coming to consciousness without pain.
                                                        Carl Jung

I never married because I have three pets at home that answer the same purpose as a husband. I have a dog that growls every morning, a parrot that swears all afternoon, and a cat that comes home late at night.   *Marie Corelli*

Let there be spaces in your togetherness.   *Kahlil Gibran*

Any marriage, happy or unhappy, is infinitely more interesting and significant than any romance, however passionate.   *W. H. Auden*

One of the best things about marriage is that it gets young people to bed at a decent hour.   *M. M. Musselman*

The majority of husbands remind me of an orangutan trying to play the violin.
Honoré de Balzac

Polygamy: an endeavour to get more out of life than there is in it.   *Elbert Hubbard*

Marriage, n: the state or condition of a community consisting of a master, a mistress, and two slaves, making, in all, two.   *Ambrose Bierce*

Marriage is a great institution, and no family should be without it.
Channing Pollock

Any married man should forget his mistakes—no use two people remembering the same thing.   *Duane Dewel*

No matter how happily a woman may be married, it always pleases her to discover that there is a nice man who wishes she were not.   *H. L. Mencken*

Marriage is three parts love and seven parts forgiveness of sins.   *Langdon Mitchell*

I married beneath me—all women do.   *Nancy, Lady Astor*

One of the best hearing aids a man can have is an attentive wife.   *Groucho Marx*

A good husband should always bore his wife.   *Fred Jacob*

There isn't a wife in the world who has not taken the exact measure of her husband, weighed him and settled him in her own mind, and knows him as well as if she had ordered him after designs and specifications of her own.   *Charles Warner*

A woman is not a whole woman without the experience of marriage. In the case of a bad marriage, you win if you lose. Of the two alternatives—bad marriage or none—I believe bad marriage would be better. It is a bitter experience and a high price to pay for fulfillment, but it is the better alternative.   *Fannie Hurst*

Maturity

One trouble with a kind of falsely therapeutic and always reassuring attitude that it is easy to fall into with old people, is the tendency to be satisfied with too little.
Kenneth Koch

Be content with what you are, and wish not change; not dread your last day, not long for it.   *Martial*

Real maturity is the ability to imagine the humanity of every person as fully as you believe in your own humanity.   *Tobias Wolff*

Strong meat belongeth to them that are of full age.   *Hebrews 5:14*

There is nothing noble about being superior to some other men. The true nobility is in being superior to your previous self.   *Hindustani proverb*

Growing up is after all only the understanding that one's unique and incredible experience is what everyone shares.   *Doris Lessing*

A mark of maturity seems to be the range and extent of one's feeling of self-involvement in abstract ideals.   *Gordon Wallport*

The mark of a mature man is the ability to give love and receive it joyously and without guilt.   *Leo Baeck*

My poetry doesn't change from place to place—it changes with the years. It's very important to be one's age. You get ideas you have to turn down—'I'm sorry, no longer'; 'I'm sorry, not yet.'   *W. H. Auden*

Maturity is the capacity to endure uncertainty.   *John Finley*

I believe that the sign of maturity is accepting deferred gratification.   *Peggy Cahn*

You don't learn to hold your own by standing on guard, but by attacking, and getting well hammered yourself.   *George Bernard Shaw*

Our judgements about things vary according to the time left us to live—that we think is left us to live.   *André Gide*

Grow up, and that is a terribly hard thing to do. It is much easier to skip it and go from one childhood to another.   *F. Scott Fitzgerald*

How many really capable men are children more than once during the day?
                                                    Napoleon Bonaparte

The immature mind hops from one thing to another; the mature mind seeks to follow through.   *Harry A. Overstreet*

One of the signs of passing youth is the birth of a sense of fellowship with other human beings as we take our place among them.   *Virginia Woolf*

It is unjust to claim the privileges of age and retain the playthings of childhood.
                                                    Samuel Johnson

Medicine and Sickness

Nature heals under the auspices of the medical profession.   *Haven Emerson*

The biggest disease today is not leprosy or tuberculosis, but rather the feeling of being unwanted.   *Mother Theresa*

Doctors are busy playing God when so few of us have the qualifications. And besides, the job is taken.   *Bernie S. Siegel, MD*

Don't defy the diagnosis, try to defy the verdict.   *Norman Cousins*

Nothing is more essential in the treatment of serious disease than the liberation of the patient from panic and forboding.   *Norman Cousins*

Better a semi-colon than a full stop.
                                        James McAuley, after a bowel cancer operation

Sickness is felt, but health not at all.   *Thomas Fuller*

The placebo cures 30% of patients—no matter what they have.   *David Kline*

To cure sometimes, to relieve often, to comfort always.   *Anon.*

Vasectomy means not ever having to say you're sorry.   *Larry Adler*

What some call health, if purchased by perpetual anxiety about diet, isn't much better than tedious disease.   *George Dennison Prentice*

It is much more important to know what sort of a patient has a disease than what sort of a disease a patient has.   *William Osler*

The desire to take medicine is perhaps the greatest feature which distinguishes man from animals.   *William Osler*

The doctor, if he forgets he is only the assistant to nature and zealously takes over the stage, may so add to what nature is already doing well that he actually throws the patient into shock by the vigour he adds to nature's forces.   *Herbert Ratner*

God heals, and the doctor takes the fees.   *Benjamin Franklin*

The history of medicine is a story of amazing foolishness and amazing intelligence.
                                                                        Jerome Tarshis

If men could get pregnant, abortion would be a sacrament.   *Florynce Kennedy*

Abortion is advocated only by persons who have themselves been born.
                                                                        Ronald Reagan

Man should not strive to eliminate his complexes, but to get in accord with them; they are legitimately what directs his contact in the world.   *Sigmund Freud*

The body never lies.   *Martha Graham*

All that is really necessary for survival of the fittest, it seems, is an interest in life, good, bad or peculiar.   *Grace Paley*

The only thing to know is how to use your neurosis.   *Arthur Adamov*

Common sense is in medicine the master workman.   *Peter Lathan*

The prime goal is to alleviate suffering, and not to prolong life. And if your treatmen
does not alleviate suffering, but only prolongs life, that treatment should be stopped.
Christian Barnard

As long as men are liable to die and are desirous to live, a physician will be made
fun of, but he will be well paid.   *Jean de la Bruyère*

After dinner, rest a while, after supper walk a mile.   *Arabic proverb*

Imprisoned in every fat man, a thin one is wildly signalling to be let out.
Cyril Connolly

Wherever a doctor cannot do good, he must be kept from doing harm.   *Hippocrates*

The student is to collect and evaluate facts. The facts are locked up in the patient.
Abraham Flexner

The practice of medicine is a thinker's art, the practice of surgery a plumber's.
Martin H. Fisher

Every surgeon carries about him a little cemetery, in which from time to time he goes
to pray, a cemetery of bitterness and regret, of which he seeks the reason for certain
of his failures.   *René Leriche*

Symptoms, then, are in reality nothing but the cry from suffering organs.
Jean-Martin Charcot

I observe the physician with the same diligence as the disease.   *John Donne*

The very first requirement in a hospital is that it should do the sick no harm.
Florence Nightingale

There are some remedies worse than the disease.   *Publilius Syrus*

To avoid delay, please have all your symptoms ready.
Notice in an English doctor's waiting-room

Sickness is a sort of early old age; it teaches us a diffidence in our earthly state.
Alexander Pope

To be sick is to enjoy monarchal prerogatives.   *Charles Lamb*

Every invalid is a physician.   *Irish proverb*

'Tis healthy to be sick sometimes.   *Henry David Thoreau*

Our doctor would never really operate unless it was necessary. He was just that way.
If he didn't need the money, he wouldn't lay a hand on you.   *Herb Shriner*

Physicians of the Utmost Fame
Were called at once, but when they came
They answered, as they took their fees,
'There is no cure for this disease.'

Hilaire Belloc

A good gulp of hot whisky at bedtime—it's not very scientific, but it helps.

Alexander D. Fleming

I enjoy convalescence. It is the part that makes the illness worthwhile.

George Bernard Shaw

A general flavour of mild decay,
But nothing local, as one may say.

Oliver Wendell Holmes

One of the first duties of the physician is to educate the masses not to take medicine.

William Osler

I was sick, and ye visited me.

Matthew 25:36

There is a great difference between a good physician and a bad one; yet very little between a good one and none at all.

Arthur Young

Nature, time and patience are the three great physicians.

Proverb

So many come to the sickroom thinking of themselves as men of science fighting disease and not as healers with a little knowledge helping nature to get a sick man well.

Sir Auckland Geddes

No doctor takes pleasure in the health even of his friends.

Montaigne

It requires a great deal of faith for a man to be cured by his own placebos.

John L. McClenahan

It is very difficult to slow down. The practice of medicine is like the heart muscle's contraction—it's all or none.

Bela Schick

Those in the United States who, by and large, have the best medical care and advice readily available to them at the least expense are the families of the specialists in internal medicine. These families use less medicine and undergo less surgery on the whole than any other group, rich or poor.

Edward C. Lambert

Nothing is more fatal to health than an overcare of it.

Benjamin Franklin

Doctor, feel my purse.

Jane Ace

The sorrow which has no vent in tears may make other organs weep.

Henry Maudsley

There is some reason to believe there is greater safety in this branch of medicine from modest, unassuming ignorance, than from a meddling presumption which frequently accompanies a little learning.

Samuel Bard

A person seldom falls sick but the bystanders are animated with a faint hope that he will die.

Ralph Waldo Emerson

In my youth, once, when I had a really exquisite toothache, I suddenly realized that my tooth had temporarily become the centre of the universe, that its outcries were more important than anything else, and that I would do absolutely anything to placate it. And as one gets older and starts worrying about cancer, one becomes more and more conscious of the fragility of the whole body, and with that consciousness comes a new and degrading kind of fear. It is degrading because it strengthens the desire to survive on any terms, and the desire to survive on any terms is the most base of all our instincts.

Otto Friedrich

If a man thinks about his physical or moral state, he usually discovers that he is ill.

Goethe

I reckon being ill is one of the greatest pleasures of life, provided one is not too ill and is not obliged to work till one is better.

Samuel Butler

We are usually the best men when in the worst health.

English proverb

Some of the papers presented at today's medical meeting tell us what we already know, but in a much more complicated manner.

Alphonse Raymond Dochez

A human being who is first of all an invalid is all body; therein lies his inhumanity and his debasement.

Thomas Mann

Invalids live longest.

German proverb

A vigorous five-mile walk will do more good for an unhappy but otherwise healthy adult than all the medicine and psychology in the world.

Paul Dudley White

We firmly believe that therapy is education rather than healing; that it is growth rather than treatment.

Arnold Lazarus and Alan Fay

Ask many of us who are disabled what we would like in life and you would be surprised how few would say, 'Not to be disabled.' We accept our limitations.

Itzhak Perlman

What is dangerous about tranquillizers is that whatever peace of mind they bring is packaged peace of mind. Where you buy a pill and buy peace with it, you get conditioned to cheap solutions instead of deep ones.

Max Lerner

The tongue ever turns to the aching tooth.

Proverb

So long as the body is affected through the mind, no audacious device, even of the most manifestly dishonest character, can fail of producing occasional good to those who yield to it an implicit or even a partial faith.

Oliver Wendell Holmes

Tranquillizers do not change our environment, nor do they change our personalities. They merely reduce our responsiveness to stimuli. They dull the keen edge of the angers, fears, or anxiety with which we might otherwise react to the problems of living. Once the response has been dulled, the irritating surface noise of living muted or eliminated, the spark and brilliance are also gone.   *Indra Devi*

I am in a moment of pretty wellness.   *Horace Walpole*

Health is the thing that makes you feel that now is the best time of the year.
                    Franklin Pierce Adams

When you hear hoofbeats, think of horses before zebras.
                    Medical maxim quoted by Harley S. Smyth

When we are sick our virtues and our vices are in abeyance.   *Vauvenargues*

Most things get better by themselves. Most things, in fact, are better by morning.
                    Lewis Thomas

In medicine, sins of commission are mortal, sins of omission venial.
                    Theodore Tronchin

It is the duty of a doctor to prolong life and it is not his duty to prolong the act of dying.   *Thomas, Lord Horder*

I came, I saw, I concurred.   *Irvine H. Page*

Disease often tells its secrets in a casual parenthesis.   *Wilfred Trotter*

Meetings and Partings

Goodnight! Goodnight! Parting is such sweet sorrow
That I shall say goodnight 'til it be morrow.   *Shakespeare, 'Romeo and Juliet'*

Man's feelings are always purest and most glowing in the hour of meeting and of farewell.   *Jean Paul Richter*

Visits always give pleasure—if not the arrival, the departure.   *Portuguese proverb*

There's a kind of release
And a kind of torment in every goodbye for every man.   *C. Day Lewis*

Parting is all we know of heaven
And all we need of hell.   *Emily Dickinson*

The joys of meeting pay the pangs of absence;
Else who could bear it?   *Nicholas Rowe*

We only part to meet again.   *John Gay*

Departure should be sudden.   *Benjamin Disraeli*

A feeling of sadness and longing
That is not akin to pain,
And resembles sorrow only
As the mist resembles the rain.   *Henry Wadsworth Longfellow*

A little while with grief and laughter,
And then the day will close;
The shadows gather . . . what comes after
No man knows.   *Donald R. P. Marquis*

Memory

Forgetfulness transforms every occurrence into a non-occurrence.   *Plutarch*

How is it that we remember the least triviality that happens to us, and yet not remember
how often we have recounted it to the same person?   *La Rochefoucauld*

I never forgive, but I always forget.   *Arthur James Balfour*

In memory, everything seems to happen to music.   *Tennessee Williams*

Living in the past has one thing in its favour—it's cheaper.   *Old saying*

Memory is the diary that we all carry about with us.   *Oscar Wilde*

One always begins to forgive a place as soon as it's left behind.   *Charles Dickens*

Reminiscences make one feel so deliciously aged and sad.   *George Bernard Shaw*

Memory, of all the powers of the mind, is the most delicate and frail.   *Ben Jonson*

Gratitude is the heart's memory.   *French proverb*

The true art of memory is the art of attention.   *Samuel Johnson*

A man must get a thing before he can forget it.   *Oliver Wendell Holmes*

It isn't so astonishing, the number of things that I can remember, as the number of
things I can remember that aren't so.   *Mark Twain*

For the sense of smell, almost more than any other, has the power to recall memories
and it is a pity that we use it so little.   *Rachel Carson*

I have a remarkable memory; I forget everything. It is wonderfully convenient. It is
as though the world were constantly renewing itself for me.   *Jules Renard*

It is commonly seen by experience that excellent memories do often accompany weak judgements.   *Montaigne*

There must be at least 500 million rats in the United States; of course, I am speaking only from memory.   *Edgar Wilson Nye*

Nostalgia is a seductive liar.   *George W. Ball*

The past is a work of art, free of irrelevancies and loose ends.   *Max Beerbohm*

Oh longing for places that were not
Cherished enough in that fleeting hour
How I long to make good from afar
The forgotten gesture, the additional act.   *Rainer Maria Rilke*

'The horror of that moment,' the King went on, 'I shall never, never forget!' 'You will, though,' the Queen said, 'if you don't make a memorandum of it.'   *Lewis Carroll*

Only by keeping the past alive in our memories can we choose what to discard and what to retain in our present way of life.   *Lady Cilento*

If a man can remember what he worried about last week, he has a very good memory.
                                                                              Anon.

That which we remember of our conduct is ignored by our closest neighbour; but that which we have forgotten having said, or even what we never said, will cause laughter even into the next world.   *Marcel Proust*

That which is bitter to endure may be sweet to remember.   *Thomas Fuller*

We forget because we must
And not because we will.   *Matthew Arnold*

Not the power to remember, but its very opposite, the power to forget, is a necessary condition for our existence.   *Sholem Asch*

Memory is the thing you forget with.   *Alexander Chase*

The palest ink is better than the best memory.   *Chinese proverb*

The advantage of a bad memory is that one enjoys several times the same good thing for the first time.   *Friedrich Nietzsche*

Everyone complains of his lack of memory, but nobody of his want of judgement.
                                                                         La Rochefoucauld

Our memories are independent of our wills. It is not so easy to forget.
                                                                   Richard Brinsley Sheridan

Nostalgia isn't what it used to be.   *Simone Signoret*

God gave us memories that we might have roses in December. *James M. Barrie*

To want to forget something is to think of it. *French proverb*

What is forgiven is usually well remembered. *Louis Dudek*

Men

Dennis Thatcher, husband of Margaret Thatcher, when asked who wore the pants in his house, said 'I do, and I also wash and iron them.'

I only like two kinds of men; domestic and foreign. *Mae West*

It is men who face the biggest problems in the future, adjusting to their new and complicated role. *Anna Ford*

Macho does not prove mucho. *Zsa Zsa Gabor*

No man thinks there is much ado about nothing when the ado is about himself.
Anthony Trollope

Nothing is so silly as the expression of a man who is being complimented.
André Gide

The follies which a man regrets most, in his life, are those which he didn't commit when he had the opportunity. *Helen Rowland*

The male sex still constitute in many ways the most obstinate vested interest one can find. *Lord Longford*

What is a highbrow? He is a man who has found something more interesting than women. *Edgar Wallace*

The beauty of stature is the only beauty of men. *Montaigne*

Men become old, but they never become good. *Oscar Wilde*

Men are what their mothers made them. *Ralph Waldo Emerson*

Men's men: be they gentle or simple, they're much of a muchness. *George Eliot*

To be a man will continue to demand a heroic heart as long as mankind is not quite human. *Julius Fucik (before he was beheaded)*

A gentleman does things no gentleman should do in a way only a gentleman can.
Luigi Banzini

The right man is the one that seizes the moment. *Goethe*

Every man in the world is better than someone else, and not as good as someone else.
William Saroyan

This is the worst pain a man can suffer: to have insight into much and power over nothing.
Herodotus

Probably the only place where a man can feel really secure is in a maximum security prison, except for the imminent threat of release.
Germaine Greer

The only things that distinguish us from the rest of the animals, Madam is our habit of drinking when we are not thirsty and making love at any time.
Beaumarchais

There was never any reason to believe in any innate superiority of the male, except his superior muscle.
Bertrand Russell

I like men to behave like men. I like them strong and childish.
Françoise Sagan

Celibacy bestows on a man the qualified freedom of a besieged city where one sometimes has to eat rats.
Sean O'Faolain

Men build bridges and throw railroads across deserts, and yet they contend successfully that the job of sewing on a button is beyond them. Accordingly, they don't have to sew buttons.
Heywood Broun

As vivacity is the gift of women, gravity is that of men.
Joseph Addison

The desire of a man for a woman is not directed at her because she is a human being, but because she is a woman. That she is a human being is of no concern to him.
Immanuel Kant

Two things control man's nature: instinct and experience.
Blaise Pascal

In his private heart no man much respects himself.
Mark Twain

When I was young, I used to have successes with women because I was young. Now I have successes with women because I am old. Middle age was the hardest part.
Artur Rubinstein

A man who has been the indisputable favourite of his mother keeps for life the feeling of a conqueror.
Sigmund Freud

We love women in proportion to their degree of strangeness to us.
Charles Baudelaire

At twenty a man is a peacock, at thirty a lion, at forty a camel, at fifty a serpent, at sixty a dog, at seventy an ape, at eighty, nothing at all.
Baltasar Gracián

Inconsistency is the only thing in which men are consistent.
Horatio Smith

There are three classes of men—lovers of wisdom, lovers of honour, lovers of gain.
Plato

Men always talk about the most important things to perfect strangers.

G. K. Chesterton

Men are made by nature unequal. It is vain, therefore, to treat them as if they were equal.
J. A. Froude

That all men are equal is a proposition to which, at ordinary times, no sane individual has ever given his assent.
Aldous Huxley

Men and Women

A man is never so weak as when a woman is telling him how strong he is. *Anon.*

The sexes and the generations are a great disappointment to each other.

Frank Dalby Davison

Eve left Adam, to meet the Devil in private. *Alexander Pope*

I should like to see any kind of a man, distinguishable from a gorilla that some good and even pretty woman could not shape a husband out of. *Oliver Wendell Holmes*

It is a truth universally acknowledged, that a single man in possession of a good fortune, must be in want of a wife.
Jane Austen

Manly men and womanly women are still here but feeling nervous. *Mason Cooley*

There is more difference within the sexes than between them. *Ivy Compton-Burnett*

When women go wrong, men go right after them. *Mae West*

Women are never disarmed by compliments. Men always are. *Oscar Wilde*

Breathes there a man with hide so tough
Who says two sexes aren't enough? *Samuel Hoffenstein*

If men and women are to understand each other, to enter into each other's nature with mutual sympathy, and to become capable of genuine comradeship, the foundation must be laid in youth.
Havelock Ellis

American women expect to find in their husbands a perfection that English women only hope to find in their butlers.
W. Somerset Maugham

Women have very little idea of how much men hate them. *Germaine Greer*

Women have one great advantage over men. It is commonly thought that if they marry they have done enough, and need career no further. If a man marries, on the other hand, public opinion is all against him if he takes this view. *Rose Macaulay*

What is most beautiful in virile men is something feminine; what is most beautiful in feminine women is something masculine.   *Susan Sontag*

In our civilization, men are afraid that they will not be men enough and women are afraid that they might be considered only women.   *Theodor Reik*

A woman knows how to keep quiet when she is in the right, whereas a man, when he is in the right, will keep on talking.   *Chazai*

A woman means by unselfishness chiefly taking trouble for others; a man means not giving trouble to others. Thus each sex regards the other as basically selfish.
                                                                              C. S. Lewis

Failing to be there when a man wants her is a woman's greatest sin, except to be there when he doesn't want her.   *Helen Rowland*

There is probably nothing like living together for blinding people to each other.
                                                                    Ivy Compton-Burnett

Perhaps one of the reasons why men don't go to doctors and psychiatrists as often as women is that they don't need to. Women generally do a brilliant job of man-maintenance.   *Beatrice Faust*

Behind every great man there is a surprised woman.   *Maryon Pearson*

Behind every successful man you'll find a woman who has nothing to wear.
                                                                            Harold Coffin

If a man hears much that a woman says, she is not beautiful.   *Henry S. Haskins*

Living with a man requires that you spend all day every day putting down the toilet seat.   *Kathy Lette*

Men have a much better time of it than women. For one thing, they marry later. For another thing, they die earlier.   *H. L. Mencken*

There is no word equivalent to 'cuckold' for women.   *Joseph Epstein*

He and I had an office so tiny that an inch smaller and it would have been adultery.
                                                                          Dorothy Parker

A man is a person who will pay two dollars for a one-dollar item he wants. A woman will pay one dollar for a two-dollar item she doesn't want.   *William Binger*

A woman may very well form a friendship with a man, but for this to endure, it must be assisted by a little physical antipathy.   *Friedrich Nietzsche*

When I was very young, I kissed my first woman, and smoked my first cigarette on the same day. Believe me, never since have I wasted any more time on tobacco.
                                                                        Arturo Toscanini

The double standard of morality will survive in this world so long as the woman whose husband has been lured away is favoured with the sympathetic tears of other women, and a man whose wife has made off is laughed at by other men.   *H. L. Mencken*

Flirtation—attention without intention.   *Max O'Neil*

All women become like their mothers. That is their tragedy. No man does. That's his.
Oscar Wilde

As the faculty of writing has chiefly been a masculine endowment, the reproach of making the world miserable has always been thrown upon the women.
Samuel Johnson

Though statisticians in our time
Have never kept the score
Man wants a great deal here below
And Woman even more.   *James Thurber*

A good cigar is as great a comfort to a man as a good cry is to a woman.
Edward Bulwer-Lytton

A man should be taller, older, heavier, uglier and hoarser than his wife.
Edgar Watson Howe

Even the wisest men make fools of themselves about women, and even the most foolish women are wise about men.   *Theodor Reik*

I love men, not because they are men, but because they are not women.
Christina, Queen of Sweden

The Mind

Common sense is the collection of prejudices acquired by age 18.   *Albert Einstein*

Curiosity is a lust of the mind.   *Thomas Hobbes*

Gluttony is an emotional escape, a sign something is eating us.   *Peter de Vries*

The heart of a statesman should be in his head.   *Napoleon Bonaparte*

Minds, like bodies, will often fall into a pimpled, ill-conditioned state from mere excess of comfort.   *Charles Dickens*

Of course, he seems to have quite a mind of his own and that is probably where he is weakest.   *Arnold Schoenberg*

That is the consolation of a little mind; you have the fun of changing it without impeding the progress of mankind.   *Frank Moore Colby*

The flesh endures the storms of the present alone; the mind, those of the past and future as well as the present.   *Epicurus*

The mind of man is capable of anything—because everything is in it, all the past as well as all the future.   *Joseph Conrad*

Then comes Winston with his hundred horsepower mind and what can I do?
Stanley Baldwin (of Churchill)

We know the human brain is a device to keep the ears from grating on one another.
Peter de Vries

One man who has a mind and knows it can always beat ten men who haven't and don't.   *George Bernard Shaw*

When the mind is thinking, it is talking to itself.   *Plato*

I am not absent-minded. It is the presence of mind that makes me unaware of everything else.   *G. K. Chesterton*

Our unconsciousness is like a vast subterranean factory with intricate machinery that is never idle, where work goes on day and night from the time we are born until the moment of our death.   *Milton R. Sapirstein*

Only an incompetent mind is content to express itself incompetently.   *J. M. Barker*

A great many open minds should be closed for repairs.   *Toledo Blade*

If you keep your mind sufficiently open, people will throw a lot of rubbish into it.
William A. Orton

Some minds remain open long enough for the truth not only to enter but to pass through by way of a ready exit without pausing anywhere along the route.
Sister Elizabeth Kenny

The perversion of the mind is only possible when those who should be heard in its defence are silent.   *Archibald MacLeish*

Our minds are lazier than our bodies.   *La Rochefoucauld*

Strength is a matter of the made-up mind.   *John Beecher*

What we think and feel and are is to a great extent determined by the state of our ductless glands and our viscera.   *Aldous Huxley*

The feeling of inferiority rules the mental life and can be clearly recognized as the sense of incompleteness and unfulfillment, and in the uninterrupted struggle both of individuals and of humanity.   *Alfred Adler*

Discipline does not mean suppression and control, nor is it adjustment to a pattern or ideology. It means a mind that sees 'what is' and learns from 'what was'.

Jiddu Krishnamurti

That which enters the mind through reason can be corrected. That which is admitted through faith, hardly ever. *Santiago Ramón y Cajal*

Minorities

A woman who is found without her veil in some regions of Islam will, it is reported, raise her skirt to cover her face. *Raymond Mortimer*

10 persons who speak make more noise than 10,000 who are silent.

Napoleon Bonaparte

I want to be the white man's brother, not his brother-in-law.

Martin Luther King, Jr

The nations which have put mankind and posterity most in their debt have been small states—Israel, Athens, Florence, Elizabethan England. *Dean William R. Inge*

How a minority,
Reaching majority,
Seizing authority,
Hates a minority! *Leonard H. Robbins*

In the country of the blind, the one-eyed man is king. *Erasmus*

By gnawing through a dyke, even a rat may drown a nation. *Edmund Burke*

The thing we have to fear in this country, to my way of thinking, is the influence of the organized minorities, because somehow or other the great majority does not seem to organize. They seem to feel that they are going to be effective because of their own strength, but they give no expression of it. *Alfred E. Smith*

We must indeed all hang together, or most assuredly we shall all hang separately.

Benjamin Franklin

A minority may be right, and a majority is always wrong. *Henrik Ibsen*

Governments exist to protect the rights of minorities. The loved and the rich need no protection—they have many friends and few enemies. *Wendell Phillips*

It is always the minorities that hold the key of progess; it is always through those who are unafraid to be different that advance comes to human society.

Raymond B. Fosdick

A minority group has 'arrived' only when it has the right to produce some fools and scoundrels without the entire group paying for it. *Carl T. Rowan*

Shall we judge a country by the majority, or by the minority? By the minority, surely.
Ralph Waldo Emerson

Never in the field of human conflict was so much owed by so many to so few.
Winston Churchill (House of Commons, August 20, 1940)

One dog barks at something, the rest bark at him.   *Chinese proverb*

The nail that sticks out is hammered down.   *Japanese proverb*

Mistakes and Blunders

The weak have one weapon: the errors of those who think they are strong.
Georges Bidault

Nothing is so simple that it cannot be misunderstood.   *Freeman Teague, Jr.*

Too much talk will include errors.   *Burmese proverb*

What is the use of running when you are on the wrong road?   *Old saying*

Great services are not cancelled by one act or by one single error.
Benjamin Disraeli

Any man whose errors take ten years to correct, is quite a man.
J. Robert Oppenheimer (of Albert Einstein)

There is nothing wrong with making mistakes. Just don't respond with encores.
Anon.

I beseech you, in the bowels of Christ, think it possible you may be mistaken.
Oliver Cromwell

Men are men, they needs must err.   *Euripides*

A clever man commits no minor blunders.   *Goethe*

There is no error so monstrous that it fails to find defenders among the ablest men. Imagine a congress of eminent celebrities such as More, Bacon, Grotius, Pascal, Cromwell, Bossuet, Montesquieu, Jefferson, Napoleon, Pitt, etc. The result would be an Encyclopedia of Errors.   *Lord Acton*

Most men would rather be charged with malice than with making a blunder.
Josh Billings

It is very easy to forgive others their mistakes. It takes more gut and gumption to forgive them for having witnessed your own.   *Jessamyn West*

Things could be worse. Suppose your errors were counted and published every day, like those of a baseball player.   *Anon.*

It's over, and can't be helped, and that's one consolation, as they always say in Turkey, when they cut the wrong man's head off.   *Charles Dickens*

In Canberra, even the mistakes are planned by the National Capital Development Commission.   *Alan Fitzgerald*

Don't ever take a fence down until you know why it was put up.   *Robert Frost*

Money

Be the business never so painful, you may have it done for money.   *Thomas Fuller*

But then one is always excited by descriptions of money changing hands. It's much more fundamental than sex.   *Nigel Dennis*

God makes, and apparel shapes: but it's money that finishes the man.

Thomas Fuller

If a man has money, it is usually a sign too, that he knows how to take care of it; don't imagine his money is easy to get simply because he has plenty of it.

Edgar Watson Howe

Of all the narks known to psychological science, there is none worse than the man who seeks to set himself above his fellows by loftily declaring that he despises money, doesn't want money, and wouldn't know what to do with it if someone left it to him in a will.   *Eleanor Dark*

Inflation is determined by money supply growth.   *Roger Bootle*

Laws go where dollars please.   *Portuguese proverb*

Money can't buy friends, but you can get a better class of enemy.   *Spike Milligan*

Money is not an aphrodisiac: the desire it may kindle in a female eye is more for the cash than the carrier.   *Marya Mannes*

Money is the fruit of evil as often as the root of it.   *Henry Fielding*

Money, like a queen, gives rank and beauty.   *Latin proverb*

Riches are for spending.   *Francis Bacon*

Some people's money is merited
And other people's is inherited.   *Ogden Nash*

There is only one thing for a man to do who is married to a woman who enjoys spending money, and that is to enjoy earning it.   *Edgar Watson Howe*

To be clever enough to get all that money, one must be stupid enough to want it.

G. K. Chesterton

Why is there so much month left at the end of the money?   *Anon.*

Money is the poor people's credit card.   *Marshall McLuhan*

A man is rich in proportion to the things he can afford to let alone.

Henry David Thoreau

Money is like a sixth sense, and you can't make use of the other five without it.

W. Somerset Maugham

Money swore an oath that nobody who did not love it should ever have it.

Irish proverb

I'm so happy to be rich, I'm willing to take all the consequences.

Howard Ahmanson

I haven't heard of anybody who wants to stop living on account of the cost.

Kin Hubbard

It isn't enough for you to love money—it's also necessary that money should love you.   *Baron Rothschild*

Philanthropist: a rich (and usually bald) old gentleman who has trained himself to grin while his conscience is picking his pocket.   *Ambrose Bierce*

The darkest hour of any man's life is when he sits down to plan how to get money without earning it.   *Horace Greeley*

The petty economies of the rich are just as amazing as the silly extravagances of the poor.   *William Feather*

Money is human happiness in the abstract.   *Arthur Schopenhauer*

Money is the most egalitarian force in society. It confers power on whoever holds it.   *Roger Starr*

Bankruptcy is a legal proceeding in which you put your money in your pants pocket and give your coat to your creditors.   *Joey Adams*

Money, like matter, is indestructible.   *G. F. Amsberg*

I don't like money actually, but it quiets my nerves.   *Joe Louis*

Money isn't everything—but it's a long way ahead of what comes next.

Edmund Stockdale

In the bad old days, there were three easy ways of losing money—racing being the quickest, women the pleasantest and farming the most certain. *William Pitt Amherst*

We forget that money gives its value—that someone exchanged work for it.

Neal O'Hara

Money is something you got to make in case you don't die.   *Max Asnes*

If you would know what the Lord God thinks of money, you have only to look at those to whom he gives it.   *Maurice Baring*

Making money is fun, but it's pointless if you don't use the power it brings.

John Bentley

Make money and the whole world will conspire to call you a gentleman.

Mark Twain

I never been in no situation where havin' money made it any worse.   *Clinton Jones*

Money is the wise man's religion.   *Euripides*

Money, it turned out, was exactly like sex; you thought of nothing else if you didn't have it and thought of other things if you did.   *James Baldwin*

A feast is made for laughter, and wine maketh merry: but money answereth all things.

Ecclesiastes 10:19

Neither a borrower nor a lender be
For loan oft loses both itself and friend,
And borrowing dulls the edge of husbandry.   *Shakespeare, 'Hamlet'*

Never invest your money in anything that eats or needs repairing.   *Billy Rose*

Money is always there but the pockets change; it is not in the same pockets after a change, and that is all there is to say about money.   *Gertrude Stein*

Men are more often bribed by their loyalties and ambitions than by money.

Robert H. Jackson

Money dignifies what is frivolous if unpaid for.   *Virginia Woolf*

How do you make a million? You start with $900,000.

Stephen Lewis to Morton Shulman

When you have told anyone you have left him a legacy, the only decent thing to do is to die at once.   *Samuel Butler*

He that maketh haste to be rich shall not be innocent.   *Proverbs 28:20*

Money is good for bribing yourself through the inconveniences of life.

Gottfried Reinhardt

There's nothing an economist should fear so much as applause.   *Herbert Marshall*

You can't force anyone to love you or to lend you money.   *Jewish proverb*

With money in your pocket, you are wise, and you are handsome, and you sing well too.   *Jewish proverb*

If the rich could hire other people to die for them, the poor would make a wonderful living.   *Jewish proverb*

The farmer's way of saving money: to be owed by someone he trusted.
Hugh MacLennan

Gentlemen prefer bonds.   *Andrew Mellon*

When you want really big money, you usually find yourself talking to people who didn't go to Eton.   *An English banker*

A good mind possesses a kingdom: a great fortune is a great slavery.   *Seneca*

When it is a question of money, everybody is of the same religion.   *Voltaire*

Money is like muck—not good unless it be spread.   *Francis Bacon*

Morality and Ethics

A truth that's told with bad intent—beats all the lies you can invent.   *William Blake*

An election is a moral horror, as bad as a battle except for the blood; a mud bath for every soul concerned in it.   *George Bernard Shaw*

An improper mind is a perpetual feast.   *Logan Pearsall Smith*

Every man has his moral backside too, which he doesn't expose unnecessarily but keeps covered as long as possible by the trousers of decorum.   *G. C. Lichtenberg*

In statesmanship get formalities right, never mind about the moralities.   *Mark Twain*

It is a public scandal that gives offence and it is no sin to sin in secret.   *Molière*

Moral indignation is, in most cases, 2% moral, 48% indignation and 50% envy.
Vittorio de Sica

Morality is the theory that every human act must be either right or wrong and that 99% of them are wrong.   *H. L. Mencken*

Of moral purpose I see no trace in Nature. That is an article of exclusively human manufacture—and very much to our credit.   *Thomas Huxley*

One of the misfortunes of our time is that in getting rid of false shame, we have killed off so much real shame as well.   *Louis Kronenberger*

Strait is the gate, and narrow is the way, which leadeth unto life, and few there be
that find it.   *Matthew 7:14*

The flea, though he kill none, he does all the harm he can.   *John Donne*

The only people who should really sin
Are the people who can sin with a grin.   *Ogden Nash*

The so-called new morality has too often the old immorality condoned.
                                                                                                                Lord Shawcross

To act without rapacity, to use knowledge with wisdom, to respect interdependence,
to operate without hubris and greed are not simply moral imperatives. They are an
accurate scientific description of the means of survival.   *Barbara Ward*

If some great power would agree to make me always think what is true and do what
is right, on condition of being some sort of clock and wound up every morning before
I got out of bed, I should close instantly with the offer.   *Thomas Huxley*

We have two kinds of morality side by side: one which we preach but do not practice,
and the other which we practice but seldom preach.   *Bertrand Russell*

There are ten commandments, right? Well, it's like an exam. You get eight out of ten,
you're just about top of the class.   *Mordecai Richler*

A man does not have to be an angel in order to be a saint.   *Albert Schweitzer*

No man is so exquisitely honest or upright in living but that ten times in his life he
might not lawfully be hanged.   *Montaigne*

It is often easier to fight for principles than to live up to them.   *Adlai Stevenson*

Only that which does not teach, which does not cry out, which does not condescend,
which does not explain, is irresistible.   *William Butler Yeats*

Quality—in its classic Greek sense—how to live with grace and intelligence, with
bravery and mercy.   *Theodore H. White*

What is morality in any given time or place? It is what the majority then and there
happen to like, and immorality is what they dislike.   *Alfred North Whitehead*

No morality can be founded on authority, even if the authority were divine.
                                                                                                                            A. J. Ayer

In any assembly the simplest way to stop transacting business and split the ranks is
to appeal to a principle.   *Jacques Barzun*

He who would do good to another must do it in minute particulars: general good is
the plea of the scoundrel, hypocrite and flatterer. For art and science cannot exist but
in minutely organized particulars.   *William Blake*

You've got to be brave and you've got to be bold. Brave enough to take your chance on your own discrimination—what's right and what's wrong, what's good and what's bad.   *Robert Frost*

We have left undone those things which we ought to have done; and we have done those things we ought not to have done; and there is no health in us.
                                                        Book of Common Prayer

Most people sell their souls and live with a good conscience on the proceeds.
                                                        Logan Pearsall Smith

This world is white no longer, and it will never be white again.   *James Baldwin*

Below the navel there is neither religion nor truth.   *Italian proverb*

It is customary these days to ignore what should be done in favour of what pleases us.   *Plautus*

What is morality but immemorial custom? Conscience is the chief of conservatives.
                                                        Henry David Thoreau

What you get free costs too much.   *Jean Anouilh*

You cannot receive a shock unless you have an electric affinity for that which shocks you.   *Henry David Thoreau*

Even moderation ought not to be practised to excess.   *Anon.*

When a blind man carries the lame man, both go forward.   *Swedish proverb*

Resignation is selfishness under another name, it is cowardice under a white veil of goodness.   *Louisa Lawson*

Shame and guilt are noble emotions essential in the maintenance of civilized society, and vital for the development of some of the most refined and elegant qualities of human potential—generosity, service, self-sacrifice, unselfishness and duty.
                                                        Willard Gaylen

If your morals make you dreary, depend on it they are wrong.
                                                        Robert Louis Stevenson

Do not be too moral. You may cheat yourself out of much life. So aim above morality. Be not simply good; be good for something.   *Henry David Thoreau*

Moral courage is a more rare commodity than bravery in battle or great intelligence.
                                                        Robert F. Kennedy

Morality is not respectability.   *George Bernard Shaw*

Moral indignation—jealousy with a halo.   *H. G. Wells*

Nobody does nothing for nobody for naught.   *Peter Lord*

The man who is anybody and who does anything is surely going to be criticized, vilified, and misunderstood. This is part of the penalty for greatness, and every man understands, too, that it is no proof of greatness.   *Elbert Hubbard*

Music

Beethoven can write music, thank God—but he can do nothing else on earth.
Ludwig van Beethoven

The public doesn't want new music; the main thing that it demands of a composer is that he be dead.   *Arthur Honegger*

I have sat through an Italian opera, til, for sheer pain, and inexplicable anguish, I have rushed out into the noisiest places of the crowded street, to solace myself with sounds which I was not obliged to follow and get rid of the distracting torment of endless, fruitless, barren attention!   *Charles Lamb*

All I can say is—sing 'em muck! It's all they can understand.
Nellie Melba to Clara Butt before her Australian tour

Let us not forget that the greatest composers were also the greatest thieves. They stole from everyone and everywhere.   *Pablo Casals*

A symphony is a stage play with the parts written for instruments instead of for actors.
Colin Wilson

An ear for music is very different from a taste for music. I have no ear whatever; I could not sing an air to save my life; but I have the intensest delight in music, and can detect good from bad.   *Samuel Taylor Coleridge*

Classic music is th' kind that we keep thinkin'll turn into a tune.   *Frank McKinney*

Discord occasions a momentary distress to the ear, which remains unsatisfied, and even uneasy, until it hears something better.   *Charles Burney*

Discord occasions a momentary distress to the ear, which remains unsatisfied, and even uneasy, until it hears something better. I am convinced . . . that provided the ear be at length made amends, there are few dissonances too strong for it. Disharmony, to paraphrase Bergson's statement about disorder, is simply a harmony to which many are unaccustomed.   *John Cage*

Canned music is like audible wallpaper.   *Alistair Cooke*

Don't play what's there, play what's not there.   *Miles Davis*

From Mozart I learnt to say important things in a conversational way.
George Bernard Shaw

Generally music feedeth that disposition of the spirits which it findeth.

Francis Bacon

God tells me how he wants the music played—and you get in his way.

Arturo Toscanini

Handel was a man of the world; but Bach was a world of a man.   *Arnold Stevenson*

I am sure my music has a taste of codfish in it.   *Edvard Grieg*

I do not mind what language an opera is sung in so long as it is the language I don't understand.   *Edward Appleton*

In the Negro melodies of America I find all that is needed for a great and noble school of music.   *Antonin Dvorak*

It is the best of all trades to make songs, and the second best to sing them.

Hilaire Belloc

Jazz came to America 300 years ago in chains.   *Paul Whiteman*

Jazz is about the only form of art existing today in which there is freedom of the individual without the loss of group contact.   *Dave Brubeck*

Jazz is the only music in which the same note can be played night after night but differently each time.   *Ornette Coleman*

Jazz will endure just as long as people hear it through their feet instead of their brains.

John Philip Sousa

Mozart is sunshine.   *Antonin Dvorak*

Music sweeps by me as a messenger
Carrying a message that is not for me.   *George Eliot*

Mozart's music gives us permission to live.   *John Updike*

Music is a strange thing. I would almost say it is a miracle. For it stands halfway between thought and phenomenon, between spirit and matter.   *Heinrich Heine*

Music is another planet.   *Alphonse Daudet*

Music is the art of thinking with sounds.   *Jules Combarieu*

Music is well said to be the speech of angels.   *Thomas Carlyle*

Music touches places beyond our touching.   *Keith Bosley*

Music with dinner is an insult, both to the cook and the violinist.   *G. K. Chesterton*

Never compose anything unless the not composing of it becomes a positive nuisance to you.
Gustav Holst

Nothing is better than music. . . . It has done more for us than we have the right to hope for.
Nadia Boulanger

Rests always sound well.
Arnold Schoenberg

Swans sing before they die—
'twere no bad thing,
Did certain persons die before they sing.
Samuel Taylor Coleridge

The basic difference between classical music and jazz is that in the former the music is always graver than its performance—whereas the way jazz is performed is always more important than what is being played.
André Previn

The devil does not stay where music is.
Martin Luther

The Sonata is an essentially dramatic art form, combining the emotional range in vivid presentation of a full-size stage drama with the terseness of a short story.
Donald Francis Tovey

The sonatas of Mozart are unique; they are too easy for children, and too difficult for artists.
Artur Schnabel

Too many pieces of music finish too long after the end.
Igor Stravinsky

Throughout my career, nervousness and stage-fright have never left me before playing. And each of the thousands of concerts I have played at, I feel as bad as I did the very first time.
Pablo Casals

Twelve Highlanders and a bagpipe make a rebellion.
Scottish proverb

Wagner has lovely moments but awful quarters of an hour.
Gioacchino Rossini

Who is there that, in logical words, can express the effect music has on us? A kind of inarticulate, unfathomable speech, which leads us to the edge of the Infinite and lets us for moments gaze into that!
Thomas Carlyle

You know what you do when you shit; singing is the same thing, only up!
Enrico Caruso

After silence, that which comes nearest to expressing the inexpressible is music.
Aldous Huxley

When people hear good music, it makes them homesick for something they never had, and never will have.
Edgar Watson Howe

Light quirks of music, broken and uneven,
Make the soul dance upon a jig of heaven.
Alexander Pope

Who hears music, feels his solitude peopled at once.   *Robert Browning*

Richard Wagner, a musician who wrote music which is better than it sounds.

Mark Twain

One cannot judge 'Lohengrin' from a first hearing, and I certainly do not intend to hear it a second time.   *Gioacchino Rossini*

Opera purges men of those hesitations and worries which make it difficult for them to acknowledge their importance to themselves. A good performance of an opera, that is, provides a language for us to speak of ourselves as we have always known we should speak.   *Hamish Swanston*

I love all those demented old dames of the old operas. They are looney, but the music is wonderful.   *Joan Sutherland*

No one can any longer write in the fat style of Strauss. That was killed by Stravinsky. He stripped the body of much of its clothes. Music is the craft of building structures with sound and that is what Stravinsky represents.   *Vladimir Nabokov*

A nation creates music—the composer only arranges it.   *Mikhail Glinka*

Sentimentally I am disposed to harmony; but organically I am incapable of a tune.

Charles Lamb

Music produces a kind of pleasure which human nature cannot do without.

Confucius

Conductors must give unmistakable and suggestive signals to the orchestra, not choreography to the audience.   *George Szell*

Music is the shorthand of emotion.   *Leo Tolstoy*

For most singers the first half of the career involves extending one's repertoire, the second half trimming it.   *Ethan Mordden*

How wonderful opera would be if there were no singers.   *Gioacchino Rossini*

Opera in English is, in the main, just about as sensible as baseball in Italian.

H. L. Mencken

Music is only sound expressing certain patterns, so to what extent is that sound architecture and to what extent theatre?   *Arthur Brown*

A jazz musician is a juggler who uses harmonies instead of oranges.   *Benny Green*

Music is a language by whose means messages are elaborated, that such messages can be understood by the many but sent out only by few, and that it alone among all the languages unites the contradictory character of being at once intelligible and untranslatable—these facts make the creator of music a being like the gods.

Claude Levi-Strauss

Music is your own experience, your thoughts, your wisdom. If you don't live it, it won't come out of your horn.   *Charlie Parker*

The good composer is slowly discovered, the bad composer is slowly found out.
Ernest Newman

The function of pop music is to be consumed.   *Pierre Boulez*

Oboe—an ill wind that nobody blows good.   *Anon.*

Music first and last should sound well, should allure and enchant the ear. Never mind the inner significance.   *Thomas Beecham*

I am tired before the concert, not afterward.   *Artur Rubinstein*

Music, the greatest good that mortals know,
And all of heaven we have below.   *Joseph Addison*

What we play is life.   *Louis Armstrong*

I know that the twelve notes in each octave and the varieties of rhythm offer me opportunities that all of human genius will never exhaust.   *Igor Stravinsky*

Had I learned to fiddle, I should have done nothing else.   *Samuel Johnson*

The notes I handle no better than many pianists. But the pauses between the notes—ah, that is where the art resides!   *Artur Schnabel*

Chamber music—a conversation between friends.   *Catherine Drinker Bowen*

Mozart is the human incarnation of the divine force of creation.   *Goethe*

I write as a sow piddles.   *Wolfgang Amadeus Mozart*

I am an arrogant and impatient listener, but in the case of a few composers, a very few, when I hear a work I do not like, I am convinced that it is my own fault. Verdi is one of those composers.   *Benjamin Britten*

Music hath charms to soothe a savage breast,
To soften rocks, or bend a knotted oak.   *William Congreve*

Harpists spend half their life tuning and the other half playing out of tune.   *Anon.*

She was an aging singer who had to take every note above 'A' with her eyebrows.
Montague Glass

Going to the opera, like getting drunk, is a sin that carries its own punishment with it and that a very severe one.   *Hannah More*

Opera is when a guy gets stabbed in the back and instead of bleeding he sings.
Ed Gardner

I think popular music in this country is one of the few things in the twentieth century that have made giant strides in reverse.   *Bing Crosby*

If a literary man puts together two words about music, one of them will be wrong.
Aaron Copland

Music is given to us specifically to make order of things, to move from an anarchic, individualistic state to a regulated, perfectly concious one, which alone insures vitality and durability.   *Igor Stravinsky*

Nature

The course of nature is the art of God.   *Edward Young*

After a debauch of thundershower, the weather takes the pledge and signs it with a rainbow.   *Thomas Bailey Aldrich*

From the intrinsic evidence of His creation, the Great Architect of the Universe now begins to appear as a pure mathematician.   *Sir James Jeans*

Is ditchwater dull? Naturalists with microscopes have told me that it teems with quiet fun.   *G. K. Chesterton*

It is not necessarily those lands which are the most fertile or most favored climate that seem to me the happiest, but those in which a long stroke of adaptation between man and his environment has brought out the best qualities of both.   *T. S. Eliot*

Like a gardener, I believe that what goes down must come up.
Lynwood L. Giacomini

Never try to return to nature; nature never stands still.   *Margaret Preston*

Nature is not human-hearted.   *Lao-tzu*

Nature, with equal mind,
Sees all her sons at play,
Sees man control the wind,
The wind sweep man away.   *Matthew Arnold*

The chess-board is the world; the pieces are the phenomena of the universe; the rules of the game are what we call the Laws of Nature. The player on the other side is hidden from us. We know that his play is always fair, just and patient. But also we know, to our cost, that he never overlooks a mistake, or makes the smallest allowance for ignorance.   *Thomas Huxley*

The sky is the daily bread of the eyes.   *Ralph Waldo Emerson*

The unnatural—that too is natural.   *Goethe*

There is one glory of the sun and another glory of the moon and another glory of the stars: for one star differeth from another star in glory.   *1 Corinthians 15:41*

There is something haunting in the light of the moon; it has all the dispassionateness of a disembodied soul, and something of its inconceivable mystery.   *Joseph Conrad*

The universe is not hostile, nor yet is it friendly. It is simply indifferent.
John Hughes Holmes

In nature there are neither rewards nor punishments—there are consequences.
Robert G. Ingersoll

Monotony is the law of nature. Look at the monotonous manner in which the sun rises. The monotony of necessary occupations is exhilarating and life-giving.
Gandhi

Men argue, nature acts.   *Voltaire*

Nature is usually wrong.   *James McNeill Whistler*

Speak to the earth, and it shall teach thee.   *Job 12.8*

Flowers have an expression of countenance as much as men or animals. Some seem to smile, some have a sad expression, some are pensive and diffident, others again are plain, honest and upright.   *Henry Ward Beecher*

Gie me a spark o' nature's fire,
That's a' the learning I desire.   *Robert Burns*

Light may be shed on man and his origins.   *Charles Darwin*

I have called this principle, by which each slight variation, if useful, is preserved, by the term natural selection.   *Charles Darwin*

Nature is reckless of the individual.   *Ralph Waldo Emerson*

I wanted to say something about the universe. There's God, angels, plants . . . and horseshit.   *Zero Mostel*

When elephants fight it is the grass that suffers.   *African saying*

The dinosaur's eloquent lesson is that if some bigness is good, an overabundance of bigness is not necessarily better.   *Eric Johnston*

Who are we? We find that we live on an insignificant planet of a humdrum star lost in a galaxy tucked away in some forgotten corner of a universe in which there are far more galaxies than people.   *Carl Sagan*

A vacuum is a hell of a lot better than some of the stuff that nature replaces it with.
Tennessee Williams

We cannot command Nature except by obeying her.   *Francis Bacon*

The mastery of nature is vainly believed to be an adequate substitute for self-mastery.
Reinhold Niebuhr

Nature thrives on patience; man on impatience.   *Paul Boese*

The soil, in return for her service, keeps the tree tied to her; the sky asks nothing and
leaves it free.   *Rabindranath Tagore*

What mighty battles have I seen and heard waged between the trees and the west
wind—an Iliad fought in the fields of air.   *Edith M. Thomas*

Grass is the forgiveness of nature—her constant benediction. Forests decay, harvests
perish, flowers vanish, but grass is immortal.   *Brian Ingalls*

I frequently tramped eight or ten miles through the deepest snow to keep an appoint-
ment with a beech tree, or a yellow birch, or an old acquaintance among the pines.
Henry David Thoreau

The whole of nature is a conjugation of the verb to eat, in the active and passive.
Dean William R. Inge

The universe is like a safe to which there is a combination, but the combination is
locked up in the safe.   *Peter de Vries*

When the oak is felled the whole forest echoes with its fall, but a hundred acorns are
sown in silence by an unnoticed breeze.   *Thomas Carlyle*

Deep in their roots,
All flowers keep the light.   *Theodore Roethke*

By nature's kindly disposition, most questions which it is beyond man's power to
answer do not occur to him at all.   *George Santayana*

To demand 'sense' is the hallmark of nonsense. Nature does not make sense. Nothing
makes sense.   *Ayn Rand*

If allowed to survive, this grass will produce enough oxygen for two students to breathe
for one semester.   *Lawn sign, University of Iowa*

The bluebird carries the sky on his back.   *Henry David Thoreau*

There is nothing in which the birds differ more from man than the way in which they
can build and yet leave a landscape as it was before.   *Robert Lynd*

The greatest joy in nature is the absence of man.   *Bliss Carman*

When a man wantonly destroys a work of man we call him a vandal; when a man
destroys one of the works of God, we call him a sportsman.   *Joseph Wood Krutch*

Man is a complex being: he makes deserts bloom and lakes die. *Gil Stern*

Nature never did betray the heart that loved her. *William Wordsworth*

Newspapers and Journalism

Freedom of the press in Britain is freedom to print such of the proprietor's prejudices as the advertisers don't object to. *Hannen Swaffer*

Newspapers have developed what might be called a vested interest in catastrophe. If they can spot a fight, they play up that fight. If they can uncover a tragedy, they will headline that tragedy. *Harry A. Overstreet*

Everything you read in the newspapers is absolutely true, except for that rare story of which you happen to have first-hand knowledge. *Erwin Knoll*

I must say I try not to read the newspapers at all. I think they cause brain damage . . . We don't know how bad for us the information is that bombards us every day. I work on the view that if something really significant has happened somebody'll tell you about it. *Blanche d'Alpuget*

Burke said there were three Estates in Parliament; but in the reporters' gallery yonder, there sat a fourth Estate more important than them all. *Thomas Carlyle*

The typical Australian newspaper reader has a mental age of 12. Write only in the active voice. Never use a sentence longer than 12 words. Never use a word that a child could not understand. *Sir John Williams to Keith Dunstan*

Remember, son, many a good story has been ruined by over-verification. *James Gordon Bennett*

Don't be afraid to make a mistake, your readers might like it. *William Randolph Hearst*

To be a working journalist one needs tact, aplomb, a wide general knowledge, an inventive mind, a faculty for quick action, a nose for news, an ear for scandal, and a mouth for drinking purposes. Also a pencil and some paper. The last three items are absolutely essential. *Lennie Lower*

The sports page records people's accomplishments, the front page usually records nothing but man's failures. *Earl Warren*

If some great catastrophe is not announced every morning, we feel a certain void. 'Nothing in the paper today,' we sigh. *Paul Valéry*

Carelessness is not fatal to journalism, nor are clichés, for the eye rests lightly on them. But what is intended to be read once can seldom be read more than once; a journalist has to accept the fact that his work, by its very todayness, is excluded from any share in tomorrow. *Cyril Connolly*

Journalists are born. Why, nobody knows.   *Lennie Lower*

An editor—a person employed on a newspaper, whose business it is to separate the wheat from the chaff, and to see that the chaff is printed.   *Elbert Hubbard*

The day you write to please everyone you no longer are in journalism. You are in show business.   *Frank Miller, Jr.*

News is the first rough draft of history.   *Benjamin Bradlee*

It is a newspaper's duty to print the news and raise hell.   *Wilbur F. Storey*

What you see is news, what you know is background, what you feel is opinion.
Lester Markel

Freedom of the press is guaranteed only to those who own one.   *A. J. Liebling*

A good newspaper is a nation talking to itself.   *Arthur Miller*

The first essence of journalism is to know what you want to know; the second, is to find out who will tell you.   *John Gunther*

Today's reporter is forced to become an educator more concerned with explaining the news than with being first on the scene.   *Fred Friendley*

A writer who takes up journalism abandons the slow tempo of literature for a faster one and the change will do him harm. By degrees the flippancy of journalism will become a habit and the pleasure of being paid on the nail and more especially of being praised on the nail, grow indispensable.   *Cyril Connolly*

Observation

'Tis distance lends enchantment to the view,
And robes the mountain in its azure hue.   *Thomas Campbell*

All of us are watchers—of television, of time clocks, of traffic on the freeway—but few are observers. Everyone is looking, not many are seeing.   *Peter M. Leschak*

As a man is, so he sees.   *William Blake*

My evening visitors, if they cannot see the clock, should find the time in my face.
Ralph Waldo Emerson

I keep six honest serving-men
They taught me all I know;
Their names are What and Why and When
And How and Where and Who   *Rudyard Kipling*

It is the theory that decides what can be observed.   *Albert Einstein*

The difference between landscape and landscape is small, but there's a great difference in the beholders.   *Ralph Waldo Emerson*

The eyes are the window of the soul.   *Old saying*

The eyes believe themselves; the ears believe other people.   *German proverb*

The eye sees only what the mind is prepared to comprehend.   *Robertson Davies*

The things we see are the mind's best bet as to what is out front.   *Adelbert Ames*

You can observe a lot just by watching.   *Yogi Berra*

The eye is the jewel of the body.   *Henry David Thoreau*

The ear tends to be lazy, craves the familiar and is shocked by the unexpected; the eye, on the other hand, tends to be impatient, craves the novel and is bored by repetition.   *W. H. Auden*

The eyes indicate the antiquity of the soul.   *Ralph Waldo Emerson*

To become the spectator of one's own life is to escape the suffering of life.
Oscar Wilde

One must always tell what one sees. Above all, which is more difficult, one must always see what one sees.   *Charles Péguy*

A fool sees not the same tree that a wise man sees.   *William Blake*

Cultivated men and women who do not skim the cream of life, and are attached to the duties, yet escape the harsher blows, make acute and balanced observers.
George Meredith

People only see what they are prepared to see.   *Ralph Waldo Emerson*

The lower classes of men, though they do not think it worthwhile to record what they perceive, nevertheless perceive everything that is worth noting; the difference between them and a man of learning often consists in nothing more than the latter's facility for expression.   *G. C. Lichtenberg*

There's none so blind as those who won't see.   *English proverb*

Opinion

Do not choose to be wrong for the sake of being different.   *Lord Samuel*

I am always prepared to recognise that there can be two points of view—mine, and one that is probably wrong.   *John Gorton*

New opinions are always suspected, and usually opposed, without any other reason but because they are not already common.   *John Locke*

So many men, so many opinions.   *Terence*

Three Spaniards, four opinions.   *Spanish proverb*

We are so vain that we even care for the opinion of those we don't care for.
Marie Ebner Von Eschenbach

One should respect public opinion in so far as it is necessary to avoid starvation and to keep out of prison, but anything that goes beyond this is voluntary submission to an unnecessary tyranny.   *Bertrand Russell*

Public opinion, a vulgar, impertinent, anonymous tyrant who deliberately makes life unpleasant for anyone who is not content to be the average man.
Dean William R. Inge

You've no idea what a poor opinion I have of myself—and how little I deserve it.
W. S. Gilbert

Predominant opinions are generally the opinions of the generation that is vanishing.
Benjamin Disraeli

To be positive: to be mistaken at the top of one's voice.   *Ambrose Bierce*

When I want your opinion I'll give it to you.   *Laurence J. Peter*

The sound of tireless voices is the price we pay for the right to hear the music of our own opinions.   *Adlai Stevenson*

It is always considered a piece of impertinence in England if a man of less than two or three thousand a year has any opinions at all upon important subjects.
Sydney Smith

The pressure of public opinion is like the pressure of the atmosphere; you can't see it—but all the same, it is sixteen pounds to the square inch.   *James Russell Lowell*

The right to be heard does not automatically include the right to be taken seriously.
Hubert Humphrey

The world is not run by thought, nor by imagination, but by opinion.
Elizabeth Drew

'No' and 'Yes' are words quickly said, but they need a great amount of thought before you utter them.   *Baltasar Gracián*

I disapprove of what you say, but I will defend to the death your right to say it.
Voltaire

It is not truth, but opinion that can travel the world without a passport.

Walter Raleigh

There never were two opinions alike in all the world, no more than two hours or two grains: the most universal quality is diversity.   *Montaigne*

A difference of opinion is what makes horse racing and missionaries.   *Will Rogers*

Public opinion is a compound of folly, weakness, prejudice, wrong feeling, right feeling, obstinacy, and newspaper paragraphs.   *Robert Peel*

The foolish and the dead alone never change their opinions.   *James Russell Lowell*

All empty souls tend to extreme opinion.   *William Butler Yeats*

Too often we . . . enjoy the comfort of opinion without the discomfort of thought.

John F. Kennedy

Opinions cannot survive if one has no chance to fight for them.   *Thomas Mann*

There are a great many opinions in this world, and a good half of them are professed by people who have never been in trouble.   *Mavis Gallant*

Optimism and Pessimism

In the midst of winter, I finally learned that there was in me an invincible summer.

Albert Camus

One cloud is enough to eclipse all the sun.   *Thomas Fuller*

It's no good crying over spilt milk; all we can do is bail up another cow.

J. B. Chifley

When I look in the glass I see that every line in my face means pessimism, but in spite of my face—that is my experience—I remain an optimist.   *Richard Jefferies*

An optimist is a guy
that has never had
much experience.   *Don Marquis*

An optimist is a fellow who believes what's going to be will be postponed.

Kin Hubbard

Pessimist—one who, when he has the choice of two evils, chooses both.

Oscar Wilde

My pessimism goes to the point of suspecting the sincerity of the pessimists.

Jean Rostand

A pessimist is one who has been compelled to live with an optimist.

Elbert Hubbard

Pessimism is only the name that men of weak nerves give to wisdom.

Elbert Hubbard

When it is dark enough, you can see the stars. *Charles A. Beard*

There is not enough darkness in all the world to put out the light of even one small candle. *Robert Alden*

When things come to the worst, they generally mend. *Susanna Moodie*

The optimist claims we live in the best of all possible worlds, and the pessimist fears this is true. *James Branch Cabell*

Still round the corner there may wait,
A new road, or a secret gate. *J. R. R. Tolkien*

When Fortune empties her chamberpot on your head, smile and say 'We are going to have a summer shower.' *John A. Macdonald*

The world gets better every day—then worse again in the evening. *Kin Hubbard*

A man he seems of cheerful yesterdays
And confident tomorrows. *William Wordsworth*

There is a budding morrow in midnight. *John Keats*

Order and Organization

It is much safer to obey than to rule. *Thomas à Kempis*

Let all things be done decently and in order. *Corinthians 14:40*

There is no right to strike against the public safety by anybody, anywhere, anytime. *Calvin Coolidge*

When liberty destroys order, the hunger for order will destroy liberty. *Will Durant*

Those who are fond of setting things to rights have no great objection to setting them wrong. *William Hazlitt*

To have his path made clear for him is the aspiration of every human being in our beclouded and tempestuous existence. *Joseph Conrad*

Our laws make law impossible; our liberties destroy all freedom; our property is organized robbery; our morality an impudent hypocrisy; our wisdom is administered by inexperienced or mal-experienced dupes; our power wielded by cowards and weaklings; and our honour false in all its points. I am an enemy of the existing order for good reasons.   *George Bernard Shaw*

Crude classifications and false generalizations are the curse of organized life.
H. G. Wells

Timing, degree and conviction are the three wise men in this life.   *R. I. Fitzhenry*

We put things in order—God does the rest. Lay an iron bar east and west, it is not magnetized. Lay it north and south and it is.   *Horace Mann*

I must create a system, or be enslaved by another man's.   *William Blake*

Out of intense complexities intense simplicities emerge.   *Winston Churchill*

There is no course of life so weak and sottish as that which is managed by order, method and discipline.   *Montaigne*

Large organization is loose organization. Nay, it would be almost as true to say that organization is always disorganization.   *G. K. Chesterton*

Originality

Originality is the art of concealing your sources.   *Anon.*

Utter originality is, of course, out of the question.   *Ezra Pound*

We do not inherit this land from our ancestors; we borrow it from our children.
Haida saying

Why can't somebody give us a list of things that everybody thinks and nobody says, and another list of things that everybody says and nobody thinks.
Oliver Wendell Holmes

Originality is nothing but judicious imitation. The most original writers borrowed one from another. The instruction we find in books is like fire. We fetch it from our neighbours, kindle it at home, communicate it to others and it becomes the property of all.   *Voltaire*

Originality does not consist in saying what no one has ever said before, but in saying exactly what you think yourself.   *James Stephens*

What a good thing Adam had—when he said a good thing, he knew nobody had said it before.   *Mark Twain*

All cases are unique and very similar to others.   *T. S. Eliot*

I invent nothing. I rediscover.   *Auguste Rodin*

There is nothing new under the sun.   *Ecclesiastes 1:9*

When people are free to do as they please, they usually imitate each other. Originality is deliberate and forced, and partakes of the nature of a protest.   *Eric Hoffer*

All profoundly original work looks ugly at first.   *Clement Greenberg*

Riding hard for glory.   *Irving Layton*

What is originality? Undetected plagiarism.   *Dean William R. Inge*

The dogmas of the quiet past are inadequate to the stormy present. The occasion is piled high with difficulty, and we must rise with the occasion. As our case is new, so we must think anew and act anew. We must disenthrall ourselves.

Abraham Lincoln

Ownership and Possession

You got a harem of seventy girls, you don't get to know any of them very well.

Billy Rose (on the hazards of over-diversification on the Stock Market)

It is preoccupation with possession, more than anything else, that prevents men from living freely and nobly.   *Bertrand Russell*

Ownership is to fear (*tener es temer*).   *Spanish proverb*

Broad acres are a patent of nobility; and no man but feels more of a man in the world if he have a bit of ground that he can call his own. However small it is on the surface, it is 4000 miles deep; and that is a very handsome property.

Charles Dudley Warner

The landscape should belong to the people who see it all the time.   *Le Roi Jones*

Whatever is not nailed down is mine. Whatever I can pry loose is not nailed down.

Collis P. Huntington

I don't want to own anything that won't fit into my coffin.   *Fred Allen*

Lives based on having are less free than lives based either on doing or on being.

William James

The possession of gold has ruined fewer men than the lack of it.

Thomas Bailey Aldrich

The want of a thing is perplexing enough, but the possession of it is intolerable.

John Vanbrugh

Our life on earth is, and ought to be, material and carnal. But we have not yet learned to manage our materialism and carnality properly; they are still entangled with the desire for ownership.
E. M. Forster

Keep a thing seven years and you will find a use for it.
Anon.

You must lose a fly to catch a trout.
George Herbert

He who wants a rose must respect the thorn.
Persian proverb

A man never feels the want of what it never occurs to him to ask for.
Arthur Schopenhauer

I feel when people say 'bigger and better' they should say 'bigger and badder'.
Marie Elizabeth Kane, thirteen years old

People are so overwhelmed with the prestige of their instruments that they consider their personal judgement of hardly any account.
Wyndham Lewis

Can anything be so elegant as to have few wants, and to serve them one's self?
Ralph Waldo Emerson

Painters and Painting

Buy old masters. They fetch a better price than old mistresses.
Lord Beaverbrook

Every time I paint a portrait I lose a friend.
John Singer Sargent

There is nothing more difficult for a truly creative painter than to paint a rose, because before he can do so he has first to forget all the roses that were ever painted.
Henri Matisse

If you could say it in words there would be no reason to paint.
Edward Hopper

Everyone wants to understand painting. Why don't they try to understand the singing of birds? People love the night, a flower, everything that surrounds them without trying to understand them. But painting—that they *must* understand.
Pablo Picasso

I cannot pretend to feel impartial about colours. I rejoice with the brilliant ones and am genuinely sorry for the poor browns.
Winston Churchill

I hope with all my heart there will be painting in heaven.
Jean Baptiste Corot

Painting is a blind man's profession. He paints not what he sees, but what he feels, what he tells himself about what he has seen.
Pablo Picasso

Painting, n: the art of protecting flat surfaces from the weather and exposing them to the critic.
Ambrose Bierce

To say to the painter that Nature is to be taken as she is, is to say to the player that he may sit on the piano.   *James McNeill Whistler*

I paint objects as I think them, not as I see them.   *Pablo Picasso*

The most celebrated, widely reproduced and universally recognisable political painting of the 20th century is Picasso's *Guernica,* and it didn't change Franco's regime one inch or shorten his life by so much as one day.   *Robert Hughes*

There are three kinds of people in the world: those who can't stand Picasso, those who can't stand Raphael and those who've never heard of either of them.
                                                                    John White

I dream my painting, and then I paint my dream.   *Vincent van Gogh*

For me, painting is a way to forget life. It is a cry in the night, a strangled laugh.
                                                                    Georges Rouault

Landscape painting is the obvious resource of misanthropy.   *William Hazlitt*

I paint from the top down. First the sky, then the mountains, then the hills, then the houses, then the cattle, and then the people.   *Grandma Moses*

A good painter is to paint two main things, namely men and the working of man's mind.   *Leonardo da Vinci*

I do not paint a portrait to look like the subject, rather does the person grow to look like his portrait.   *Salvador Dali*

All colours are the friends of their neighbours and the lovers of their opposites.
                                                                    Marc Chagall

The purest and most thoughtful minds are those which love colour the most.
                                                                    John Ruskin

Don't judge a picture by its title—nude gods and goddesses are only unclothed models.
                                                                    Margaret Preston

Sir, when their backsides look good enough to slap, there's nothing more to do.
                                                                    Peter Paul Rubens

A painter who has the feel of breasts and buttocks is saved.   *Auguste Renoir*

Never believe what an artist says, only what he paints.   *Fred Williams*

Modern art is what happens when painters stop looking at girls and persuade themselves they have a better idea.   *John Ciardi*

A picture is worth exactly what some sucker will pay for it, not a penny more and not a penny less.   *Robert Hughes*

Parenthood

A Jewish man with parents alive is a 15–year-old boy, and will remain a 15–year-old boy until they die.
Philip Roth

A rich child often sits in a poor mother's lap.
Spanish proverb

Every beetle is a gazelle in the eyes of its mother.
Moorish proverb

Parentage is a very important profession, but no test of fitness for it is ever imposed in the interests of the children.
George Bernard Shaw

Parents accept their obsolescence with the best grace they can muster. . . they do all they can to make it easy for the younger generation to surpass the older, while secretly dreading the rejection that follows.
Christopher Lasch

Parents are sometimes a bit of a disappointment to their children. They don't fulfil the promise of their early years.
Anthony Powell

Parenthood remains the greatest single preserve of the amateur.
Alvin Toffler

The best brought-up children are those who have seen their parents as they are. Hypocrisy is not the parents' first duty.
George Bernard Shaw

Everyone likes to think that he has done reasonably well in life, so that it comes as a shock to find our children believing differently. The temptation is to tune them out; it takes much more courage to listen.
John D. Rockefeller III

You don't have to deserve your mother's love. You have to deserve your father's. He's more particular.
Robert Frost

I demand for the unmarried mother, as a sacred channel of life, the same reverence and respect as for the married mother; for Maternity is a cosmic thing and once it has come to pass, our conventions must not be permitted to blaspheme it.   *Ben Lindsey*

Who takes the child by the hand takes the mother by the heart.
German proverb

Diogenes struck the father when the son swore.
Robert Burton

When one has not had a good father, one must create one.
Friedrich Nietzsche

Perhaps host and guest is really the happiest relation for father and son.
Evelyn Waugh

Mother is the name for God in the lips and hearts of children.
William Makepeace Thackeray

To bring up a child in the way he should go, travel that way yourself once in a while.
Josh Billings

Anything which parents have not learned from experience they can now learn from their children.   *Anon.*

A father is a banker provided by nature.   *French proverb*

To become a father is not hard,
To be a father is, however.   *Wilhelm Busch*

Our sons, who so easily recognize our errors, and rightly denounce them, will have to confess their own, later on, and they may be as bad as ours, perhaps worse.
                    Bruce Hutchison

A mother who is really a mother is never free.   *Honoré de Balzac*

God could not be everywhere and therefore he made mothers.   *Jewish proverb*

Parenthood is like the modern stonewashing process for denim jeans. You may start out crisp, neat and tough, but you end up pale, limp and wrinkled.   *Kerry Cue*

The first half of our lives is ruined by our parents and the second half by our children.
                    Clarence S. Darrow

Tired mothers find that spanking takes less time than reasoning and penetrates sooner to the seat of the memory.   *Will Durant*

Every parent is at some time the father of the unreturned prodigal, with nothing to do but keep his house open to hope.   *John Ciardi*

The fundamental defect of fathers is that they want their children to be a credit to them.   *Bertrand Russell*

Don't limit a child to your own learning, for he was born in another time.
                    Rabbinical saying

An ounce of mother is worth a pound of clergy.   *Spanish proverb*

No matter how old a mother is, she watches her middle-aged children for signs of improvement.   *Florida Scott-Maxwell*

Whatever you would have your children become, strive to exhibit in your own lives and conversation.   *Lydia H. Sigourney*

Train a child in the way he should go, and when he is old he will not depart from it.
                    Proverbs 12:4

I must study politics and war, that my sons may have the liberty to study mathematics and philosophy, geography, natural history, and naval architecture, navigation, commerce, and agriculture, in order to give their children a right to study painting, poetry, music, architecture, statuary, tapestry and porcelain.   *John Adams*

The thing about having a baby is that thereafter you have it.   *Jean Kerr*

The best way to bring up some children is short.   *Anthony J. Pettito*

What the mother sings to the cradle goes all the way down to the coffin.
Henry Ward Beeche-

The mother-child relationship is paradoxical and, in a sense, tragic. It requires the most intense love on the mother's side, yet this very love must help the child grow away from the mother and to become fully independent.   *Erich Fromm*

Who doesn't desire his father's death?   *Fyodor Dostoevsk_*

Insanity is hereditary—you can get it from your children.   *Sam Levinson*

Parents are the bones on which children cut their teeth.   *Peter Ustino*

Your children need your presence more than your presents.   *Jesse Jackson*

Babies teach their parents an enormous amount. I grew up thinking my parents taught me things, but the reverse is true.   *Judy Davi_*

It is the malady of our age that the young are so busy teaching us that they have no time left to learn.   *Eric Hoffe_*

Passion and the Heart

What our age lacks is not reflection but passion.   *Søren Kierkegaard*

It is with our passions as it is with fire and water—they are good servants, but bad masters.   *Roger l'Estrange*

The happiness of a man in this life does not consist in the absence but in the mastery of his passions.   *Alfred, Lord Tennyson*

The ruling passion, be it what it will,
The ruling passion conquers reason still.   *Alexander Pope*

There is no passion like that of a functionary for his function. *Georges Clemenceau*

An intense feeling carries with it its own universe, magnificent or wretched as the case may be.   *Albert Camus*

He disliked emotion, not because he felt lightly, but because he felt deeply.
John Buchan

People don't ask for facts in making up their minds. They would rather have one good soul-satisfying emotion than a dozen facts.   *Robert Keith Leavit_*

If we resist our passions, it is more due to their weakness than to our strength.
La Rochefoucauld

A sentimentalist is simply one who desires to have the luxury of an emotion without paying for it.   *Oscar Wilde*

Is it not strange
That desire should so many years outlive performance?
                                                    Shakespeare, 'Henry IV' Part II

The world is a comedy to those who think; a tragedy to those who feel.
                                                                Horace Walpole

Follow your heart, and you perish.   *Margaret Laurence*

Many of our commentators are polarised between their genitals and their minds; they seem to have suffered a complete heart bypass.   *Caroline Jones*

Fanaticism consists in redoubling your efforts when you have forgotten your aim.
                                                            George Santayana

Disappointments should be cremated, not embalmed.   *Henry S. Haskins*

Artificial manners vanish the moment the natural passions are touched.
                                                            Maria Edgeworth

Hands have not tears to flow.   *Dylan Thomas*

A good heart is better than all the heads in the world.   *Edward Bulwer-Lytton*

Where the mind is past hope, the heart is past shame.   *John Lyly*

Nobody has ever measured, even poets, how much a heart can hold.
                                                            Zelda Fitzgerald

The logic of the heart is absurd.   *Julie de Lespinasse*

Our hearts were drunk with a beauty
Our eyes could never see.   *George W. Russell*

The same heart beats in every human breast.   *Matthew Arnold*

The heart has its reasons which reason knows nothing of.   *Blaise Pascal*

Man *becomes* man only by the intelligence, but he *is* man only by the heart.
                                                        Henri Frédéric Amiel

From the solitude of the wood, (Man) has passed to the more dreadful solitude of the heart.   *Loren Eiseley*

Seeing's believing, but feeling's the truth.   *Thomas Fuller*

We are adhering to life now with our last muscle—the heart.   *Djuna Barnes*

The great art of life is sensation, to feel that we exist, even in pain.   *Lord Byron*

Weak people cannot be sincere.   *La Rochefoucauld*

Patience

Patience and passage of time do more than strength and fury.   *Jean de la Fontaine*

Patience is a bitter plant but it has sweet fruit.   *Old proverb*

Patience, that blending of moral courage with physical timidity.   *Thomas Hardy*

The slow rhythm of waiting.   *Adrian Cowell*

What can't be cured, must be endured.   *Old saying*

Have patience with all things, but chiefly have patience with yourself. Do not lose courage in considering your own imperfections, but instantly set about remedying them—every day begin the task anew.   *St. Francis de Sales*

Patience makes a woman beautiful in middle age.   *Elliot Paul*

Life on the farm is a school of patience; you can't hurry the crops or make an ox in two days.   *Henri Fournier Alain*

There is nothing so bitter, that a patient mind cannot find some solace for it.
                                                                Seneca

Patience has its limits. Take it too far, and it's cowardice.   *George Jackson*

With time and patience the mulberry leaf becomes a silk gown.   *Chinese proverb*

People in a hurry cannot think, cannot grow, nor can they decay. They are preserved in a state of perpetual puerility.   *Eric Hoffer*

Never cut what you can untie.   *Joseph Joubert*

I am as poor as Job, my lord, but not so patient.   *Shakespeare, 'Henry IV' Part II*

Patience under evil is tacit encouragement of evil, and to submit to pain is to sanction torture.   *Louisa Lawson*

The more haste, the less speed.   *John Heywood*

Hasten slowly.   *Augustus Caesar*

There are no short cuts to Heaven, only the ordinary way of ordinary things.
                                                            Vincent McNabe

Never think that God's delays are God's denials. Hold on; hold fast; hold out. Patience is genius.   *Comte de Buffon*

Patriotism and Nationalism

Ireland is the old sow that eats her farrow. *James Joyce*

I have never understood why one's affections must be confined, as once with women, to a single country. *John Kenneth Galbraith*

One of the great attractions of patriotism—it fulfills our worst wishes. In the person of our nation we are able, vicariously, to bully and cheat. Bully and cheat, what's more, with a feeling that we are profoundly virtuous. *Aldous Huxley*

Patriotism is not short, frenzied outbursts of emotion, but the tranquil and steady dedicaton of a lifetime. *Adlai Stevenson*

True patriotism hates injustice in its own land more than anywhere else.
Clarence Darrow

A nation is a body of people who have done great things together. *Ernest Renan*

Each man must for himself alone decide what is right and what is wrong, which course is patriotic and which isn't. You cannot shirk this and be a man. *Mark Twain*

The French have a passion for revolution but an abhorrence of change. *Old saying*

God made the ocean, but the Dutch made Holland. *Dutch proverb*

The Creator made Italy with designs by Michelangelo. *Mark Twain*

Men may be linked in friendship. Nations are linked only by interests.
Rolf Hochhuth

What makes a nation great is not primarily its great men, but the stature of its innumerable mediocre ones. *José Ortega y Gasset*

Nationalism is both a vital medicine and a dangerous drug. *Geoffrey Blainey*

I'm troubled. I'm dissatisfied. I'm Irish. *Marianne Moore*

The mind supplies the idea of a nation, but what gives this idea its sentimental force is a community of dreams. *André Malraux*

My favourite example (of 'expatriatism') is James Joyce, who left Ireland at nineteen and never came back. But he spent the rest of his life writing about Ireland from the perspective of living in Paris. *Karl Beveridge*

A nation is a body of people who have done great things together in the past and hope to do great things together in the future. *Frank Underhill*

The Swiss are not a people so much as a neat, clean, quite solvent business.
William Faulkner

Ireland is a fatal disease; fatal to Englishmen and doubly fatal to Irishmen.
George Moore

Peace

There is no such thing as inner peace, there is only nervousness and death.

Fran Lebowitz

When fire and water are at war it is the fire that loses.   *Spanish proverb*

Before the war, and especially before the Boer War, it was summer all the year round.

George Orwell

One sword keeps another in the sheath.   *George Herbert*

Peace is a virtual, mute, sustained victory of potential powers against probable greeds.

Paul Valéry

Peace is not an absence of war, it is a virtue, a state of mind, a disposition for benevolence, confidence, justice.   *Benedict Spinoza*

There are no makers of peace because the making of peace is at least as costly as the making of war—at least as exigent.   *Daniel Berrigan*

Once you hear the details of victory, it is hard to distinguish it from a defeat.

Jean-Paul Sartre

The peace of the man who has foresworn the use of the bullet seems to me not quite peace, but a canting impotence.   *Ralph Waldo Emerson*

Where they make a desert, they call it peace.   *Tacitus*

That they may have a little peace, even the best dogs are compelled to snarl occasionally.   *William Feather*

Peace: in international affairs, a period of cheating between two periods of fighting.

Ambrose Bierce

They sicken of the calm who know the storm.   *Dorothy Parker*

Personal Appearance

A fair exterior is a silent recommendation.   *Publilius Syrus*

Bald as the bare mountain tops are bald, with a baldness full of grandeur.

Matthew Arnold

But Shelley had a hyperthyroid face.   *John C. Squire*

He had but one eye, and the pocket of prejudice runs in favour of two.

Charles Dickens

His ears made him look like a taxi cab with both doors open.

Howard Hughes (of Clark Gable)

The fifty-year-old woman's face tells us not only that she has lived fifty years but where and how she has lived it.   *Germaine Greer*

The secret of ugliness consists not in irregularity, but in being uninteresting.

Ralph Waldo Emerson

(Abraham Lincoln's) weathered face was homely as a plowed field.

Stephen Vincent Benét

Every man over forty is responsible for his face.   *Abraham Lincoln*

Don't blame the mirror if your face is faulty.   *Nikolai Vasilyevich Gogol*

People are like birds—from a distance, beautiful: from close up, those sharp beaks, those beady little eyes.   *Richard J. Needham*

Consider the lilies of the field, how they grow; they toil not, neither do they spin. And yet I say unto you, that even Solomon in all his glory was not arrayed like one of these.   *Matthew 6:28,29*

The world is a looking glass and gives back to every man the reflection of his own face.   *William Makepeace Thackeray*

He that has a great nose thinks everybody is speaking of it.   *Thomas Fuller*

There's one thing about baldness—it's neat.   *Don Herold*

One's eyes are what one is, one's mouth what one becomes.   *John Galsworthy*

Hair is another name for sex.   *Vidal Sassoon*

It is only shallow people who do not judge by appearances. The true mystery of the world is the visible, not the invisible.   *Oscar Wilde*

Clothes and manners do not make the man; but, when he is made, they greatly improve his appearance.   *Henry Ward Beecher*

Any man may be in good spirits and good temper when he's well dressed. There ain't much credit in that.   *Charles Dickens*

Why don't you get a haircut; you look like a chrysanthemum.   *P. G. Wodehouse*

Her face looks as if it had worn out two bodies.   *New England saying*

A man cannot dress, without his ideas get clothed at the same time.

Laurence Sterne

Where's the man could ease the heart
Like a satin gown? *Dorothy Parker*

Let me be dressed fine as I will,
Flies, worms, and flowers, exceed me still. *Isaac Watts*

Philosophy

A blind man in a dark room—looking for a black hat which isn't there.
Lord Bowen

In other words, apart from the known and the unknown, what else is there?
Harold Pinter

The unrest which keeps the never-stopping clock metaphysics going is the thought that
the non-existence of this world is just as possible as its existence.   *William James*

It takes a very unusual mind to undertake the analysis of the obvious.
Alfred North Whitehead

All philosophy lies in two words, sustain and abstain. *Epictetus*

In philosophy an individual is becoming himself. *Bernard Lonergan*

Romanticism is the expression of man's urge to rise above reason and common sense,
just as rationalism is the expression of his urge to rise above theology and emotion.
Charles Yost

Science is what you know, philosophy is what you don't know.   *Bertrand Russell*

Here is the beginning of philosophy: a recognition of the conflicts between men, a
search for their cause, a condemnation of mere opinion . . . and the discovery of a
standard of judgement. *Epictetus*

Anything that comes easy, comes wrong. *Josephine Tessier*

To teach how to live with uncertainty, and yet without being paralyzed by hesitation,
is perhaps the chief thing that philosophy in our age can still do for those who study
it. *Bertrand Russell*

All philosophies, if you ride them home, are nonsense; but some are greater nonsense
than others. *Samuel Butler*

It is easy to build a philosophy. It doesn't have to run.   *Charles F. Kettering*

I've developed a new philosophy—I only dread one day at a time.
Charles M. Schulz

A man of business may talk of philosophy; a man who has none may practise it.

Alexander Pope

Philosophy—the purple bullfinch in the lilac tree.   *T. S. Eliot*

Philosophy has a fine saying for everything—for Death it has an entire set.

Laurence Sterne

Three passions, simple but overwhelmingly strong, have governed my life: the longing for love, the search for knowledge and unbearable pity for the suffering of mankind.

Bertrand Russell

I have a simple philosophy. Fill what's empty. Empty what's full. And scratch where it itches.   *Alice Roosevelt Longworth*

In North America there is the general belief that everything can be fixed, that life can be fixed up. In Europe, the view is that a lot can't be fixed up and that living properly is not necessarily a question of mastering the technology so much as learning to live gracefully within the constraints that the species invents.   *Jonathan Miller*

Every day look at a beautiful picture, read a beautiful poem, listen to some beautiful music, and if possible, say some reasonable thing.   *Goethe*

When you have only two pennies left in the world, buy a loaf of bread with one, and a lily with the other.   *Chinese proverb*

The opposite of a correct statement is a false statement. But the opposite of a profound truth may well be another profound truth.   *Niels Bohr*

The philosophy of one century is the common sense of the next.

Henry Ward Beecher

Philosophy is a good horse in the stable, but an errant jade on a journey.

Oliver Goldsmith

Philosophy will clip an Angel's wings
Conquer all mysteries by rule and line,
Empty the haunted air, the gnomed mine—
Unweave a rainbow.   *John Keats*

Adversity's sweet milk, philosophy.   *Shakespeare, 'Romeo and Juliet'*

Philosophy is doubt.   *Montaigne*

Be a philosopher but, amid all your philosophy be still a man.   *David Hume*

The philosopher is Nature's pilot—and there you have our difference; to be in hell is to drift: to be in heaven is to steer.   *George Bernard Shaw*

Being wrong is just an occupational hazard of being a philosopher.

Ronald Samuel Laura

One's task is not to turn the world upside down, but to do what is necessary at the given place and with a due consideration of reality.   *Dietrich Bonhoeffer*

Photography

Instead of just recording reality, photographs have become the norm for the way things appear to us, thereby changing the very idea of reality and of realism.
                                                                            Susan Sontag

The virtue of the camera is not the power it has to transform the photographer into an artist, but the impulse it gives him to keep on looking.   *Brooks Atkinson*

You see someone on the street, and essentially what you notice about them is the flaw.
                                                                            Diane Arbus

If you scratch a great photograph, you find two things: a painting and a photograph.
                                                                            Janet Malcolm

The camera makes everyone a tourist in other people's reality, and eventually in one's own.   *Susan Sontag*

Photography records the gamut of feelings written on the human face—the beauty of the earth and skies that man has inherited; and the wealth and confusion man has created. It is a major force in explaining man to man.   *Edward Steichen*

All I wanted was to connect my moods with those of Paris. Beauty pains and when it pained most, I shot.   *Ernst Haas*

Photographers deal in things which are continually vanishing and when they have vanished there is no contrivance on earth which can make them come back again.
                                                                    Henri Cartier Bresson

Photographers, along with dentists, are the two professions never satisfied with what they do. Every dentist would like to be a doctor and inside every photographer is a painter trying to get out.   *Pablo Picasso*

Life is not about significant details, illuminated in a flash, fixed forever. Photographs are.   *Susan Sontag*

I really believe there are things nobody would see if I didn't photograph them.
                                                                            Diane Arbus

Poets and Poetry

A drainless shower
of light is poesy; 'tis the supreme of power;
'tis might half slumb'ring on its own right arm.   *John Keats*

A good poem is a contribution to reality. The world is never the same once a good poem has been added to it. A good poem helps to change the shape and significance of the universe, helps to extend everyone's knowledge of himself and the world around him.   *Dylan Thomas*

If Galileo had said in verse that the world moved, the Inquisition might have let him alone.   *Thomas Hardy*

In poetry, you must love the words, the ideas and the images and rhythms with all your capacity to love anything at all.   *Wallace Stevens*

Poetry is the song of a mind, singing to other minds.   *A. R. Chisholm*

Poetry is not a profession, it's a destiny.   *Mikhail Dudan*

Poetry is the language of a state of crisis.   *Stephane Mallarmé*

Poetry must be as new as foam, and as old as the rock.   *Ralph Waldo Emerson*

To earn his keep, a poet has to be
Himself, his age, and his society.   *John Manifold*

The mind that finds its way to wild places is the poet's; but the mind that never finds its way back is the lunatic's.   *G. K. Chesterton*

When a poet's mind is perfectly equipped for its work, it is constantly amalgamating disparate experiences.   *T. S. Eliot*

I don't really feel my poems are mine at all. I didn't create them out of nothing. I owe them to my relations with other people.   *Robert Graves*

There's no money in poetry, but then there's no poetry in money either.
                                                                                                            Robert Graves

The essentials of poetry are rhythm, dance and the human voice.   *Earle Birney*

'A poet's at his best dead drunk:
   So here's a go!' smooth Flaccus said.
A half-truth on the edge of bunk—
   A poet's best when he is dead!   *Hugh McCrae*

A poet dares to be just so clear and no clearer; he approaches lucid ground warily, like a mariner who is determined not to scrape his bottom on anything solid. A poet's pleasure is to withhold a little of his meaning, to intensify by mystification. He unzips the veil from beauty, but does not remove it. A poet utterly clear is a trifle glaring.
                                                                                                                E. B. White

Most joyful let the Poet be,
It is through him that all men see.   *William Ellery Channing*

Most people do not believe in anything very much and our greatest poetry is given to us by those that do.   *Cyril Connolly*

The poet is the priest of the invisible.   *Wallace Stevens*

A good poet is someone who manages, in a lifetime of standing out in thunderstorms, to be struck by lightning five or six times.   *Randall Jarrell*

Poetry should be common in experience but uncommon in books.   *Robert Frost*

For what is a poem but a hazardous attempt at self-understanding: it is the deepest part of autobiography.   *Robert Penn Warren*

When a great poet has lived, certain things have been done once for all, and cannot be achieved again.   *T. S. Eliot*

Before verse can be human again it must learn to be brutal.   *J. M. Synge*

No honest poet can ever feel quite sure of the permanent value of what he has written: he may have wasted his time and messed up his life for nothing.   *T. S. Eliot*

Poetry is all nouns and verbs.   *Marianne Moore*

I wish our clever young poets would remember my homely definitions of prose and poetry; that is, prose—words in their best order; poetry—the best words in their best order.   *Samuel Taylor Coleridge*

When you write in prose you say what you mean. When you write in rhyme you say what you must.   *Oliver Wendell Holmes*

The courage of the poet is to keep ajar the door that leads into madness.
                                                            Christopher Morley

Science is for those who learn; poetry for those who know.   *Joseph Roux*

Popular poets are the parish priests of the Muse, retailing her ancient divinations to a long since converted public.   *George Santayana*

Reason respects the differences, and imagination the similitudes of things.
                                                          Percy Bysshe Shelley

The poet's mind is . . . a receptacle for seizing and storing up numberless feelings, phrases, images, which remain there until all the particles which can unite to form a new compound are present together.   *T. S. Eliot*

Of our conflicts with others we make rhetoric; of our conflicts with ourselves we make poetry.   *William Butler Yeats*

Poetry is a mug's game.   *T. S. Eliot*

A poem begins with a lump in the throat; a homesickness or a lovesickness. It is a reaching-out toward expression; an effort to find fulfillment. A complete poem is one where an emotion has found its thought and the thought has found words.

Robert Frost

An art in which the artist by means of rhythm and great sincerity can convey to others the sentiment which he feels about life.   *John Masefield*

Poetry is a profession generally regarded as being too sacred to be paid for in mere money.   *Les A. Murray*

It is Homer who has chiefly taught other poets the art of telling lies skilfully.

Aristotle

Writing free verse is like playing tennis with the net down.   *Robert Frost*

To have great poets there must be great audiences too.   *Walt Whitman*

Poets aren't very useful,
Because they aren't consumeful or very produceful.   *Ogden Nash*

Poetry is a way of taking life by the throat.   *Robert Frost*

Poetry is the opening and closing of a door, leaving those who look through to guess what is seen during a moment.   *Carl Sandburg*

Poetry is the journal of a sea animal living on land, wanting to fly in the air.

Carl Sandburg

There are nine and sixty ways of constructing tribal lays,
And every single one of them is right.   *Rudyard Kipling*

Poetry is the impish attempt to paint the colour of the wind.   *Maxwell Bodenheim*

For me, poetry is an evasion of the real job of writing prose.   *Sylvia Plath*

Politeness and Manners

He who says what he likes shall hear what he does not like.   *English proverb*

Modesty: the gentle art of enhancing your charm by pretending not to be aware of it.

Oliver Herford

Never speak of a man in his own presence. It is always indelicate, and may be offensive.

Samuel Johnson

The opposite of talking is not listening. The opposite of talking is waiting.

Fran Lebowitz

(Politeness is) a tacit agreement that people's miserable defects, whether moral or intellectual, shall on either side be ignored and not be made the subject of reproach.

Arthur Schopenhauer

Good manners are made up of petty sacrifices. *Ralph Waldo Emerson*

Manners are the hypocrisy of a nation. *Honoré de Balzac*

Politeness is good nature regulated by good sense. *Sydney Smith*

If a man didn't make sense, the Scotch felt it was misplaced politeness to try to keep him from knowing it. Better that he be aware of his reputation, for this would encourage reticence which goes well with stupidity. *J. K. Galbraith*

A man must have very eminent qualities to hold his own without being polite.

Jean de la Bruyère

Ah, men do not know how much strength is in poise
That he goes the farthest who goes far enough. *James Russell Lowell*

Questioning is not the mode of conversation among gentlemen. *Samuel Johnson*

I don't care what people do in the bedroom as long as they don't do it in the streets and frighten the horses. *Mrs. Patrick Campbell*

There is always a best way of doing everything, if it be only to boil an egg. Manners are the happy ways of doing things. *Ralph Waldo Emerson*

There is not a single outward mark of courtesy that does not have a deep moral basis.

Goethe

Good breeding consists in concealing how much we think of ourselves and how little we think of the other person. *Mark Twain*

Charming people live up to the very edge of their charm, and behave as outrageously as the world will let them. *Logan Pearsall Smith*

Etiquette means behaving yourself a little better than is absolutely essential.

Will Cuppy

I can't stand a naked light bulb, any more than I can stand a rude remark or a vulgar action. *Tennessee Williams*

Rudeness is the weak man's imitation of strength. *Eric Hoffer*

Chivalry is the most delicate form of contempt. *Albert Guérard*

A true gentlemen is one who is never unintentionally rude. *Oscar Wilde*

Chivalry is a poor substitute for justice, if one cannot have both. Chivalry is something like the icing on cake, sweet, but not nourishing. *Nellie McClung*

(A gentleman) is any man who wouldn't hit a woman with his hat on.   *Fred Allen*

This is the final test of a gentleman: his respect for those who can be of no possible service to him.   *William Lyon Phelps*

A gentleman is mindful no less of the freedom of others than of his own dignity.
Livy

What is the test of good manners? Being able to bear patiently with bad ones.
Solomon ibn Gabirol

The attributes of a great lady may still be found in the rule of the four S's: Sincerity, Simplicity, Sympathy, and Serenity.   *Emily Post*

Politicians

Politicians cannot help being clowns. Political activity is essentially absurd.
Donald Horne

90% of the politicians give the other 10% a bad reputation.   *Henry Kissinger*

A politician is a person with whose politics you don't agree; if you agree with him, he is a statesman.   *David Lloyd George*

All political lives, unless they are cut off in midstream at a happy juncture, end in failure.   *Enoch Powell*

Politicians are the same all over. They promise to build a bridge even where there is no river.   *Nikita Khrushchev*

Probably the most distinctive characteristic of the successful politician is selective cowardice.   *Richard Harris*

Reagan won because he ran against Jimmy Carter. Had he run unopposed he would have lost.   *Mort Sahl*

Successful democratic politicians are insecure and intimidated men. They advance politically only as they placate, appease, bribe, seduce, bamboozle or otherwise manage to manipulate the demanding and threatening elements in their constituencies.
Walter Lippman

The British House of Lords is the British Outer Mongolia for retired politicians.
Tony Bennett

The first requirement of a statesman is that he be dull. This is not always easy to achieve.   *Dean Acheson*

The Australians appear to a man to regard their politicians as time-serving crooks or simple-minded hirelings.   *Jim Cameron*

A Conservative is a fellow who is standing athwart history yelling 'Stop!'
William F. Buckley, Jr

Greater love hath no man than this, that he lay down his friends for his political life
Jeremy Thorpe

It is a wise philosopher who can recognise his theory, 'the pet child of his brain', after it has been the plaything of politicians.
Sir Frederick Egglestor

Now that all the members of the press are so delighted I lost, I'd like to make a statement. As I leave you I want you to know—just think how much you'll be missing You won't have Nixon to kick around anymore because, gentlemen, this is my last press conference.
Richard Nixon
(After losing the California gubernatorial race in 1962.
He was elected President in 1968.)

The public meeting is part of the continuous educative process that politicians have to engage in.
Gough Whitlam

I have been driven many times to my knees by the overwhelming conviction that I had nowhere else to go. My own wisdom, and that of all about me seemed insufficient for the day.
Abraham Lincoln

If we are strong, our strength will speak for itself. If we are weak, words will be no help.
John F. Kennedy

Our Congressmen are the finest body of men money can buy.   *Maury Amsterdam*

A politician . . . one that would circumvent God.   *Shakespeare, 'Hamlet'*

I shall never ask, never refuse, nor ever resign an office.   *George Washington*

Politicians are always dealing with things which they don't understand.
R. G. Menzies

A disposition to preserve, and an ability to improve, taken together, would be my standard of a statesman.
Edmund Burke

Whenever a man has cast a longing eye on office, a rottenness begins in his conduct.
Thomas Jefferson

Whin a man gets to be my age, he ducks political meetin's, an' reads th' papers an' weighs th' ividence an' th' argymints—pro-argymints an' con-argymints, an' makes up his mind ca'mly, an' votes th' Dimmycratic Ticket.
Finley Peter Dunne

He knows nothing; he thinks he knows everything—that clearly points to a political career.
George Bernard Shaw

A councillor ought not to sleep the whole night through—a man to whom the populace is entrusted, and who has many responsibilities.
Homer

One of the luxuries of a politican's life is that you see yourself as others see you.

Joe Clark

If I believe in something, I will fight for it with all I have. But I do not demand all or nothing. I would rather get something than nothing. Professional liberals want the fiery debate. They glory in defeat. The hardest job for a politician today is to have the courage to be a moderate. It's easy to take an extreme position.

Hubert Humphrey

Politicians cannot be compelled to be honest.   *D. J. Killen*

You do not know, you cannot know, the difficulty of the life of a politician. It means every minute of the day or night, every ounce of your energy. There is no rest, no relaxation. Enjoyment? A politician does not know the meaning of the word.

Nikita Khrushchev

It is expecting too much of a politician to be sincerely interested in the free flow of information.   *Graham Perkin*

A politician divides mankind into two classes: tools and enemies.

Friedrich Nietzsche

An honest politician is one who when he is bought will stay bought.

Simon Cameron

The art of statesmanship is to foresee the inevitable and to expedite its occurrence.

Talleyrand

Since a politician never believes what he says, he is surprised when others believe him.   *Charles de Gaulle*

Power is a drug on which the politicians are hooked. They buy it from the voters, using the voters' own money.   *Richard J. Needham*

a politician is an arse upon which everyone has sat except a man.   *e. e. cummings*

A ginooine statesman should be on his guard, if he must hev beliefs, not to b'lieve 'em too hard.   *James Russell Lowell*

More men have been elected between Sundown and Sunup than ever were elected between Sunup and Sundown.   *Will Rogers*

Macdonald's Law: Never write a letter if you can help it, and never destroy one.

John A. Macdonald

He is a pragmatist. He is not right wing, nor left wing, nor any wing.

Robert Stanfield

Politicians make good company for a while just as children do—their self-enjoyment is contagious. But they soon exhaust their favourite subjects—themselves.

Garry Wills

Your representative owes you, not his industry only, but his judgement; and he betrays instead of serving you if he sacrifices it to your opinion. *Edmund Burke*

The most important office is that of private citizen. *Louis D. Brandeis*

I'm not an old, experienced hand at politics. But I am now seasoned enough to have learned that the hardest thing about any political campaign is how to win without proving that you are unworthy of winning. *Adlai Stevenson*

Never retract, never explain, never apologize—get the thing done and let them howl *Nellie McClung*

A Conservative is a man who will not look at the new moon, out of respect for that ancient institution, the old one. *Douglas Jerrold*

Politics

All I know is I'm not a Marxist. *Karl Marx*

The fact that a reactionary can sometimes be right is a little less recognized that the fact that a liberal can be . . . *Joseph Gies*

An independent is a guy who wants to take the politics out of politics. *Adlai Stevenson*

Any woman who understands the problems of running a home will be nearer to understanding the problems of running a country. *Margaret Thatcher*

I just received the following wire from my generous Daddy 'Dear Jack: Don't buy a single vote more than necessary. I'll be damned if I am going to pay for a landslide. ' *John F. Kennedy*

Politics is both a fine art and an inexact science. *R. G. Menzies*

In politics it is necessary either to betray one's country or the electorate. I prefer to betray the electorate. *Charles de Gaulle*

Nobody is qualified to become a statesman who is entirely ignorant of the problems of wheat. *Socrates*

Politics is a blood sport. *Aneurin Bevan*

Politics is supposed to be the second oldest profession. I have come to realize that it bears a very close resemblance to the first. *Ronald Reagan*

Politics is the diversion of trivial men who, when they succeed at it, become important in the eyes of more trivial men. *George Jean Nathan*

Politics is both fraud and vision. *Donald Horne*

The heaviest penalty for deciding to engage in politics is to be ruled by someone inferior to yourself. *Plato*

The Labour Party is going about the country stirring up apathy. *William Whitelaw*

The radical invents the views. When he has worn them out, the conservative adopts them. *Mark Twain*

The trouble with socialists is that they let their bleeding hearts go to their bloody heads. *Tommy Douglas (Canadian politician)*

Politics is theatre: it tends to reflect life, but also to exaggerate some of its genuine emotions, as well as its superficialities, for dramatic effect and advantage.
Nicholas Whitlam and John Stubbs

There cannot be a crisis next week. My schedule is already full. *Henry Kissinger*

Three people marooned on a desert island would soon reinvent politics.
Mason Cooley

We're eyeball to eyeball, and I think the other fellow just blinked. *Dean Rusk*

What matters in Politics is what men actually do—sincerity is no excuse for acting unpolitically, and insincerity may be channelled by politics into good results.
Bernard Crick

When Cicero (Marcus Tullius Cicero 106–43 BC) was in 64 BC running for consul of Rome he was reported to be advised by his 'campaign manager' that the voters 'had rather you lied to them than refused them.' *Anon.*

The essential ingredient of politics is timing. *Pierre Elliott Trudeau*

It was a storm in a tea cup, but in politics we sail in paper boats.
Harold Macmillan

Party-spirit . . . which at best is but the madness of many for the gain of a few.
Alexander Pope

Practical politics consists in ignoring facts. *Henry Adams*

Ultimately politics in a democracy reflects values much more than it shapes them.
Arnold A. Rogow

Politics is not a good location or a vocation for anyone lazy, thin-skinned or lacking a sense of humour. *John Bailey*

A question which can be answered without prejudice to the government is not a fit question to ask. *John G. Diefenbaker*

I have never found, in a long experience of politics, that criticism is ever inhibited by ignorance. *Harold Macmillan*

Politics, as a practice, whatever its professions, has always been the systematic organization of hatreds.   *Henry Adams*

Politics, and the fate of mankind, are shaped by men without ideals and without greatness.   *Albert Camus*

If you ever injected truth into politics you would have no politics.   *Will Rogers*

The sad duty of politics is to establish justice in a sinful world.   *Reinhold Niebuhr*

There is no worse heresy than that the office sanctifies the holder of it.   *Lord Acton*

Poetry was the maiden I loved, but politics was the harridan I married.
Joseph Howe

Damn your principles! Stick to your party!   *Benjamin Disraeli*

Politics is a field where action is one long second best and where the choice constantly lies between two blunders.   *John Morley*

Politics is the science of how who gets what, when and why.   *Sidney Hillman*

It is hard to escape the conclusion that in Australia, Parliaments are now mainly of ritualistic significance and the significance of the peculiarly parliamentary part of Australian democracy is quite slight.   *Donald Horne*

Politics is the gizzard of society, full of gut and gravel.   *Henry David Thoreau*

A week is a long time in politics.   *Harold Wilson*

The more you read about politics, the more you got to admit that each party is worse than the other.   *Will Rogers*

In academic life you seek to state absolute truths; in politics you seek to accommodate truth to the facts around you.   *Pierre Elliott Trudeau*

Politics. The diplomatic name for the law of the jungle.   *Ely Culbertson*

There is a certain satisfaction in coming down to the lowest ground of politics, fo⁻ then we get rid of cant and hypocrisy.   *Ralph Waldo Emerson*

In politics a community of hatred is almost always the foundation of friendships.
Alexis de Tocqueville

Politics has got so expensive that it takes lots of money to even get beat with.
Will Rogers

Honest statesmanship is the wise employment of individual meannesses for the public good.   *Abraham Lincoln*

Politics is war without bloodshed, and war is politics with blood.   *Mao Tse-Tung*

Here is bureaucracy rampant and Parliament couchant.   *D. J. Killen, M.P.*

Congress is so strange. A man gets up to speak and says nothing. Nobody listens, then everybody disagrees.   *Boris Marshalov*

This organization (United Nations) is created to prevent you from going to hell. It isn't created to take you to heaven.   *Henry Cabot Lodge, Jr.*

It will not be any European statesman who will unite Europe: Europe will be united by the Chinese.   *Charles de Gaulle*

There is no excitement anywhere in the world, short of war, to match the excitement of the American presidential campaign.   *Theodore White*

(Election) campaigns are like childbirth. Before you remember how awful it is, you're back in there having another one.   *Margaret Whitlam*

A dictatorship is a country where they have taken the politics out of politics.   *Sam Himmel*

Vote for the man who promises least; he'll be the least disappointing.   *Bernard Baruch*

What counts is not necessarily the size of the dog in the fight—it's the size of the fight in the dog.   *Dwight D. Eisenhower*

Someone asked me . . . how I felt and I was reminded of a story that a fellow townsman of ours used to tell—Abraham Lincoln. They asked him how he felt once after an unsuccessful election. He said he felt like a little boy who has stubbed his toe in the dark. He said that he was too old to cry, but it hurt too much to laugh.   *Adlai Stevenson*

Democracy is good. I say this because other systems are worse.   *Jawaharlal Nehru*

There are two problems in my life. The political ones are insoluble and the economic ones are incomprehensible.   *Alexander Douglas-Home*

The lady's not for turning.   *Margaret Thatcher*

I have never regarded politics as the arena of morals. It is the arena of interests.   *Aneurin Bevan*

In politics, a straight line is the shortest distance to disaster.   *John P. Roche*

In order to become the master, the politician poses as the servant.   *Charles de Gaulle*

You know very well that whether you are on page one or page thirty depends on whether they fear you. It is just as simple as that.   *Richard Nixon*

If people have to choose between freedom and sandwiches they will take sandwiches.   *Lord Boyd-Orr*

Once upon a time my political opponents honored me as possessing the fabulous intellectual and economic power by which I created a worldwide depression all by myself.   *Herbert Hoover*

In our age there is no such thing as 'keeping out of politics'. All issues are political issues.   *George Orwell*

Deep down he is shallow.   *Political saying*

As I learnt very early in my life in Whitehall, the acid test of any political question is: What is the alternative?   *Lord Trent*

Dirksen's Three Laws of Politics: 1. Get elected. 2. Get re-elected. 3. Don't get mad, get even.   *Senator Everett Dirksen*

Politics is no game for the faint-hearted, or for those whose stomachs turn to water when they read an unkind leading article.   *R. J. Southey*

The (US) Senate is the last primitive society in the world. We still worship the elders of the tribe and honour the territorial imperative.   *Eugene McCarthy*

To the victor belong the spoils of the enemy.   *William L. Marcy*

I pledge you, I pledge myself, to a new deal for the American people. Let us all here assembled constitute ourselves prophets of a new order of competence and courage. This is a call to arms.
Franklin D. Roosevelt, accepting Presidential nomination, 1932

A statesman is an easy man,
He tells his lies by rote;
A journalist makes up his lies
And takes you by the throat;
So stay at home and drink your beer
And let the neighbours vote.   *William Butler Yeats*

Politics is more dangerous than war, for in war you are only killed once.
Winston Churchill

Money is the mother's milk of politics.   *Jesse Unruh*

One fifth of the people are against everything all the time.   *Robert F. Kennedy*

Those who make peaceful revolution impossible will make violent revolution inevitable.   *John F. Kennedy*

Poverty

Sex is the poor man's opera.   *Italian proverb*

Hunger is insolent, and will be fed.   *Alexander Pope*

If you've ever really been poor, you remain poor at heart all your life.

Arnold Bennett

Poor men's reasons are not heard.   *Thomas Fuller*

Only the poor will help the poor.   *Frank Hardy*

The rich would have to eat money, but luckily the poor provide food.

Russian proverb

There were times my pants were so thin I could sit on a dime and tell if it was heads
or tails.   *Spencer Tracy*

Poverty makes you sad as well as wise.   *Bertolt Brecht*

The child was diseased at birth—stricken with an hereditary ill that only the most vital
men are able to shake off. I mean poverty—the most deadly and prevalent of all
diseases.   *Eugene O'Neill*

There is no scandal like rags, nor any crime so shameful as poverty.

George Farquhar

The poor on the borderline of starvation live purposeful lives. To be engaged in a
desperate struggle for food and shelter is to be wholly free from a sense of futility.

Eric Hoffer

It is easy enough to say that poverty is no crime. No, if it were, men wouldn't be
ashamed of it. It's a blunder, though, and is punished as such.   *Jerome K. Jerome*

What the rich dislike in the pressure of the poor is the unbearable reflection of their
own condition.   *Jacques Delaruelle*

The poor don't know that their function in life is to exercise our generosity.

Jean-Paul Sartre

Poverty is an anomaly to rich people: it is very difficult to make out why people who
want dinner do not ring the bell.   *Walter Bagehot*

Short of genius, a rich man cannot imagine poverty.   *Charles Péguy*

The conspicuously wealthy turn up urging the character-building value of privation for
the poor.   *J. K. Galbraith*

Modern poverty is not the poverty that was blest in the Sermon on the Mount.

George Bernard Shaw

The poor will always be with you.   *John 12:8*

This is one of the bitter curses of poverty: it leaves no right to be generous.

George Gissing

The best way to help the poor is not to become one of them.

Mining magnate, Lang Hancock

Power

He who despises his own life is soon master of another's.   *English proverb*

Men will fawn where there is power.   *William Forster*

Horsepower was a wonderful thing when only horses had it.   *Anon.*

It is not power that corrupts but fear. The fear of losing power corrupts those who wield it, and fear of the scourge of power corrupts those who are subject to it.
Aung San Suu Kyi (winner of 1991 Nobel Peace Prize)

In any group there are master and followers. Even the right side rather dislikes the man who stands alone.   *Shirley Hazzard, 'The Transit of Venus'*

Many a man's strength is in opposition, and when he faileth, he groweth out of use.
Francis Bacon

Never doubt that a small group of committed citizens can change the world. Indeed, it is the only thing that ever has.   *Margaret Mead*

Not hammer strokes, but dance of the water sings the pebbles into perfection.
Rabindranath Tagore

People exercise an unconscious selection in being influenced.   *T. S. Eliot*

Power in America today is control of the means of communication.   *Theodore White*

A formula for measuring international power is essential: ironically the most useful formula is warfare. Until the function of warfare is appreciated, the search for a more humane and more efficient way of measuring power it likely to be haphazard.
Geoffrey Blainey

The best effect of fine persons is felt after we have left their presence.
Ralph Waldo Emerson

The fault, dear Brutus, is not in our stars,
But in ourselves, that we are underlings.   *Shakespeare, 'Julius Caesar*

The tyrant dies and his rule is over; the martyr dies and his rule begins.
Søren Kierkegaard

Unused power slips imperceptibly into the hands of another.   *Konrad Heider*

Who controls the past controls the future.
Who controls the present controls the past.   *George Orwell*

Power never takes a back step—only in the face of more power.   *Malcolm X*

Power is always right, weakness always wrong. Power is always insolent and despotic.
Noah Webster

Power only tires those who don't exercise it.   *Pierre Elliott Trudeau*

The only justification in the use of force is to reduce the amount of force necessary
to be used.   *Alfred North Whitehead*

Not believing in force is the same as not believing in gravitation.   *Leon Trotsky*

The first principle of a civilized state is that the power is legitimate only when it is
under contract.   *Walter Lippmann*

He was one of those men who possess almost every gift, except the gift of the power
to use them.   *Charles Kingsley*

Force is never more operative than when it is known to exist but is not brandished.
Alfred Thayer Mahan

The main task of a free society is to civilize the struggle for power. Slavery of the
acquiescent majority to the ruthless few is the hereditary state of mankind; freedom,
a rarely acquired characteristic.   *R. H. S. Crossman*

Power corrupts the few, while weakness corrupts the many.   *Eric Hoffer*

His countenance was like lightning, and his raiment white as snow.   *Matthew 28:3*

Power is the recognition of necessity.   *Abraham Rotstein*

If absolute power corrupts absolutely, where does that leave God?   *George Daacon*

Power is the ultimate aphrodisiac.   *Henry Kissinger*

Liberal—a power worshipper without power.   *George Orwell*

Power is like a woman you want to stay in bed with forever.   *Patrick Anderson*

The illegal we do immediately, the unconstitutional takes a little longer.
Henry Kissinger

Power tends to connect; absolute power connects absolutely.   *Peter Newman*

Praise and Flattery

A rich man's joke is always funny.   *Thomas Edward Brown*

Be advised that all flatterers live at the expense of those who listen to them.
Jean de la Fontaine

In lapidary inscriptions a man is not upon oath.   *Samuel Johnson*

Let us now praise famous men, and our fathers that begat us.   *Ecclesiasticus 44:1*

In the art of biography, the idolater is just as objectionable as the debunker.
Norman Lindsay

Self-praise is no recommendation.   *Old saying*

Among the smaller duties in life, I hardly know any one more important than that of not praising when praise is not due.   *Sydney Smith*

Praise to the undeserving is severe satire.   *Benjamin Franklin*

It's pleasant to hear these nice words while I'm still alive. I'd rather have the taffy than the epitaphy.   *Chauncey Depew*

Commendation, n: the tribute that we pay to achievements that resemble, but do no equal, our own.   *Ambrose Bierce*

Applause is the spur of noble minds, the end and aim of weak ones.
Charles Caleb Colton

The meanest, most contemptible kind of praise is that which first speaks well of a man, and then qualifies it with a 'but'.   *Henry Ward Beecher*

He who gladly does without the praise of the crowd will not miss the opportunity of becoming his own fan.   *Karl Kraus*

Flattery is all right—if you don't inhale.   *Adlai Stevenson*

The advantage of doing one's praising to oneself is that one can lay it on so thick and exactly in the right places.   *Samuel Butler*

Some praise at morning what they blame at night.   *Alexander Pope*

What really flatters a man is that you think him worth flattery.
George Bernard Shaw

Our credulity is greatest concerning the things we know least about. And since we know least about ourselves, we are ready to believe all that is said about us. Hence the mysterious power of both flattery and calumny.   *Eric Hoffer*

Some fellows pay a compliment like they expected a receipt.   *Kin Hubbard*

I can live for two months on a good compliment.   *Mark Twain*

A compliment is a gift, not to be thrown away carelessly unless you want to hurt the giver.   *Eleanor Hamilton*

'Tis an old maxim in the schools,
That flattery's the food of fools—
Yet now and then your men of wit
Will condescend to take a bit.

Jonathan Swift

The true test of independent judgement is being able to dislike someone who admires
us.   *Sydney J. Harris*

Once in a century a man may be ruined or made insufferable by praise. But surely
once a minute something generous dies for want of it.   *John Masefield*

Few human beings are proof against the implied flattery of rapt attention.

Jack Woodford

Some natures are too good to be spoiled by praise.   *Ralph Waldo Emerson*

To be praised by ignorance is the last insult.   *Lionel Lindsay*

It is simpler and easier to flatter men than to praise them.   *Jean Paul Richter*

Prayer

There are few men who dare to publish to the world the prayers they make to Almighty
God.   *Montaigne*

To Mercy, Pity, Peace and Love
All pray in their distress.   *William Blake*

Do not pray for tasks equal to your powers but for powers equal to your tasks.

John Flynn

It is not well for a man to pray cream and live skim milk.   *Henry Ward Beecher*

Pray, v: to ask that the laws of the universe be annulled in behalf of a single petitioner
confessedly unworthy.   *Ambrose Bierce*

O Lord, please don't let anything happen today.
                Bishop F.F. Goe (supposedly uttered by him every morning)

We offer up prayers to God only because we have made Him after our own image.
We treat Him like a Pasha, or a Sultan, who is capable of being exasperated and
appeased.   *Voltaire*

The fewer the words, the better the prayer.   *Martin Luther*

In prayer we call ourselves 'worms of the dust', but it is only on a sort of tacit
understanding that the remark shall not be taken at par.   *Mark Twain*

Give us grace and strength to preserve. Give us courage and gaiety and the quiet mind. Spare to us our friends and soften to us our enemies. Give us the strength to encounter that which is to come, that we may be brave in peril, constant in tribulation, temperate in wrath and in all changes of fortune, and down to the gates of death, loyal and loving to one another.   *Robert Louis Stevenson*

I have lived to thank God that all my prayers have not been answered.
                                                                    Jean Ingelow

God punishes us mildly by ignoring our prayers and severely by answering them.
                                                              Richard J. Needham

What men usually ask of God when they pray is that two and two not make four.
                                                                        Anon.

Don't pray for rain—dam it.   *Bishop James Moorhouse*

In certain trying circumstances, urgent circumstances, desperate circumstances, profanity furnishes a relief denied even to prayer.   *Mark Twain*

Prejudice and Bigotry

An antisemite is a person who hates Jews more than is absolutely necessary.
                                                                  Jewish proverb

I am 52 years of age. I am a bishop in the Anglican Church, and a few people might be constrained to say that I was reasonably responsible. In the land of my birth, I cannot vote.   *Bishop Desmond Tutu*

Prejudice—in the race relations context—is an *attitude* and is *learned in society*. Racists are not born and no child is by nature intolerant. Their racial dislike and intolerance have to be cultivated.   *Colin Tatz*

It is a great shock at the age of 5 or 6 to find that in a world of Gary Coopers you are the Indian.   *James Baldwin*

Never try to reason the prejudice out of a man. It was not reasoned into him, and cannot be reasoned out.   *Sydney Smith*

Since my little daughter is only half Jewish, would it be alright if she went into the pool only up to her waist?
                        Groucho Marx (applying for membership in a Country Club)

There are only two ways to be quite unprejudiced and impartial. One is to be completely ignorant. The other is to be completely indifferent.   *Charles Curtis*

Prejudice is the child of ignorance.   *William Hazlitt*

Passion and prejudice govern the world; only under the name of reason.
                                                                    John Wesley

How it infuriates a bigot, when he is forced to drag out his dark convictions!
Logan Pearsall Smith

Everyone is a prisoner of his own experiences. No one can eliminate prejudices—just recognize them.
Edward R. Murrow

We are chameleons, and our partialities and prejudices change places with an easy and blessed facility.
Mark Twain

Fortunately for serious minds, a bias recognized is a bias sterilized.
A. Eustace Haydon

Without the aid of prejudice and custom, I should not be able to find my way across the room.
William Hazlitt

One may no more live in the world without picking up the moral prejudices of the world than one will be able to go to hell without perspiring.
H. L. Mencken

We hate some persons because we do not know them; and will not know them because we hate them.
Charles Caleb Colton

The mind of a bigot is like the pupil of the eye; the more light you pour upon it, the more it will contract.
Oliver Wendell Holmes, Jr.

It is not healthy when a nation lives within a nation, as coloured Americans are living inside America. A nation cannot live confident of its tomorrow if its refugees are among its own citizens.
Pearl Buck

Pride

You must stir it and stump it,
and blow your own trumpet,
or trust me, you haven't a chance.
W. S. Gilbert

Pride is seldom delicate: it will please itself with very mean advantages.
Samuel Johnson

The truly proud man is satisfied with his own good opinion, and does not seek to make converts to it.
William Hazlitt

Pride is the mask of one's own faults.
Jewish proverb

Pride is the direct appreciation of oneself.
Arthur Schopenhauer

There is a certain noble pride, through which merits shine brighter than through modesty.
Jean Paul Richter

The sun will set without thy assistance.   *The Talmud*

When a proud man hears another praised, he feels himself injured.   *English proverb*

A confessional passage has probably never been written that didn't stink a little bit of the writer's pride in having given up his pride.   *J. D. Salinger*

I do not believe that any peacock envies another peacock his tail, because every peacock is persuaded that his own tail is the finest in the world. The consequence of this is that peacocks are peaceable birds.   *Bertrand Russell*

Pride, perceiving humility honourable, often borrows her cloak.   *Thomas Fuller*

There is a paradox in pride: it makes some men ridiculous, but prevents others from becoming so.   *Charles Caleb Colton*

Pride had rather go out of the way than go behind.   *Thomas Fuller*

Progress

He that will not apply new remedies must expect new evils, for time is the greatest innovator.   *Francis Bacon*

If it is to be,
It is up to me.   *William H. Johnson*

All that is human must retrograde if it does not advance.   *Edward Gibbon*

Ambition can creep as well as soar.   *Edmund Burke*

New roads; new ruts.   *G. K. Chesterton*

Progress, far from consisting in change, depends on retentiveness. Those who cannot remember the past are content to repeat it.   *George Santayana*

The new electronic interdependence recreates the world in the image of a global village.
                                                                  Marshall McLuhan

All progress is based upon the universal innate desire on the part of every organism to live beyond its income.   *Samuel Butler*

This world of ours is a new world, in which the unit of knowledge, the nature of human communities, the order of society, the order of ideas, the very notions of society and culture have changed, and will not return to what they have been in the past. What is new is new, not because it has never been there before, but because it has changed in quality.   *J. Robert Oppenheimer*

And from the discontent of man
The world's best progress springs.   *Ella Wheeler Wilcox*

Every gain made by individuals or society is almost instantly taken for granted.
Aldous Huxley

Do not seek to follow in the footsteps of the men of old; seek what they sought.
Matsuo Basho

Once you sink that first stake, they'll never make you pull it up.   *Robert Moses*

Flight is the only true sensation that men have achieved in modern history.
James Dickey

The fundamental magic of flying is a miracle that has nothing to do with any of its practical purposes—purposes of speed, accessibility and convenience—and will not change as they change.   *Anne Morrow Lindbergh*

The really great visual experience today is to fly over a huge city and look down into the night. It's like a tremendous jubilant Christmas tree. You just feel life is worth living—when you come down you may have some doubts.   *Gyorgy Kepes*

A great devotee of the gospel of getting on.   *George Bernard Shaw*

The century on which we are entering can be and must be the century of the common man.   *Henry A. Wallace*

To spur a willing horse.   *Latin proverb*

Removing the faults in a stage-coach may produce a perfect stage-coach, but it is unlikely to produce the first motor car.   *Edward de Bono*

Progress might have been all right once, but it's gone on too long.   *Ogden Nash*

Is it progress if a cannibal uses knife and fork?   *Stanislaw Lec*

A thousand things advance; nine hundred and ninety-nine retreat; that is progress.
Henri Frédéric Amiel

The simple faith in progress is not a conviction belonging to strength, but one belonging to acquiescence and hence to weakness.   *Norbert Wiener*

The major advances in civilization are processes which all but wreck the societies in which they occur.   *Alfred North Whitehead*

Behold the turtle. He makes progress only when he sticks his neck out.
James Bryant Conant

Always remember that the soundest way to progress in any organization is to help the man ahead of you to get promoted.   *L. S. Hamaker*

What saves a man is to take a step. Then another step. It is always the same step, but you have to take it.   *Antoine de Saint-Exupéry*

Daring ideas are like chessmen moved forward. They may be beaten, but they ma͞
start a winning game.   *Goethe*

The rule is jam tomorrow and jam yesterday—but never jam today.   *Lewis Carrod*

The art of progress is to preserve order amid change, and to preserve change amid
order.   *Alfred North Whitehead*

Now here, you see, it takes all the running you can do to keep in the same place. If
you want to get somewhere else, you must run at least twice as fast as that!
                                                            Lewis Carrod

It so happens that the world is undergoing a transformation to which no change that
has yet occurred can be compared, either in scope or in rapidity.   *Charles de Gaulle*

Modern kitchen—where the pot calls the kettle chartreuse.   *Anor.*

If Jesus Christ were to come today, people would not even crucify him. They would
ask him to dinner, and hear what he had to say, and make fun of him.
                                                        Thomas Carlyle

Man is flying too fast for a world that is round. Soon he will catch up with himself
in a great rear-end collision and Man will never know that what hit him from behind
was Man.   *James Thurber*

Every step of progress the world has made has been from scaffold to scaffold, and
from stake to stake.   *Wendell Phillips*

Today every invention is received with a cry of triumph which soon turns into a cry
of fear.   *Bertolt Brecat*

Once a man would spend a week patiently waiting if he missed a stage coach, but
now he rages if he misses the first section of a revolving door.   *Simeon Strunsky*

The reasonable man adapts himself to the world; the unreasonable one persists in trying
to adapt the world to himself. Therefore all progress depends upon the unreasonable
man.   *George Bernard Shaw*

There is no royal road to anything. One thing at a time, and all things in succession.
That which grows slowly endures.   *J. G. Hollard*

Growth for the sake of growth is the ideology of the cancer cell.   *Edward Abbey*

The world owes all its onward impulses to men ill at ease. The happy man inevitably
confines himself within ancient limits.   *Nathaniel Hawthorne*

That which comes into the world to disturb nothing deserves neither respect nor
patience.   *René Char*

Occasionally we sigh for an earlier day when we could just look at the stars without
worrying whether they were theirs or ours.   *Bill Vaughan*

Every year it takes less time to fly across the Atlantic, and more time to drive to the
office.   *Anon.*

Proof and Certainty

The quest for certainty blocks the search for meaning. Uncertainty is the very condition to impel man to unfold his powers.
Erich Fromm

There are no facts, only interpretations.
Friedrich Nietzsche

Statistics are no substitute for judgement.
Henry Clay

Get your facts first, and then you can distort 'em as much as you please.
Mark Twain

'For example' is not proof.
Jewish proverb

A half truth, like half a brick, is always more forcible as an argument than a whole one. It carries better.
Stephen Leacock

You are all you will ever have for certain.
June Havoc

Doubt is not a pleasant condition, but certainty is.
Voltaire

To believe with certainty we must begin with doubting.
Stanislaus, King of Poland

Modest doubt is call'd
The beacon of the wise.
Shakespeare, 'Troilus and Cressida'

What men want is not knowledge, but certainty.
Bertrand Russell

Psychiatry

A neurotic is the man who builds a castle in the air. A psychotic is the man who lives in it. And a psychiatrist is the man who collects the rent.
Anon.

A psychiatrist is a man who goes to the Folies-Bergère and looks at the audience.
Mervyn Stockwood

I am going to give my psychoanalyst one more year, then I'm going to Lourdes.
Woody Allen

Neurosis is always a substitute for legitimate suffering.
Carl Jung

Psychiatrists classify a person as neurotic if he suffers from his problems in living, and a psychotic if he makes others suffer.
Thomas Szasz

Schizophrenic behaviour is a special strategy that a person invents in order to live in an unlivable situation.
R. D. Laing

If you talk to God, you are praying; if God talks to you, you have schizophrenia.
Thomas Szasz

The psychiatrist must become a fellow traveller with his patient.   *R. D. Laing*

Those modern analysts, they charge so much! In my day, for five marks Freud himself would treat you. For ten marks he would treat you and press your pants. For fifteen marks Freud would let you treat *him*—that included a choice of any two vegetables.
Woody Allen

Psychiatry enables us to correct our faults by confessing our parents' shortcomings.
Laurence J. Peter

Psychoanalysis is confession without absolution.   *G. K. Chesterton*

Psychiatry is the care of the id by the odd.   *Anon.*

The point of therapy is get unhooked, not to thrash around on how you got hooked.
Maryanne Walters

The four-letter word for psychotherapy is 'talk'.   *Anon.*

I can feel guilty about the past, apprehensive about the future, but only in the present can I act. The ability to be in the present moment is a major component of mental wellness.   *Abraham Maslow*

Mental health problems do not affect three or four out of every five persons, but one out of one.   *William Menninger*

The trouble with being a hypochondriac these days is that antibiotics have cured all the good diseases.   *Caskie Stinnet*

The best cure for hypochondria is to forget about your own body and get interested in someone else's.   *Goodman Ace*

Depression is the inability to construct a future.   *Rollo May*

Depression is rage spread thin.   *Paul Tillich*

Fortunately, analysis is not the only way to resolve inner conflicts. Life itself remains a very effective therapist.   *Karen Horney*

Anyone who goes to a psychiatrist ought to have his head examined.
Sam Goldwyn

Quips and Comments

No, Groucho is not my real name. I am breaking it in for a friend.   *Groucho Marx*

I have admired W.C. Fields since the day he advanced upon Baby LeRoy with an ice pick. Any man who hates dogs and babies can't be all bad.   *Leo Rosten*

One bliss for which
there is no match
is when you itch
to up and scratch.   *Ogden Nash*

Only mediocrity can be trusted to be always at its best.   *Max Beerbohm*

Only two things are infinite, the universe and human stupidity, and I'm not sure about
the former.   *Albert Einstein*

Sometimes a cigar is only a cigar.   *Sigmund Freud*

The blind man is laughing at the bald head.   *Persian proverb*

If it's a boy, I'll call it after myself. If it's a girl I'll call it Victoria after our Queen.
But if, as I strongly suspect, it's nothing but piss and wind, I'll call it after you.
                    Sir George Reid, after being asked, in regard to his protuberant belly,
                                        'What are you going to call it, George?'

There ain't no answer. There ain't gonna be any answer. There never has been an
answer. That's the answer.   *Gertrude Stein*

We are the people our parents warned us about.   *Graffiti*

Worthless as wither'd weeds.   *Emily Brontë*

You must lose a fly to catch a trout.   *George Herbert*

A diplomat these days is nothing but a head waiter who is allowed to sit down
occasionally.   *Peter Ustinov*

A man surprised is half beaten.   *Thomas Fuller*

A nimble sixpence is better than a slow shilling.   *English proverb*

Brevity is the soul of lingerie.   *Dorothy Parker*

Every path has its puddle.   *Old saying*

Every time I look at you I get a fierce desire to be lonesome.   *Oscar Levant*

Evil spelled backward is live.   *Graffiti*

Forgetting of a wrong is a mild revenge.   *Thomas Fuller*

He looked at me as if I was a side dish he hadn't ordered.   *Ring Lardner, Jr.*

Heat, madam! It was so dreadful that I found there was nothing for it but to take off
my flesh and sit in my bones.   *Sydney Smith*

I am an atheist. I don't believe in Zeus.   *Graffiti*

I don't deserve this award, but I have arthritis, and I don't deserve that either.

Jack Benny

I don't know much about being a millionaire, but I'll bet I'd be darling at it.

Dorothy Parker

I never said 'I want to be alone.' I only said, 'I want to be left alone.' There is all the difference. *Greta Garbo*

In baiting a mousetrap with cheese, always leave room for the mouse. *Saki*

In the ant's house, the dew is a flood. *Old saying*

India is a geographical term. It is no more a United Nation than the Equator.

Winston Churchill

Judas needed the money for a sick friend. *Graffiti*

'What will you have?' said the waiter,
Reflectively picking his nose.
'I'll have two boiled eggs, you bastard.
You can't put your fingers in those.' *George Wallace*

It is a sobering thought that, when Mozart was my age, he had been dead for two years. *Tom Lehrer*

Show me a man with both feet on the ground and I'll show you a man who can't put his pants on. *Arthur K. Watson*

My idea of an agreeable person is a person who agrees with me. *Benjamin Disraeli*

Alimony: the cash surrender value of a husband. *Anon.*

Kiss principle: Keep it simple, stupid. *Anon.*

Nothing is impossible for the person who doesn't have to do it. *Weller's Law*

His shortcoming is his long staying. *Anon.*

He has all of the virtues I dislike and none of the vices I admire.

Winston Churchill

Sherard Blaw, the dramatist who had discovered himself, and who had given so unstintingly of his discovery to the world. *Saki*

The Right Honourable gentleman is indebted to his memory for his jests and to his imagination for his facts. *Richard Brinsley Sheridan*

Her face was her chaperone. *Rupert Hughes*

Angels fly because they take themselves lightly. *G. K. Chesterton*

When people don't want to come, nothing will stop them.   *Sol Hurok*

Venice is like eating an entire box of chocolate liqueurs in one go.   *Truman Capote*

More and more these days I find myself pondering on how to reconcile my net income with my gross habits.   *John Kirk Nelson*

A verbal contract isn't worth the paper it's written on.   *Sam Goldwyn*

Epigram: a wisecrack that has played Carnegie Hall.   *Oscar Levant*

Include me out.   *Sam Goldwyn*

A hole is nothing at all, but you can break your neck in it.   *Austin O'Malley*

You keep asking us who called the cook a bastard; what we want to know is who called the bastard a cook.   *Anonymous Australian soldier*

In uplifting, get underneath.   *George Ade*

If there were any justice in the world, people would be able to fly over pigeons for a change.   *Anon.*

When the mouse laughs at the cat there's a hole nearby.   *Nigerian proverb*

Fatigue is the best pillow.   *Hindu proverb*

The ugliest of trades have their moments of pleasure. Now, if I was a grave digger, or even a hangman, there are some people I could work for with a great deal of enjoyment.   *Douglas Jerrold*

What happens to the hole when the cheese is gone?   *Bertolt Brecht*

God made me on a morning when he had nothing else to do.   *C. F. Lloyd*

When Babe Ruth was asked in 1930 how he felt about making more money than the President of the United States, he replied 'I had a better year than he did.'

Nothing succeeds like one's own successor.   *Clarence H. Hincks*

Whom the gods wish to destroy, they first call promising.   *Cyril Connolly*

In California everyone goes to a therapist, is a therapist, or is a therapist going to a therapist.   *Truman Capote*

We also serve who only punctuate.   *Brian Moore*

Every director bites the hand that lays the golden egg.   *Sam Goldwyn*

If Roosevelt were alive he'd turn in his grave.   *Sam Goldwyn*

There's a wonderful family called Stein,
There's Gert, and there's Epp and there's Ein:
Gert's poems are bunk,
Epp's statues are junk,
And no one can understand Ein.

Anon

Automatic simply means that you can't repair it yourself.

Frank Capra

A thick skin is a gift from God.

Konrad Adenauer

While you're saving your face you're losing your ass.
Never trust a man whose eyes are too close to his nose.
I never trust a man unless I've got his pecker in my pocket.
Better inside the tent pissing out than outside the tent pissing in.

Lyndon B. Johnson

Parsley
is gharsley.

Ogden Nash

Oats, n.s. A grain which in England is generally given to horses, but in Scotland
supports the people.

Samuel Johnson

Coffee in England is just toasted milk.

Anon

Old statisticians never die; they are simply seasonally adjusted.

Ken Wiltshire

Some people approach every problem with an open mouth.

Adlai Stevenson

The butler entered the room, a solemn procession of one.

P. G. Wodehouse

And what's a butterfly? At best,
He's but a caterpillar, drest.

John Grey

If I look like this, I need the trip.

Gloria Swanson (of her passport photo)

As old as the itch.

English proverb

Early to bed, early to rise, work like hell, and advertise.

Laurence J. Peter

Land rights for gay whales.

Margret RoadKnight's slogan for the 'ultimate cause'

When you have got an elephant by the hind leg, and he is trying to run away, it is
best to let him run.

Abraham Lincoln

Too much of a good thing can be wonderful.

Mae West

All would live long, but none would be old.

Proverb

Bland as a Jesuit, sober as a hymn.

William Ernest Henley

I never forget a face, but in your case I'll make an exception.

Groucho Marx

'Are you lost daddy?' I asked tenderly.
'Shut up,' he explained.   *Ring Lardner*

Geography is about maps,
But biography is about chaps.   *Edmund Clerihew Bentley*

In the world of mules there are no rules.   *Ogden Nash*

There are some people so addicted to exaggeration that they can't tell the truth without
lying.   *Josh Billings*

Since the house is on fire let us warm ourselves.   *Italian saying*

I used to be snow-white . . . but I drifted.   *Mae West*

Equal opportunity is good, but special privilege even better.   *Anna Chennault*

A man of words and not of deeds,
Is like a garden full of weeds.   *English proverb*

I don't see what's wrong with giving Bobby a little experience before he starts to
practise law.   *John F. Kennedy (after appointing his brother Attorney General)*

Shake a bridle over a Yorkshireman's grave, and he'll rise and steal a horse.
                                                          Lancashire proverb

An indecent mind is a perpetual feast.   *Old saying*

If you can't bite, don't show your teeth.   *Yiddish proverb*

Only the shallow know themselves.   *Oscar Wilde*

Don't quote me; that's what you heard, not what I said.   *Lawrence K. Frank*

Thin people are beautiful but fat people are adorable.   *Jackie Gleason*

I had always assumed that cliché was a suburb of Paris, until I discovered it to be a
street in Oxford.   *Philip Guedalla*

He'd give the devil ulcers.   *Anon.*

When I'm good, I'm very good, but when I'm bad, I'm better.   *Mae West*

Reality

Human kind cannot bear very much reality.   *T. S. Eliot*

The stern, bare horrors of reality, from which there was no awakening.
                                       Henry Handel Richardson, 'Ultima Thule'

If anything is poisoning our lives and weakening our society, it is reality—and not the fabrication of television writers and producers. *Martin Maloney*

There is no reality except the one contained within us. That is why so many people live such an unreal life. They take the images outside them for reality and never allow the world within to assert itself. *Hermann Hesse*

There is sometimes little to choose between the reality of illusion and the illusion of reality. *Patrick White, 'The Aunt's Story*

Nothing which is at all times and in every way agreeable to us can have objective reality. It is of the very nature of the real that it should have sharp corners and rough edges, that it should be resistant, should be itself. Dream-furniture is the only kind on which you never stub your toes or bang your knee. *C. S. Lewis*

Facts as facts do not always create a spirit of reality, because reality is a spirit. *G. K. Chesterton*

We take our shape, it is true, within and against that cage of reality bequeathed us at our birth, and yet it is precisely through our dependence on this reality that we are most endlessly betrayed. *James Baldwin*

You too must not count overmuch on your reality as you feel it today, since, like that of yesterday, it may prove an illusion for you tomorrow. *Luigi Pirandello*

All our interior world is reality—and that perhaps more so than our apparent world. *Marc Chagall*

The field of consciousness is tiny. It accepts only one problem at a time. Get into a fist fight, put your mind on the strategy of the fight, and you will not feel the other fellow's punches. *Antoine de Saint-Exupéry*

I like reality. It tastes of bread. *Jean Anouilh*

To see what is in front of one's nose needs a constant struggle. *George Orwell*

We do not fight for the real but for shadows we make
A flag is a piece of cloth and a word is a sound,
But we make them something neither cloth nor a sound
Tokens of love and hate, black sorcery stones. *Stephen Vincent Benét*

Reason

A life based on reason will always require to be balanced by an occasional bout of violent and irrational emotion, for the instinctual tribes must be satisfied. *Cyril Connolly*

Analysis kills spontaneity. The grain once ground into flour springs and germinates no more. *Henri Frédéric Amiel*

Facts do not cease to exist because they are ignored. *Aldous Huxley*

Where I cannot satisfy my reason, I love to humour my fancy. *Sir Thomas Browne*

When the human mind exists in the light of reason and no more than reason, we may say with absolute certainty that Man and all that made him will be in that instant gone.
Loren Eiseley

I have hardly ever known a mathematician who was capable of reasoning. *Plato*

Reason is God's gift, but so are the passions. Reason is as guilty as passion.
Cardinal Newman

The man who is master of his passions is Reason's slave. *Cyril Connolly*

Human reason needs only to will more strongly than fate, and she is fate.
Thomas Mann

Reason deserves to be called a prophet; for in showing up the consequence and effect of our actions in the present, does it not tell us what the future will be?
Arthur Schopenhauer

The difference between the reason of man and the instinct of the beast is this, that the beast does but know, but the man knows that he knows. *John Donne*

Reason is also choice. *John Milton*

Reason is an emotion for the sexless. *Heathcote Williams*

The last advance of reason is to recognize that it is surpassed by innumerable things; it is feeble if it cannot realize that. *Blaise Pascal*

All our reasoning ends in surrender to feeling. *Blaise Pascal*

Rebellion, Revolution and Reform

A nation without the means of reform is without the means of survival.
Edmund Burke

Every reform was once a private opinion, and when it shall be a private opinion again, it will solve the problem of the age. *Ralph Waldo Emerson*

Revolution never relieves misery, but increases it. *Martin Boyd*

Not actual suffering but the hope of better things incites people to revolt.
Eric Hoffer

The most dangerous moment for a bad government is when it begins to reform.
Alexis de Tocqueville

There are a thousand hacking at the branches of evil to one who is striking at the roots. *Henry David Thoreau*

Thinkers prepare the revolution; bandits carry it out. *Mariano Azuela*

Inferiors revolt in order that they may be equal, and equals that they may be superior. *Aristotle*

Resistance to tyrants is obedience to God. *Benjamin Franklin*

In almost any society, I think, the quality of the non-conformists is like to be just as good as, and no better than that of the conformists. *Margaret Mead*

Whatever little we have gained, we have gained by agitation, while we have uniformly lost by moderation. *Daniel O'Connell*

Every generation revolts against its fathers and makes friends with its grandfathers. *Lewis Mumford*

One revolution is like one cocktail, it just gets you organized for the next. *Will Rogers*

Revolution is the festival of the oppressed. *Germaine Greer*

A reformer is one who sets forth cheerfully toward sure defeat. *Richard S. Childs*

The overwhelming pressure of mediocrity, sluggish and indomitable as a glacier, will mitigate the most violent, and depress the most exalted revolution. *T. S. Eliot*

It is possible for a single individual to defy the whole might of an unjust empire to save his honour, his religion, his soul, and lay the foundation for that empire's fall or its regeneration. *Gandhi*

It is essential to the triumph of reform that it shall never succeed. *William Hazlitt*

It is a dangerous thing to reform anyone. *Oscar Wilde*

Reformers have the idea that change can be achieved by brute sanity. *George Bernard Shaw*

It is not the prisoners who need reformation, it is the prisons. *Oscar Wilde*

By gnawing through a dyke, even a rat may drown a nation. *Edmund Burke*

Radicalism is the opium of the middle class. *Christina Stead, 'Letty Fox: Her Luck'*

All reform except a moral one will prove unavailing. *Thomas Carlyle*

I hold it, that a little rebellion now and then is a good thing, and as necessary in the political world as storms in the physical. *Thomas Jefferson*

Riots are the voices of the unheard.   *Martin Luther King, Jr.*

If we should promise people nothing better than only revolution, they would scratch their heads and say, 'Isn't it better to have good goulash?'   *Nikita Khrushchev*

A trade unionist who is not a militant is not worth his salt.   *Clarrie O'Shea*

Big Brother is watching you.   *George Orwell*

Religion

A firm belief attracts facts. They come out iv holes in the ground an' cracks in th' wall to support belief, but they run away fr'm doubt.   *Finley Peter Dunne*

Don't wait for the Last Judgment. It takes place every day.   *Albert Camus*

A minister is coming down every generation nearer and nearer to the common level of the useful citizen—no oracle at all, but a man of more than average moral instincts, who if he knows anything, knows how little he knows.   *Oliver Wendell Holmes*

Religion is, in all cases, a matter of diet and climate.   *Marcus Clarke*

Faith consists in believing when it is beyond the power of reason to believe. It is not enough that a thing be possible for it to be believed.   *Voltaire*

He was of the faith chiefly in the sense that the Church he currently did not attend was Catholic.   *Kingsley Amis*

God does not need a religion.   *Harry Hooton*

Heathen, n. A beknighted creature who has the folly to worship something that he can see and feel.   *Ambrose Bierce*

I'm not really a Jew; just Jew-ish, not the whole hog.   *Jonathan Miller*

If you can't believe in God the chances are your God is too small.   *J. B. Phillips*

It is extremely difficult for a Jew to be converted, for how can he bring himself to believe in the divinity of—another Jew?   *Heinrich Heine*

Man is a venerating animal. He venerates as easily as he purges himself. When they take away from him the gods of his fathers, he looks for others abroad.   *Max Jacob*

My own mind is my own church.   *Thomas Paine*

One's religion is whatever he is most interested in.   *James M. Barrie*

Religion is the way we honour our ancestors' errors.   *Mark M. Otoysao*

The church exists for the sake of those outside it.

William Temple (Archbishop of Canterbury)

The writers against religion, whilst they oppose every system, are wisely careful never to set up any of their own.   *Edmund Burke*

The idea that He would take his attention away from the universe in order to give me a bicycle with three speeds is just so unlikely I can't go along with it.

Quentin Crisp

The Pope is barely Catholic enough for some converts.   *John Ayscough*

The test for a prophet is in the Bible. It is this. 'When a prophet speaketh in the name of the Lord, if the thing follow not, nor come to pass, that is the thing which the Lord hath not spoken.'   *Anon.*

The three great apostles of practical atheism, that make converts without persecuting and retain them without preaching are Wealth, Health and Power.

Charles Caleb Colton

To tolerate everything is to teach nothing.   *Dr. F. J. Kinsman*

Heresy is the perpetual hair-shirt of the church.   *Ernest Scott*

When people cease to believe in God, they don't believe in nothing; they believe in anything.   *G. K. Chesterton*

Zen is a way of liberation, concerned not with discovering what is good or bad or advantageous, but what is.   *Alan Watts*

Each religion, by the help of more or less myth which it takes more or less seriously, proposes some method of fortifying the human soul and enabling it to make its peace with its destiny.   *George Santayana*

The good news is that Jesus is coming back. The bad news is that he's really pissed off.   *Bob Hope*

The merit claimed for the Anglican Church is that, if you let it alone, it will let you alone.   *Ralph Waldo Emerson*

Most people believe that the Christian commandments are intentionally a little too severe—like setting a clock half an hour ahead to make sure of not being late in the morning.   *Søren Kierkegaard*

Three things are good in little measure and evil in large: yeast, salt and hesitation.

The Talmud

Mystic: a person who is puzzled before the obvious, but who understands the non-existent.   *Elbert Hubbard*

Faith means intense, usually confident, belief that is not based on evidence sufficient to command assent from every reasonable person.   *Walter Kaufmann*

Men will wrangle for religion, write for it, fight for it, die for it, anything but live for it.   *Charles Caleb Colton*

I have never yet met a healthy person who worries very much about his health or a really good person who worries much about his own soul.   *J. B. S. Haldane*

Men are idolaters, and want something to look at and kiss and hug, or throw themselves down before; they always did, they always will, and if you don't make it of wood, you must make it of words.   *Oliver Wendell Holmes*

The various modes of worship which prevailed in the Roman world were all considered by the people as equally true; by the philosopher as equally false; and by the magistrate as equally useful.   *Edward Gibbon*

Nothing in human life, least of all in religion, is ever right until it is beautiful.
                                              Harry Emerson Fosdick

I think if you ask people what their concept of heaven is, they would say, if they are honest, that it is a big department store, with new things every week—all the money to buy them, and maybe a little more than the neighbours.   *Erich Fromm*

We have grasped the mystery of the atom, and rejected the Sermon on the Mount.
                                              Omar Bradley

Religion is a great force—the only real motive force in the world; but you must get at a man through his own religion, not through yours.   *George Bernard Shaw*

It must require an inordinate share of vanity and presumption after enjoying so much that is good and beautiful on earth, to ask the Lord for immortality in addition to it all.   *Heinrich Heine*

Oysters are more beautiful than any religion . . . there's nothing in Christianity or Buddhism that quite matches the sympathetic unselfishness of an oyster.   *Saki*

Don't be agnostic—be something.   *Robert Frost*

A gentle Quaker, hearing a strange noise in his house one night, got up and discovered a burglar busily at work. He went and got his gun, came back and stood quietly in the doorway. 'Friend,' he said, 'I would do thee no harm for the world, but thou standest where I am about to shoot.'   *James Hines*

Better no religion at all—if such be possible—than one which concedes equal rights beyond the grave and denies them here.   *'Tom Collins' (Joseph Furphy)*

Religion is a way of walking, not a way of talking.   *Dean William R. Inge*

Puritanism—the haunting fear that someone, somewhere may be happy.
                                              H. L. Mencken

The worst moment for the atheist is when he is really thankful, and has nobody to thank. *Dante Gabriel Rossetti*

The mystery of the beginning of all things is insoluble by us; and I for one must be content to remain agnostic. *Charles Darwin*

Religion converts despair, which destroys, into resignation, which submits.
Lady Blessington

For the wonderful thing about saints is that they were human. They lost their tempers, got angry, scolded God, were egotistical or testy or impatient in their turns, made mistakes and regretted them. Still they went on doggedly blundering toward heaven.
Phyllis McGinley

With soap baptism is a good thing. *Robert G. Ingersoll*

When a man is freed of religion, he has a better chance to live a normal and wholesome life. *Sigmund Freud*

The Church of England is the Tory party at prayer. *Anon*

A Unitarian very earnestly disbelieves what everyone else believes.
W. Somerset Maugham

While I cannot be regarded as a pillar, I must be regarded as a buttress of the church, because I support it from outside. *Lord Melbourne*

Atheism is rather in the lip than in the heart of Man. *Francis Bacon*

There's no reason to bring religion into it. I think we ought to have as great a regard for religion as we can, so as to keep it out of as many things as possible.
Sean O'Casey

If the thunder is not loud, the peasant forgets to cross himself. *Russian proverb*

Religion is the opiate of the people. *Karl Marx*

Psychology is the theology of the 20th century. *Harry Hooton*

Infidel, n: in New York, one who does not believe in the Christian religion; in Constantinople, one who does. *Ambrose Bierce*

An atheist is a man who has no invisible means of support. *Fulton Sheen*

Yes, I am a Jew, and when the ancestors of the right honourable gentlemen were brutal savages in an unknown land, mine were priests in the Temple of Solomon.
Benjamin Disraeli

As for a future life, every man must judge for himself between conflicting vague possibilities. *Charles Darwin*

My theology, briefly,
Is that the universe
Was dictated
But not signed.   *Christopher Morley*

My atheism, like that of Spinoza, is true piety towards the universe and denies only
gods fashioned by men in their own image, to be servants of their human interests.
                                                         George Santayana

There is a crack in everything God has made.   *Ralph Waldo Emerson*

Christianity might be a good thing if anyone ever tried it.   *George Bernard Shaw*

The voice of the people is the voice of God. (*Vox populi, vox dei.*)   *Latin proverb*

I'm not ok—you're not ok, and that's ok.   *Rev. William Sloane Coffin*

Men prefer to believe that they are degenerated angels, rather than elevated apes.
                                                         W. Winwood Roade

Let's all give God a great big hand. I've seen the last page of the bible and it's going
to turn out all right.   *Anon.*

You have not converted a man because you have silenced him.   *John Morley*

I consider myself a Hindu, Christian, Moslem, Jew, Buddhist, and Confucian.
                                                         Gandhi

Repentance and Apology

From listening comes wisdom and from speaking, repentance.   *Old saying*

There are people who are very resourceful
At being remorseful,
And who apparently feel that the best way to make friends
Is to do something terrible and then make amends.   *Ogden Nash*

He's half absolv'd
Who has confess'd.   *Matthew Prior*

It is a very delicate job to forgive a man, without lowering him in his estimation, and
yours too.   *Josh Billings*

The sinning is the best part of repentance.   *Arabic proverb*

Apology is only egotism wrong side out.   *Oliver Wendell Holmes*

Apologize, v: to lay the foundation for a future offence.   *Ambrose Bierce*

Apology—a desperate habit, and one that is rarely cured. *Oliver Wendell Holmes*

No sensible person ever made an apology. *Ralph Waldo Emerson*

Repentance is for little children. *Adolf Eichmann*

Repentance is but want of power to sin. *John Dryden*

Make it a rule of life never to regret and never look back. Regret is an appalling waste of energy; you can't build on it; it's good only for wallowing in.
Katharine Mansfield

If I die, I forgive you: if I recover, we shall see. *Spanish proverb*

It is a good rule in life never to apologize. The right sort of people do not want apologies, and the wrong sort take a mean advantage of them. *P. G. Wodehouse*

God will pardon me. It's his business. *Heinrich Heine (as he died,*

Retirement

Cessation of work is not accompanied by cessation of expenses. *Cato the Elder*

You can't put off being young until you retire. *Philip Larkin*

The role of a retired person is no longer to possess one. *Simone de Beauvoir*

When men reach their sixties and retire, they go to pieces. Women just go right on cooking. *Gail Sheehy*

Retirement: statutory senility. *Emmett O'Donnell*

Two weeks is about the ideal length of time to retire. *Alex Comfort*

(The Queensland Gold Coast's) air of affluent decay as its aging retirees retreat in late afternoon to their fortified penthouses is a sight that ought to keep most people working until they die. *Michael Sexton*

Absence of occupation is not rest,
A mind quite vacant is a mind distress'd. *William Cowper*

Don't think of retiring from the world until the world will be sorry that you retire.
Samuel Johnson

Far from the madding crowd's ignoble strife.
Retirement, rural quiet, friendship, books. *James Thomson*

Few men of action have been able to make a graceful exit at the appropriate time.
Malcolm Muggeridge

Dismiss the old horse in good time, lest he fail in the lists and the spectators laugh.
Horace

I try to learn one new thing a week to balance the one thing I forget a week, but lately I forget three things a week.   *Joseph Gies*

Ruin

Nations have passed away and left no traces,
And history gives the naked cause of it—
One single simple reason in all cases;
They fell because their peoples were not fit.   *Rudyard Kipling*

So in the Libyan fable it is told
That once an eagle, stricken with a dart,
Said, when he saw the fashion of the shaft,
'With our own feathers, not by others' hands,
Are we now smitten.'   *Aeschylus (from Aesop)*

No man is demolished but by himself.   *Thomas Bentley*

What does not destroy me, makes me strong.   *Friedrich Nietzsche*

I never was ruined but twice—once when I lost a lawsuit, and once when I gained one.   *Voltaire*

There is nothing so costly to the state as a ruined life.   *Catherine Helen Spence*

All men that are ruined are ruined on the side of their natural propensities.
Edmund Burke

My downfall raises me to infinite heights.   *Napoleon Bonaparte*

Candour and generosity, unless tempered by due moderation, lead to ruin.   *Tacitus*

Italians come to ruin most generally in three ways—women, gambling and farming. My family chose the slowest one.   *Pope John XXIII*

Sanity and Insanity

One is healthy when one can laugh at the earnestness and zeal with which one has been hypnotized by any single detail of one's life.   *Friedrich Nietzsche*

When we remember that we are all mad, the mysteries disappear and life stands explained.   *Mark Twain*

Madness is part of all of us, all the time, and it comes and goes, waxes and wanes.

Otto Friedrich

A man should not strive to eliminate his complexes, but to get into accord with them: they are legitimately what directs his conduct in the world.   *Sigmund Freud*

Work and love—these are the basics; waking life is a dream controlled.

George Santayana

Outside, among your fellows, among strangers, you must preserve appearances, a hundred things you cannot do; but inside, the terrible freedom!

Ralph Waldo Emerson

Sanity is very rare; every man almost, and every woman, has a dash of madness.

Ralph Waldo Emerson

Mad, bad and dangerous to know.   *Lady Caroline Lamb (of Lord Byron)*

We are all born mad. Some remain so.   *Samuel Beckett*

There is a pleasure sure,
In being mad, which none but madmen know!   *John Dryden*

Scholars and Scholarship

He not only overflowed with learning, but stood in the slop.

Sydney Smith of Macaulay

If we wish to know the force of human genius, we should read Shakespeare. If we wish to see the insignificance of human learning, we may study his commentators.

William Hazlitt

The clever men at Oxford
Know all there is to be knowed—
But they none of them know as half as much
As intelligent Mr. Toad.   *Kenneth Grahame*

Academic economists have about the status and reliability of astrologers or the readers of Tarot cards. If the medical profession was as lacking in resources as the economists, we would not have advanced very far beyond the provision of splints for broken arms.

Barry O. Jones

A man should keep his little brain attic stocked with all the furniture that he is likely to use, and the rest he can put away in the lumber-room of his library, where he can get it if he wants it.   *Arthur Conan Doyle*

What is research, but a blind date with knowledge?   *Will Henry*

If I had read as much as other men, I should have known no more than they.

Thomas Hobbes

Deep-versed in books
And shallow in himself.   *John Milton*

Learning is the knowledge of that which none but the learned know.

William Hazlitt

I would live to study, not study to live.   *Francis Bacon*

Almost all important questions are important precisely because they are not susceptible
to quantitative answer.   *Arthur Schlesinger, Jr.*

Science and Technology

All science is either Physics or stamp-collecting.   *Lord Kelvin*

As far as the laws of Mathematics refer to reality, they are not certain, and as far as
they are certain, they do not refer to reality.   *Albert Einstein*

He had read Shakespeare and found him weak in chemistry.   *H. G. Wells*

I am sorry to say there is too much point to the wise crack that life is extinct on other
planets because their scientists were more advanced than ours.   *John F. Kennedy*

If all the arts aspire to the condition of music, all the sciences aspire to the condition
of mathematics.   *George Santayana*

If the human race wants to go to Hell in a basket, technology can help it get there by
jet.   *Charles M. Allen*

In science, all facts, no matter how trivial or banal, enjoy democratic equality.

Mary McCarthy

Life exists in the universe only because the carbon atom possesses certain exceptional
properties.   *James Jeans*

Light is the ultimate messenger of the universe.   *BBC World Service*

Most science is only high falutin' nature studies.   *Stephen Strauss*

My advice is to look out for engineers—they begin with sewing machines and end up
with the atomic bomb.   *Marcel Pagnol*

Never try to walk across a river just because it has an average depth of four feet.

Martin Friedman

Reason, observation, and experience—the Holy Trinity of Science.

Robert G. Ingersoll

Science is built of facts the way a house is built of bricks; but an accumulation of facts is no more science than a pile of bricks is a house.   *Henri Poincaré*

Science without religion is lame, religion without science is blind.   *Albert Einstein*

Scientific discovery consists in the interpretation for our own convenience of a system of existence which has been made with no eye to our convenience at all.

Norbert Wiener

The means by which we live have outdistanced the ends for which we live. Our scientific power has outrun our spiritual power. We have guided missiles and misguided men.   *Martin Luther King, Jr.*

The scientific theory I like best is that the rings of Saturn are composed entirely of lost airline luggage.   *Mike Russell*

The simplest schoolboy is now familiar with truths for which Archimedes would have sacrificed his life.   *Ernest Renan*

The world that science is making may be disgusting but it is the world in which we have to live and it condemns to futility all who are too blind to notice it.

Margaret Preston

Technology—the knack of so arranging the world that we don't have to experience it.

Max Frisch

The great tragedy of Science: the slaying of a beautiful hypothesis by an ugly fact.

Thomas Huxley

Technology means the systematic application of scientific or other organized knowledge to practical tasks.   *J. K. Galbraith*

Whenever science makes a discovery, the devil grabs it while the angels are debating the best way to use it.   *Alan Valentine*

Science cannot stop while ethics catches up—and nobody should expect scientists to do all the thinking for the country.   *Elvin Stackman*

Science must constantly be reminded that her purposes are not the only purposes and that the order of uniform causation which she has use for, and is therefore right in postulating, may be enveloped in a wider order, on which she has no claim at all.

William James

Science is the attempt to make the chaotic diversity of our sense-experience correspond to a logically uniform system of thought.   *Albert Einstein*

Though many have tried, no one has ever yet explained away the decisive fact that science, which can do so much, cannot decide what it ought to do.

Joseph Wood Krutch

It may be bizarre, but in my opinion, science offers a sure path to God and religion.

Paul Davies

Technology can be used to promote greater economic equity, more freedom of choice, and participatory democracy. Conversely, it can be used to intensify the worst aspects of a competitive society, to widen the gap between rich and poor, to make democratic goals irrelevant, and institute a technocracy.   *Barry O. Jones*

The new electronic interdependence recreates the world in the image of a global village.

Marshall McLuhan

Research is the process of going up alleys to see if they are blind.   *Marston Bates*

Research is to see what everybody has seen, and to think what nobody else has thought.

Albert Szent-Gyorgyi

No scientific theory achieves public acceptance until it has been thoroughly discredited.

Douglas Yates

The first rule of intelligent tinkering is to save all the parts.   *Paul R. Ehrlich*

Computers can figure out all kinds of problems, except the things in the world that just don't add up.   *James Magary*

The World would be a safer place,
If someone had a plan,
Before exploring Outer Space,
To find the Inner Man.   *E. Y. Harburg*

No amount of experimentation can ever prove me right; a single experiment can prove me wrong.   *Albert Einstein*

I think and think for months and years. Ninety-nine times, the conclusion is false. The hundredth time I am right.   *Albert Einstein*

There is more than a mere suspicion that the scientist who comes to ask metaphysical questions and turns away from metaphysical answers may be afraid of those answers.

Gregory Zilboorg

In science the credit goes to the man who convinces the world, not to the man to whom the idea first occurs.   *William Osler*

The perfect computer has been developed. You just feed in your problems, and they never come out again.   *Al Goodman*

Electric clocks reveal to you
Precisely when your fuses blew.   *Leonard Schiff*

The telephone is the most important single technological resource of later life.

Alex Comfort

$E = mc^2$: Energy equals mass times the speed of light squared.   *Albert Einstein*

Space isn't remote at all. It's only an hour's drive away if your car could go straight upwards.   *Fred Hoyle*

It is very seldom that the same man knows much of science, and about the things that were known before science came.   *Lord Dunsany*

A science which hesitates to forget its founders is lost.   *Alfred North Whitehead*

Pollution is nothing but resources we're not harvesting.   *Buckminster Fuller*

Medieval Technology? The Middle Ages invented, among other things, the crank, the horse collar, eyeglasses, the flying buttress, the stirrup, the windmill, the wheelbarrow, printing, firearms, paper, the canal lock, the compass, the rudder, the mechanical clock, the spinning wheel, and the treadle.   *Joseph and Frances Gies*

The best defence against the atom bomb is not to be there when it goes off.

The British Army Journal

A few observations and much reasoning lead to error; many observations and a little reasoning to truth.   *Alexis Carrel*

The most important of my discoveries have been suggested to me by my failures.

Sir Humphrey Davy

Basic research is what I'm doing when I don't know what I'm doing.

Wernher von Braun

Sit down before fact as a little child, be prepared to give up every preconceived notion, follow humbly wherever and to whatever abyss nature leads, or you shall learn nothing.

Thomas Huxley

If I have seen farther it is by standing on the shoulders of giants.   *Isaac Newton*

The Sea

The ocean and I have many pebbles
To find and wash off and roll into shape.   *William Stafford*

The sea possesses a power over one's moods that has the effect of a will.
The sea can hypnotize. Nature in general can do so.   *Henrik Ibsen*

Roll on, thou deep and dark blue ocean—roll!
Ten thousand fleets sweep over thee in vain;
Man marks the earth with ruin—his control
Stops with the shore. *Lord Byron*

The sea—the truth must be confessed—has no generosity. No display of manly qualities—courage, hardihood, endurance, faithfulness—has ever been known to touch its irresponsible consciousness of power. *Joseph Conrad*

Being in a ship is being in a jail, with the chance of being drowned.
Samuel Johnson

Only fools and passengers drink at sea. *Alan Villiers*

Love the sea? I dote upon it—from the beach. *Douglas Jerrold*

I liked to sail alone. The sea was the same as a girl to me—I did not want anyone else along. *E. B. White*

I do not love the sea. The look of it is disquieting. There is something in the very sound of it that stirs the premonition felt while we listen to noble music; we become inexplicably troubled. *H. M. Tomlinson*

The only cure for seasickness is to sit on the shady side of an old church in the country.
Anon.

I have observed, on board a steamer, how men and women easily give way to their instinct for flirtation, because water has the power of washing away our sense of responsibility, and those who on land resemble the oak in their firmness behave like floating seaweed when on the sea. *Rabindranath Tagore*

A poor woman from Manchester, on being taken to the seaside, is said to have expressed her delight on seeing for the first time something of which there was enough for everybody. *John Lubbock*

There's never an end for the sea. *Samuel Beckett*

The Seasons

April is the cruellest month,
breeding Lilacs out of the dead land,
mixing memory and desire
stirring dull roots with Spring rain. *T. S. Eliot*

Autumn wins you best by this: its mute
Appeal to sympathy for its decay. *Robert Browning*

Honest Winter, snow-clad, and with the frosted beard, I can welcome not uncordially; But that long deferment of the calendar's promise, that weeping gloom of March and April, that bitter blast outraging the honour of May how often has it robbed me of heart and hope?   *George Gissing*

No one thinks of Winter when the grass is green.   *Rudyard Kipling*

No Winter lasts forever, no Spring skips its turn. April is a promise that May is bound to keep, and we know it.   *Hal Borland*

The nicest thing about the promise of spring is that sooner or later she'll have to keep it.   *Mark Beltaire*

Now is the winter of our discontent
Made glorious summer by this sun of York.   *Shakespeare, 'King Richard III'*

Every April, God rewrites the Book of Genesis.   *Anon.*

The changing year's progressive plan
Proclaims mortality to man.   *Horace*

Summer is the mother of the poor.   *Italian proverb*

Take a winter as you find him and he turns out to be a thoroughly honest fellow with no nonsense in him: and tolerating none in you, which is a great comfort in the long run.   *James Russell Lowell*

Summer ends, and Autumn comes, and he who would have it otherwise would have high tide always and a full moon every night.   *Hal Borland*

June's too soon, July's too late—for summer.   *Siberian saying*

April,
Comes like an idiot, babbling, and strewing flowers.   *Edna St. Vincent Millay*

Autumn arrives in the early morning, but spring at the close of a winter's day.
                                                              Elizabeth Bowen

Autumn is the bite of a harvest apple.   *Christina Petrowsky*

May is a pious fraud of the almanac
A ghastly parody of real Spring
Shaped out of snow and breathed with eastern wind.   *James Russell Lowell*

The first day of spring was once the time for taking the young virgins into the fields, there in dalliance to set an example in fertility for Nature to follow. Now we just set the clock an hour ahead and change the oil in the crankcase.   *E. B. White*

Secrets and Secrecy

What is told in the ear of a man is often heard 100 miles away. *Chinese saying*

Two things a man cannot hide: that he is drunk, and that he is in love. *Antiphanes*

Nothing is so burdensome as a secret. *French proverb*

It is a secret in the Oxford sense. You may tell it to only one person at a time.
Oliver Franks

I know that's a secret, for it's whispered everywhere. *William Congreve*

All the knowledge I possess everyone else can acquire, but my heart is all my own.
Goethe

Shy and unready men are great betrayers of secrets; for there are few wants more
urgent for the moment than the want of something to say. *Henry Taylor*

In the mind and nature of a man a secret is an ugly thing, like a hidden physical
defect. *Isak Dinesen*

Be secret and exult,
Because of all things known
That is most difficult. *William Butler Yeats*

If you wish to preserve your secret, wrap it up in frankness. *Alexander Smith*

Where secrecy reigns, carelessness and ignorance delight to hide—skill loves the light.
Daniel C. Gelman

Whatsoever ye have spoken in darkness shall be heard in the light; and that which ye
have spoken in the ear in closets shall be proclaimed upon the housetops.
Luke 12:13

Even in your thought, do not curse the king, nor in your bedchamber curse the rich;
for a bird of the air will carry your voice, or some winged creature tell the matter.
Ecclesiastes 10:20

Self and Self-Knowledge

A man cannot be comfortable without his own approval. *Mark Twain*

An old man concludeth from his knowing mankind that they know him too, and that
maketh him very wary. *Lord Halifax*

A sick man that gets talking about himself, a woman that gets talking about her baby,
and an author that begins reading out of his own book, never know when to stop.
Oliver Wendell Holmes

Each man must look to himself to teach him the meaning of life. It is not something discovered; it is something moulded.   *Antoine de Saint-Exupéry*

Egotism: the art of seeing in yourself what others cannot see.   *George Higgins*

Every one is bound to bear patiently the results of his own example.   *Phaedrus*

He who is in love with himself has at least this advantage he won't encounter many rivals.   *G. C. Lichtenberg*

Nobody is more nauseating than the self-made man who is made of self.
David Crosby

No him, no me.   *Dizzy Gillespie (of Louis Armstrong)*

Man who man would be, must rule the empire of himself.   *Percy Bysshe Shelley*

No man does anything from a single motive.   *Samuel Taylor Coleridge*

Nobody can honestly think of himself as a strong character because, however successful he may be in overcoming them, he is necessarily aware of the doubts and temptations that accompany every important choice.   *W. H. Auden*

We carry with us the wonders we seek without us.   *Sir Thomas Browne*

What the collective age wants, allows and approves, is the perpetual holiday from the self.   *Thomas Mann*

When a man is wrapped up in himself he makes a pretty small package.
John Ruskin

Who's not sat tense before his own heart's curtain?   *Rainer Maria Rilke*

If a man really knew himself he would utterly despise the ignorant notions others might form on a subject in which he had such matchless opportunities for observation
George Santayana

With every physical pain, my moral fibre unravels a little.   *Mason Cooley*

I have never seen a greater monster or miracle in the world than myself. *Montaigne*

We are all serving a life sentence in the dungeon of self.   *Cyril Connolly*

One may understand the cosmos, but never the ego; the self is more distant than any star.   *G. K. Chesterton*

We judge ourselves by our motives and others by their actions.   *Dwight Morrow*

There is nothing noble about being superior to some other man. The true nobility is in being superior to your previous self.   *Hindu proverb*

Self-confidence is the first requisite to great undertakings.   *Samuel Johnson*

Never to talk of oneself is a form of hypocrisy.   *Friedrich Nietzsche*

Goethe said there would be little left of him if you were to discard what he owed to others.   *Charlotte Cushman*

Be yourself. Who else is better qualified?   *Frank J. Giblin II*

I don't think anyone is free—one creates one's own prison.   *Graham Sutherland*

I am I plus my circumstances.   *José Ortega y Gasset*

I think somehow we learn who we really are and then live with that decision.
Eleanor Roosevelt

There is nothing will kill a man so soon as having nobody to find fault with but himself.   *George Eliot*

I am as bad as the worst, but, thank God, I am as good as the best.   *Walt Whitman*

A man can stand a lot as long as he can stand himself. He can live without hope, without friends, without books, even without music, as long as he can listen to his own thoughts.   *Axel Munthe*

If you really do put a small value upon yourself, rest assured that the world will not raise your price.   *Anon.*

If I am not for myself, who will be?   *Pirke Avot*

The greatest success is successful self-acceptance.   *Ben Sweet*

Compassion for myself is the most powerful healer of them all.
Theodore Isaac Rubin

Self-respect is the root of discipline: the sense of dignity grows with the ability to say no to oneself.   *Abraham J. Heschel*

If you know nothing, be pleased to know nothing.   *John Newlove*

I am more afraid of my own heart than of the Pope and all his cardinals. I have within me the great Pope, Self.   *Martin Luther*

The happy man is he who knows his limitations, yet bows to no false gods.
Robert Service

Most men, when praising others warmly, are unconsciously praising images struck from the die of their own ideas of themselves.   *Daniel Deniehy*

Nobody knows what's in him until he tries to pull it out. If there's nothing, or very little, the shock can kill a man.   *Ernest Hemingway*

Blessed are they who heal us of self-despisings. Of all services which can be done to man, I know of none more precious.   *William Hale White*

When three people call you an ass, put on a bridle.   *Spanish proverb*

A complete life may be one ending in so full an identification with the not-self that there is no self left to die.   *Bernard Berenson*

A show of envy is an insult to oneself.   *Yevgeny Yevtushenko*

Maturity consists of no longer being taken in by oneself.
Kajetan von Schlaggenberg

Our own interests are still an exquisite means for dazzling our eyes agreeably.
Blaise Pascal

To penetrate one's being, one must go armed to the teeth.   *Paul Valéry*

Men at some time are masters of their fates:
The fault, dear Brutus, is not in our stars,
But in ourselves, that we are underlings.   *Shakespeare, 'Julius Caesar'*

Self-reverence, self-knowledge, self-control—these three alone lead to sovereign power.
Alfred, Lord Tennyson

There are limits to self-indulgence, none to self-restraint.   *Gandhi*

Integrity simply means a willingness not to violate one's identity.   *Erich Fromm*

The important thing is not what they think of me, it is what I think of them.
Victoria, Queen of England

I think Dostoevsky was right, that every human being must have a point at which he stands against the culture, where he says, this is me and the damned world can go to hell.   *Rollo May*

O wad some Pow'r the giftie gie us
To see oursels as others see us.
It wad frae money a blunder free us,
And foolish notion.   *Robert Burns*

Self-respecting people do not care to peep at their reflections in unexpected mirrors, or to see themselves as others see them.   *Logan Pearsall Smith*

Self-command is the main elegance.   *Ralph Waldo Emerson*

No one can make you feel inferior without your consent.   *Eleanor Roosevelt*

I am better than my reputation.   *Friedrich von Schiller*

I know I'm not exactly a bombshell, but one has to make the best of what one's got.

Joan Sutherland

Be thine own palace, or the world's thy jail.   *John Donne*

Do not make yourself so big. You are not so small.   *Jewish proverb*

Individualism is rather like innocence; there must be something unconscious about it.

Louis Kronenberger

I am as my Creator made me, and since He is satisfied, so am I.   *Minnie Smith*

I live in the crowds of jollity, not so much to enjoy company as to shun myself.

Samuel Johnson

I refuse to try to explain everything, because if you know too much about yourself, you become impotent. Better not to know what it is that makes you tick.

Paul Wunderlich

Every man shall bear his own burden.   *Galatians 6:5*

I seem to have an awful lot of people inside me.   *Edith Evans*

There is no crime of which I do not deem myself capable.   *Goethe*

I shall stay the way I am
Because I do not give a damn.   *Dorothy Parker*

I have been a selfish being all my life, in practice, though not in principle.

Jane Austen

God knows, I'm no the thing I should be,
Nor am I even the thing I could be.   *Robert Burns*

In the main it is not by introspection but by reflecting on our living in common with others that we come to know ourselves. What is revealed? It is an original creation. Freely the subject makes himself what he is, never in this life is the making finished, always it is in process, always it is a precarious achievement that can slip and fall and shatter.   *Bernard Lonergan*

I'm a vague, conjunctured personality, more made up of opinions and academic prepossessions than of human traits and red corpuscles.   *Woodrow Wilson*

to be nobody but yourself—in a world which is doing its best, night and day, to make you everybody else—means to fight the hardest battle which any human being can fight, and never stop fighting.   *e. e. cummings*

Learn what you are, and be such.   *Pindar*

My great mistake, the fault for which I can't forgive myself, is that one day I ceased my obstinate pursuit of my own individuality.   *Oscar Wilde*

A man must learn to forgive himself. *Arthur Davison Ficke*

I have come back again to where I belong; not an enchanted place, but the walls are strong. *Dorothy H. Rath*

There's only one corner of the universe you can be certain of improving and that's your own self. *Aldous Huxley*

It is not only the most difficult thing to know oneself, but the most inconvenient one, too. *Josh Billings*

To know oneself, one should assert oneself. *Albert Camus*

Every new adjustment is a crisis in self-esteem. *Eric Hoffer*

There is no greater delight than to be conscious of sincerity on self-examination. *Mencius*

Whatever you may be sure of, be sure of this—that you are dreadfully like other people. *James Russell Lowell*

All life is the struggle, the effort to be itself. The difficulties which I meet with in order to realize my existence are precisely what awaken and mobilize my activities, my capacities. *José Ortega y Gasset*

My closest relation is myself. *Terence*

Sex

I'll wager that in ten years it will be fashionable again to be a virgin. *Barbara Cartland*

Is sex dirty? Only if it is done right. *Woody Allen*

No sex is better than bad sex. *Attributed to Germaine Greer*

Sara could commit adultery at one end and weep for her sins at the other, and enjoy both operations at once. *Joyce Cary*

Sex is an emotion in motion. *Mae West*

A post-feminist lover is one who tends to insist on a Vietnamese meal and a French movie before sex. *Wendy Harmer*

Sex, unlike justice, should not be seen to be done. *Evelyn Laye*

A radical celibate is a person with a sense of humour. *Ita Buttrose*

There will be sex after death; we just won't be able to feel it. *Lily Tomlin*

Two-parent sex appeared on the scene about 500,000,000 years ago.

Mark Jerome Walters

When she raises her eyelids it's as if she were taking off all her clothes.   *Colette*

Sex is the great amateur art.   *David Cort*

Of all sexual aberrations, perhaps the most peculiar is chastity.   *Rémy de Gourmont*

I've looked on a lot of women with lust. I've committed adultery in my heart many times. This is something God recognizes I will do—and I have done it—and God forgives me for it.   *Jimmy Carter*

The big difference between sex for money and sex for free is that sex for money usually costs a lot less.   *Brendan Francis*

Whatever else can be said about sex, it cannot be called a dignified performance.

Helen Lawrenson

Sex—the poor man's polo.   *Clifford Odets*

Lord, make me chaste—but not yet.   *St. Augustine*

The natural man has only two primal passions—to get and beget.   *William Osler*

Amoebas at the start were not complex—
They tore themselves apart and started sex.   *Arthur Guiterman*

Every animal is sad after intercourse.   *Latin proverb*

As a matter of biology, if something bites you it is probably female.

Scott M. Kruse

Sex ought to be a wholly satisfying link between two affectionate people from which they emerge unanxious, rewarded, and ready for more.   *Alex Comfort*

When a man tells me he's run out of steam in the sex department, I'll tell him, 'Count your blessings; you've escaped from the clutches of a cruel tyrant. Enjoy!'

Richard J. Needham

While a person does not give up on sex, sex does not give up on the person.

Gabriel García Márquez

Silence

Be silent and safe—silence never betrays you.   *John Boyle O'Reilly*

Silence is as full of potential wisdom and wit as the unhewn marble of great sculpture.

Aldous Huxley

The silent dog is the first to bite.   *Old saying*

We need a reason to speak, but none to keep silent.   *Pierre Nicole*

Silence is the unbearable repartee.   *G. K. Chesterton*

That man's silence is wonderful to listen to.   *Thomas Hardy*

I believe in the discipline of silence and could talk for hours about it.
George Bernard Shaw

He has the gift of quiet.   *John Le Carré*

I'm exhausted from not talking.   *Sam Goldwyn*

The cruellest lies are often told in silence.   *Robert Louis Stevenson*

Nature has given to men one tongue, but two ears, that we may hear from others twice
as much as we speak.   *Epictetus*

Silence is the most perfect expression of scorn.   *George Bernard Shaw*

Speech may be barren; but it is ridiculous to suppose that silence is always brooding
on a nestful of eggs.   *George Eliot*

Silence propagates itself, and the longer talk has been suspended, the more difficult it
is to find anything to say.   *Samuel Johnson*

The most silent people are generally those who think most highly of themselves.
William Hazlitt

The greatest triumphs of propaganda have been accomplished, not by doing something,
but by refraining from doing. Great is truth, but still greater, from a practical point of
view, is silence about truth.   *Aldous Huxley*

Men fear silence as they fear solitude, because both give them a glimpse of the terror
of life's nothingness.   *André Maurois*

Silence is deep as Eternity; speech, shallow as Time.   *Thomas Carlyle*

Better silent than stupid.   *German proverb*

It is a great misfortune neither to have enough wit to talk well nor enough judgement
to be silent.   *Jean de la Bruyère*

I have noticed that nothing I never said ever did me any harm.   *Calvin Coolidge*

One of the best ways to persuade others is with your ears.   *Dean Rusk*

It is easier to talk than to hold one's tongue.   *Greek proverb*

The pause—that impressive silence, that eloquent silence, that geometrically progressive silence which often achieves a desired effect where no combination of words, howsoever felicitous, could accomplish it.   *Mark Twain*

Sleep

The feeling of sleepiness when you are not in bed, and can't get there, is the meanest feeling in the world.   *Edgar Watson Howe*

Did anyone ever have a boring dream?   *Ralph Hodgson*

The sleep of a labouring man is sweet, whether he eat little or much; but the abundance of the rich will not suffer him to sleep.   *Ecclesiastes 5:12*

Sleep that knits up the ravelled sleave of care,
The death of each day's life, sore labour's bath,
Balm of hurt minds, great nature's second course,
Chief nourisher in life's feast.   *William Shakespeare, 'Macbeth'*

Weariness
Can snore upon the flint, when resty sloth
Finds the down pillow hard.   *Shakespeare, 'Cymbeline'*

One of the most adventurous things left is to go to bed, for no one can lay a hand on our dreams.   *E. V. Lucas*

Sleeping is no mean art. For its sake one must stay awake all day.   *Friedrich Nietzsche*

Sleep faster, we need the pillows.   *Jewish proverb*

That we are not much sicker and much madder than we are is due exclusively to that most blessed and blessing of all natural graces, sleep.   *Aldous Huxley*

I never sleep in comfort save when I am hearing a sermon or praying to God.   *Rabelais*

Sleep—kinsman thou to death and trance and madness.   *Alfred, Lord Tennyson*

Thou hast been called, O sleep! the friend of woe;
But 'tis the happy who have called thee so.   *Robert Southey*

Yet a little sleep, a little slumber, a little folding of the hands to sleep.   *Proverbs 6:10*

Sleep takes off the costume of circumstance, arms us with terrible freedom, so that every will rushes to deed. A skillful man reads his dreams for his self-knowledge; yet not the details, but the quality. What part does he play in them—a cheerful, manly part, or a poor, drivelling part? However monstrous and grotesque their apparitions. they have a substantial truth. *Ralph Waldo Emerson*

For some must watch, while some must sleep; thus runs the world away.
Shakespeare, 'Hamlet

Snobs and Snobbishness

The public has a taste for supping with the great. *Ulick O'Connor*

Laughter would be bereaved if snobbery died. *Peter Ustinov*

The true definition of a snob is one who craves for what separates men rather than for what unites them. *John Buchan*

No place in England where everyone can go is considered respectable.
George Moore

Snobs talk as if they had begotten their ancestors. *Herbert Agar*

Women really do tend to be more snobbish than men. *Margaret Whitlam*

A highbrow is a person educated beyond his intelligence. *Brander Matthews*

All the people like us are We,
And everyone else is They. *Rudyard Kipling*

The true snob never rests; there is always a higher goal to attain, and there are, by the same token, always more and more people to look down upon.
Russell Lynes

Society and Social Structure

Every generation is a secret society and has incommunicable enthusiasm, tastes and interests which are a mystery both to its predecessor and to posterity.
Arthur Chapman

Fools take to themselves the respect that is given to their office. *Aesop*

There is no such thing as a democratic gentleman; the adjective and noun are hyphenated by a drawn sword. *Joseph Furphy*

Society is commonly too cheap. We meet at very short intervals, not having had time to acquire any new value for each other. We meet at meals three times a day, and give each other a new taste of that old musty cheese that we are. *Henry David Thoreau*

A wowser is a gentleman who uses a contraceptive as a bookmark for his Bible.

Alan Marshall

An aristocracy doesn't need brains. That is why it never has them.

Martin Boyd, 'Lucinda Brayford'

Society can only exist on the basis that there is some amount of polished lying and that no one says exactly what he thinks.   *Lin Yutang*

The cocktail party—as the name itself indicates—was originally invented by dogs. They are simply bottom-sniffings raised to the rank of formal ceremonies.

Laurence Durrell

Two people can form a community by excluding a third.   *Jean-Paul Sartre*

The world has narrowed to a neighbourhood before it has broadened to a brotherhood.

Lyndon B. Johnson

There are only two families in the world, as a Grandmother of mine used to say, the haves and the have-nots.   *Miguel de Cervantes*

What is a Communist? One who hath yearnings
for equal division of unequal earnings.   *Ebenezer Elliott*

Society is composed of two great classes: those who have more dinners than appetite, and those who have more appetite than dinners.   *Sebastien Chamfort*

The complacent, the self-indulgent, the soft societies are about to be swept away with the debris of history.   *John F. Kennedy*

Society is now one polished horde,
Formed of two mighty tribes,
The Bores and the Bored.   *Lord Byron*

Society, dead or alive, can have no charm without intimacy and no intimacy without an interest in trifles.   *Arthur Balfour*

To be social is to be forgiving.   *Robert Frost*

In any civilised society, a police force is a necessary evil, but some members of it are more evil than necessary.   *Ken Buckley*

The difference between our decadence and the Russians' is that while theirs is brutal, ours is apathetic.   *James Thurber*

The cocktail party—a device for paying off obligations to people you don't want to invite to dinner.   *Charles Merrill Smith*

Vigorous societies harbour a certain extravagance of objectives.

Alfred North Whitehead

Tolerably early in life I discovered that one of the unpardonable sins, in the eyes of most people, is for a man to go about unlabeled. The world regards such a person as the police do an unmuzzled dog.   *Thomas Huxley*

Twenty per cent of the people in volunteer groups do ninety per cent of the work.
The Diamond of Psi Upsilon

Nothing is so dangerous as being too modern; one is apt to grow old-fashioned quite suddenly.   *Oscar Wilde*

Gentleman: one who never hurts anyone's feelings unintentionally.   *Anon.*

Etiquette means behaving yourself a little better than is absolutely essential.
Will Cuppy

The best things and best people rise out of their separateness; I'm against a homogenized society because I want the cream to rise.   *Robert Frost*

There are four varieties in society; the lovers, the ambitious, observers, and fools. The fools are the happiest.   *Hippolyte Taine*

Whatever people may say, the fastidious formal manner of the upper classes is preferable to the slovenly easygoing behaviour of the common middle class. In moments of crisis, the former know how to act, the latter become uncouth brutes.
Cesare Pavese

The classes that wash most are those that work least.   *G. K. Chesterton*

That's what being in the working class is all about—how to get out of it.
Neville Wran

Necessity is the constant scourge of the lower classes, ennui of the higher ones.
Arthur Schopenhauer

Society, my dear, is like salt water, good to swim in but hard to swallow.
Arthur Stringer

Only a few human beings should grow to the square mile; they are commonly planted too close.   *William T. Davis*

'Tis the final conflict! Let each stand in his place! The international working class shall be the human race!   *'The Internationale'*

Every society honours its live conformists and its dead troublemakers.
Mignon McLaughlin

In order to stand well in the eyes of the community, it is necessary to come up to a certain, somewhat indefinite, conventional standard of wealth.   *Thorstein Veblen*

Class is an aura of confidence that is being sure without being cocky. Class has nothing to do with money. Class never runs scared. It is self-discipline and self-knowledge. It's the sure-footedness that comes with having proved you can meet life.

Ann Landers

I respect kindness in human beings first of all, and kindness to animals. I don't respect the law; I have a total irreverance for anything connected with society except that which makes the roads safer, the beer stronger, the food cheaper and the old men and old women warmer in the winter and happier in the summer.   *Brendan Behan*

Every man is a consumer and ought to be a producer.   *Ralph Waldo Emerson*

Solitude

There are three things a man must do alone. Be born, die, and testify.

James J. Walker

Solitary trees, if they grow at all, grow strong.   *Winston Churchill*

We never touch but at points.   *Ralph Waldo Emerson*

I was never less alone than when by myself.   *Edward Gibbon*

In the world a man lives in his own age; in solitude in all ages.   *W. Matthews*

I never found the companion that was so companionable as solitude.

Henry David Thoreau

If from Society we learn to live
'Tis Solitude should teach us how to die;
It hath no flatterers.   *Lord Byron*

Solitude is as needful to the imagination as society is wholesome for the character.

James Russell Lowell

One can acquire everything in solitude but character.   *Stendhal*

Solitude is the profoundest fact of the human condition. Man is the only being who knows he is alone.   *Octavio Paz*

It's a rather pleasant experience to be alone in a bank at night.   *Willie Sutton*

We're all of us sentenced to solitary confinement inside our own skins, for life.

Tennessee Williams

To dare to live alone is the rarest courage; since there are many who had rather meet their bitterest enemy in the field, than their own hearts in their closet.

Charles Caleb Colton

One of the greatest necessities in America is to discover creative solitude.

Carl Sandburg

Secret, and self-contained, and solitary as an oyster.   *Charles Dickens*

Night, when words fade and things come alive, when the destructive analysis of day is done, and all that is truly important becomes whole and sound again. When man reassembles his fragmentary self and grows with the calm of a tree.

Antoine de Saint-Exupéry

Sorrow

What's gone and what's past help
should be past grief.   *Shakespeare, 'The Winter's Tale'*

About suffering they were never wrong,
The Old Masters;
How well they understood
Its human position; how it takes place
While someone else is eating or opening a window or just walking dully along.

W. H. Auden

Excessive sorrow laughs. Excessive joy weeps.   *William Blake*

He's simply got the instinct for being unhappy highly developed.   *Saki*

One cannot weep for the entire world. It is beyond human strength. One must choose.

Jean Anouilh

Should you shield the canyons from the windstorms you would never see the true beauty of their carvings.   *Elisabeth Kubler-Ross*

Sorrow makes us all children again.   *Ralph Waldo Emerson*

There are some men above grief and some men below it.   *Ralph Waldo Emerson*

Unhurt people are not much good in the world.   *Enid Starkie*

In extreme youth, in our most humiliating sorrow, we think we are alone. When we are older we find that others have suffered too.   *Suzanne Moarny*

The deeper the sorrow the less tongue it hath.   *The Talmud*

When sorrows come, they come not as single spies,
But in battalions!   *Shakespeare, 'Hamlet'*

Men who are unhappy, like men who sleep badly, are always proud of the fact.

Bertrand Russell

What man is there that does not laboriously, though all unconsciously, himself fashion the sorrow that is to be the pivot of his life.   *Maurice Maeterlinck*

Only one-fourth of the sorrow in each man's life is caused by outside uncontrollable elements, the rest is self-imposed by failing to analyze and act with calmness.
George Jackson

There is something pleasurable in calm remembrance of a past sorrow.   *Cicero*

The poor and the busy have no leisure for sentimental sorrow.   *Samuel Johnson*

While grief is fresh, every attempt to divert it only irritates.   *Samuel Johnson*

No one can keep his griefs in their prime; they use themselves up.   *E. M. Cioran*

Sorrow is a fruit; God does not allow it to grow on a branch that is too weak to bear it.   *Victor Hugo*

There are few sorrows, however poignant, in which a good income is of no avail.
Logan Pearsall Smith

Speakers and Speeches

A man does not know what he is saying until he knows what he is not saying.
G. K. Chesterton

Even so, the tongue is a little member and boasteth great things, behold, how great a matter a little fire kindleth!   *James 3:5*

He rose without a friend, and sat down without an enemy.   *Henry Grattan*

Language most shows a man: speak, that I may see thee.   *Ben Jonson*

Little said is soon amended. There is always time to add a word, never to withdraw one.   *Baltasar Gracián*

None love to speak so much, when the mood of speaking comes, as they who are naturally taciturn.   *Henry Ward Beecher*

Nothing is so unbelievable that oratory cannot make it acceptable.   *Cicero*

Speak clearly, if you speak at all;
Carve every word before you let it fall.   *Oliver Wendell Holmes*

The relationship of the toastmaster to the speaker should be the same as that of the fan to the fan dancer. It should call attention to the subject without making any particular effort to cover it.   *Adlai Stevenson*

Though old the thought and oft exprest,
'tis his at last who says it best.

James Russell Lowell

To know how to say what others only know how to think is what makes men poets
or sages; and to dare to say what others only dare to think makes men martyrs or
reformers or both.

Elizabeth Charles

Whatever is well said by another, is mine.

Seneca

Winston (Churchill) has devoted the best years of his life to preparing his impromptu
speeches.

F. E. Smith

Would you persuade, speak of interest, not of reason.

Benjamin Franklin

It is terrible to speak well and be wrong.

Sophocles

All the great speakers were bad speakers at first.

Ralph Waldo Emerson

If the announcer can produce the impression that he is a gentleman, he may pronounce
as he pleases.

George Bernard Shaw

A dull speaker, like a plain woman, is credited with all the virtues, for we charitably
suppose that a surface so unattractive must be compensated by interior blessings.

A. P. Herbert

Once you get people laughing, they're listening and you can tell them almost anything.

Herbert Gardner

I hate to be interrupted in the middle of an insult.

Sir Robert Askin

The only interruption I tolerate is applause.

Gough Whitlam

In an easy cause any man may be eloquent.

Ovid

The object of oratory alone is not truth, but persuasion.

Thomas Babington Macaulay

If no thought
your mind does visit
make your speech
not too explicit.

Piet Hein

Oratory: the art of making deep noises from the chest sound like important messages
from the brain.

H. I. Phillips

The glittering generalities of the speaker have left an impression more delightful than
permanent.

Franklin J. Dickman

Say what you have to say and the first time you come to a sentence with a grammatical
ending—sit down.

Winston Churchill

First learn the meaning of what you say, and then speak.   *Epictetus*

When a man is asked to make a speech, the first thing he has to decide is what to say.   *Gerald Ford*

I've never thought my speeches were too long; I've rather enjoyed them.
Hubert Humphrey

Blessed is the man who, having nothing to say, abstains from giving us wordy evidence of the fact.   *George Eliot*

Look wise, say nothing, and grunt. Speech was given to conceal thought.
William Osler

I have learnt a good deal from my own talk.   *Thomas Chandler Haliburton*

Speech is the small change of silence.   *George Meredith*

If you don't say anything, you won't be called on to repeat it.   *Calvin Coolidge*

In Maine we have a saying that there's no point in speaking unless you can improve on silence.   *Edmund Muskie*

If you have an important point to make, don't try to be subtle or clever. Use a pile-driver. Hit the point once. Then come back and hit it again. Then hit it a third time—a tremendous whack!   *Winston Churchill*

He draweth out the thread of his verbosity finer than the staple of his argument.
Shakespeare, 'Love's Labour's Lost'

Sport

Football combines the two worst features of American life. It is violence punctuated by committee meetings.   *George F. Will*

Great sport begins at a point where it has ceased to be healthy.   *Bertolt Brecht*

There is nothing so momentary as a sporting achievement and nothing so lasting as the memory of it.   *Greg Dening*

I hate all sports as rabidly as a person who likes sports hates common sense.
H. L. Mencken

You can't think and hit at the same time.   *Yogi Berra*

Pro football is like nuclear warfare. There are no winners, only survivors.
Frank Gifford

Horses and jockeys mature earlier than people—which is why horses are admitted to race tracks at the age of two, and jockeys before they are old enough to shave.

Dick Beddoes

Jogging is very beneficial. It's good for your legs and your feet. It's also very good for the ground. It makes it feel needed.   *Charles M. Schulz*

It you watch a game, it's fun. If you play it, it's recreation. If you work at it, it's golf

Bob Hope

Winning can be defined as the science of being totally prepared.   *George Allen*

Running for money doesn't make you run fast. It makes you run first.   *Ben Jipcho*

When you win, nothing hurts.   *Joe Namath*

The nineteenth century often turned work into sport. We, in contrast, often turn sport into work.   *Geoffrey Blainey*

Sports allow men to build up situations of emergency. What he then demands of himself is unnecessary achievement—and unnecessary sacrifice. He artificially creates the tension that he has been spared by affluent society.   *Viktor Frankl*

It is in games that many men discover their paradise.   *Robert Lynd*

International sport is war without shooting.   *George Orwell*

Fatigue makes cowards of us all.   *Vince Lombardi*

Sports do not build character. They reveal it.   *Heywood Broun*

Every time you win, you're reborn; when you lose you die a little.   *George Allen*

Becoming number one is easier than remaining number one.   *Bill Bradley*

If you aren't fired with enthusiasm, you'll be fired with enthusiasm.

Vince Lombardi

Sport is one area where no participant is worried about another's race, religion or wealth: and where the only concern is 'Have you come to play?'

Henry Roxborough

Behind every tennis player there is another tennis player.   *John McPhee*

Sport is a loathsome and dangerous pursuit.   *Barry Humphries*

Sport to many Australians is life and the rest is shadow.   *Donald Horne*

Golf is a good walk spoiled.   *Mark Twain*

A sportsman is a man who, every now and then, simply has to get out and kill something. Not that he's cruel. He wouldn't hurt a fly. It's not big enough.

Stephen Leacock

Walking is the best possible exercise. Habituate yourself to walk very far.

Thomas Jefferson

Hockey captures the essence of the Canadian experience in the New World. In a land so inescapably and inhospitably cold, hockey is the dance of life, and an affirmation that despite the deathly chill of winter we are alive.   *Bruce Kidd*

The game isn't over until it's over.   *Yogi Berra*

The race is not always to the swift nor the battle to the strong—but that's the way to bet.   *Damon Runyon*

Sport begets tumultuous strife and wrath, and wrath begets fierce quarrels and war to the death.   *Horace*

Citius, altius, fortius. (Swifter, higher, stronger.)   *Motto of the Olympic Games*

(Rowing) is, of course, an extraordinarily apt sport for men in public life, because you can face one way while going the other.   *Gough Whitlam*

Going to bed with a woman never hurt a ball player. It's staying up all night looking for them that does you in.   *Casey Stengel*

Knute Rockne liked 'bad losers.' He said 'good losers' lose too often.   *George Allen*

Ninety per cent of this game is half-mental.   *Yogi Berra*

Success

I stopped believing in Santa Claus when I was six. Mother took me to see him in a department store and he asked for my autograph.   *Shirley Temple*

Success is like a smack in the face with a wet fish. It only means trouble for an artist.

Sidney Nolan

Nothing recedes like success.   *Walter Winchell*

Perseverance, n. A lowly virtue whereby mediocrity achieves a glorious success.

Ambrose Bierce

Success for the striver washes away the effort of striving.   *Pindar*

The penalty of success is to be bored by people who used to snub you.

Nancy, Lady Astor

The secret of success is constancy to purpose.   *Benjamin Disraeli*

There are few successful adults who were not first successful children.

Alexander Chase

What is success?
To laugh often and much;
To win the respect of intelligent people and the affection of children;
To earn the appreciation of honest critics and endure the betrayal of false friends;
To appreciate beauty;
To find the best in others;
To leave the world a bit better, whether by a healthy child, a garden patch
  or a redeemed social condition;
To know even one life has breathed easier because you have lived;
That is to have succeeded.   *Ralph Waldo Emerson*

If one advances confidently in the direction of his dreams, and endeavours to live the life which he has imagined, he will meet with a success unexpected in common hours.

Henry David Thoreau

The world belongs to the enthusiast who keeps cool.   *William McFee*

Out of every fruition of success, no matter what, comes forth something to make a new effort necessary.   *Walt Whitman*

Though a tree grow ever so high, the falling leaves return to the root.

Malay proverb

Success is that old A B C—ability, breaks and courage.   *Charles Luckman*

How can they say my life isn't a success? Have I not for more than sixty years got enough to eat and escaped being eaten?   *Logan Pearsall Smith*

You always pass failure on the way to success.   *Mickey Rooney*

Of course there is no formula for success except perhaps, an unconditional acceptance of life and what it brings.   *Artur Rubinstein*

High station in life is earned by the gallantry with which appalling experiences are survived with grace.   *Tennessee Williams*

Everything bows to success, even grammar.   *Victor Hugo*

Never having been able to succeed in the world, he took his revenge by speaking ill of it.   *Voltaire*

The successful people are the ones who think up things for the rest of the world to keep busy at.   *Don Marquis*

It is no use saying 'we are doing our best.' You have got to succeed in doing what is necessary.   *Winston Churchill*

Survival is triumph enough. *Harry Crews*

It takes time to be a success, but time is all it takes. *Anon.*

There is a passion for perfection which you will rarely see fully developed; but you may note this fact, that in successful lives it is never wholly lacking. *Bliss Carman*

Nothing fails like success; nothing is so defeated as yesterday's triumphant cause.
Phyllis McGinley

The toughest thing about success is that you've got to keep on being a success.
Irving Berlin

Nothing fails like success because we don't learn from it. We learn only from failure.
Kenneth Boulding

Get place and wealth, if possible with grace;
If not, by any means get wealth and place. *Alexander Pope*

Success is not so much what you are, but rather what you appear to be. *Anon.*

I cannot give you the formula for success, but I can give you the formula for failure, which is—try to please everybody. *Herbert Bayard Swope*

Success has made failures of many men. *Cindy Adams*

A successful man is he who receives a great deal from his fellow men, usually incomparably more than corresponds to his service to them. The value of a man, however, should be seen in what he gives and not in what he is able to receive.
Albert Einstein

Success is not the result of spontaneous combustion. You must set yourself on fire.
Reggie Leach

Success is the progressive realization of a worthy ideal. *Earl Nightingale*

A great secret of success is to go through life as a man who never gets used up.
Albert Schweitzer

Failure changes for the better, success for the worse. *Seneca*

Behind every successful man there's a lot of unsuccessful years. *Bob Brown*

If people knew what they had to do to be successful, most people wouldn't.
Lord Thomson of Fleet

The secret of all victory lies in the organization of the non-obvious.
Oswald Spengler

The great secret of being useful and successful is to admit of no difficulties.
Sir George Gipps

There is only one success—to be able to spend your life in your own way.
Christopher Morley

Tact and Diplomacy

A timid question will always receive a confident answer. *Lord Darling*

'Let us agree not to step on each other's feet,' said the cock to the horse.
English proverb

I think personal diplomacy has caused a lot of mischief and harm, and has impeded the progress of peace in the world. *Paul Hasluck*

Tact is the intelligence of the heart. *Anon.*

Silence is not always tact, and it is tact that is golden, not silence. *Samuel Butler*

Diplomats are useful only in fair weather. As soon as it rains, they drown in every drop. *Charles de Gaulle*

A distinguished diplomat could hold his tongue in ten languages. *Anon.*

Negotiation in the classic diplomatic sense assumes parties more anxious to agree than to disagree. *Dean Acheson*

Diplomacy: the art of saying 'nice doggie' till you can find a rock. *Wynn Catlin*

If any pilgrim monk come from distant parts, with wish as a guest to dwell in the monastery, and will be content with the customs which he finds in the place, and does not perchance by his lavishness disturb the monastery, but is simply content with what he finds, he shall be received for as long as he desires. If, indeed, he find fault with anything, or expose it, reasonably, and with the humility of charity, the Abbott shall discuss it prudently lest perchance God had sent him for this very thing. But, if he have been found gossipy and contumacious in the time of his sojourn as guest, not only ought he not be joined to the body of the monastery, but also, it shall be said to him, honestly, that he must depart. If he does not go, let two stout monks, in the name of God, explain the matter to him. *Saint Benedict*

An ambassador is an honest man sent to lie abroad for the good of his country.
Henry Wotton

Talent

All our talents increase in the using, and every faculty both good and bad, strengthens by exercise. *Anne Brontë*

Conciseness is the sister of talent. *Anton Chekhov*

Genius does what it must, and talent does what it can. *Edward Bulwer-Lytton*

Any breakthrough achieved by the very talented will be run into the ground by the less talented. *Clive James*

There is no substitute for talent. Industry and all the virtures are of no avail.
Aldous Huxley

Talent is always conscious of its own abundance, and does not object to sharing.
Aleksandr Solzhenitsyn

The luck of having talent is not enough; one must also have a talent for luck.
Hector Berlioz

A talent somewhat above mediocrity, shrewd and not too sensitive, is more likely to rise in the world than genius, which is apt to be perturbable and to wear itself out before fruition.   *Charles Horton Cooley*

Great talents are the most lovely and often the most dangerous fruits on the tree of humanity. They hang upon the most slender twigs that are easily snapped off.
Carl Jung

Everyone has a talent. What is rare is the courage to follow the talent to the dark places where it leads.   *Erica Jong*

The crowning blessing of life—to be born with a bias to some pursuit.
S. C. Tallentyre

Taste

Everyone carries his own inch-rule of taste, and amuses himself by applying it, triumphantly, wherever he travels.   *Henry Adams*

Taste is a capacity for making bad mistakes. It is based on self-flattery.
Harold Desbrowe Annear

Good taste is the first refuge of the non-creative. It is the last-ditch stand of the artist.
Marshall McLuhan

It is good taste, and good taste alone, that possesses the power to sterilize and is always the first handicap to any creative functioning.   *Salvador Dali*

Taste is the feminine of genius.   *Edward Fitzgerald*

Taste is the enemy of creativeness.   *Pablo Picasso*

Have nothing in your houses that you do not know to be useful, or believe to be beautiful.   *William Morris*

Style is a simple way of saying complicated things.   *Jean Cocteau*

Fashion exists for women with no taste, etiquette for people with no breeding.
Queen Marie of Rumania

People care more about being thought to have good taste than about being thought either good, clever or amiable. *Samuel Butler*

We all have some taste or other, of too ancient a date to admit of our remembering that it was an acquired one. *Charles Lamb*

Good taste and humour are a contradiction in terms, like a chaste whore.
Malcolm Muggeridge

Taste cannot be controlled by law. *Thomas Jefferson*

One of the surest signs of the Philistine is his reverence for the superior tastes of those who put him down. *Pauline Kael*

One man's poison ivy is another man's spinach. *George Ade*

Taxation

The Eiffel Tower is the Empire State Building after taxes. *Anon.*

The power to tax involves the power to destroy. *John Marshall*

The art of taxation consists in so plucking the goose as to get the most feathers with the least hissing. *Jean Baptiste Colbert*

The point to remember is that what the government gives it must first take away.
John S. Coleman

Next to being shot at and missed, nothing is quite as satisfying as an income tax refund. *F. J. Raymond*

The income tax has made more liars out of the American people than golf has. Even when you make a tax form out on the level, you don't know when it's through, if you are a crook or a martyr. *Will Rogers*

Governments last as long as the under-taxed can defend themselves against the over-taxed. *Bernard Berenson*

There went out a decree from Caesar Augustus that all the world should be taxed . . . And all went to be taxed, everyone into his own city. *Luke 2:1, 3*

The promises of yesterday are the taxes of today. *William Lyon Mackenzie King*

Teachers and Teaching

First he wrought, and afterwards he taught. *Geoffrey Chaucer*

Give a man a fish and you feed him for a day. Teach man to fish and you feed him for a lifetime. *Chinese proverb*

The art of effective teaching is much rarer than the faculty of acquiring knowledge.

Charles Harpur

The school teacher is certainly underpaid as a child minder, but ludicrously overpaid as an educator.   *John Osborne*

There is no crisis to which academics will not respond with a seminar.   *Old saying*

A teacher affects eternity; he can never tell where his influence stops.   *Henry Adams*

It would be a great advantage to some schoolmasters if they would steal two hours a day from their pupils, and give their own minds the benefit of the robbery.

J. F. Boyse

If the student fails to learn the teacher fails to teach.   *Anon.*

To teach is to learn twice.   *Joseph Joubert*

The authority of those who profess to teach is often a positive hindrance to those who desire to learn.   *Cicero*

Teaching is not a lost art, but the regard for it is a lost tradition.   *Jacques Barzun*

A high-school teacher, after all, is a person deputized by the rest of us to explain to the young what sort of world they are living in, and to defend, if possible, the part their elders are playing in it.   *Emile Capouya*

He who can, does. He who cannot, teaches.   *George Bernard Shaw*

Boys are always delightful in February and March, distressing towards the end of first term, beyond hope in August, exasperating in November, when iniquity always come to light, and again not so bad in December, when one says goodbye to so many of them with regret.   *J. R. Darling, headmaster*

If you are going to be any good, you have got to like the little swine.

J. R. Darling

The secret of teaching is to appear to have known all your life what you learned this afternoon.   *Anon.*

No man can reveal to you aught but that which already lies half asleep in the dawning of your knowledge.   *Kahlil Gibran*

The first duty of a lecturer—to hand you after an hour's discourse a nugget of pure truth to wrap up between the pages of your notebooks and keep on the mantelpiece for ever.   *Virginia Woolf*

Television

All television is educational television. The question is: what is it teaching?
Nicholas Johnson

He who prides himself on giving what he thinks the public wants is often creating a fictitious demand for low standards which he will then satisfy.
Lord Reith (former Director General, BBC)

A TV programme can never be worse than its viewers; for the more stupid it is, the more stupid they are to watch it.
Clive James

Television? The word is half Latin and half Greek. No good can come of it.
C. P. Scott

Television's compelling power is its immediacy . . . this immediacy feeds the politics of emotions, gut reactions and impressions rather than the politics of logic, facts and reason; it emphasizes personality rather than issues.
Hedrick Smith

Television is the literature of the illiterate, the culture of the low-brow, the wealth of the poor, the privilege of the underprivileged, the exclusive club of the excluded masses.
Lee Loevinger

Adams' first law of television: the weight of the backside is greater than the force of the intellect.
Phillip Adams

When television is good, nothing is better. But when television is bad, nothing is worse. I invite you to sit down in front of your TV set and keep your eyes glued to that set until the station signs off. I can assure you that you will observe a vast wasteland.
Newton Minow

Television has proved that people will look at anything rather than each other.
Ann Landers

Television is a gold goose that lays scrambled eggs; and it is futile and probably fatal to beat it for not laying caviar.
Lee Loevinger

Television is chewing gum for the eyes.
Frank Lloyd Wright

In the age of television, image becomes more important than substance.
S. I. Hayakawa

Television is the first truly democratic culture—the first culture available to everybody and entirely governed by what the people want. The most terrifying thing is what people do want.
Clive Barnes

Television has a real problem. They have no page two.
Art Buchwald

Good heavens, television is something you appear on, you don't watch.
Noel Coward

Television is an invention that permits you to be entertained in your living room by people you wouldn't have in your home.   *David Frost*

Why should people pay good money to go out and see bad films when they can stay at home and see bad television for nothing?   *Sam Goldwyn*

The television commercial is the most efficient power-packed capsule of education that appears anywhere on TV.   *C. L. Gray*

Television is not the truth. Television is a god-damned amusement park. Television is a circus, a carnival, a travelling troupe of acrobats, storytellers, dancers, singers, jugglers, sideshow freaks, lion tamers and football players. We're in the boredom-killing business.   *Paddy Chayefsky*

Dictum on television scripts: We don't want it good—we want it Tuesday.
    Dennis Norden

Quite small and ineffectual demonstrations can be made to look like the beginnings of a revolution if the cameraman is in the right place at the right time.
    Gough Whitlam

Temptation

All men are tempted. There is no man that lives that can't be broken down, provided it is the right temptation, put in the right spot.   *Henry Ward Beecher*

There are several good protections against temptation, but the surest is cowardice.
    Mark Twain

Temptation rarely comes in working hours. It is in their leisure time that men are made or marred.   *W. M. Taylor*

Things forbidden have a secret charm.   *Tacitus*

After listening to thousands of pleas for pardon to offenders, I can hardly recall a case where I did not feel that I might have fallen as my fellow man had done, if I had been subjected to the same demoralizing influences and pressed by the same temptations.   *Horatio Seymour*

I have a simple principle for the conduct of life—never to resist an adequate temptation.
    Max Lerner

If the world were merely seductive, that would be easy. If it were merely challenging, that would be no problem. But I rise in the morning torn between a desire to improve (or save) the world and a desire to enjoy (or savour) the world. This makes it hard to plan the day.   *E. B. White*

The only way to get rid of a temptation is to yield to it. Resist it, and your soul grows sick with longing for the things it has forbidden to itself.   *Oscar Wilde*

Never give in, never give in, never, never, never, never—in nothing great or small, large or petty—never give in except to convictions of honour and good sense.
Winston Churchill

I generally avoid temptation unless I can't resist it.   *Mae West*

Thinking and Thought

A library is thought in cold storage.   *(Viscount) Herbert Samuel*

A man is not idle because he is absorbed in thought.
There is a visible labour and there is an invisible labour.   *Victor Hugo*

An Englishman thinks seated; a Frenchman, standing; an American, pacing; an Irishman, afterward.   *Austin O'Malley*

It is the business of thought to define things, to find the boundaries.   *Vance Palmer*

Data data everywhere but not a thought to think.   *Theodore Roszak*

One must live the way one thinks or end up thinking the way one has lived.
Paul Bourget

One thought fills immensity.   *William Blake*

Sometimes people mistake the way I talk for what I am thinking.   *Idi Amin*

Thought is the labour of the intellect, reverie is its pleasure.   *Victor Hugo*

Three minutes' thought would suffice to find this out; . . . but thought is irksome and three minutes is a long time.   *A. E. Houseman*

When thought becomes excessively painful, action is the finest remedy.
Salman Rushdie

Worrying is the most natural and spontaneous of all human functions. It is time to acknowledge this, perhaps even to learn to do it better.   *Lewis Thomas*

All thought is a feat of association; having what's in front of you bring up something in your mind that you almost didn't know you knew.   *Robert Frost*

We only think when we are confronted with a problem.   *John Dewey*

The extra calories needed for one hour of intense mental effort would be completely met by eating one oyster cracker or one half of a salted peanut.
Francis C. Benedict

Every man who says frankly and fully what he thinks is doing a public service.
Leslie Stephen

Thought is the strongest thing we have. Work done by true and profound thought—that is a real force.   *Albert Schweitzer*

When a man knows he is to be hanged in a fortnight, it concentrates his mind wonderfully.   *Samuel Johnson*

We find it hard to believe that other people's thoughts are as silly as our own, but they probably are.   *James Harvey Robinson*

Thinking is like loving and dying—each of us must do it for himself.   *Josiah Royce*

A man of action forced into a state of thought is unhappy until he can get out of it.
                                                    John Galsworthy

It is human nature to think wisely and to act in an absurd fashion.   *Anatole France*

Men use thought only to justify their wrongdoings, and speech only to conceal their thoughts.   *Voltaire*

And which of you with taking thought can add to his stature one cubit? *Luke 12:25*

The real offence, as she ultimately perceived, was her having a mind of her own at all. Her mind was to be his—attached to his own like a small garden plot to a deer park.   *Henry James*

No delight equals that of the bright intoxication when you feel your thought quick within you.   *William Sutherland*

Think wrongly, if you please, but in all cases think for yourself.   *Doris Lessing*

The thoughts that come often unsought, and, as it were, drop into the mind, are commonly the most valuable of any we have.   *John Locke*

We shall succeed only so far as we continue that most distasteful of all activity, the intolerable labour of thought.   *Learned Hand*

Profundity of thought belongs to youth, clarity of thought to old age.
                                                    Friedrich Nietzsche

Every real thought on every real subject knocks the wind out of somebody or other.
                                                    Oliver Wendell Holmes

What was once thought can never be unthought.   *Friedrich Dürrenmatt*

Many a time I have wanted to stop talking and find out what I really believed.
                                                    Walter Lippmann

Man is a slow, sloppy and brilliant thinker; the machine is fast, accurate and stupid.
                                                    William M. Kelly

Folks that blurt out just what they think wouldn't be so bad if they thought.

Kin Hubbard

Facts in books, statistics in encyclopedias, the ability to use them in men's heads.

Fogg Brackel

Knowledge is a process of piling up facts; wisdom lies in their simplification.

Martin H. Fisher

The fundamental fact about the Greek was that he had to use his mind. The ancient priests had said 'Thus far and no farther. We set the limits of thought.' The Greek said, 'All things are to be examined and called into question. There are no limits set on thought.'

Edith Hamilton

Thought is born of failure.

Lancelot Law Whyte

Speaking without thinking is shooting without taking aim.

Spanish proverb

What you think is an illusion created by your glands, your emotions and, in the last analysis, by the content of your stomach. That gray matter you're so proud of is like a mirror in an amusement park which transmits to you nothing but distorted signals from reality forever beyond your grasp.

Ayn Rand

Many highly intelligent people are poor thinkers. Many people of average intelligence are skilled thinkers. The power of a car is separate from the way the car is driven.

Edward de Bono

Belief is harder to shake than knowledge.

Adolf Hitler

Time

3 o'clock is always too late or too early for anything you want to do.

Jean-Paul Sartre

Time—whether you are burning it up by falling in love or spreading it out thin in a dentist's waiting room—is a commodity that cannot be weighed out and measured by clocks.

Joan Lindsey

Nothing is improbable until it moves into the past tense.

George Ade

Nothing really belongs to us but time, which even he has who has nothing else.

Baltasar Gracian

Time does not alter men—it merely unmasks them.

Hal Porter

The butterfly counts not months but moments,
And has time enough.

Rabindranath Tagore

The passing minute is every man's equal possession but what has once gone by is not ours.   *Marcus Aurelius*

This only is denied even to God: the power to undo the past.   *Agathon*

Time is a Test of Trouble—
But not a Remedy—
If such it proved, it proves too
There was no Melody.   *Emily Dickinson*

Time is the rider that breaks youth.   *George Herbert*

To excel the past we must not allow ourselves to lose contact with it; on the contrary, we must feel it under our feet because we raised ourselves upon it.

José Ortega y Gasset

Time is a great legalizer, even in the fields of morals.   *H. L. Mencken*

Time goes, you say? Ah no! Alas, Time stays, we go.   *Henry Austin Dobson*

Let time that makes you homely, make you sage.   *Thomas Parnell*

I don't ask for your pity, but just your understanding—no, not even that—no. Just for your recognition of me in you, and the enemy, time, in us all.   *Tennessee Williams*

All things flow, nothing abides.   *Heraclitus*

When you sit with a nice girl for two hours, you think it's only a minute. But when you sit on a hot stove for a minute, you think it's two hours. That's relativity.

Albert Einstein

There was a young lady named Bright
Who could travel much faster than light
She started one day
In the relative way
And came back on the previous night.   *Anon.*

Longevity conquers scandal every time.   *Shelby Foote*

What may be done at any time will be done at no time.   *Scottish proverb*

One of these days is none of these days.   *English proverb*

Punctuality is the thief of time.   *Oscar Wilde*

Enjoy the present hour,
Be thankful for the past,
And neither fear nor wish
Th' approaches of the last.   *Abraham Cowley*

Horus non numero nisi serenas (I count only the sunny hours).
Motto on sundial quoted by William Hazlit

The only true time which a man can properly call his own, is that which he has al
to himself; the rest, though in some sense he may be said to live it, is other people's
time, not his.
Charles Lamb

I want to go ahead of Father Time with a scythe of my own.
H. G. Wells

Time is a great teacher, but unfortunately it kills all its pupils.
Hector Berlioz

Time that is moved by little fidget wheels
Is not my Time, the flood that does not flow.
Kenneth Slessor

Time and I against any two.
Baltasar Gracián

Time discovered truth.
Seneca

Time gives good advice.
Maltese proverb

What a day may bring, a day may take away.
Thomas Fuller

Time is a kindly god.
Sophocles

Time goes by: reputation increases, ability declines.
Dag Hammarskjöld

Time cools, time clarifies; no mood can be maintained quite unaltered through the
course of hours.
Thomas Mann

Every minute starts an hour.
Paul Gondola

Time wounds all heels.
Jane Ace

The apparent serenity of the past is an oil spread by time.
Lloyd Frankenberg

Time is a sort of river of passing events, and strong is its current; no sooner is a thing
brought to sight than it is swept by and another takes its place, and this too will be
swept away.
Marcus Aurelius

It takes time to save time.
Joe Taylor

The mind of man works with strangeness upon the body of time. An hour, once t
lodges in the queer element of the human spirit, may be stretched to fifty or a hundred
times its clock length; on the other hand, an hour may be accurately represented by
the timepiece of the mind by one second.
Virginia Woolf

Travel and Travellers

All travelling becomes dull in exact proportion to its rapidity.
John Ruskin

I dislike feeling at home when I am abroad.
George Bernard Shaw

Like all great travellers, I have seen more than I remember, and remember more than I have seen. *Benjamin Disraeli*

A man travels the world in search of what he needs and returns home to find it. *George Moore*

In Paris they simply stared when I spoke to them in French; I never did succeed in making those idiots understand their own language. *Mark Twain*

Lovers of air travel find it exhilarating to hang poised between the illusion of immortality and the fact of death. *Alexander Chase*

My heart is warm with the friends I make,
And better friends I'll not be knowing;
Yet there isn't a train I wouldn't take,
No matter where it's going. *Edna St. Vincent Millay*

To many people holidays are no voyage of discovery, but a ritual of reassurance. *Phillip Adams*

The American arrives in Paris with a few French phrases he has culled from a conversational guide or picked up from a friend who owns a beret. *Fred Allen*

The crow, when travelling abroad, came back just as black. *English proverb*

The journey is the reward. *Tao saying*

The routines of tourism are even more monotonous than those of daily life. *Mason Cooley*

The time to enjoy a European trip is about three weeks after unpacking. *George Ade*

There is a ghost
That eats handkerchiefs;
It keeps you company
On all your travels. *Christian Morgenstern*

I like terra firma—the more firma, the less terra. *George S. Kaufman*

When I was at home, I was in a better place; but travellers must be content. *Shakespeare, 'As You Like It'*

I cannot agree that travel broadens the mind. However, there is no doubt that it places enormous strain on the bladder. *Phillip Adams*

To travel hopefully is a better thing than to arrive. *Robert Louis Stevenson*

The early North American Indian made a great mistake by not having an immigration bureau. *Anon.*

Travel is fatal to prejudice, bigotry and narrow-mindedness. *Mark Twain*

Every perfect traveller always creates the country where he travels.

Nikos Kazantzakis

No man should travel until he has learned the language of the country he visits, otherwise he voluntarily makes himself a great baby—so helpless and ridiculous.

Ralph Waldo Emerson

As the Spanish proverb says, 'He who would bring home the wealth of the Indies, must carry the wealth of the Indies with him.' So it is with traveling. A man must carry knowledge with him if he would bring home knowledge.   *Samuel Johnson*

How much a dunce that has been sent to roam
Excels a dunce that has been kept at home!   *William Cowper*

The traveller's-eye view of men and women is not satisfying. A man might spend his life in trains and restaurants and know nothing of humanity at the end. To know, one must be an actor as well as a spectator.   *Aldous Huxley*

My favourite thing is to go where I've never been.   *Diane Arbus*

Usually speaking, the worst-bred person in company is a young traveller just returned from abroad.   *Jonathan Swift*

For my part, I travel not to go anywhere, but to go. I travel for travel's sake. The great affair is to move.   *Robert Louis Stevenson*

I met a lot of people in Europe. I even encountered myself.   *James Baldwin*

Travel is ninety per cent anticipation and ten per cent recollection.   *Edward Streeter*

If one had but a single glance to give the world, one should gaze on Istanbul.

Alphonse de Lamartine

There is no unhappiness like the misery of sighting land again after a cheerful, careless voyage.   *Mark Twain*

Before he sets out, the traveller must possess fixed interests and facilities, to be served by travel. If he drifted aimlessly from country to country he would not travel but only wander, ramble as a tramp. The traveller must be somebody and come from somewhere so his definite character and moral traditions may supply an organ and a point of comparison for his observations.   *George Santayana*

Following the sun we left the old world.   *Inscription on one of Columbus' caravels*

When you travel, remember that a foreign country is not designed to make you comfortable. It is designed to make its own people comfortable.   *Clifton Fadiman*

Wherever I travel, I'm too late. The orgy has moved elsewhere.   *Mordecai Richler*

(Airplanes) may kill you, but they ain't likely to hurt you.   *Satchell Paige*

If you are lucky enough to have lived in Paris as a young man, then wherever you go for the rest of your life, it stays with you, for Paris is a movable feast.

Ernest Hemingway

Old men and far travellers may lie with authority. *Anon.*

Russia is the only country of the world you can be homesick for while you're still in it. *John Updike*

Trust

A promise made is a debt unpaid. *Robert W. Service*

You should never trust anyone who listens to Mahler before they're forty.

Clive James

Never trust the teller. Trust the tale. *D. H. Lawrence*

There is nothing more likely to start disagreement among people or countries than an agreement. *E. B. White*

When praying does no good, insurance does help. *Bertolt Brecht*

It is better to suffer wrong than to do it, and happier to be sometimes cheated than not to trust. *Samuel Johnson*

I think that we may safely trust a good deal more than we do. *Henry David Thoreau*

To put one's trust in God is only a longer way of saying that one will chance it.

Samuel Butler

To be trusted is a greater compliment than to be loved. *George Macdonald*

Trust me, but look to thyself. *Irish proverb*

Trust thyself only, and another shall not betray thee. *Thomas Fuller*

Make yourself necessary to somebody. *Ralph Waldo Emerson*

Trust one who has tried. *Virgil*

Truth

The truth is always libellous. *George Finey*

A misleading impression, not a lie. It was being economical with the truth.

Sir Robert Armstrong

An exaggeration is a truth that has lost its temper.   *Kahlil Gibran*

The truth is impossible to tell even when one is willing to tell it. For the truth resides in memory, and the memory is clouded with repression and a desire to embellish.
Frank Hardy

It is a difficult task, Oh citizens, to make speeches to the belly, which has no ears.
Plutarch

'It was as true', said Mr. Barkus, 'as taxes is. And nothing is truer than them.'
Charles Dickens

Many people would be more truthful were it not for their uncontrollable desire to talk.
Edgar Watson Howe

No one means all he says and yet very few say all they mean.   *Henry Adams*

Pure truth, like pure gold, has been found unfit for circulation because men have discovered that it is far more convenient to adulterate the truth than to refine themselves.   *Charles Caleb Colton*

The truth is cruel, but it can be loved and it makes free those who have loved it.
George Santayana

There are no whole truths. All truths are half-truths. It is trying to treat them as whole truths that plays the devil.   *Alfred North Whitehead*

Too much truth
Is uncouth.   *Franklin P. Adams*

Truth is a child of Time.   *Don Ford*

Time trieth truth.   *English proverb*

Truth always lags last, limping along on the arm of Time.   *Baltasar Gracián*

Truth exists. Only lies are invented.   *Georges Braque*

Truth never dies but lives a wretched life.   *Yiddish proverb*

What a myth never contains is the critical power to separate its truth from its errors.
Walter Lippman

The man who speaks the truth is always at ease.   *Persian proverb*

Every man has a right to utter what he thinks is truth, and every other man has a right to knock him down for it.   *Samuel Johnson*

Don't be consistent, but be simply true.   *Oliver Wendell Holmes*

It makes all the difference in the world whether we put truth in the first place, or in the second place. *John Morley*

Rough work, iconoclasm, but the only way to get at the truth.
Oliver Wendell Holmes

When one has no design but to speak plain truth, he may say a great deal in a very narrow compass. *Richard Steele*

One can live in this world on soothsaying but not on truth saying.
G. C. Lichtenberg

For my part, whatever anguish of spirit it may cost, I am willing to know the whole truth—to know the worst and provide for it. *Patrick Henry*

Truth has a handsome countenance but torn garments. *German proverb*

God offers to every mind its choice between truth and repose. Take which you please; you can never have both. *Ralph Waldo Emerson*

Some people handle the truth carelessly;
Others never touch it at all. *Anon.*

Truth for him was a moving target; he never aimed for the bull and rarely pierced the outer ring. *Hugh Cudlipp on William Randolph Hearst*

Seeing's believing—but feeling is God's own truth. *Irish proverb*

I tore myself away from the safe comfort of certainties through my love for truth; and truth rewarded me. *Sylvia Ashton-Warner*

Every emancipation has in it the seeds of a new slavery, and every truth easily becomes a lie. *I. F. Stone*

In every generation there has to be some fool who will speak the truth as he sees it.
Boris Pasternak

Every truth passes through three stages before it is recognized. In the first it is ridiculed, in the second it is opposed, in the third it is regarded as self-evident.
Arthur Schopenhauer

No one can bar the road to truth, and to advance its cause I'm ready to accept even death. *Aleksandr Solzhenitsyn*

The passion for truth is silenced by answers which have the weight of undisputed authority. *Paul Tillich*

A truth that's told with bad intent
Beats all the lies you can invent. *William Blake*

He who, when called upon to speak a disagreeable truth, tells it boldly and has done, is both bolder and milder than he who nibbles in a low voice and never ceases nibbling.
Johann Kaspar Lavater

We call first truths those we discover after all the others.   *Albert Camus*

As scarce as truth is, the supply has always been in excess of the demand.
Josh Billings

I speak the truth, not so much as I would, but as much as I dare; and I dare a little more, as I grow older.   *Montaigne*

Between whom there is hearty truth, there is love.   *Henry David Thoreau*

Everything has to be taken on trust; truth is only that which is taken to be true. It's the currency of living. There may be nothing behind it, but it doesn't make any difference so long as it is honoured.   *Tom Stoppard*

One truth discovered, one pang of regret at not being able to express it, is better than all the fluency and flippancy in the world.   *William Hazlitt*

If you speak the truth have a foot in the stirrup.   *Turkish proverb*

The man who fears no truths has nothing to fear from lies.   *Thomas Jefferson*

Pretty much all the honest truthtelling there is in the world is done by children.
Anon.

There are truths that are not for all men, nor for all times.   *Voltaire*

A thing is not necessarily true because a man dies for it.   *Oscar Wilde*

What I tell you three times is true.   *Lewis Carroll*

Peace if possible, but truth at any rate.   *Martin Luther*

It takes two to speak the truth—one to speak, and another to hear.
Henry David Thoreau

If you tell the truth you don't have to remember anything.   *Mark Twain*

There's such a thing as moderation, even in telling the truth.   *Vera Johnson*

Truth is something you stumble into when you think you're going some place else.
Jerry García

Who look on Truth with mortal sight
Are blinded in its blaze of light.   *Rosemary Dobson*

Truth emerges more readily from error than from confusion.   *Francis Bacon*

If you are out to describe the truth, leave elegance to the tailor.   *Albert Einstein*

I don't give them hell. I just tell the truth and they think it is hell.

Harry S. Truman

Vice

Every vice is only an exaggeration of a necessary and virtuous function.

Ralph Waldo Emerson

As for an authentic villain, the real thing, the absolute, the artist, one rarely meets him, even once in a lifetime. The ordinary bad hat is always in part a decent fellow.

Colette

It's true Heaven forbids some pleasures, but a compromise can usually be found.

Moliére

What maintains one vice would bring up two children.   *Benjamin Franklin*

Vice goes a long way tow'rd makin' life bearable. A little vice now an' thin is relished by th' best iv men.   *Finley Peter Dunne*

When I religiously confess myself to myself, I find that the best virtue I have has in it some tincture of vice.   *Montaigne*

One big vice in a man is apt to keep out a great many smaller ones.   *Bret Harte*

Vice is as much a part of human nature as folly, and pornography may be as necessary to vent vice as satire is to vent folly.   *Mavor Moore*

He who hates vice hates men.   *John Morley*

Nurse one vice in your bosom. Give it the attention it deserves and let your virtues spring up modestly around it. Then you'll have the miser who's no liar; and the drunkard who's the benefactor of a whole city.   *Thornton Wilder*

The vices we scoff at in others, laugh at us within ourselves.   *Thomas Browne*

It is the function of vice to keep virtue within reasonable grounds.   *Samuel Butler*

When our vices leave us, we flatter ourselves with the credit of having left them.

La Rochefoucauld

Many without punishment, none without sin.   *John Ray*

If individuals have no virtues, their vices may be of use to us.   *Junius*

If you don't want anyone to know it, don't do it.   *Chinese proverb*

Ill habits gather by unseen degrees,
As brooks make rivers, rivers run to seas.   *John Dryden*

Vice can be learnt, even without a teacher.   *Seneca*

There's a small choice in rotten apples.   *Shakespeare*
'The Taming of the Shrew'

Everyone has his faults which he continually repeats; neither fear nor shame can cure
them.   *Jean de la Fontaine*

Violence

It is better to be violent, if there is violence in our hearts, than to put on the cloak of
non-violence to cover impotence.   *Gandhi*

Keep violence in the mind
Where it belongs.   *Brian Aldiss*

Violence is the quest for identity. When identity disappears with technological innovation, violence is the natural recourse.   *Marshall McLuhan*

Violence is essentially wordless, and it can begin only where thought and rational
communication have broken down.   *Thomas Merton*

You know what I think about violence. For me it is profoundly moral—more moral
than compromises and transactions.   *Benito Mussolini*

Violence is just, where kindness is vain.   *Corneille*

It is unfair to blame man too fiercely for being pugnacious; he learned the habit from
Nature.   *Christopher Morley*

Is some cases non-violence requires more militancy than violence.   *César Chavez*

We are all shot through with enough motives to make a massacre, any day of the week
that we want to give them their head.   *Jacob Bronowski*

In a war of ideas it is people who get killed.   *Stanislaw J. Lec*

The private terror of the liberal spirit is invariably suicide, not murder.
Norman Mailer

Violence is, essentially, a confession of ultimate inarticulateness.   *Time Magazine*

Non-violence is a powerful and just weapon. It is a weapon unique in history, which
cuts without wounding and enobles the man who wields it. It is a sword that heals.
Martin Luther King, Jr.

Today violence is the rhetoric of the period.   *José Ortega y Gasset*

Virtue

A tragic situation exists precisely when virtue does not triumph but when it is still felt that man is nobler than the forces which destroy him.   *George Orwell*

Humility is a virtue, and it is a virtue innate in guests.   *Max Beerbohm*

The sun, though it passes through dirty places, yet remains as pure as before.
                                                                      Francis Bacon

Fatal human malice is the stable of narrative, original sin the mother-fluid of historians. But it is a risky enterprise to have to write of virtue.   *Thomas Keneally*

Virtue has its own reward, but no sale at the box office.   *Mae West*

When virtue has slept, she will get up more refreshed.   *Friedrich Nietzsche*

Few men have virtue to withstand the highest bidder.   *George Washington*

Purity is obscurity.   *Ogden Nash*

I know myself too well to believe in pure virtue.   *Albert Camus*

There are few chaste women who are not tired of their trade.   *La Rochefoucauld*

Ascetic: one who makes a necessity of virtue.   *Friedrich Nietzsche*

A virtue to be serviceable must, like gold, be alloyed with some commoner but more durable metal.   *Samuel Butler*

The Saints are the Sinners who keep on trying.   *Robert Louis Stevenson*

No doubt alcohol, tobacco, and so forth, are things that a saint must avoid, but sainthood is also a thing that human beings must avoid.   *George Orwell*

If a man has no vices, he's in great danger of making vices about his virtues, and there's a spectacle.   *Thornton Wilder*

When men grow virtuous in their old age, they only make a sacrifice to God of the devil's leavings.   *Jonathan Swift*

If virtue were its own reward, it would no longer be a human quality, but supernatural.
                                                                      Vauvenargues

Let him who believes in immortality enjoy his happiness in silence without giving himself airs about it.   *Goethe*

War

A conventional army loses if it does not win. The guerrilla wins if it does not lose.
Henry Kissinger

War and peace are more than opposites. They have so much in common that neither can be understood without the other.   *Geoffrey Blainey*

All wars are popular for the first 30 days.   *Arthur Schlesinger, Jr.*

Do not let us speak of darker days; let us speak rather of sterner days. These are not dark days: these are great days—the greatest days our country has ever lived.
Winston Churchill (October 29, 1941)

Good things, when short, are twice as good.   *Baltasar Gracián*

I have never understood disliking for war. It panders to instincts already catered for within the scope of any respectable domestic establishment.   *Alan Bennett*

If a house be divided against itself, that house cannot stand.   *Mark 3:25*

In time of war the devil makes more room in hell.   *German proverb*

In war the will is directed at an animate object that reacts.   *Karl von Clausewitz*

Let us not be deceived—we are today in the midst of a cold war.   *Bernard Baruch*

Let us therefore brace ourselves to our duties, and so bear ourselves that, if the British Empire and its Commonwealth last for a thousand years, men will still say: 'This was their finest hour.'   *Winston Churchill (House of Commons June 18, 1940)*

Morality is contraband in war.   *Gandhi*

Scots, wha hae wi' Wallace bled,
Scots, wham Bruce has aften led,
Welcome to your gory bed
Or to victorie.   *Robert Burns*

(War) is not a business in which one can take any pride or pleasure, or even pretend to. Its horror, its ghastly inefficiency, its unspeakable cruelty and misery has always appalled me, but there is nothing to do but to set one's teeth and stick it out as long as one can.   *Sir John Monash*

Television brought the brutality of war into the comfort of the living room. Vietnam was lost in the living rooms of U.S.A.—not on the battlefields of Vietnam.
Marshall McLuhan

The quickest way of ending a war is to lose it.   *George Orwell*

There never was a good war or a bad peace.   *Benjamin Franklin*

They will conquer, but they will not convince.   *Miguel de Unamuno*

We few, we happy few, we band of brothers;
For he today that sheds his blood with me;
Shall be my brother.   *Shakespeare, 'Henry V'*

Tweedle Dum and Tweedle Dee
Agreed to have a battle;
For Tweedle Dum said Tweedle Dee
Had spoiled his nice new rattle.   *Lewis Carroll*

We shall not flag or fail. We shall fight in France, we shall fight on the seas and oceans, we shall fight with growing confidence and growing strength in the air, we shall defend our island, whatever the cost may be, we shall fight on the beaches, we shall fight on the landing grounds, we shall fight in the fields and in the streets, we shall fight in the hills; we shall never surrender.   *Winston Churchill*

When the rich wage war, it's the poor who die.   *Jean-Paul Sartre*

We only win at war because we fight another government. If we fought private industry we would not last until noontime.   *R. I. Fitzhenry*

War is much too important a matter to be left to the generals.   *Georges Clemenceau*

War is mainly a catalogue of blunders.   *Winston Churchill*

War is a series of catastrophes which result in victory.   *Georges Clemenceau*

It would indeed be a tragedy if the history of the human race proved to be nothing more than the story of an ape playing with a box of matches on a petrol dump.
                    David Ormsby Gore

Either war is obsolete, or men are.   *Buckminster Fuller*

War appeals to young men because it is fundamentally auto-eroticism. *Northrop Frye*

No wars are unintended or 'accidental'. What is often unintended is the length and bloodiness of the war. Defeat too is unintended.   *Geoffrey Blainey*

A war regarded as inevitable or even probable, and therefore much prepared for, has a very good chance of eventually being fought.   *Anaïs Nin*

War is the unfolding of miscalculations.   *Barbara Tuchman*

If you know the enemy and know yourself you need not fear the results of a hundred battles.   *Sun Tzu*

Today the real test of power is not capacity to make war but capacity to prevent it.
                    Anne O'Hare McCormick

As long as war is regarded as wicked, it will always have its fascination. When it is looked upon as vulgar, it will cease to be popular. *Oscar Wilde*

What the hell difference does it make, left or right? There were good men lost on both sides. *Brendan Behan*

The supreme excellence is not to win a hundred victories in a hundred battles. The supreme excellence is to subdue the armies of your enemies without even having to fight them. *Sun Tzu*

Frankly I'd like to see the government get out of war altogether and leave the whole field to private industry. *Joseph Heller*

War is the national industry of Prussia. *Mirabeau*

It is a fearful thing to lead this great peaceful people into war, into the most terrible and disastrous of all wars, civilization itself seeming to be in the balance. But the right is more precious than peace, and we shall fight for the things which we have always carried nearest our hearts—for democracy. *Woodrow Wilson*

Sweet is war to those who have never experienced it. *Latin proverb*

The possibility of war increases in direct proportion to the effectiveness of the instruments of war. *Norman Cousins*

I don't know what effect these men will have on the enemy, but by God, they frighten *me*. *Attributed to the Duke of Wellington reviewing his troops*

Boys are the cash of war. Whoever said: 'we're not free spenders' doesn't know our like. *John Ciardi*

In time of war the first casualty is truth. *Boake Carter*

War is waged by men; not by beasts, or by gods. It is a peculiar human activity. *Frederic Manning*

It's one of the most serious things that can possibly happen to one in a battle—to get one's head cut off. *Lewis Carroll*

No one can guarantee success in war, but only deserve it. *Winston Churchill*

There is no such thing as inevitable war. If war comes it will be from failure of human wisdom. *Bonar Law*

The world will never have lasting peace so long as men reserve for war the finest human qualities. *John Foster Dulles*

War would end if the dead could return. *Stanley Baldwin*

If they want peace, nations should avoid the pinpricks that precede cannon shots. *Napoleon Bonaparte*

Sometime they'll give a war and nobody will come.   *Carl Sandburg*

A man who experiences no genuine satisfaction in life does not want peace. People court war to escape meaninglessness and boredom, to be relieved of fear and frustration.
Nels F. S. Ferre

The object of war is to survive it.   *John Irving*

So far war has been the only force that can discipline a whole community, and until an equivalent discipline is organized, I believe that war must have its way.
William James

Men love war because it allows them to look serious; because it is the only thing that stops women laughing at them.   *John Fowles*

War hath no fury like a non-combatant.   *E. C. Montague*

Most sorts of diversion in men, children and other animals, are in imitation of fighting.
Jonathan Swift

Nothing except a battle lost can be half so melancholy as a battle won.
Duke of Wellington

Human war has been the most successful of all our cultural traditions. *Robert Ardrey*

War is the trade of kings.   *John Dryden*

The whole art of war consists of guessing at what is on the other side of the hill.
Duke of Wellington

It is well that war is so terrible—we would grow too fond of it.   *Robert E. Lee*

Men grow tired of sleep, love, singing and dancing sooner than of war.   *Homer*

Most people coming out of war feel lost and resentful. What had been a minute-to-minute confrontation with yourself, your struggle with what courage you have against discomfort, at the least, and death at the other end, ties you to the people you have known in the war and makes for a time others seem alien and frivolous.
Lillian Hellman

Vice stirs up war; virtue fights.   *Vauvenargues*

In peace, sons bury their fathers; in war, fathers bury their sons.   *Herodotus*

War will exist until that distant day when the conscientious objector enjoys the same reputation and prestige that the warrior does today.   *John F. Kennedy*

The weak against the strong,
Is always in the wrong.   *Ivan Krylov*

But, in case signals can neither be seen or perfectly understood, no captain can do very wrong if he places his ship alongside the enemy. *Horatio Nelson*

Something must be left to chance; nothing is sure in a sea fight beyond all others. *Horatio Nelson*

War is like love, it always finds a way. *Bertolt Brecht*

The guerilla must live amongst the people as the fish lives in the water. *Mao Tse-Tung*

It simply is not true that war never settles anything. *Felix Frankfurter*

War does not determine who is right—only who is left. *Anon.*

There are no atheists in the foxholes. *William Thomas Cummings*

There is many a boy here today who looks on war as all glory, but boys, it is all hell. *William T. Sherman*

There will be no veterans of World War III. *Walter Mondale*

Wealth

He that maketh haste to be rich shall not be innocent. *Proverbs 28:20*

I glory more in the coming purchase of my wealth than in the glad possession. *Ben Jonson*

Ill fares the land, to hastening ills of prey
Where wealth accumulates, and men decay. *Oliver Goldsmith*

It is the wretchedness of being rich that you have to live with rich people. *Logan Pearsall Smith*

One cannot both feast and become rich. *Ashanti proverb*

Poor men seek meat for their stomach, rich men stomach for their meat. *Old saying*

Riches serve a wise man but command a fool. *Old saying*

The first wealth is health. *Ralph Waldo Emerson*

Prosperity is like the tide, being able to flood one shore only by ebbing from another. *Xavier Herbert, 'Capricornia'*

There are few sorrows, however poignant, in which a good income is of no avail. *Logan Pearsall Smith*

The human race has had long experience and a fine tradition in surviving adversity. But we now face a task for which we have little experience, the task of surviving prosperity.   *Alan Gregg*

Riches enlarge, rather than satisfy appetites.   *Thomas Fuller*

Australia is so kind that, just tickle her with a hoe, and she laughs with a harvest.
                                                                Douglas Jerrold

It is better to live rich than to die rich.   *Samuel Johnson*

We can have democracy in this country or we can have great wealth concentrated in the hands of a few, but we can't have both.   *Louis D. Brandeis*

I am opposed to millionaires, but it would be dangerous to offer me the position.
                                                                    Mark Twain

Sleep, riches and health to be truly enjoyed must be interrupted.   *Jean Paul Richter*

The wealth of a nation consists not in its mass of material things, but in its system. The natural resources of South America are not inferior to those of the United States, but the wealth of the two regions is vastly different. The land of India is far richer than that of Japan, but the comparative wealth of the two nations is reversed.
                                                                George Brockway

I have enough money to get by. I'm not independently wealthy, just independently lazy, I suppose.   *Montgomery Clift*

I have no complex about wealth. I have worked hard for my money, producing things people need. I believe that the able industrial leader who creates wealth and employment is more worthy of historical notice than politicians or soldiers.   *Paul Getty*

I was born into it and there was nothing I could do about it. It was there, like air or food, or any other element. The only question with wealth is what you do with it.
                                                                John D. Rockefeller, Jr.

Riches do not consist in the possession of treasures, but in the use made of them.
                                                                Napoleon Bonaparte

I wish to become rich, so that I can instruct the people and glorify honest poverty a little, like those kind-hearted, fat, benevolent people do.   *Mark Twain*

In big houses in which things are done properly, there is always the religious element. The diurnal cycle is observed with more feeling when there are servants to do the work.   *Elizabeth Bowen*

Wickedness and Cruelty

The weakest and most timorous are the most revengeful and implacable.
Thomas Fuller

The springs of fascism will always bubble quietly in the darker earth of human nature.
Peter Ryan

Man is worse than an animal when he is an animal.   *Rabindranath Tagore*

Men are always wicked at bottom unless they are made good by some compulsion.
Niccolo Machiavelli

God bears with the wicked, but not forever.   *Cervantes*

Weak men are apt to be cruel because they stick at nothing that may repair the ill effect of their mistakes.   *George, Lord Halifax*

All cruelty springs from weakness.   *Seneca*

I must be cruel
Only to be kind.   *Shakespeare, 'Hamlet'*

We are oftener treacherous through weakness than through calculation.
La Rochefoucauld

When we do evil,
We and our victims
Are equally bewildered.   *W. H. Auden*

Half of the harm that is done in this world
Is due to people who want to feel important.
They don't mean to do harm—but the harm does not interest them.   *T. S. Eliot*

We all have flaws, and mine is being wicked.   *James Thurber*

Why inflict pain on oneself, when so many others are ready to save us the trouble?
George W. Pacaud

Will and Determination

Men never cling to their dreams with such tenacity as at the moment when they are losing faith in them and know it, but do not dare confess it to themselves.   *Anon.*

Nothing and no one can destroy the Chinese people. They are relentless survivors.
Pearl Buck

Nothing is easy to the unwilling.   *Thomas Fuller*

The greatest intellectual capacities are only found in connection with a vehement and passionate will.   *Arthur Schopenhauer*

The spirit indeed is willing, but the flesh is weak.   *Matthew 26:41*

The difference between perseverance and obstinacy is that one often comes from a strong will, and the other from a strong won't.   *Henry Ward Beecher*

This free-will business is a bit terrifying anyway. It's almost pleasanter to obey, and make the most of it.   *Ugo Betti*

Fall seven times, stand up eight.   *Japanese proverb*

Where the willingness is great, the difficulties cannot be great.   *Niccolo Machiavelli*

The will is the strong blind man who carries on his shoulders the lame man who can see.   *Arthur Schopenhauer*

Obstinacy is the result of the will forcing itself into the place of the intellect.
                                                                 Arthur Schopenhauer

Make voyages. Attempt them. There's nothing else.   *Tennessee Williams*

Do what you can, with what you have, where you are.   *Theodore Roosevelt*

Our strength is often composed of the weakness that we're damned if we are going to show.   *Mignon McLaughlin*

Nothing in the world can take the place of persistence. Talent will not; nothing is more common than unsuccessful men of talent. Genius will not; unrewarded genius is almost a proverb. Education will not; the world is full of educated derelicts. Persistence and determination alone are omnipotent.   *Calvin Coolidge*

All happiness depends on courage and work. I have had many periods of wretchedness, but with energy and above all with illusions, I pulled through them all.
                                                                 Honoré de Balzac

Man is both determined and self-determining.   *Stein and Vidichon*

Don't let your will roar when your power only whispers.   *Thomas Fuller*

Those who live are those who fight.   *Victor Hugo*

If you start to take Vienna—take Vienna.   *Napoleon Bonaparte*

If you would convince others, seem open to conviction yourself.   *Lord Chesterfield*

You have to pay the price—but if you do you can only win.   *Frank Leahy*

Victory—a matter of staying power.   *Elbert Hubbard*

In war, as in life, it is often necessary, when some cherished scheme has failed, to take up the best alternative open, and if so, it is folly not to work for it with all your might.   *Winston Churchill*

A dominant personality doesn't have to believe in its own will. All it needs is the inability to recognise the existence of anybody else's.   *Clive James*

Wisdom and the Wise

A man's ruin lies in his tongue.   *Egyptian saying*

A sage has one advantage; he is immortal. If this is not his century, many others will be.   *Baltasar Gracián*

A wise man always throws himself on the side of his assailants. It is more his interests than it is theirs to find his weak point.   *Ralph Waldo Emerson*

A wise man, to accomplish his end, may even carry his foe on his shoulder.
Panchatantra

Ah, men do not know how much strength is in poise,
That he goes the farthest who goes far enough.   *James Russell Lowell*

I gave my beauty and my youth to men. I am going to give my wisdom and experience to animals.   *Brigitte Bardot*

It wasn't raining when Noah built the ark.   *Howard Ruff*

Knowledge can be communicated but not wisdom.   *Hermann Hesse*

Le raison avant la passion—Reason over passion.   *Pierre Elliott Trudeau*

Let my heart be wise. It is the gods' best gift.   *Euripides*

Never since the time of Copernicus have so many experts been so wrong so often with so little humility.
Anonymous saying at the totally unpredicted collapse of the Berlin Wall

Night is the mother of counsels.   *George Herbert*

Some folks are wise and some are otherwise.   *Tobias Smollett*

The more specific you are, the more general it'll be.   *Diane Arbus*

Wisdom, especially in the initiative stages, is with the minority—indeed, it is generally the thought of a single mind.   *Catherine Helen Spence*

The question of commonsense is always 'what is it good for?'—a question which would abolish the rose and be answered triumphantly by the cabbage.

James Russell Lowell

The tigers of wrath are wiser than the horses of instruction.   *William Blake*

There was only one catch and that was Catch-22, which specified the concern for one's own safety in the face of dangers that were real and immediate was the process of a rational mind.   *Joseph Heller*

Wisdom is always an overmatch for strength.   *Phaedrus*

Wisdom comes alone through suffering.   *Aeschylus*

The road to wisdom? Well, it's plain
And simple to express:
Err
And err
And err again
But less
And less
And less.   *Piet Hein*

A wise man hears one word and understands two.   *Jewish proverb*

The art of being wise is the art of knowing what to overlook.   *William James*

Through wisdom a house is built and through understanding it is established.

Proverbs 24:3

Great men are not always wise.   *Job 32:9*

A wise man gets more use from his enemies than a fool from his friends.

Baltasar Gracián

Who is wise? He that learns from everyone.
Who is powerful? He that governs his passions.
Who is rich? He that is content.
Who is that? Nobody.   *Benjamin Franklin*

Not to know certain things is a great part of wisdom.   *Hugo Grotius*

It is characteristic of wisdom not to do desperate things.   *Henry David Thoreau*

A word to the wise is infuriating.   *Anon.*

The wise only possess ideas; the greater part of mankind are possessed by them.

Samuel Taylor Coleridge

Learning passes for wisdom among those who want both.   *William Temple*

It is not wise to be wiser than is necessary.   *Philippe Quinault*

A wise man sees as much as he ought, not as much as he can.   *Montaigne*

A proverb is one man's wit and all men's wisdom.   *John Russell*

Almost every wise saying has an opposite one, no less wise, to balance it.
George Santayana

We should be careful to get out of an experience only the wisdom that is in it—and stop there, lest we be like the cat that sits down on a hot stovelid. She will never sit down on a hot stove-lid again—and that is well; but also she will never sit down on a cold one anymore.   *Mark Twain*

All human wisdom is summed up in two words—wait and hope.
Alexandre Dumas the Elder

It's taken me all my life to understand that it is not necessary to understand everything.
René Coty

What a man knows at fifty that he did not know at twenty is for the most part incommunicable.   *Adlai Stevenson*

Nine-tenths of wisdom consists in being wise in time.   *Theodore Roosevelt*

Deliberate often—decide once.   *Latin proverb*

Nothing contributes so much to tranquilize the mind as a steady purpose—a point on which the soul may fix its intellectual eye.   *Mary Wollstonecraft Shelley*

Knowledge comes, but wisdom lingers.   *Alfred, Lord Tennyson*

In much wisdom is much grief: and he that increaseth knowledge increaseth sorrow.
Ecclesiastes 1:18

I prefer the errors of enthusiasm to the indifference of wisdom.   *Anatole France*

The wise have a solid sense of silence and the ability to keep a storehouse of secrets Their capacity and character are respected.   *Baltasar Graciár*

My father used to say: Son, if you are not bright, you've got to be methodical (Defusing argument when challenged and proved right.)   *Robert Sachs*

Everyone whose deeds are more than his wisdom, his wisdom endures. And everyone whose wisdom is more than his deeds, his wisdom does not endure.   *The Talmud*

Wit

If the camel once gets his nose in a tent, his body will soon follow.

Saudi Arabian proverb

If you laid every economist in the country end to end you would still not reach a conclusion.   *Salvadore Nasello*

Irrevocable as a haircut.   *Lynwood L. Giacomini*

If it's me against 48, I feel sorry for the 48.

Margaret Thatcher (when out-voted at a world conference)

Men never think their fortunes too great, nor their wit too little.   *Thomas Fuller*

The banalities of a great man pass for wit.   *Alexander Chase*

The wit makes fun of other persons; the satirist makes fun of the world; the humorist makes fun of himself.   *James Thurber*

When I appear in public people expect me to neigh, grind my teeth, paw the ground and swish my tail—none of which is easy.   *Princess Anne*

Wit consists in knowing the resemblance of things which differ and the difference of things which are alike.   *Madame de Staël*

Melancholy men are of all others the most witty.   *Aristotle*

If you want to be witty, work on your character and say what you think on every occasion.   *Stendhal*

The well of true wit is truth itself.   *George Meredith*

What is perfectly true is perfectly witty.   *La Rochefoucauld*

Wit is the sudden marriage of ideas which, before their union, were not perceived to have any relation.   *Mark Twain*

True wit is Nature to advantage dress'd
What oft was thought, but ne'er so well express'd.   *Alexander Pope*

A man often runs the risk of throwing away a witticism if he admits that it is his own.

Jean de la Bruyère

Wit is the epitaph of an emotion.   *Friedrich Nietzsche*

Wit has truth in it; wisecracking is simply calisthenics with words.   *Dorothy Parker*

Wit is far more often a shield than a lance.   *Anon.*

What is an epigram? A dwarfish whole,
Its body brevity, and wit its soul.   *Samuel Taylor Coleridge*

Brevity is the soul of wit.   *Shakespeare, 'Hamlet'*

Belief in form, but disbelief in content—that's what makes an aphorism charming.
Friedrich Nietzsche

Women

A woman is as old as she looks before breakfast.   *Edgar Watson Howe*

A woman's strength is the irresistible might of weakness.   *Ralph Waldo Emerson*

A woman, the more careful she is about her face, is commonly the more careless about
her house.   *Ben Jonson*

Feminism is the most revolutionary idea there has ever been. Equality for women
demands a change in the human psyche, more profound than anything Marx dreamed
of. It means valuing parenthood as much as we value banking.   *Polly Toynbee*

From birth to 18 a girl needs good parents. From 18 to 35, she needs good looks.
From 35 to 55, good personality. From 55 on, she needs good cash. I'm saving my
money.   *Sophie Tucker*

I've got a woman's ability to stick to a job and get on with it when everyone else
walks off and leaves it.   *Margaret Thatcher*

In the sex-war, thoughtlessness is a weapon of the male, vindictiveness of the female.
Both are reciprocally generated, but a woman's desire for revenge outlasts all other
emotion. Yet when every unkind word about women has been said, we have still to
admit, with Byron, that they are nicer than men. They are more devoted, more unselfish
and more emotionally sincere. When the long fuse of cruelty, deceit and revenge is
set alight, it is male thoughtlessness which has fired it.   *Cyril Connolly*

No woman marries for money; they are all clever enough, before marrying a millionaire, to fall in love with him first.   *Cesare Pavese*

People call me a feminist whenever I express sentiments that differentiate me from a
doormat or a prostitute.   *Rebecca West*

The battle for women's rights has been largely won.   *Margaret Thatcher*

The great and almost only comfort about being a woman is that one can always pretend
to be more stupid than one is and no one is surprised.   *Freya Stark*

The great question which I have not been able to answer, despite my 30 years of
research into the feminine soul, is 'what does a woman want'?   *Sigmund Freud*

There is in every true woman's heart a spark of heavenly fire, which lies dormant in the broad daylight of prosperity, but which kindles up and beams and blazes in the dark hour of adversity.
Washington Irving

Time and trouble will tame an advanced young woman. But an advanced old woman is uncontrollable by any force.
Dorothy L. Sayers

We don't love a woman for what she says, but we like what she says because we love her.
André Maurois

What one beholds of a woman is the least part of her.
Ovid

Where young boys plan for what they will achieve and attain, young girls plan for whom they will achieve and attain.
Charlotte Perkins

Women can do everything; men can do the rest.
Russian proverb

Have you any notion how many books are written about women in the course of one year? Have you any notion how many are written by men? Are you aware that you are, perhaps, the most discussed animal in the universe?
Virginia Woolf

A woman is the only thing I am afraid of that I know will not hurt me.
Abraham Lincoln

The most popular image of the female despite the exigencies of the clothing trade is all boobs and buttocks, a hallucinating sequence of parabolae and bulges.
Germaine Greer

A woman never sees what we do for her, she only sees what we don't do.
Georges Courteline

You have to go back to the Children's Crusade in 1212 AD to find as unfortunate and fatuous an attempt at manipulated hysteria as the Women's Liberation Movement.
Helen Lawrenson

A woman is always buying something.
Ovid

Educating a beautiful woman is like pouring honey into a fine Swiss watch: everything stops.
Kurt Vonnegut

By nice women . . . you probably mean selfish women who have no more thought for the underprivileged, overworked women than a pussycat in a sunny window for the starving kitten in the street. Now in that sense I am not a nice woman, for I do care.
Nellie McClung

A kiss can be a comma, a question mark or an exclamation point. That's a basic spelling that every woman should know.
Mistinguett

A beautiful woman who is pleasing to men is good only for frightening fish when she falls into the water.
Zen proverb

Whether women are better than men I cannot say—but I can say they are certainly no worse.
Golda Meir

Of my two 'handicaps', being female put many more obstacles in my path than being black.
Shirley Chisholm

The toughest thing about being a housewife is you have no place to stay home from.
Patricia C. Beudoin

The economic dependence of women is perhaps the greatest injustice that has been done to us, and has worked the greatest injury to the race.
Nellie McClung

Whatever women do they must do twice as well as men to be thought half as good. Luckily, this is not difficult.
Charlotte Whitton

All women's dresses are merely variations on the eternal struggle between the admitted desire to dress and the unadmitted desire to undress.
Lin Yutang

If you can make a woman laugh you can do anything with her.
Nicol Williamson

Woman is at once apple and serpent.
Heinrich Heine

The more underdeveloped the country, the more overdeveloped the women.
J. K. Galbraith

One is not born a woman—one becomes one.
Simone de Beauvoir

Nature says to a woman: 'Be beautiful if you can, wise if you want to, but be respected, that is essential.'
Beaumarchais

A modest woman, dressed out in all her finery, is the most tremendous object of the whole creation.
Oliver Goldsmith

No country can advance unless its women advance.
Maie Casey

You don't know a woman until you have had a letter from her.
Ada Levenson

Housework is what woman does that nobody notices unless she hasn't done it.
Evan Esar

If the women's movement can be summed up in a single phrase, it is 'the right to choose'.
Beatrice Faust

The woman who thinks she is intelligent demands equal rights with men. A woman who is intelligent does not.
Colette

Most women still need a room of their own and the only way to find it may be outside their own home.
Germaine Greer

Women are the true maintenance class. Society is built upon their acquiescence and upon their small and necessary labours.
Sally Kempton

It is hard to fight an enemy who has outposts in your head.   *Sally Kempton*

A woman past forty should make up her mind to be young—not her face.
Billie Burke

There is nothing enduring in life for a woman except what she builds in a man's heart.
Judith Anderson

I know the nature of women;
When you want to, they don't want to;
And when you don't want to, they desire exceedingly.   *Terence*

Convent girls never leave the Church, they just become feminists. I learned that in Australia.   *Blanche d'Alpuget*

My vigour, vitality and cheek repel me. I am the kind of woman I would run from.
Nancy, Lady Astor

I have met with women who I really think would like to be married to a poem, and to be given away by a novel.   *John Keats*

A beautiful woman should break her mirror early.   *Baltasar Gracián*

Age cannot wither her, nor custom stale her infinite variety; other women cloy the appetites they feed, but she makes hungry where most she satisfies.
Shakespeare, 'Antony and Cleopatra'

I don't know of anything better than a woman if you want to spend money where it will show.   *Kin Hubbard*

In our civilization men are afraid they will not be men enough, and women are afraid they might be considered only women.   *Theodor Reik*

It takes all the fun out of a bracelet if you have to buy it yourself.   *Peggy Joyce*

The cave-dweller's wife complained that he hadn't dragged her anywhere in months.
Laurence J. Peter

There is but an hour a day between a good housewife and a bad one.
English proverb

If a woman likes another woman, she's cordial. If she doesn't like her, she's very cordial.   *Irvin S. Cobb*

Next to the wound, what women make best is the bandage.   *Barbey d'Aurevilly*

Social science affirms that a woman's place in society marks the level of civilization.
Elizabeth Cady Stanton

Nobody objects to a woman being a good writer or sculptor or geneticist if at the same time she manages to be a good wife, good mother, good looking, good tempered, well groomed and unaggressive.   *Leslie M. McIntyre*

When thou goest to woman, take thy whip.   *Friedrich Nietzsche*

It was a woman who drove me to drink—and, you know, I never even thanked her.
                                                                        W. C. Fields

If I had my way, I would put them all behind bras.
                    Chief Justice Sir Leslie Herron, on women's liberation

Each suburban housewife spends her time presiding over a power plant sufficient to have staffed the palace of a Roman emperor with a hundred slaves. *Margaret Mead*

Boys don't make passes at female smart-asses.   *Letty Cottin Pogrebin*

As a woman, to be competitive is to be passive.   *Marianne Partridge*

Women are like elephants. They are interesting to look at, but I wouldn't like to own one.   *W. C. Fields*

No woman can call herself free who does not own and control her body. No woman can call herself free until she can choose consciously whether she will or will not be a mother.   *Margaret Sanger*

Women are most adorable when they are afraid; that's why they frighten so easily.
                                                                        Ludwig Borne

Can we today measure devotion to husband and children by our indifference to everything else?   *Golda Meir*

Women are perfectly well aware that the more they seem to obey the more they rule.
                                                                        Jules Michelet

Some women blush when they are kissed; some call for the police; some swear; some bite. But the worst are those who laugh.   *Anon.*

What will not woman, gentle woman dare
When strong affection stirs her spirit up?   *Robert Southey*

Women keep a special corner of their hearts for sins they have never committed.
                                                                    Cornelia Otis Skinner

Nature is in earnest when she makes a woman.   *Oliver Wendell Holmes*

The only question left to be settled now is, are women persons? *Susan B. Anthony*

Women do not find it difficult nowadays to behave like men, but they often find it extremely difficult to behave like gentlemen.   *Compton Mackenzie*

In various stages of her life, a woman resembles the continents of the world. From 13 to 18, she's like Africa—virgin territory, unexplored; from 18 to 30, she's like Asia—hot and exotic; from 30 to 45, she's like America—fully explored and free with her resources; from 45 to 55, she's like Europe—exhausted, but not without places of interest; after 55, she's like Australia—everybody knows it's down there but nobody much cares.   *Al Boliska*

When a woman dresses up for an occasion, the man should become the black velvet pillow for the jewel.   *John Weitz*

Woman's place is in the wrong.   *James Thurber*

There are no ugly women, only lazy ones.   *Helena Rubenstein*

A woman without a man is like a fish without a bicycle.   *Gloria Steinem*

I dress for women—and I undress for men.   *Angie Dickinson*

The average girl would rather have beauty than brains because she knows the average man can see much better than he can think.   *Ladies' Home Journal*

She was not a woman likely to settle for equality when sex gave her an advantage.
                                                                              Anthony Delano

Whether they give or refuse, women are glad to have been asked.   *Ovid*

One can find women who have never had a love affair, but it is rare indeed to find any who have had only one.   *La Rochefoucauld*

The mirror is the conscience of women; they never do a thing without first consulting it.   *Moritz G. Saphir*

Simpson succeeded in proving that there was no harm in giving anaesthetics to men, because God put Adam into a deep sleep when He extracted his rib. But male ecclesiastics remained unconvinced as regards the sufferings of women, at any rate in childbirth.   *Bertrand Russell*

The cleverest woman finds a need for foolish admirers.   *Anon.*

Women who set a low value on themselves make life hard for all women.
                                                                              Nellie McClung

Women have simple tastes. They get pleasure out of the conversation of children in arms and men in love.   *H. L. Mencken*

Women are the cowards they are because they have been semi-slaves for so long. The number of women prepared to stand up for what they really think, feel, experience, with a man they are in love with is still very small.   *Doris Lessing*

Woman's normal occupations in general run counter to creative life, or contemplative life, or saintly life.   *Anne Morrow Lindbergh*

Men know that women are an overmatch for them, and therefore they choose the weakest or the most ignorant. If they did not think so, they never could be afraid of women knowing as much as themselves.   *Samuel Johnson*

If woman had no existence save in the fiction written by men, one would imagine her a person of the utmost importance; very various; heroic and mean; splendid and sordid; infinitely beautiful and hideous in the extreme; as great as a man, some think even better.   *Virginia Woolf*

No man is as anti-feminist as a really feminine woman.   *Frank O'Connor*

The ideal woman which is in every man's mind is evoked by a word or phrase or the shape of her wrist, her hand. The most beautiful description of a woman is by understatement. Remember, all Tolstoy ever said to describe Anna Karenina was that she was beautiful and could see in the dark like a cat. Every man has a different idea of what's beautiful, and it's best to take the gesture, the shadow of the branch, and let the mind create the tree.   *William Faulkner*

Words and Language

Words are far worse than drugs; there is no hope of surfeit or remorse.
                                                                Gwen Harwood

A word is not the same with one writer as with another. One tears it from his guts. The other pulls it out of his overcoat pocket.   *Charles Péguy*

Language is the Rubicon that divides man from beast.   *Max Müller*

Dialect words—those terrible marks of the beast to the truly genteel. *Thomas Hardy*

Eloquence is the language of nature, and cannot be learned in the schools; but rhetoric is the creature of art, which he who feels least will most excel in.
                                                          Charles Caleb Colton

For words, like Nature, half reveal
And half conceal the Soul within.   *Alfred Lord Tennyson*

He multiplieth words without knowledge.   *Job 35:16*

If you were to make little fishes talk, they would talk like whales. *Oliver Goldsmith*

In the beginning was the Word and the Word was with God, and the Word was God.
                                                                John 1:1

Languages are the pedigree of nations.   *Samuel Johnson*

Let thy speech be short, comprehending much in few words.   *Ecclesiasticus*

Letter-writing is the only device for combining solitude with good company.

Lord Byron

Man is a creature who lives not upon bread alone, but principally by catch words.

Robert Louis Stevenson

Many terms which have now dropped out of favour will be revived, and those that are at present respectable, will drop out, if useage so choose with whom resides the decision and the judgment and the code of speech.   *Horace*

Numbers constitute the only universal language.   *Nathanael West*

Soft words are hard arguments.   *Thomas Fuller*

Thanks to words, we have been able to rise above the brutes; and thanks to words, we have often sunk to the level of the demons.   *Aldous Huxley*

The adjective is the banana peel of the parts of speech.   *Clifton Fadiman*

The limits of my language are the limits of my mind. All I know is what I have words for.   *Ludwig Wittgenstein*

The art of translation lies less in knowing the other language than in knowing your own.   *Ned Rorem*

The two most beautiful words in the English language are 'cheque enclosed'.

Dorothy Parker

The medium is the message.   *Marshall McLuhan*

The stroke of the whip maketh marks in the flesh; but the stroke of the tongue breaketh the bones. Many have fallen by the edge of the sword; but not so many as have fallen by the tongue.   *Ecclesiasticus*

The thoughtless are rarely wordless.   *Howard W. Newton*

We must have a better word than 'prefabricated', why not 'ready-made'?

Winston Churchill

We must think things not words, or at least we must constantly translate our words into the facts for which they stand, if we are to keep to the real and the true.

Oliver Wendell Holmes

Words are the small change of thought.   *Jules Renard*

Words should be weighed and not counted.   *Yiddish proverb*

Since the concepts people live by are derived only from perceptions and from language and since the perceptions are received and interpreted only in light of earlier concepts, man comes pretty close to living in a house that language built. *Russell R. W. Smith*

If a conceptual distinction is to be made, the machinery for making it ought to show itself in language. If a distinction cannot be made in language, it cannot be made conceptually.

N. R. Hanson

Often I am struck in amazement about a word: I suddenly realize that the complete arbitrariness of our language is but a part of the arbitrariness of our own world in general.

Christian Morgenstern

Understanding is nothing else than conception caused by speech.   *Thomas Hobbes*

Language is to the mind more than light is to the eye.   *William Gibson*

Who does not know another language, does not know his own.   *Goethe*

To me, the term 'middle-class' connotes a safe, comfortable, middle-of-the road policy. Above all, our language is 'middle-class' in the middle of our road. To drive it to one side or the other or even off the road, is the noblest task of the future.

Christian Morgenstern

Similes are like songs of love:
They much describe, they nothing prove.

Matthew Prior

Words are the physicians of a mind diseased.   *Aeschylus*

A language is a dialect with its own army and navy.   *Max Weinreich*

'When I use a word,' Humpty Dumpty said in rather a scornful tone, 'it means just what I choose it to mean—neither more nor less.'
'The question is,' said Alice, 'whether you can make words mean so many different things.'
'The question is,' said Humpty Dumpty, 'which is to be master—that's all.'

Lewis Carroll

The word is half his that speaks, and half his that hears it.   *Montaigne*

A single word often betrays a great design.   *Jean Baptiste Racine*

Words once spoken, can never be recalled.   *Wentworth Dillon*

Some words are like the old Roman galleys; large-scaled and ponderous. They sit low in the water even when their cargo is light.   *William Jovanovich*

It's as interesting and as difficult to say a thing well as to paint it. There is the art of lines and colours, but the art of words exists too, and will never be less important.

Vincent van Gogh

The difference between the right word and the almost right word is the difference between lightning and the lightning bug.   *Mark Twain*

Words, like eyeglasses, blur everything that they do not make clear.   *Joseph Joubert*

There is only one way to degrade mankind permanently and that is to destroy language.
Northrop Frye

The limits of my language mean the limits of my world.   *Ludwig Wittgenstein*

More than kisses, letters mingle souls.   *John Donne*

To have another language is to possess a second soul.   *Charlemagne*

I wonder what language truck drivers are using, now that everyone is using theirs?
Beryl Pfizer

The two words 'information' and 'communication' are often used interchangeably, but they signify quite different things. Information is giving out; communication is getting through.   *Sydney J. Harris*

England and America are two countries separated by the same language.
George Bernard Shaw

The Englishman loves to roll his tongue around the word, 'extraordinary'. It so pleases him that he is reluctant to finish the sound which goes on into harmonics and overtones. The North American publisher is likewise inclined.   *R. I. Fitzhenry*

Words are feminine; deeds are masculine.   *Baltasar Gracián*

Let it not be said that I have said nothing new. The arrangement of the material is new.   *Blaise Pascal*

When an idea is wanting, a word can always be found to take its place.   *Goethe*

Speech is civilization itself. The word, even the most contradictory word, preserves contact—it is silence which isolates.   *Thomas Mann*

In certain trying circumstances, urgent circumstances, desperate circumstances, profanity furnishes a relief denied even to prayer.   *Mark Twain*

Like stones, words are laborious and unforgiving, and the fitting of them together, like the fitting of stones, demands great patience and strength of purpose and particular skill.   *Edmund Morrison*

Great literature is simply language charged with meaning to the utmost possible degree.
Ezra Pound

One way of looking at speech is to say it is a constant stratagem to cover nakedness.
Harold Pinter

The downtrodden, who are the great creators of slang, hurl pithiness and colour at poverty and oppression.   *Anthony Burgess*

Slang is language which takes off its coat, spits on its hands—and goes to work.
Carl Sandburg

Man's command of the language is most important. Next to kissing, it's the most exciting form of communication.   *Oren Arnold*

'Plain English'—everybody loves it, demands it—from the other fellow.
                                                                Jacques Barzun

Words are as recalcitrant as circus animals, and the unskilled trainer can crack his whip at them in vain.   *Gerald Brenan*

The magic of the tongue is the most dangerous of all spells. *Edward Bulwer-Lytton*

A word after a word after a word is power.   *Margaret Atwood*

You have to fall in love with hanging around words.   *John Ciardi*

Language is the armoury of the human mind; and at once contains the trophies of its past, and the weapons of its future conquests.   *Samuel Taylor Coleridge*

Everyone hears only what he understands.   *Goethe*

When I feel inclined to read poetry, I take down my dictionary. The poetry of words is quite as beautiful as the poetry of sentences.   *Oliver Wendell Holmes*

Language most shows a man; speak that I may see thee.   *Ben Jonson*

True eloquence consists of saying all that should be, not all that could be, said.
                                                            La Rochefoucauld

Even if language is a living evolving organism, we don't have to embrace all the changes that occur during our lifetimes. If language is so alive, it can get sick.
                                                    Christopher Lehmann-Haupt

Our language, one of our most precious natural resources, deserves at least as much protection as our woodlands, streams and whooping cranes.   *James Lipton*

His words were softer than oil, yet they were drawn swords.   *Psalms 55:21*

Language is an inventory of human experience.   *L. W. Lockhart*

Change is legitimate and inevitable, for our language is a mighty river, picking up silt and flotsam here and discarding it there, but growing ever wider and richer.
                                                            Robert MacNeil

The grossest thing in our gross national product today is our language. It is suffering from inflation.   *James Reston*

A word has its use,
Or, like a man, it will soon have a grave.   *Edward Arlington Robinson*

No matter how eloquently a dog may bark, he cannot tell you that his parents were poor but honest.   *Bertrand Russell*

Most people have to talk so they won't hear. *May Sarton*

Every utterance is an event, and no two events are precisely alike. The extreme view, therefore, is that no word ever means the same thing twice. *Louis B. Saloman*

It is with words as with sunbeams. The more they are condensed, the deeper they burn. *Robert Southey*

If you can teach me a new word, I'll walk all the way to China to get it. *Turkish proverb*

I have always suspected that correctness is the last refuge of those who have nothing to say. *Friedrich Wasiman*

Work

By working faithfully eight hours a day you may eventually get to be a boss and work 12 hours a day. *Robert Frost*

Everything considered, work is less boring than amusing oneself. *Charles Baudelaire*

A windmill is eternally at work to accomplish one end, although it shifts with every variation of the weather cock, and assumes 10 different positions in a day. *Charles Caleb Colton*

A good horse should be seldom spurred. *Thomas Fuller*

All work is seed sown. It grows and spreads, and sows itself anew. *Thomas Carlyle*

Chop your own wood and it will warm you twice.
(Carved on the cypress wood mantel in Henry Ford's home, Fairlane)

Give the labourer his wage before his perspiration be dry. *Muhammad*

The worst thing about work in the house or the home is that whatever you do, it is destroyed, laid waste or eaten within 24 hours. *Alexandra Hasluck*

If you want a work well done, select a busy man: the other kind has no time. *Elbert Hubbard*

Most people work the greater part of their time for a mere living; and the little freedom which remains to them so troubles them that they use every means of getting rid of it. *Goethe*

No fine work can be done without concentration and self-sacrifice and toil and doubt. *Max Beerbohm*

No task, rightly done, is truly private. It is part of the world's work. *Woodrow Wilson*

One machine can do the work of 50 ordinary men. No machine can do the work of one extraordinary man.   *Anon.*

One of the saddest things is, the only thing a man can do for 8 hours a day, day after day, is work. You can't eat 8 hours a day nor drink for 8 hours a day, nor make love for 8 hours.   *William Faulkner*

The only place where success comes before work is a dictionary.   *Vidal Sassoon*

Routine is the god of every social system; it is the seventh heaven of business, the essential component in the success of every factory, the ideal of every statesman.
Alfred North Whitehead

The monarchy is a labour-intensive industry.   *Harold Wilson*

The test of a vocation is the love of the drudgery it involves. *Logan Pearsall Smith*

They say hard work never hurt anybody, but I figure why take the chance.
Ronald Reagan

Unionism, seldom if ever, uses such powers as it has to ensure better work; almost always it devotes a large part of that power to safeguarding bad work.
H. L. Mencken

Work is of two kinds: first, altering a position of matter at or near the earth's surface relatively to other such matter; second, telling other people to do so. The first kind is unpleasant and ill-paid; the second is pleasant and highly paid.   *Bertrand Russell*

As a remedy against all ills—poverty, sickness, and melancholy—only one thing is absolutely necessary: a liking for work.   *Charles Baudelaire*

They intoxicate themselves with work so they won't see how they really are.
Aldous Huxley

Most people like hard work, particularly when they're paying for it.
Franklin P. Jones

We work to become, not to acquire.   *Elbert Hubbard*

If one defines the term 'dropout' to mean a person who has given up serious effort to meet his responsibilities, then every business office, government agency, golf club and university faculty would yield its quota.   *John W. Gardner*

Hasten slowly, and without losing heart, put your work twenty times upon the anvil.
Nicolas Boileau

How many years of fatigue and punishment it takes to learn the simple truth that work, that disagreeable thing, is the only way of not suffering in life, or at all events, of suffering less.   *Charles Baudelaire*

Miracles sometimes occur, but one has to work terribly hard for them.

Chaim Weizmann

Beware all enterprises that require new clothes.   *Henry David Thoreau*

Employment is nature's physician, and is essential to human happiness.   *Galen*

Work is the grand cure of all the maladies and miseries that ever beset mankind.

Thomas Carlyle

The secret of being miserable is to have leisure to bother about whether you are happy
or not. The cure for it is occupation.   *George Bernard Shaw*

Chance favours only those who know how to court her.   *Charles Nicolle*

Work is man's most natural form of relaxation.   *Dagobert Runes*

Work is not man's punishment. It is his reward and his strength, his glory and his
pleasure.   *George Sand*

If a man loves the labour of his trade, apart from any question of success or fame,
the gods have called him.   *Robert Louis Stevenson*

When white-collar people get jobs, they sell not only their time and energy, but their
personalities as well. They sell by week, or month, their smiles and their kindly
gestures, and they must practise prompt repression of resentment and aggression.

C. Wright Mills

He that can work is a born king of something.   *Thomas Carlyle*

Love of bustle is not industry.   *Seneca*

The joy about our work is spoiled when we perform it not because of what we produce
but because of the pleasure with which it can provide us, or the pain against which it
can protect us.   *Paul Tillich*

Productive work is the central purpose of a rational man's life, the central value that
integrates and determines the hierarchy of all his other values. Reason is the source,
the precondition of his productive work—pride is the result.   *Ayn Rand*

By the work one knows the workman.   *Jean de la Fontaine*

Because it is less structured than work, leisure time leaves workaholics at a loss for
what to do. Workaholics practically climb the wall when they can't work.

Marilyn Machlowitz

Workaholics commit slow suicide by refusing to allow the child inside them to play.

Dr. Laurence Susser

Man works primarily for his own self-respect and not for others or for profit . . . the person who is working for the sake of his own satisfaction, the money he gets in return serves merely as fuel, that is, as a symbol of reward and recognition, in the last analysis, of acceptance by one's fellowmen.   *Otto Rank*

In a professional once engaged, the performance of the job comes first.
                                                                                  Garson Kanin

If a little labour, little are our gains.
Man's fortunes are according to his pains.   *Robert Herrick*

Work is the curse of the drinking classes.   *Oscar Wilde*

A man must love a thing very much if he not only practises it without any hope of fame and money, but even practises it without any hope of doing it well.
                                                                              G. K. Chesterton

A hobby is hard work you wouldn't do for a living.   *Anon.*

A task becomes a duty from the moment you suspect it to be an essential part of that integrity which alone entitles a man to assume responsibility.   *Dag Hammarskjöld*

God gave man work, not to burden him, but to bless him, and useful work, willingly, cheerfully, effectively done, has always been the finest expression of the human spirit.
                                                                          Walter R. Courtenay

Work is more fun than fun.   *Noel Coward*

When more and more people are thrown out of work, unemployment results.
                                                                              Calvin Coolidge

Man's usual routine is to work and to dream and work and dream.
                                                                            Raymond Queneau

We can redeem anyone who strives unceasingly.   *Goethe*

The Gods rank work above virtues.   *Hesiod*

Anyone can do any amount of work provided it isn't the work he is supposed to be doing at that moment.   *Robert Benchley*

It is not upon thee to finish the work; neither art thou free to abstain from it.
                                                                              The Talmud

Work banishes those three great evils, boredom, vice, and poverty.   *Voltaire*

Amateurs hope. Professionals work.   *Garson Kanin*

Work is love made visible. And if you cannot work with love but only with distaste, it is better that you should leave your work and sit at the gate of the temple and take alms of those who work with joy.   *Kahlil Gibran*

There is dignity in work only when it is work freely accepted.   *Albert Camus*

If a man will not work, he shall not eat.   *2 Thessalonians 3:10*

Anyone who is honestly seeking a job and can't find it, deserves the attention of the United States government, and the people.   *John F. Kennedy*

Work is the inevitable condition of human life, the true source of human welfare.
Leo Tolstoy

He who shuns the millstone, shuns the meal.   *Erasmus*

Rest is the sweet sauce of labour.   *Plutarch*

God gives every bird its food, but he does not throw it into the nest.   *J. G. Holland*

When your work speaks for itself, don't interrupt.   *Henry J. Kaiser*

I work as my father drank.   *George Bernard Shaw*

While I am busy with little things, I am not required to do greater things.
St. Francis de Sales

For it is commonly said: accomplished labours are pleasant.   *Cicero*

A people so primitive that they did not know how to get money except by working for it.   *George Ade*

Work expands so as to fill the time available for its completion.
C. Northcote Parkinson

If all the year were playing holidays
To sport would be as tedious as to work.   *Shakespeare, 'Henry IV' Part I*

I am only an average man, but, by George, I work harder at it than the average man.
Theodore Roosevelt

Work is accomplished by those employees who have not yet reached their level of incompetence.   *Laurence J. Peter*

When I was a young man I observed that nine out of ten things I did were failures. I didn't want to be a failure, so I did ten times more work.   *George Bernard Shaw*

The worst crime against working people is a company which fails to operate at a profit.
Samuel Gompers

How do I work? I grope.   *Albert Einstein*

It is the privilege of any human work which is well done to invest the doer with a certain haughtiness. He can well afford not to conciliate, whose faithful work will answer for him.   *Ralph Waldo Emerson*

Work and love—these are the basics. Without them there is neurosis.   *Theodor Reik*

The effectiveness of work increases according to geometric progression if there are no interruptions.   *André Maurois*

Writers and Writing

The art of writing is the art of discovering what you believe.   *David Hare*

I keep six honest serving men. (They taught me all I know);
Their names are What and Why and When and How and Where and Who.
Rudyard Kipling

Agatha Christie has given more pleasure in bed than any other woman.
Nancy Banks-Smith

An original writer is not one who imitates nobody, but one whom nobody can imitate
de Chateaubriand

Autobiography is a preemptive strike against biographers.   *Barbara G. Harris*

You need a skin as thin as a cigarette paper to write a novel and the hide of an elephant to publish it.   *Frank Dalby Davison*

Dr. Johnson's sayings would not appear so extraordinary were it not for his bow-wow way.   *Henry Herbert*

Every other author may aspire to praise; the lexicographer can only hope to escape reproach.   *Samuel Johnson*

I am being frank about myself in this book. I tell of my first mistake on page 850.
Henry Kissinger

I am not learning definitions as established in even the latest dictionaries. I am not a dictionary-maker. I am a person a dictionary-maker has to contend with. I am a living evidence in the development of language.   *William Stafford*

I have this feeling of wending my way or plundering through a mysterious jungle of possibilities when I am writing. This jungle has not been explored by previous writers. It never will be explored. It's endlessly varying as we progress through the experience of time. These words that occur to me come out of my relation to the language which is developing even as I am using it.   *William Stafford*

I have tried lately to read Shakespeare, and found it so intolerably dull that it nauseated me.   *Charles Darwin*

In Ireland, a writer is looked upon as a failed conversationalist.   *Anon.*

It is a sad fact about our culture that a poet can earn much more money writing or talking about his art than he can by practising it.   *W. H. Auden*

Make 'em laugh; make 'em cry; make 'em wait.   *Charles Reade*

Many a fervid man writes books as cold and flat as graveyard stones.
Elizabeth Barrett Browning

Memoirs: the backstairs of history.   *George Meredith*

No tears and the writer, no tears and the reader.   *Robert Frost*

The pen is mightier than the sword.   *Edward Bulwer-Lytton*

The work of Henry James has always seemed divisible by a simple dynastic arrangement into three reigns: James 1st, James 2nd, and the Old Pretender.
Philip Guedalla

There are three difficulties in authorship: to write anything worth the publishing, to find honest men to publish it, and to get sensible men to read it.   *C. C. Colton*

This morning I took out a comma and this afternoon I put it back again.
Oscar Wilde

Thought flies and words go on foot.   *Julien Green*

To write is to become disinterested. There is a certain renunciation in art.
Albert Camus

What I like in a good author is not what he says, but what he whispers.
Logan Pearsall Smith

When my journal appears, many statues must come down.   *Duke of Wellington*

Writers aren't exactly people, they're a whole lot of people trying to be one person.
F. Scott Fitzgerald

Writing is not a profession but a vocation of unhappiness.   *Georges Simenon*

Writing is one of the easiest things: erasing is one of the hardest.
Rabbi Israel Salanter

Writing is turning one's worst moments into money.   *J. P. Donleavy*

You cannot write in the chimney with charcoal.   *Russian proverb*

The truth is, we've not really developed a fiction that can accommodate the full tumult, the zaniness and crazed quality of modern experience.   *Saul Bellow*

Take care of the sense and the sounds will take of care themselves.   *Lewis Carroll*

There is today an extraordinary interest with the data of modern experience per se. Our absorption in our contemporary historical state is very high right now. It's not altogether unlike a similar situation in seventeenth century Holland, where wealthy merchants wanted their portraits done with all their blemishes included. It is the height of egotism, in a sense, to think even one's blemishes are of significance. So today Americans seem to want their writers to reveal all their weaknesses, their meannesses, to celebrate their very confusions. And they want it in the most direct possible way—they want it served up neat, as it were, without the filtering and generalizing power of fiction.   *Saul Bellow*

I can write better than anyone who can write faster, and I can write faster than anyone who can write better.   *A. J. Liebling*

Writing: I certainly do rewrite my central myth in every book, and would never read or trust any writer who did not also do so.   *Northrop Frye*

Every human being has hundreds of separate people living under his skin. The talent of a writer is his ability to give them their separate names, identities, personalities and have them relate to other characters living with him.   *Mel Brooks*

There is one last thing to remember: writers are always selling somebody out.
                                                                    Joan Didion

The writer must write what he has to say, not speak it.   *Ernest Hemingway*

Writers should be read—but neither seen nor heard.   *Daphne du Maurier*

A person who publishes a book appears willfully in public with his pants down.
                                                          Edna St. Vincent Millay

The beginning is easy; what happens next is much harder.   *Anon.*

There should be two main objectives in ordinary prose writing: to convey a message and to include in it nothing that will distract the reader's attention or check his habitual pace of reading—he should feel that he is seated at ease in a taxi, not riding a temperamental horse through traffic.   *Robert Graves and Allan Hodge*

A story is never an accurate translation of life, it is always larger than life, so never spoil a good one for the sake of truth.   *Alan Marshall*

The writer is committed when he plunges to the very depths of himself with the intent to disclose, not his individuality, but his person in the complex society that conditions and supports him.   *Jean-Paul Sartre*

I struggled in the beginning. I said I was going to write the truth, so help me God. And I thought I was. I found I couldn't. Nobody can write the absolute truth.
                                                                    Henry Miller

For a dyed-in-the-wool author nothing is as dead as a book once it is written . . . she is rather like a cat whose kittens have grown up. While they were a-growing she was passionately interested in them but now they seem hardly to belong to her—and probably she is involved with another batch of kittens as I am involved with other writing.   *Rumer Godden*

Every author, however modest, keeps a most outrageous vanity chained like a madman in the padded cell of his breast.   *Logan Pearsall Smith*

Never believe anything a writer tells you about himself. A man comes to believe in the end the lies he tells himself about himself.   *George Bernard Shaw*

I am always at a loss to know how much to believe of my own stories.
   Washington Irving

That's not writing, that's typing.   *Truman Capote (on Jack Kerouac)*

There is an accuracy that defeats itself by the overemphasis of details. I often say that one must permit oneself, and quite advisedly and deliberately, a certain margin of misstatement.   *Benjamin N. Cardozo*

I suppose some editors are failed writers—but so are most writers.   *T. S. Eliot*

I think with my right hand.   *Edmund Wilson*

Writers are the engineers of human souls.   *Joseph Stalin*

I quote others in order to better express my own self.   *Montaigne*

A great many people now reading and writing would be better employed in keeping rabbits.   *Edith Sitwell*

The process of writing a book is infinitely more important than the book that is completed as a result of the writing, let alone the success or failure that book may have after it is written . . . the book is merely a symbol of the writing. In writing the book, I am living. I am growing. I am tapping myself. I am changing. The process is the product.   *Theodore Isaac Rubin*

Writing is no trouble: you just jot down ideas as they occur to you. The jotting is simplicity itself—it is the occurring which is difficult.   *Stephen Leacock*

Writing, when properly managed (as you may be sure I think mine is) is but a different name for conversation.   *Laurence Sterne*

My method is to take the utmost trouble to find the right thing to say, and then to say it with the utmost levity.   *George Bernard Shaw*

Caesar had perished from the world of men
Had not his sword been rescued by his pen.   *Henry Vaughan*

Every great and original writer, in proportion as he is great and original, must himself create the taste by which he is to be relished.   *William Wordsworth*

Writers write to influence their readers, their preachers, their auditors, but always, at bottom, to be more themselves.   *Aldous Huxley*

We are as much informed of a writer's genius by what he selects as by what he originates.   *Ralph Waldo Emerson*

In any really good subject, one has only to probe deep enough to come to tears.   *Edith Wharton*

He is limp and damp and milder than the breath of a cow.   *Virginia Woolf (of E. M. Forster,*

The most essential gift for a good writer is a built-in, shockproof shit detector. This is the writer's radar and all great writers have had it.   *Ernest Hemingway*

Get black on white.   *Guy de Maupassant*

It is a sobering thought that each of us gives his hearers and his readers a chance to look into the inner working of his mind when he speaks or writes.   *J. M. Barker*

Read over your compositions, and when you meet a passage which you think is particularly fine, strike it out.   *Samuel Johnson*

When you're a writer, you no longer see things with the freshness of the normal person. There are always two figures that work inside you, and if you are at all intelligent you realize that you have lost something. But I think there has always been this dichotomy in a real writer. He wants to be terribly human, and he responds emotionally but at the same time there's this cold observer who cannot cry.   *Brian Moore*

When I am dead, I hope it may be said:
'His sins were scarlet, but his books were read.'   *Hilaire Belloc*

The best part of every author is in general to be found in his book, I assure you.   *Samuel Johnson*

The obscurity of a writer is generally in proportion to his incapacity.   *Quintilian*

Life cannot defeat a writer who is in love with writing—for life itself is a writer's love until death.   *Edna Ferber*

Just get it down on paper, and then we'll see what to do with it.
   Maxwell Perkins (advice to Marcia Davenport,

Advice to young writers who want to get ahead without any annoying delays: don't write about Man, write about a man.   *E. B. White*

Vigorous writing is concise. A sentence should contain no unnecessary words, a paragraph no unnecessary sentences, for the same reason that a drawing should have no unnecessary lines and a machine no unnecessary parts. This requires not that the writer make all his sentences short, or that he avoid all detail and treat his subjects only in outline, but that every word tell. *William Strunk*

Tennessee Williams said if he got rid of his demons, he would lose his angels.
Dakin Williams

Self-expression is for babies and seals, where it can be charming. A writer's business is to affect the reader. *Vincent McHugh*

There is but one art, to omit. *Robert Louis Stevenson*

A man really writes for an audience of about ten persons. Of course if others like it, that is clear gain. But if those ten are satisfied, he is content.
Alfred North Whitehead

It is in the hard rockpile labour of seeking to win, hold, or deserve a reader's interest that the pleasant agony of writing comes in. *John Mason Brown*

Write something, even if it's just a suicide note. *Anon.*

Flaubert had infinite correction to perform. *Roland Barthes*

Nature, not content with denying him the ability to think, has endowed him with the ability to write. *A. E. Housman*

There have always been other, more lively, more accessible, more insistent arts than writing; literature has withstood their seductions. *Gough Whitlam*

When an author is yet living, we estimate his powers by his worst performance; and when he is dead, we rate them by his best. *Samuel Johnson*

How vain it is to sit down to write when you have not stood up to live.
Henry David Thoreau

A writer is someone who can make a riddle out of an answer. *Karl Kraus*

The challenge for the writer is to adapt his ancient and difficult craft to a generation that is largely insensitive to its virtues and to a popular audience increasingly distracted by the pace, immediacy and materialism of contemporary life. *Gough Whitlam*

Style is the hallmark of a temperament stamped upon the material at hand.
André Maurois

Every writer, without exception, is a masochist, a sadist, a peeping Tom, an exhibitionist, a narcissist, an injustice collector and a depressed person constantly haunted by fears of unproductivity. *Edmund Bergler*

My novels point out that the world consists entirely of exceptions. *Joyce Cary*

Less is more.   *Robert Browning*

We like that a sentence should read as if its author, had he held a plough instead of a pen, could have drawn a furrow deep and straight to the end.
Henry David Thoreau

The reason a writer writes a book is to forget a book and the reason a reader reads one is to remember it.   *Thomas Wolfe*

I work every day—or at least I force myself into office or room. I may get nothing done, but you don't earn bonuses without putting in time. Nothing may come for three months, but you don't earn the fourth without it.   *Mordecai Richler*

John the Baptist pretending to be Karl Marx. *Anonymous description of G. B. Shaw*

Every word she writes is a lie, including 'and' and 'the'.
Mary McCarthy (of Lillian Hellman)

It fell dead from the Press.   *Old bookseller saying*

When you put down the good things you ought to have done, and leave out the bad things you did do—well, that's memoirs.   *Will Rogers*

Journalism allows its readers to witness history. Fiction gives its readers an opportunity to live it.   *John Hersey*

His (the writer's) standard of fidelity to the truth should be so high that his invention, out of his experience, should produce a truer account than anything factual can be.
Ernest Hemingway

When a writer ceases to be disturbing to the status quo—or rather, unless a writer does disturb things as they are and so prevent stagnation—he doesn't rank as either great or creative.   *Miles Franklin*

The life of a writer is tragic: the more we advance, the farther there is to go and the more there is to say, the less time there is to say it.   *Gabrielle Roy*

It is only through fiction and the dimension of the imaginary that we can learn something real about individual experience. Any other approach is bound to be general and abstract.   *Nicola Chiaromonte*

When the style is fully formed, if it has a sweet undersong, we call it beautiful, and the writer may do what he likes in words or syntax.   *Oliver Wendell Holmes*

I have only made this letter rather long because I have not had time to make it shorter.
Blaise Pascal

It makes a great difference in the force of a sentence whether a man be behind it or no.   *Ralph Waldo Emerson*

Footnotes, the little dogs yapping at the heels of the text.   *William James*

I like prefaces. I read them. Sometimes I do not read any further.   *Malcolm Lowry*

If you write to satisfy your soul, you will satisfy your readers. Not that one ever does succeed in satisfying one's own soul.   *Mary Grant Bruce*

What is written without effort is in general read without pleasure.   *Samuel Johnson*

Proper words in proper places, make the true definition of a style.   *Jonathan Swift*

They're fancy talkers about themselves, writers. If I had to give young writers advice, I would say don't listen to writers talking about writing or themselves.
Lillian Hellman

The business of writing is one of the four or five most private things in the world.
Ethel Wilson

I conceive that the right way to write a story for boys is to write so that it will not only interest boys but strongly interest any man who has ever been a boy. That immensely enlarges the audience.   *Mark Twain*

He claimed his modest share of the general foolishness of the human race.
Irving Howe (of Thomas Hardy)

There are two kinds of writers—the great ones who can give you truths, and the lesser ones, who can only give you themselves.   *Clifton Fadiman*

My own experience is that once a story has been written, one has to cross out the beginning and the end. It is there that we authors do most of our lying . . . one must ruthlessly suppress everything that is not concerned with the subject. If, in the first chapter, you say there is a gun hanging on the wall, you should make quite sure that it is going to be used further on in the story.   *Anton Chekhov*

(Writing)—the art of applying the seat of the pants to the seat of the chair.
Mary Heaton Vorse

All a writer has to do to get a woman is to say he's a writer. It's an aphrodisiac.
Saul Bellow

Publication is a self-invasion of privacy.   *Marshall McLuhan*

It has been said that writing comes more easily if you have something to say.
Sholem Asch

I've put my genius into my life; I've only put my talent into my works.
Oscar Wilde

Fundamentally, all writing is about the same thing: it's about dying, about the brief flicker of time we have here, and the frustrations that it creates.   *Mordecai Richler*

I am what libraries and librarians have made me, with a little assistance from a professor of Greek and a few poets.   *B. K. Sandwell*

Our society, like decadent Rome, has turned into an amusement society, with writers chief among the court jesters—not so much above the clatter as part of it.

Saul Bellow

If you would be a reader, read; if a writer, write.   *Epictetus*

A writer and nothing else: a man alone in a room with the English language, trying to get human feelings right.   *John K. Hutchens*

How can I know what I think till I see what I say?   *E. M. Forster*

Please, never despise the translator. He's the mailman of human civilization.

Alexander Pushkin

The waste basket is a writer's best friend.   *Isaac Bashevis Singer*

The llama is a woolly sort of fleecy hairy goat
With an indolent expression and an undulating throat—
Like an unsuccessful literary man.   *Hilaire Belloc*

If a man means his writing seriously, he must mean to write well. But how can he write well until he learns to see what he has written badly. His progress toward good writing and his recognition of bad writing are bound to unfold at something like the same rate.   *John Ciardi*

Words and sentences are subjects of revision; paragraphs and whole compositions are subjects of prevision.   *Barrett Wendell*

There is nothing more dangerous to the formation of a prose style than the endeavour to make it poetic.   *J. Middleton Murry*

The most original thing a writer can do is write like himself. It is also his most difficult task.   *Robertson Davies*

Now as through this world I ramble,
I see lots of funny men,
Some rob you with a six gun
Some with a fountain pen.   *Woody Guthrie*

It is the function of art to renew our perception. What we are familiar with we cease to see. The writer shakes up the familiar scene, and, as if by magic, we see a new meaning in it.   *Anaïs Nin*

Better to write for yourself and have no public, than to write for the public and have no self.   *Cyril Connolly*

I have cultivated my hysteria with joy and terror.   *Charles Baudelaire*

Writing has power, but its power has no vector. Writers can stir the mind, but they can't direct it. Time changes things, God changes things, the dictators change things, but writers can't change anything.   *Isaac Bashevis Singer*

A good writer is basically a story-teller, not a scholar or a redeemer of mankind.

Isaac Bashevis Singer

I believe the writer . . . should always be the final judge. I have always held to that position and have sometimes seen books hurt thereby, but at least as often helped. The book belongs to the author.   *Maxwell Perkins*

You have to throw yourself away when you write.   *Maxwell Perkins*

A memorandum is written to protect the writer—not to inform his reader.

Dean Acheson

I write for myself and strangers. The strangers, dear Readers, are an after-thought.

Gertrude Stein

The great enemy of clear language is insincerity. When there is a gap between one's real and one's declared aims, one turns as if it were instinctively to long words and exhausted idioms, like a cuttlefish squirting out ink.   *George Orwell*

A novel must be exceptionally good to live as long as the average cat.

Hugh MacLennan

You praise the firm restraint with which they write—
I'm with you, there, of course:
They use the snaffle and the curb all right,
But where's the bloody horse?   *Roy Campbell*

At least half the mystery novels published violate the law that the solution, once revealed, must seem to be inevitable.   *Raymond Chandler*

On the trail of another man, the biographer must put up with finding himself at every turn: any biography uneasily shelters an autobiography within it.

Paul Murray Kendall

The editorial job has become, unlike the ancient age when one judged what one read, a job of making judgements on outlines, ideas, reputations, previous books, scenarios, treatments, talk and promises.   *Sam Vaughan*

An editor should tell the author his writing is better than it is. Not a lot better, a little better.   *T. S. Eliot*

Writing is a solitary occupation. Family, friends and society are the natural enemies of a writer. He must be alone, uninterrupted and slightly savage if he is to sustain and complete an undertaking.   *Laurence Clark Powell*

Just as there is nothing between the admirable omelette and the intolerable, so with autobiography.   *Hilaire Belloc*

How can you write if you can't cry?   *Ring Lardner*

I think it's bad to talk about one's present work, for it spoils something at the root of the creative act. It discharges the tension.   *Norman Mailer*

As for my next book, I am going to hold myself from writing it till I have it impending in me: grown heavy in my mind like a ripe pear, pendant, gravid, asking to be cut or it will fall.   *Virginia Woolf*

No man understands a deep book until he has seen and lived at least part of its contents.
Ezra Pound

Writing is easy: all you do is sit staring at the blank sheet of paper until the drops of blood form on your forehead.   *Gene Fowler*

Your manuscript is both good and original; but the parts that are good are not original, and the parts that are original are not good.   *Samuel Johnson*

Youth

Blessed are the young, for they shall inherit the national debt.   *Herbert Hoover*

When a man of 40 falls in love with a girl of 20, it isn't her youth he is seeking but his own.   *Lenore Coffee*

Whom the gods love, die young, no matter how long they live.   *Elbert Hubbard*

Young folk, silly folk; old folk, cold folk.   *Old saying*

In early youth, as we contemplate our coming life, we are like children in a theatre before the curtain is raised, sitting there in high spirits and eagerly waiting for the play to begin.   *Arthur Schopenhauer*

How ruthless and hard and vile and right the young are.   *Hal Porter*

Young men think old men fools and old men know young men to be so.   *Anon*

It takes a long time to become young.   *Pablo Picasso*

The belief that youth is the happiest time of life is founded upon a fallacy. The happiest person is the person who thinks the most interesting thoughts, and we grow happier as we grow older.   *William Lyon Phelps*

When I was a boy of fourteen, my father was so ignorant I could hardly stand to have the old man around. But when I got to be twenty-one, I was astonished at how much the old man had learned in seven years.   *Mark Twain*

It is essential that we enable young people to see themselves as participants in one of the most exciting eras in history, and to have a sense of purpose in relation to it.
Nelson Rockefeller

This is a youth-oriented society, and the joke is on them because youth is a disease from which we all recover.   *Anon.*

Oh, to be only half as wonderful as my child thought I was when he was small, and only half as stupid as my teenager now thinks I am.   *Rebecca Richards*

When I was younger, I could remember anything, whether it had happened or not.
Mark Twain

The deepest definition of youth is life as yet untouched by tragedy.
Alfred North Whitehead

Only the young die good.   *Oliver Herford*

I am constantly amazed when I talk to young people to learn how much they know about sex and how little about soap.   *Billie Burke*

The joy of the young is to disobey—but the trouble is that there are no longer any orders.   *Jean Cocteau*

To keep clear of concealment, to keep clear of the need of concealment, to do nothing that he might not do out on the middle of Boston Common at noonday—I cannot say how more and more that seems to me to be the glory of a young man's life. It is an awful hour when the first necessity of hiding anything comes. The whole life is different thenceforth. When there are questions to be feared and eyes to be avoided and subjects that must not be touched, then the bloom of life is gone. Put off that day as long as possible. Put if off forever if you can.   *Phillips Brooks*

Youth has become a class.   *Roger Vadim*

The 'teenager' seems to have replaced the Communist as the appropriate target for public controversy and foreboding.   *Edgar Z. Friedenberg*

Everyone believes in his youth that the world really began with him, and that all merely exists for his sake.   *Goethe*

It is not possible for civilization to flow backward while there is youth in the world. Youth may be headstrong, but it will advance its allotted length.   *Helen Keller*

You never see the old austerity
That was the essence of civility;
Young people hereabouts, unbridled, now
Just want.   *Molière*

The young always have the same problem—how to rebel and conform at the same time. They have now solved this by defying their parents and copying one another.
Quentin Crisp

One boy's a boy, two boys are half a boy; three boys are no boy at all.
Charles A. Lindbergh, Senior

Trouble is, kids feel they have to shock their elders and each generation grows up into
something harder to shock.   *Cal Craig*

I do beseech you to direct your efforts more to preparing youth for the path and less
to preparing the path for the youth.   *Ben Lindsey*

To the young all things are new, and if their minds are not injured by their upbringing,
they respond with wonder and delight to what is eternal in the beauty of all kingdoms.
                                                                       Martin Boyd

The interests of childhood and youth are the interests of mankind.
                                                            Edmund Storer James

The youth gets together this material to build a bridge to the moon, or perchance, a
palace or temple on earth, and at length, the middle-aged man concludes to build a
woodshed with them.   *Henry David Thoreau*

Don't laugh at a youth for his affectations; he's only trying on one face after another
till he finds his own.   *Logan Pearsall Smith*

If one could recover the uncompromising spirit of one's youth, one's greatest indignation would be for what one has become.   *André Gide*

It is always self-defeating to pretend to the style of a generation younger than your
own; it simply erases your own experience in history.   *Renata Adler*

It's all that the young can do for the old, to shock them and keep them up to date.
                                                            George Bernard Shaw

What though youth gave love and roses
Age still leaves us friends and wine.   *Thomas More*

Index